Roving With Roger

Helen Abbot Lapham (center) leads her husband, Roger Dearborn Lapham, as they literally "tread out the grapes" for winemaking at a favorite taverna during their residency in Greece where he was Marshall Plan Chief of Mission in 1950-1952. On his left is Betty Jane Peurifoy, wife of the U. S. Ambassador to Greece, John E. Peurifoy.

Roving With Roger

by

HELEN ABBOT LAPHAM

46237

Published by Cameron & Co., San Francisco

To my dear husband,
without whom there would have been no "Roving,"
and to my daughter, Carol,
who insisted that I write this book.

HELEN ABBOT LAPHAM

ROGER DEARBORN LAPHAM
1883—1966

AN EDITOR'S NOTE

The Roger in "Roving With Roger" is Roger Dearborn Lapham; the fellow rover and author is his wife, Helen Abbot Lapham. Together for nearly fifty-nine years, ending with his death, April 16, 1966, they shared day-to-day, personal roles in some of the most eventful vagaries of recent U.S. history: violent labor-management strife on San Francisco's waterfront; chaos of Washington, D.C., during World War II; bareknuckle politics of big city mayoralty; formation of The United Nations; Marshall Plan reconstruction of Greece, and attempts to salvage China on the eve of the Communist takeover.

In the course of partisan participation in local and world events, their separate and remarkable personalities almost universally excited affection and admiration from friend and begrudging foe, alike. And opponents came in a wide range of political animosities because the Lapham Style was confrontation, shunning equivocation and exquisite finesse.

The common leavening in the sometimes shattering candor they both shared was humor, integrity of principle and a sense of scrupulous fairness. At that point, however, their manner parted. Helen Abbot Lapham contributed dignity in perfect complement to her husband's irrepressible ebullience; a highly successful counterpoint often noted by press editorializing everywhere the Laphams operated as a team — London, San Francisco, Washington, Shanghai, Athens ...

Roger Dearborn Lapham's monumental effervescence reflected from his whole being and it permeated his every activity. He was a big, broad-shouldered man, square-jawed, deep-voiced, and from early life with a great shock of white hair.

His trademark was frighteningly flamboyant, hand-painted neckties denying the conservative cut and cloth of custom-tailored suits. An expert bridge player, he sometimes opened bids without looking at his cards and he never sorted a hand. For nearly two decades, he was rated by sports columnists among California's ten top golfers; he was a passionate golfer and so convinced by the beauty of Western courses that he alone was responsible for getting the U.S.G.A. Annual Amateur to Pebble Beach in 1929 — a brilliant success and the first time it had been played West of the Mississippi.

But at no time did his enthusiasms erupt more volcanically than when he danced. Dancing was one of his major instruments of domestic and international communications — whether "fancy dancing" with the Queen of Greece at a palace ball, or with her youngest subjects in a remote village square.

His ebullience, however, was disciplined by timing which raised antics to superb showmanship. For example, faced as Mayor of San Francisco with a recall attempt by a disgruntled newspaper publisher, he publicly signed a street petition for his own recall — much to the delight of the electorate in the boisterous campaign. Confidence in Mayor Lapham was reaffirmed at the polls by a trouncing plurality.

Confidence and respect he regularly engendered at all political levels including that of four U.S. Presidents — Hoover, Roosevelt, Truman and Eisenhower. Among his assignments by them: shipping official in the United States Food Administration after World War I; member of the predecessor National Defense Mediation Board, and subsequently leading industry representative of the National War Labor Board during World War II; and post-war Chief of Mission, Economic Cooperation Administration, first in China and then Greece.

In part this trust was based on his great skill in simplifying complicated subjects, both in his own mind and in those of others. This deftness was particularly conspicuous at his many press conferences. Typically, he asked and answered his own questions — including leading ones — before they were framed by the appreciative reporters.

His introduction to national prominence, however, stemmed initially from a paradox: schooling in turbulent labor relations while President of the American-Hawaiian Steamship company. Part of his thirteen-year tenure — he later became Chairman of the Board — coincided with some of the bitterest and bloodiest strikes in U.S. labor history, the acrimonious waterfront stoppages of 1934 and 1936 in San Francisco. All intercoastal shipping was involved, but his company — the West Coast's oldest and largest line — was a principle target.

Characteristically, he tackled the problem head on and with honesty that gradually won the respect, if not always compliance, of the opposing labor leadership. Finally, a melodramatic move captured the imagination of the rank and file, too. Today — thirty-five years later — the event is still recalled by reminiscing longshoremen in San Francisco hiring halls. And it is still spoken of simply as "The Great Debate".

The Great Debate took place at the most flammable point of what later was dubbed "The Hundred Days Strike". The lone debaters on the public platform were Roger Dearborn Lapham, representing the Waterfront Employers' Association, and Harry Bridges, the nationally controversial President of the International Longshoremen's and Warehousemen's Union, CIO. The auditorium was filled to standing-room capacity by an estimated 17,000 union members and sympathizers; in the middle of that hostile audience sat Helen Abbot Lapham, virtually alone in silent support of her husband's position. His appearance triggered jeers which quickly subsided as he opened with, "Boys, I know you're against me, but . . . . " and then gave the employers' side of the issues.

The bold clash proved to be a successful gambit in moves that settled the paralyzing strike a month or so later. Meanwhile, the Lapham reputation for courageous sportsmanship and frankness was strongly imprinted in the minds of local labor — a deciding factor seven years later when the wealthy shipping executive won a landslide mayoralty victory over San Francisco's deeply entrenched political machine.

The other effect of The Great Debate was immediate focus of a then strike-tormented nation on the capabilities of this western maverick. As *Time Magazine*, *Saturday Evening Post* and numerous other national publications subsequently paraphrased: "That was the day Roger Dearborn Lapham walked on to the political stage." He and his companion-in-roving stormed that stage — often triumphantly — for the next sixteen years until restless retirement.

He came by his zest for daring and venture honestly. He was born December 6, 1883 in his grandmother's home on East 68th Street, New York City. A few months later his family moved to Spuyten Duyvil, overlooking the confluence of the Hudson and Harlem Rivers, which was then a rural area. The family later returned to New York City in order to send the children to good schools.

Four uncles of his mother, Antoinette Dearborn Lapham, were sea captains; the family organized the American-Hawaiian Steamship Company while young Lapham was in his teens. And it was from the deck of an uncle's cargoliner that he viewed San Francisco's Golden

Gate after a voyage 'Round the Horn. The young mariner became an Instant Westerner.

The compass rose of chance and intent kept swinging his career back to the West until it finally fixed on San Francisco in 1920. He was a dedicated San Franciscan for the remainder of his life — a devotion equally shared and still observed today by Helen Abbot Lapham. Meanwhile, he had graduated from Harvard and had served as a World War I infantry captain — at the cost of being gassed, and temporarily blinded for two weeks.

Predictably, a progeny distinguished each in his or her own right resulted from the Lapham marriage in 1907: two sons and two daughters today increased by eleven grandchildren and seven great-grandchildren. The sons followed the formidable example of their father in creating business careers. The eldest, Lewis, a former President of Grace Lines, is now Vice-Chairman of Bankers Trust of New York; Roger, Jr., is Chairman of the Board, Frank B. Hall & Company of California, and Vice President and a Director of its namesake company, the world's fourth largest insurance brokerage firm.

Continuously for nearly six decades, Helen Abbot Lapham eagerly and fully participated in every tumultuous twist and turn of their joined life; adding to it at the many way points of frequent joy and inevitable sorrow her own ingredients of dignity stiffened by courage, and candor softened by humor. A lesser companion, hearing the beat of such rapid drumming, might well have broken step. "Roving With Roger" is an autobiographical monument to her constancy.

A final note. One might expect a memoir authored by an octogenarian to be ghost-written or at the very least, a product of heavy collaboration. In fact the 800-page original manuscript was written over the last five years by the author without editorial assistance of any kind. Furthermore, it was typewritten by her own hand — a skill learned with great pride when she was sixty years old! The factual detail of the text, which makes the recollections so authentic and fascinating, were provided by a lifelong habit of saving memorabilia and keeping journals.

Thus the editor's role has been only the one of a guide through the labyrinths of publishing and printing. The greatest reward of the guiding — as many before have discovered in contact with Helen Abbot Lapham — is the unabashed affection and admiration of the guide for the guided.

San Francisco, June, 1971   *Bart Benedict, Editor.*

CONTENTS

I. EARLY YEARS

II. MAYORALTY PERIOD (1943—1948)

III. ECA—CHINA AND GREECE (1948—1952)

IV. RETIREMENT ROVINGS (1953—1966)

ILLUSTRATIONS

I
EARLY YEARS

1

MEETING ROGER

I F I had been born in the late 18th instead of the late 19th Century, I would undoubtedly have worked a cross-stitch sampler reading

"Helen B. Abbot is my name
America my Nation.
Brooklyn my Home and Dwelling Place,
But Heaven my Destination."

I have been told, and see no reason to doubt that I was born at 144 Carroll Street, Brooklyn, although the Brooklyn Bureau of Statistics, even after the dollar I sent them to search the records, denies that I was ever born at all. But at least I remember the move to 1146 Dean Street when I was seven, and from then on I lived the typical life of an uninhibited Brooklyn girl: roller skating up and down the block after the cobble stones had been changed to asphalt, watching the statue of General Grant go up in Bedford Square with the tail of his horse originally placed upside down in a most untenable position, walking back and forth to Miss Rounds' School on Clinton Avenue, from which I graduated in 1901, and spending marvellous summer months in Noroton, Connecticut.

Those Noroton days were carefree and wonderful, all except the Sundays which meant: church at half-past ten, Sunday School at twelve, a long hot walk home (we didn't use the horses on Sunday), changing from the good Sunday-go-to-Meeting clothes, and finally the pretty well congealed remains of Sunday dinner.

On the Sabbath, I was not allowed to read anything except my Sunday School library book or "Pilgrim's Progress" for the rest of the day, nor to play any sort of a game. If I transgressed, I had to learn either a hymn or a Psalm. I must have been born into original sin, for I still know practically every verse of every well-known hymn, and many, many parts of the Bible.

One event which stands out most clearly in my mind during those early summers was a Temperance Sunday when I was about twelve years old. After a rousing talk on the evils of alcohol and tobacco, all the little children were invited to come up and sign the pledge forever adjuring those wiles of Satan. We all sang:

> *"Tobacco is a filthy weed,*
> *Straight from the Devil sprang the seed.*
> *It soils your fingers, spoils your clothes,*
> *And makes a chimney of your nose."*

... and everyone went up to sign except my bosom friend Edna Capen and me. My father, having been abroad year after year, thought a little wine with water was good, even for children; and Edna's German grandfather always served it at dinner, so we saw no harm in it. So why should we renounce something of which our families so evidently approved? (And aside from that, we had smoked cornsilk behind the barn for years without spoiling a single clo', so why give that up?)

The Superintendent pled with us. Everyone else prayed for us. But we two poor little outcasts, standing up in the aisle with the tears streaming down our faces, still refused to sign. To this day, I don't know how we found the courage not to. Or as Edna said to me as we sat with a cocktail in our hands not so long ago, "Aren't you glad we never signed the pledge, Helen? We'd both have broken it, of course, but raised as we were, I'll bet neither of us would ever really have enjoyed a drink."

And yet as a matter of fact, my up-bringing was no stricter than that of other girls of my generation. My father was a delightful man who had read enormously, wrote both charming and amusing poetry and other articles. He also had a keen sense of humor which he displayed one Sunday shortly after the Temperance affair by taking Edna and me for a picnic in the woods after church. We both had such a delicious sense of guilt at missing Sunday School, that we enjoyed every minute of it.

How my mother ever lived through those last years in Noroton I will never know. Within five years she lost her father, her adored only-brother and two girl babies. In spite of these tragedies, she kept house for her mother (who had "nervous prostration" or whatever it may be called today), her mother's trained nurse, her brother's widow and little girl—as well as for her own husband and two children. And the house had only one bathroom!

My sister Dorothy—five years my junior—was a good little girl, but I was what the psychologists now term "uncooperative" although the good old New England word "ornery" comes much closer to the mark. I was a tomboy. I climbed trees and tore my clothes, and practically everything I did made somebody nervous. So I remember early in my teens vowing that no matter what *my* children did, I would never, never say "Don't do that, it makes me nervous." (That is a promise I really think I kept pretty well, although it took a good deal of self-restraint later on when they were old enough to have automobiles.)

As I look back on it, the memory of restrictions has faded as does the memory of pain; no one could have had a happier or more care-free girlhood, and I still see Noroton in a haze of golden light.

In February, 1899, we went abroad for four unforgettable months. My father was a designer and importer of French china, connected with the Haviland factories in Limoges. He went to Europe every year, generally alone, but this time he took my mother, my nine-year-old sister and me with him. He left us in Paris for a month while he went to Limoges where we joined him in April. That month in Paris was sheer delight.

I had always been an avid reader, and was steeped in stories of France: "The Chaplet of Pearls," "Under the Red Robe," "A Gentleman of France," "Old Court Life in France." And I saw my dream world come true. I was allowed to go around by myself and I spoke enough schoolgirl French to get by. I spent hours in the Louvre—not filled

3

for me with great masterpieces of art, but peopled by the long dead Kings and Queens who emerged from the shadowy past and let me watch them. Starry-eyed, I wandered from room to room. Late one afternoon I happened to find myself alone in one of the more remote wings when the great bell of St. Germain LAuxerrois began to toll—the signal for the Massacre of St. Bartholomew! Frightened almost out of my wits—for I had no white armband on my sleeve—I ran like a bat out of hell and burst into the Salon Carre' to the rather apathetic amazement and amusement of the patient copyists.

Then came a month in Limoges where my French improved considerably. My mother spoke very little and was shy about it. My sister was in the *"J'aime, tu aimes, il aime"* stage. My father's French was fluent but terrible; however, with his usual quick wit, he was able to make a pun when his host, M. Gerard, broke a glass at dinner one night, and turning to my father said *"C'est vous qui a casse' la verre."*

"Pas moi," said my father. *"Au contraire c'est vous qui a casse' la ver-i-te'!"*

Hardly anyone in Limoges spoke English in those far off days, so a good deal of the daily ordering and shopping devolved on me, and it stood me in good stead two years later in college.

We stayed in the Hotel de la Paix, and the big event of the day was watching the Cuirassiers ride out each morning on their black horses, their sabres shining in the sun, their horse-tail plumes streaming out in the breeze, and the Regimental Band playing the "Marche Lorraine." A heady sight for a fourteen-year-old American girl, and Brooklyn—even Noroton—seemed a bit tame ever afterwards.

The next two years were scholastically busy ones, because I was preparing for Smith College. The entrance requirements had just been changed, and I found that I had to have either a science or a third language. Therefore, in my last year of school I was taking Latin, French and two years of German in one. But there were also blissfully happy Saturdays with wonderful matinees (gallery seats 35¢)—"The Heart of Maryland," "Secret Service," "Rupert of Hentzau," "Old

4

Heidelberg" and other tear-jerkers. (If you used less than three handkerchiefs, the afternoon had been a failure.) As a substitute for nonexistent movies or radios, almost everyone of the young crowd played some sort of an instrument. And we sang. Oh, how we sang! All the good old songs: "Seeing Nellie Home," "The Spanish Cavalier," "A Hot Time in the Old Town"—and all of us knew every single word of verse and chorus. A simple life? Yes, but none of us knew enough not to enjoy every minute of it.

In the summer of 1901 I spent two weeks with my dear girlhood friend, Edna Capen and, through her, met my husband-to-be, Roger Lapham. Of course, neither of us suspected at the time that we would marry. If he had, I don't think I would ever have seen him again because girls just didn't exist for him then. His whole interest was golf. But I thought him "too, too divine." I begged a tiny snapshot of him from Edna, and wore it in a heart-shaped silver locket around my neck for the next four years.

Roger entered Harvard the same year I entered Smith, and I never saw him again until after we were both graduated even though all the beaux I had were Harvard men. In fact one Harvard beau claimed to be fascinated with my Brooklyn accent, and kept urging me to repeat my favorite rhyme:

"The doity boid sat on a doity coib, eating a doity, doity woim.
If the doity boid eats any more doity woims, the doity boid
*   will boist,"*

but he disappeared after the third repetition, and I never saw him again. (However my accent must have remained unsullied, for when I took Greek lessons in Athens later, my teacher said I was the only person she had ever heard who spoke Greek with a Brooklyn accent.)

I really enjoyed college for the first three years, although I was generally second best in everything. I played on the scrub basketball team. I never made the lead in the college plays, but I was asked to join both the French Club and a "literary" society.

However, the latter wasn't a complete victory. After having heard a wonderful play I had written, the club passed a resolution at the very next meeting saying that the recent offerings by some of their members had fallen so far below their standards, that a higher type of literary output would be expected from now on. From then on I concentrated on French and history.

Science and higher mathematics meant no more to me then than they do now. And my father, fortunately, was far ahead of his time and his advice was what I would give any non-professional woman today: "Never mind algebra, geometry or trigonometry. All you really need to know is how to balance your check book. Concentrate on languages. Learn to speak at least one well, for you will use it all your life, and only wish you spoke many others." How right he was! Nothing I have ever learned since (except my typing, almost 40 years later) has been of greater use to me in many places than my French.

By senior year I was ready to quit. I didn't seem to have as much collegiate spirit as I should. True, the scenery around Northampton was beautiful, but I'd seen it, and oh! the winters were so long, and so cold, and the spring so late in coming. But my father had had to go to work when he was fourteen. He had four girls and no sons; and I was to have the education the eldest son would have had. So I stayed on and graduated in 1905 in a white Princess dress with a stiff boned collar, a sweeping skirt, and a single American Beauty rose in the hand.

The summer of 1905, I again visited my beloved friend and college roommate, Edna Capen, in Noroton, and the two Lapham brothers, Roger and Jack, drove down from their home in New Canaan every day to take us to play tennis and swim at Shippan Point. Jack was a superb horseman, but all Roger seemed to know about a horse was its head from its tail. One memorable day he nearly joined the horses by cramping the wheels under the buckboard and driving around and around in circles. I don't know which was the more confused, he or the horse.

Roger never talked much. (He wasn't the conversationalist then that he was later to become.) But even though he was almost tone-

6

deaf (the only two tunes he really recognized were the "Star Spangled Banner" and "Fair Harvard") he did sing to me:

"Stay little birdie, stay with me—and my little birdie be.
I will treat you very well and give you a cage wherein to
  dwell."

I couldn't really take it as a proposal, but it did give me hope.

That fall he started coming over to Brooklyn to see me. From his home at 15 W. 56th Street, New York, to 1146 Dean Street, Brooklyn, was a real trek in those days, because the subway was not finished until a year or so later. Edna's mother insisted that if he came once he was interested, but if he came twice, he was serious! But he still didn't talk much, and I wore myself out trying to find a topic I could really get him started on; after I had exhausted all my from-the-teeth-out remarks—such as "Which would you rather do, go up in an airplane or down in a submarine?"—I discovered that the only thing which really interested him was golf. Eventually I learned to listen quietly to all the "71-73 shots" he had taken for the afternoon eighteen.

Then the miracle happened. He asked me to go to a football game on a *Saturday* afternoon! (I found out afterward that it was too cold to play golf.) On the way out of the Stadium a horse almost bit me— or at least I thought it was going to—so I screamed. That evening he asked me to marry him.

With the proposal came the warning that it would be some time before we could marry. He was just starting with the American-Hawaiian Steamship Company, and furthermore I should realize that he did not intend to stay in the East any longer than he could help it. He had been to the Pacific Coast twice, had fallen in love with it, and wanted to live there. So . . . I could take it or leave it. Although I'd never been further West than St. Louis, I was willing to take a chance. I said "Yes."

2

MARRIAGE AND THE FIRST ROVINGS

FOLLOWING our engagement, Roger was away for several months during the next year and a half. He spent quite a bit of time on the Isthmus of Tehuantepec, where A-H was transshipping cargo to San Francisco and Seattle. Meanwhile I was collecting my trousseau, and learning to play what my girl friends and I called "Bridge Whist," (each hostess proudly presenting the prize, a pair of *real silk* stockings, at the end of each session).

We were finally married in Brooklyn on October 30, 1907, by the same minister who had married my father and mother. We spent our two-week honeymoon at the Lake Placid Club. Perfect weather with canoeing on the lake the first week, and then heavy snow for my first and last attempts at skiing.

On our return we went to live with Roger's family at 15 West 56th Street. Jack was in his last year at Williams; Elinor, the elder sister, was at Farmington; and Ruth, the youngest, was at home with a governess and going to school. It didn't take me long to find out how little I had learned about bridge—in spite of the six pairs of stockings I had acquired—for all of Roger's family were A-1 players and took their game very seriously. For the most part they suffered me in silence as I ruined game after game for them.

But that winter taught me a good deal besides bridge, for I grew to know and love Roger's parents as I never would have in any other way. Mother Lapham I loved from the start, and saw a great deal of her as she had had an operation for appendicitis the previous September. She still had to spend much time in bed or on the chaise-longue in her bedroom where I had long, long visits and talks with her. Father Lapham I came to love little by little as I got used to him. At first I was frightened to death of him. (When my family asked me what he was like, I said, "a retired brigand.")

With Mother Lapham rarely at dinner except on her Wednesday opera nights, I usually presided with a butler breathing down my neck, something to which I was totally unaccustomed. In my home, dinner had been a relaxed event with a good deal of conversation; my father was witty and amusing, my mother an appreciative audience, and Dorothy and I had been taught to describe some experience which we had had during the day as interestingly as possible. So I chatted along gaily at the Lapham's, dropping my remarks into a deep well of silence, and finding my plate whisked away when I had no more than touched my food. By the end of the winter I had lost eight pounds—but that was all to the good, as I weighed 150 when I graduated. I also won this appraisal from my father-in-law: "Daughter, When I first knew you, I thought you had a brain. I now realize it is nothing but a glib tongue!"

In May 1908 we took a furnished house in Pelham Manor. After Edna Capen and Jack Lapham were married in October, they moved into a house a block away. I was pregnant by then, and my eldest son, Lewis, was born the following March in my old home in Brooklyn. Edna's eldest, Johnny, was born that October. My Carol came the next June. Then Edna's second son, David, arrived on Johnny's first birthday. A dear friend of ours, Alma Colbron, who also lived in Pelham, was in the same "interesting condition" at the same times and as often as we were. We must have been a sight as we pushed our baby-carriages up and down the Esplanade with our out-sized stomachs. At any rate we called a taxi to take us to lunch one day, and after one look at the three of us, the driver never shifted out of low gear!

In October 1910, Roger was transferred to Seattle, and off we started on a six day trip. The entourage and equipment included two Irish maids, who were sisters; nursing bottles; and zinc-lined boxes of Walker-Gordon milk, which had to be iced at every station.

9

There were a great many prayers to the Holy Mother and the Blessed Saints to protect us from Indians and all the other dangers of the wild country for which we were headed. And one totally unforeseen incident did arise. Roger and I got out at some little whistle-stop in Washington, and were chatting with the brakeman—most fortunately for us—when the train quietly started to pull out. The brakeman yelled to a passenger on the observation platform to pull the emergency cord. He did only after a bit of persuasion. We had to race after the train and finally caught it at a water tank, which was as far as it was going anyhow. But we didn't know that and to make matters worse, I was nursing Carol. I could hardly blame my two nice Irish girls for being a bit on the frantic side when we rejoined them.

We had only a year and a half in Seattle, but I adored every moment of it. I was furnishing my first house and I saw most of my wedding presents for the first time since we had been married. We made friends. We bought a car and both learned to drive at the same time. And having been thoroughly prepared for the constant rain, I didn't mind it a bit.

After we had been there a year, Roger asked me one night if I would like to go East on a trip with him the following week! I just couldn't believe it. When I had left New York, I had bade my family an eternal farewell—whoever saw anyone again when they were separated by a continent? Much as I loved Seattle, New York and everything about it seemed pretty glamorous, and on the visit I permanently flattened my slightly pug nose against those enchanting Fifth Avenue shop windows.

My father and mother came out to visit us in Seattle later that year, and my sister Dorothy and a friend of hers in the spring. By that time I knew I was going to have my third baby, and was slightly discouraged as I had just been slated to dance the leading role in the yearly Kermess. It had all been good fun up to then. Golf tournaments in more-British-than-England Victoria. The Potlatch celebration when I stayed up all night for the first time in my life and saw the dawn come up over Puget Sound. But it was too good to last.

About the fifth month of my pregnancy Roger was again transferred, this time to Los Angeles. I was in a quandary. Lewis was just three, Carol not quite two, and the new baby was due in July. How could I move all my goods and chattels and children, go to Los Angeles, find a house, furnish it, and find a new and unknown doctor in less than four months? So I didn't. Roger had to report in Los Angeles at once, and I decided to go back to Brooklyn for my accouchement the last of July. I closed the house and shipped the furniture to Roger via A-H. Dorothy and her friend were there to help me, but our getaway was nothing if not hectic.

An hour before train time, I discovered that there was a mixup in our train ticket. I was telephoning frantically to the A-H agent to do something about it.

In the midst of the confusion, dear little Lewis came up to cling to my skirts and murmuring something which I didn't even try to listen to. Being in a complete frenzy, I simply put my foot under his little behind and hoisted him quietly into the other room. He landed sitting down, too surprised even to cry. When we finally got off, I shut and locked myself into my compartment, leaving other members of our party to cope with the children. Lewis completed his happy day by getting hold of a bottle of Phenolax, eating six or seven nice, sweet pink pills. No one had the courage to tell me until they had spent the rest of the day with him in the bathroom.

Brooklyn seemed a haven of rest. I engaged an excellent nurse at $35 a month. That was an outrageous price at the time, but she had had six months of child-care training. I was willing to pay it before I told her I was expecting my third child and would be moving to Los Angeles as soon as I could after the baby's birth! It might even have gone up to $40 if she had known those two facts.

Early in July, I went up to New Canaan, presumably for a quiet weekend. Roger had just arrived from the West. It was the night of

July 4th. I gave birth to a daughter on a kitchen table which had been carried up to my bedroom. I had come all the way East to have my own obstetrician but was attended instead by a country doctor and village nurse! My sister-in-law, Edna, was the witness. She reported that I said nothing under the anaesthetic except: "The Lord is my shepherd, I shall not want." In view of this reassurance, I named the new baby, Edna.

It was the middle of August before I could rejoin Roger in Los Angeles. The trip West, even with Frances Monahan and Nora to take care of the children, was a nightmare.

Roger met us, a dirty, dishevelled crew, and took us to the Beverly Hills Hotel where we had nice rooms, but oh! the heat, and the dust, and the everlasting rustle and flap of those horrid fan palms.

I was nursing Edna, and dashing into town between feedings to hunt for a house to rent. Each prospect seemed more impossible than the last. Few of them had more than one maid's room and most of them none at all. At perhaps one out of four the real estate agent (or "realtor" as I learned to say) would tell me with pride: "Now *this house* is absolutely free from tuberculosis." I inferred that most of the others weren't.

Finally we bought one at 615 South Manhattan Place, at that time on the outskirts of civilization and with nothing beyond but oil wells. It was a comfortable, attractive house, but it had a few drawbacks which we discovered by degrees; among them was a cesspool, of which I only became aware when the front lawn suddenly began to sink and the air was permeated with a most peculiar odor. Even then it took my next-door neighbor to tell me what the trouble was! Then there was an assessment when we were connected with the city sewage system and another when the street was paved.

I didn't like Los Angeles. I didn't like the climate which, after three children in a little over three years, I found very enervating. I didn't like the people. They didn't like me much either, for Roger had been there as a young, good-looking, free, extra man for five months, and to have to give him up when he produced a wife and three children was more than they could bear. They resented me bitterly and made no bones about showing it. I had almost no social life. Roger played golf almost every Saturday and Sunday. I was really lonely so I spent most of my days reading French books from the library, making dresses for the little girls, and playing the piano. My father, mother and sister came out late that winter and took a house for several months, which helped. But I still didn't like Los Angeles. Nor did I ever change my mind during the two years and a half we lived there.

There were, of course, a few bright spots. For instance, when I invited Carol, aged three-and-a-half, to repeat a hymn I had taught her for some visiting relatives, she arose and nothing loath, recited:

> "Onward Christian soldiers, marching as to war,
> With the cross of Jesus going on before.
> 'Gainst the line of crimson they can't prevail,
> Three cheers for Harvard, and down with Yale!"

The relatives did think it a bit odd, but I explained that it was just the result of the influence of her two parents, and let it go at that.

One famous evening Roger brought a classmate out for dinner— Clarence Dillon, of Dillon Reed. Hot as it was, he was impeccably dressed in a black suit and a three inch high stiff collar. He couldn't have been more solemn if he had been an undertaker. He told us a story of an experience he had had shortly after he was married. While standing with his mother-in-law at a small station in Wisconsin waiting for a local train to Chicago, a Chicago-Northwestern express rushed by. It hit a St. Bernard dog, which hit his mother-in-law, who in turn hit him and knocked him into a stanchion giving him a concussion. After several days in the hospital he began to sit up and wondered why no one from the railroad had been to see him. So he consulted his lawyer, who got in touch with the lawyer for the railroad. The very bland answer was that the road was in no way responsible, as the train had not injured the two people, and the dog was not their "accredited agent!" Then his lawyer dug up an ordinance—passed probably in the 1850's but never repealed—that no train should proceed through that station at more than ten miles an hour! Shortly after that, Clarence was invited to lunch with the Chicago-Northwestern attorney. The net result was a year in Europe for Clarence, his wife and his mother-in-law.

Clarence told the story without a change of expression so it was no time for me to shriek with laughter, but I was so convulsed I choked on my food, and had to leave the table to take my mirth elsewhere.

In the summer of 1914 the assassination at Sarajevo passed almost unnoticed. But I still remember exactly where I was standing when Roger telephoned me to say that the Germans had invaded Belgium, that France had declared war, and England was expected to go in at any moment. At first, strange as it seems, our sympathy was with the Germans—hemmed in on all sides, etc. But it didn't last long as the reports of the atrocities in Belgium began to trickle in.

The war didn't affect us in any particular way. In fact, the high point of the fall to my mind was my first visit to San Francisco, for I fell in love with the city at first sight. It was so beautiful, the air was so exhilarating, and above all it was so gay. We dined at old Tait's on O'Farrell Street, and from the little Chinese girls passing around ripe olives to the curtained boxes upstairs, it seemed to me the ultimate in glamor.

On my return to Los Angeles, I decided to teach Lewis to read, and young as Carol was, she said she wanted to learn, too. I had a couple of books called the "See and Say Method." I still think it the best and easiest method possible, because it gives even the youngest an indelible impression of the association of sight and sound. Each letter of the alphabet was shown both in caps and small letters, plus a picture describing the sound. For instance, under "M" was a cow with the caption, "The cow says 'M-M-M-oo' and this letter sounds like mmm"; "S" was a snake that said, "S-S-S," so that little by little the children could read a whole simple sentence simply by sounding it all out. Once I asked Carol to give me a word with a frog sound (gu-gu-gu), and after a moment's thought, she drawled, "Gar-bage"—correct, if not pretty.

Finally, finally Roger was moved to San Francisco, in January 1915, just before the opening of the Panama Pacific International Exposition. I felt as if I had died and gone to heaven. I met people. They were nice to me. I had learned enough by that time to know that if you want to have friends you have to show friendliness; or as one of the older women I met said, "I will entertain anyone who is properly introduced to me once; after that, it's up to her."

We rented a furnished house on Buchanan Street. The two older children went to kindergarten around the corner on Pacific Avenue and I no longer nursed the baby. We went to the Exposition over and over with a gay group of young people; to Del Monte for golf tournaments; and oh! what fun it all was! We took a house in San Mateo for the summer, and still another in San Francisco for the winter of 1915-1916. But again it was too good to last. Early in the summer of 1916 we went East, supposedly for six weeks. But as all the American-Hawaiian ships were under charter, there was no business for Roger to come back to, so we just stayed on in New Canaan and New York with Roger's family.

In January 1917, we went off to South America, leaving Lewis with my mother in Brooklyn and the two little girls with Mrs. Lapham in New York. My chief preparations for the trip—aside from 25 Spanish lessons at the Berlitz School, and buying thin clothes—were anti-typhoid shots and a smallpox vaccination, which took violently, as did my first permanent. (The permanent was six hours in the doing, cost $30, and I had 130 curls. I came out at the end of the day completely exhausted and looking more like a Hottentot than the original species. In fact, when I had my first shampoo in Rio, the operator was so appalled as my snaky locks frizzed tighter and tighter under the water, he called everyone in the beauty shop to come and look at the unholy spectacle.)

It was a queer, rather unhappy trip. We sailed on the "Vauban," a Lamport and Holt liner whose Captain had been captured by the Germans in the first week of the war. He had been released on parole and had broken it. The U-Boats were operating in the South Atlantic and they had promised to hang our Captain from the yard-arm if they caught him, so we sailed a zigzag course with all the portholes blacked out. Even lighting a cigarette on deck after dark was strictly taboo. Our life-boats were assigned, of course, and one of the few bright spots of the trip came when the other woman at our table, a Bostonian who fancied herself tremendously (and was traveling to South America in January with two fur coats) asked our little steward: "Whose life-boat am I in?"

"That would be the Captain's things, Madame" said he, adding as she preened herself, thinking it was just as it should be; "It'll be the last, you know Madame, to leave the ship."

In New York it had been rumored that we had been sunk on leaving Para, but we reached Rio safely and entered the harbor at sunrise one morning. What a sight it was! Sugar Loaf rising sheer from the sea, and the Organ Mountains with the pink light on them, was something never to be forgotten.

Rio was hot; boiling, blazing hot. São Paulo was hot; they tried to serve me beer in a glass out of which the barman had just shaken a mouse. Santos was hot; Roger played roulette at Guaraja, sticking to #17 "The Black Alaska" number, which never came up once, while I stood by with the perspiration pouring off me, partly from the heat and partly from worrying about the drain on our letter of credit.

We went from Rio to Montevideo on a horrid little 5,000-ton ship, the "Byron," which rolled and pitched and successfully kept me in my berth for most of the five days. I didn't like that ship. I didn't like the location of the bathroom, which was next to the galley. I didn't like having a two-thirds-hatched chicken pop out of the softboiled egg I ordered for breakfast. Later in the day I might have risen above it, but not before coffee!

After nearly three weeks in Buenos Aires, which gave me a good chance to practice my Berlitz Spanish, we took the train for Valparaiso, running through a swarm of locusts, and changing to a narrow gauge train at 4 a.m. at Mendoza to cross the Andes.

A few days in Valparaiso, a trip to Vina del Mar for the races, and then homeward bound on the Chilean steamer "Huasco." We had been able to get reservations only because our friends in Buenos Aires had had to stay on unexpectedly and had turned theirs over to us.

When Roger received the tickets for one of the only two staterooms aboard with baths, he had been warned that the room would probably have been sold four or five times; be sure to have all our luggage put in it, and to take possession of the cabin at least four hours before sailing time. So we went out and I sat, with a face like Medusa that would have turned anyone but a South American to stone at just one glance. But not the Argentinos nor the Chileños! It simply excited them to frenzied flights of Spanish oratory, during which I gave the Spanish equivalent for "*J'y suis, j'y reste.*"

We stopped every day at one of the nitrate ports—Iquique, Arica, Mollendo, Antofagasta, Callao—anchored in the bays from 6 a.m. to 6 p.m., and then taking off cross-seas just before dinner. By that time I was prostrate on my bed and summoned up courage to dress only when Roger promised me champagne the minute I got to the table.

Our last stop before the Canal was Paita, the miles-down-the-river port of Guayaquil, where we hung over the side and bargained for Panama hats. When we got to Colon, we learned to our horror that there had been yellow fever at Guayaquil and we had to remain aboard ship for another day to fulfill our quarantine requirement. By that time the food, which had been put on board at Panama on the way down, had either spoiled or given out, so we were reduced to *Panqueques* with palm syrup for all three meals a day. The United Fruit ship on which we sailed for New Orleans seemed like luxury incarnate, and the food fit for the gods.

3

WORLD WAR I AND LONDON

NOW it was no longer a question of *if*, but *when* the United States would declare war. Roger had told me that if we were not in it by the time we returned from South America, he was going to France to drive an ambulance. But war was declared the day we arrived in New Orleans, April 5th, and after a few days in San Antonio where Jack and Edna were then living, we went on to New York. Two weeks later Roger signed up for the first Officers Training Camp at Plattsburg.

I took a furnished house in New Canaan for the summer, and when he graduated as a Captain in September and was assigned to Camp Upton on Long Island, I took another house in Bellport, 17 miles away. It was a General Grant era house, modernized as to bathrooms; a pleasant summer residence, which couldn't have been nicer in the crisp, sunny October days. But what a winter it turned out to be!

Roger generally got home for Saturday and Sunday (unless he had forgotten to fill the water buckets, or his miserable Major discovered some other minor omission he could be nasty about). If he wasn't able to get off, I took the children over to see him. He commanded Company M of the 77th Division—New York City draft troops of nine nationalities, some of them not even speaking English.

His Colonel was Colonel Smedberg, Regular Army, from San Francisco. I was so impressed with his rank, that I always thought of him as at least six feet tall. (When I met him after the war, he wasn't even as tall as I was!) I introduced the children to him one day, and he asked them if they could identify the different Army ranks. They couldn't, so he said he'd tell them in a way they'd never forget.

"Think, children," said he, "of a ladder leaning against a tree. A Lieutenant has one bar on his shoulder—the first rung of the ladder.

A Captain has two—he is one step further up. A Major wears a leaf from the tree, a Colonel an eagle from above, and a General one or more of the stars in the sky."

Early in December the weather began to worsen (this was brought home to me when Lewis, whom I had put in the little Public School, came home and asked if he was sewed into his clothes for the winter. I assured him he wasn't, which he seemed to think made him an outcast, as all the other boys were! From Christmas week until the first of February the thermometer never went above 20°. It snowed and froze and snowed again.

At last the thaw came in the middle of March, and with it the feeling that the 77th would be going overseas at almost any time. I knew by then that I was to have a fourth child, my "War Baby," but decided not to tell Roger for two reasons: first, because he had too much on his mind anyhow; and second, because, between the suspense of waiting for the inevitable parting, and driving 17 miles to Upton day after day through hub-deep slushy, sticky mud, I was by no means sure I would get through my pregnancy.

The 77th left the last of April, and I moved back to another house in New Canaan for the summer and settled the children. Then I went to the Pacific Coast to collect my household goods stored in both Los Angeles and San Francisco. I wanted to take an apartment in New York, furnish it and settle down at least for the duration.

The summer was quiet, but seemed terribly long. I did some Red Cross work, but heard very little from Roger except indirectly through the Company M Ladies Auxiliary meetings which, as the Captain's wife, I conducted once a month in New York. The various relatives of the members of Company M attended, and I was supposed to keep them happy and amused for two hours. I was at my wits' end as to how to do it, since I had no information to impart. There was a piano in our meeting room, so I took down lots of music and played all the good old war songs: "Long, Long Trail," "Tipperary," "Over There," etc., which they all sang with gusto.

Then they would all start handing me letters they had received for me to read aloud. It was a ticklish job as I never knew what information I would run across. For example, one man, who had married just before he left, wrote his wife, and when I read the letter, his parents heard of his marriage for the first time! Another wrote: "Our Captain is a good old guy." (Roger was 35.) "He always sees that we get fed before we march anywhere." But the prize was, "Well, Toots, I suppose you think I am spending my time taking a roll in the hay with these French mamzells. Well, Toots, I ain't, for the hay stinks, and I ain't seen a mamzell yet who was any better'n you." But all of them, without exception ended "God, how my feet hurt."

My birthday was the 13th of September and I received many letters and telegrams. One was from the War Office. It said, "Deeply regret to inform you that your husband Captain Roger D. Lapham was seriously wounded in action August 15. This Department has no further information."

I got in touch with my father-in-law immediately, and he started the wheels rolling. By the end of the day we knew Roger and most of his company had been gassed while waiting to be relieved from their position in Haute Savoie. The New Canaan postmaster gave us the first news. His son was a medical orderly who had recognized Roger's name and identified him to his father as "the son of that family in the big house next to the ball field." He went on to say that the Captain had been gassed, was blinded, but conscious and able to talk.

The Red Cross confirmed what we had learned. So that when the New York Herald-Tribune came out the next week with the headline: "CAPTAIN ROGER LAPHAM KILLED IN ACTION," at least we knew it wasn't true. That very morning I got a letter from Roger telling me he was in a hospital in Tours, had recovered his sight, and was due for leave on the Riviera. His death was denied the next day, in two lines on the sixth page.

In October I moved to New York, staying in my mother's apartment on 58th Street while furnishing my own. It was anything but a cheery time. Flu was at its height—many of my kind friends asked me if I wasn't scared to death . . . "For it's fatal, you know, to anyone who is pregnant." The funerals in New York went through 58th Street on their way to the cemetery; the three children had chicken-pox; I hadn't heard from Roger since September—taking one thing with another, I didn't seem to be able to sleep very well.

I moved into my own apartment on 67th Street November 1st, celebrated the false Armistice on the 7th, the real one on the 11th by a champagne dinner at my in-law's, and went straight from their apartment to Miss Lippincott's small private hospital, where Roger Jr. was born at five minutes of twelve!

I couldn't believe that I had had a boy. So the doctor picked him up by the heels, shook him in front of my face and asked, "What do you think now?"

Now I had two holiday babies. Or as Roger Jr. put it several years later, "I notice, Edna, they hang out the flags on our birthdays, but not for those other children." (Poor Lewis and Carol!)

My cable telling Roger of the birth of his son was the first time he knew he had even been expecting one, because my letters had been held up during those last hectic weeks of the war. His cabled reply arrived just before Thanksgiving. So great was my relief that I let down for the first time, went into hysterics, and gave my two-week old baby a grand case of colic as a result.

In January, Roger was asked to go to London as a shipping expert for the Hoover Food Administration. He was demobilized in June and exchanged the cold rain of France for the cold rain of London. At the end of June I sailed to join him, taking ten-year-old Lewis with me, after settling the other children and the maids in a small house in New Canaan.

We took a "service flat" in St. James' Court within a few blocks of Buckingham Palace. It was a truly wonderful summer. Roger's dose of mustard gas had left him with a dreadful cough which would have

21

turned into TB had he not had that good old Dearborn-State-of-Maine constitution. The weather was England's best and he lost the cough by degrees. Lewis went by himself every morning to watch the "Changing of the Guard" at the Palace. The Victory Parade took place—General Pershing leading it on his jet black horse, all his unit marching behind him with fixed bayonets, not one of them under six feet tall and all specially trained for the occasion. Foch was there; Haig and Beatty were there; and between crying and cheering, I couldn't speak above a whisper for the next two days.

We had nice weekend trips into the country, and in August we visited the Continent with Roger's Chief, Mr. Flesh, and his wife. We went first to Holland where the men left us while they went up to Germany, and then to Paris and out to the various areas where Roger had been just a year before. He even found the very foxhole he had quit just before he was gassed!

October saw the conclusion of the London job, and we headed back to New York for Roger's introduction to his 11-month-old son, who fortunately was the living image of him, and was able to say "Da-da," which of course we translated as "Gee, Dad, how nice to meet you!"

Our rather charming duplex apartment, which had been more than adequate the year before, seemed a bit crowded with the addition of a large man and a small baby. So after another freezing cold winter in New York—with the side streets impassable, garbage thrown out anywhere on increasingly dirty snow, a cross-town car frozen in on 42nd Street for weeks—we decided enough was too much. As soon as summer came, we would retrace our steps to the Golden Gate. We had gone East for six weeks, and stayed four years!

4

ATHERTON AND JACKSON STREET
(1920 — 1930)

IN 1920 we rented an unfurnished house on Jackson Street, and lived in it winters for ten years. In 1923, after two more summer rentals, we bought a house in Atherton, 30 miles south of San Francisco. At last I had a place to leave the summer clothes in winter and vice versa, to say nothing of the impedimenta we had collected since 1907. We had been married for 16 years, and this was the 16th place I had kept house in. Now you can understand why the title of this book is "ROVING WITH ROGER."

The next ten years were busy, happy ones. The Atherton house had no pretensions to style. It was roomy and comfortable with two large sleeping porches which were used as dormitories—one for the boys and their friends, and one for the girls. Domestic help was easy to get and inexpensive in those days. I had a fine old-time Chinese cook who adored the boys but would have none of the girls. (When Lewis went off to boarding school in 1923, Old Tim stood beside me with tears in his eyes and said, "Louie one velly good-looking boy. Little Loger good-looking too. But that Carol—she look just like you." My ego was so deflated that my tears dried even before they fell!)

In 1924, my sister-in-law wrote and asked: "How much money have you got saved up? Don't you think we need a Sabbatical leave from our Lapham husbands? Why don't we go to Europe?" Both of us having been brought up as good, thrifty Presbyterians in the New England atmosphere of Noroton, we each had a nice little nest egg tucked away in the savings bank. We decided to go. Father Lapham added

23

to the travel funds when we got to New York in October on condition that we hired our own car and driver in Paris. We agreed and got the handsomest (and stupidest) driver with the most stylish and worst functioning car in the whole city. It had to be in low gear to go up the Champs Elysees!

With the exception of a trip to Verdun and one through the Chateau country to Limoges, we concentrated on Paris and shopping. Limoges was included because my father's old partner, M. Gerard, was still living (my father had died in 1914) and my mother was most anxious that I should see the Gerards again for old times' sake.

We stayed at the Hotel de la Paix, and as far as I could see, absolutely nothing had changed in twenty-five years, except that I could now appreciate how completely provincial a well-to-do French family could be. The Gerards couldn't believe that the good old black lace numbers we wore to the dinner they gave us had been bought in such outlandish places as San Francisco and San Antonio! Surely they came from Paris! They asked the usual question: "Were we much troubled by Indians?"

They were sure we were too well dressed and had too stylish a car to be up to any good. Our invitation to the married daughter, who was in her middle thirties, to motor back to Paris with us, was greeted with sheer, unadulterated horror! She was keen on the idea. Her husband was taking their two boys off shooting for the weekend, and she had not been to Paris (only six hours away by train) in the 15 years of her married life. But she didn't have a prayer, not with two "loose women" like us!

In 1925, Roger became President of the American-Hawaiian Steamship Company. Although the headquarters had been moved from New York to San Francisco, so in the following years he spent almost as much time in New York as he did in San Francisco. Two or three times a year I went with him. One October I spent several weeks with my mother in her charming little home in Washington, Connecticut. Though I have become a loyal Californian, I always resent it when people who have not seen New England in the fall insist that there is no true beauty outside the State of California.

24

In the winter of 1927, I went abroad again, this time with my mother-in-law. We had a fine six-week trip which included an audience with the Pope, a motor trip from Rome to Paris with a stop at Chartres on Good Friday, and ten days in Paris (where, after being blessed by the Pope in Rome and six Cardinals in Chartres, we felt we had received absolution for some time to come, so we turned into real devils and went to the Folies Bergeres)!

We met a charming young couple, the Bryan Reids from Chicago, who had crossed on the "Saturnia" with us, and with whom we had had many a good bridge game from Rome on as they were following the same route we were. Bryan played a good natural game, but Margaret had been taking lessons, and her favorite remarks after she had raised Bryan and gone down: "but Bryan, I had normal expectancy!" So after seeing the hordes of cats in Trajan's Forum in Rome, I bought a small stuffed kitten and sent it to them with the following jingle:

> *"I'm a kitten from Trajan's old Forum*
> *And I really should be there right now;*
> *300 like me make a quorum,*
> *We live there together—and how!*
> *Don't look at my figure too closely,*
> *I know I should diet or bant.*
> *Let me whisper a secret jocosely,*
> *I suspect I'm the least bit enceinte.*
> *I suppose my Expectancy's Normal,*
> *So cut out that line "It's not done";*
> *With but nine lives one can't be too formal,*
> *And us kittens just must have our fun."*

But to get back to the "Folies"; I really didn't want Mother Lapham to go, as I knew the kind of show it was—the kind she didn't like. But Argentina was dancing, she was anxious to see her, and so we all went. The first act was all right except for a couple of awfully funny off-color skits which she fortunately didn't understand, but I knew what the second would be like, and suggested she leave. But no; she wanted to see Argentina who was last on the bill. Sure enough the showgirls came out in the middle of the act enveloped from head to foot in ostrich feather capes shading from pale pink to crimson, removed them, and stood stark naked except for a diamond G-string.

"My Patience," said mother, "let me out! This is no place for one of the heads of the YWCA." I said: "You can't get out; shut your eyes, it won't last long," and popped an ammonia capsule under her nose. She recovered, and enjoyed Argentina; but I am sure she agreed with Bryan who said as we went out, "You know, Mrs. Lapham, most of them would honestly look better with brassieres."

We got home in time to see Lewis graduate from Hotchkiss, and that fall he entered Yale. Carol, who had graduated from Miss Burke's School in San Francisco in June, went to the Spence School in New York for a year before entering Smith in 1928. Edna went to the Santa Barbara Girls' School. Our large family gatherings were a thing of the past.

The year 1929 dawned and what a year that turned out to be! Carol made her debut with a large ball at the Burlingame Club in June. Later that month we bought our home in San Francisco—3680 Jackson Street, a beautiful pinkish brick Georgian house overlooking the Presidio and the Golden Gate. Here we have lived ever since—with the exception of three years in Washington, one in China, two in Greece, and several two- or three-month trips to Asia, Australia, Africa, and once completely around the world.

In August the National Amateur Golf Championship was held at Pebble Beach. Roger had won his long-fought victory to have it held in the West. He had been a member of the United States Golf Association, was then President of the Northern California Golf Association and, as such, the official host for the occasion.

There were many problems he had to solve, one of the greatest being how to legally provide alcoholic beverages for the whole thirsty crowd?

It was during Prohibition so no one could sell liquor. After many tentative plans, a solution was found—the "Hook'n Eye" Club was founded, based on and named for everyone's burning question: "How can I . . . get a drink?" The President of the Del Monte Properties Company provided a small cottage for the Club House. The Chief of Police had no cause to interfere with anyone who wanted to give liquor away. The day was saved.

Players and spectators came from all over, many in private cars. No one had ever had it better, and the Calcutta Pool, sold the night before the qualifying round, reached astronomic proportions—or as one man said, "If I hold up a left finger it means I bid $100. If it's a right finger it's $1,000. But I don't hold up my left hand much!"

Early in October 1929, we moved into our beautiful Jackson Street home. We made no structural changes, but did completely redecorate. One of the four former owners—the house was built in 1910 and was as nearly earthquake-proof as possible—had evidently had a great flair for color and ornamentation. My redecorating included removal of: 26 griffons' heads from the dining room mantelpiece; 12 strips of polychrome fruit and flowers from the small inserts in the panelling; 6 gold griffons' heads holding a blue velvet rope in their teeth from the stairway; a large polychrome basket of flowers from the lunette in the panelled living room; and all the gold paint from the linen-fold columns in the foyer. My contractor said that if he could only salvage all that gold paint, he wouldn't have to charge me a cent for his services.

One thing I needed was plenty of room for our books, and there seemed to be no bookcases in the living room. One end was solid panelling, the other covered by two enormous French paintings of a gentleman handing a lady into a boat and subsequently into a Temple of Love. But the happiest of surprises awaited me: the panelling was hinged, the paintings removable, and behind them bookcases reached from floor to ceiling. My birthday came just before we moved in, and the bookcase discovery was the best possible gift I could have had.

Roger's cousin was being married in San Antonio October 30, (our anniversary, too) and I decided to take Roger Jr. to the wedding rather than leave him to rattle around alone at home. There was one condition. He mustn't ask me a single question during the entire trip! He agreed, but I am not sure that it wasn't worse because he bought a 25¢ book at the station entitled "3,000 Little Known Facts" and read aloud to me steadily for the next two days. He would begin: "Mother, did you know? . . . Oh, I forgot! Listen, Mother: 'Maurice de Saxe had 365 illegi-ti-mate children' . . . that must have been one every day for a year!"

We reached San Antonio on the 28th, and on October 29th all hell broke loose on the New York stock market. Henry Lapham, the bridegroom's father, spent the whole day on the telephone being besought to bail out one or another of his friends who were trading on margin.

That night the young bridegroom-to-be said he was so nervous he didn't want to sleep alone, and could he use the other bed in my room in the Jack Lapham's guest cottage? I answered definitely *not*. In the first place, I didn't think his bride would fancy the idea at all. Secondly, I didn't want him. I could hear him snoring even in his own room, and I got enough of that at home. So I gave him 10 grains of sodium bromide, told him he would sleep like a top, and firmly closed my door behind him.

The pretty wedding went off just as happily as if the stock market had not crashed, and the next day Roger Jr., Mrs. Lapham Senior and I left for home. She was very anxious to see the house. I was equally anxious to enlist her marvellous taste in helping me place furniture. A good deal of thought was needed in arranging the large pieces I had and the others that I had ordered. The living room was 45 x 30. Her suggestions were both practical and artistic, and even today almost everything is just where she placed it.

The decade ended as '29 passed on into '30. The market rallied a bit from time to time, and even though many small traders were wiped out, few people saw the handwriting on the wall. Most felt that everything would soon be back to normal—as if the '20's had ever been normal! President Hoover assured us all that "Prosperity was just around the corner." People were still buying bootleg liquor or making bathtub gin. And the motto was not Henry of Navarre's famous "two chickens in every pot," but "two cars in every garage."

That summer was another gay, busy one: the house filled with young people; all sorts of golf tournaments and subsequent dinners at the Menlo Country Club; and many outdoor parties of our own—one of which I will never forget. Everyone was wandering around the grounds after a Sunday luncheon, when a large snake meandered across the grass. Shrieks from everyone, as we still had rattlers appear every once in a while. But one man walked over to it, took a good look, and said, "Helen, it's a gopher snake and we have lots of gophers. Do you mind if I take it home?" I acceded with pleasure. He promptly picked it up, rolled it, and put it in his pocket where it remained peacefully. But all of us fought a bit shy of him for the rest of the afternoon.

In September I took my Edna East on her way to boarding-school in France. She had been entered for Miss Nixon's, a good American school in Florence, but at the last moment I was notified that they had no room for her, so did the best I could, and got her into a very small school, "Les Mandariniers" in Juan-Les-Pins. Roger had telephoned her from San Francisco to say goodbye, but we had left so early for the steamer that he missed her. Two days later he put in the first shore-to-ship call from San Francisco to the "Teutonic." My Edna was so amazed that she didn't really grasp what was happening. She was sure that one of the people on board was playing a joke on her!

The school was anything but a success, and how the poor child stuck it out for five months I will never know. I don't think she could have, had it not been for the kindness of Mrs. Bruce Barton who was staying at the school with her own two children. All the girls Edna's age had been withdrawn due to war scare in the Mediterranean. The headmaster was very strange. He chewed all his food thirty times, and ended his meals with a huge glass of agar-agar and water, ingesting it very slowly, after everyone else had finished their meal. The system may have been all right for him, but added to the amount of pasta fed to the girls by the Italian cook, it put thirty pounds on my daughter.

In December Carol told me that she did not want to go back to college because 'she had to hunch up her shoulders so high to keep her ears warm, it was ruining her posture!' Of course Northampton is cold, and the winters are long. And one excuse is as good as another. But I was quite sure that this one had a name—Ernst Ophuls—of whom she had seen more and more as the summer went on. I finally persuaded her to go back to finish her sophomore year, and get her credits for junior year at the Sorbonne in case she wanted to go the following fall. But when the time came she didn't, so that was that.

In the meantime I had told her that, no matter how interested she was in Ernst, I had planned for a long time to take her abroad, and I wasn't going to be cheated out of it. She agreed with pleasure, so in February 1931, she, Mrs. Lapham and I sailed for Italy on the "Conte Biancomano." They disembarked at Naples, while I went on to Villefranche to see Edna's school, and pick her up to take her with us on our long motor trip.

Edna met me at the steamer, and even though I hadn't seen her since September, one look at her 160 pounds and all I could say was, "Oh! Edna!" To which she replied, "Yes Mother, I know, but I'm going to lose it." And how that dear child worked at it—eating only one real meal a day. By the time we got to Vienna I was able to buy her some pretty clothes that fitted—those she had worn ever since leaving home most certainly didn't.

After two delightful weeks in Rome, we started off on our tour in a good Packard with a fine chauffeur-guide. He was a Russian, formerly in the Czar's Guard, who had escaped from Russia after a three-week cross-country walk into Austria. At one point, he eluded a spy in Vienna by crawling out the window of a restroom. He was related to many of the big European families, had dinner clothes, and was quite prepared to act as escort to restaurants, the opera or the theatre. But I felt that Mrs. Lapham did not take too much stock in his adventures, and was rather against her daughter-in-law and granddaughters fraternizing with him. However, he really was invaluable. He spoke many languages, knew the right places to go to at the right times for lunch, tea or dinner, and for $5.00 wangled a visa for Edna, which we had forgotten to get, at the Italian-Austrian frontier.

We drove through the hill towns at a leisurely rate, spent ten days in Florence, a freezing cold week in Venice, and then on to Vienna. We spent one night en route, while Boris changed from right- to left-hand driving, supplied us with Austrian schillings which we hadn't drawn before leaving Italy, ordered our dinner from the German menu, and ended the day by coming to our rooms to remind us to look out the window, as there was an eclipse of the full moon!

Vienna was divine. We went everywhere, saw everything, ordered clothes like mad. And I bought linen and lingerie for Carol, even though she had gone into a silent Lapham mood and I could not find out if she had an "understanding" or not. But I based my reasoning on her keen disappointment at not getting the mail she expected at all our different stops. We never knew what happened, but it all came in one large batch in Vienna, and her spirits soared from then on.

From Vienna we drove on to Munich, stopping overnight at Linz, where I discovered that my few words of German were taken at their face value. All through Europe, Carol had wanted cold milk to drink, but nowhere had anyone ever heard of drinking cold milk. Then someone told me we could get it in Germany or Austria if we asked for *"Mutter's milch."* So that night in Linz I did, and our waiter looked as if I had hit him in the face with a wet towel. He repeated *"Mutter's Milch?"* I said *"Ja,"* and he disappeared for a long time, finally returning with half a teacup full of a pale blue watery liquid. . . . I wasn't surprised that it had taken him so long to find it. I watched Carol. She took a taste, said it tasted very queer, warm and sort of sweetish, and she guessed she wouldn't drink it. I agreed with her decision, but have never thought to ask her since if she knew what is really was!

Mother Lapham was a wonderful traveling companion, always enthusiastic, always ready to try anything at least once. She was even willing to listen to Carol and me play some of the piano duets we had bought in Italy. Schubert's "Marche Militaire" was our *piece de resistance* with which we brought our tea-time concert to a triumphant conclusion. We went sightseeing every morning, lunched at a good restaurant, and then she returned to the hotel for a long rest, while Carol, Edna and I had fittings, window-shopped, or did some of the things that involved too much walking for her. She had only one failing. Any foreign language could have been Chinese or Greek as far as she was concerned, and I spent a geat deal of time hauling her out of *"Herren,"* and trying to convince her that she was a Dame, and *"Damen"* was where she belonged! But it just never seemed to register. Only once did the girls and I make the same mistake. That was when we went into the wrong outhouse in the courtyard of a very second-class small Inn in the Tyrol, and were yelled at by the proprietor, but by that time all I could say was *"Zu spaht."*

Several days before we got to Nuremberg, I developed a peculiar ailment. I itched all over, just as if I had poison ivy, but with no visible signs of inward discomfort. We asked the hotel to get us an English-speaking doctor. A nice little spade-bearded German was produced, who instantly diagnosed my condition as more pasta in Italy than my system could assimilate and that I should stay in Nuremberg for ten days. He would give me piqueurs, and cure me completely. I said that unfortunately we were leaving the next day, but I would consult a doctor as soon as we got to Paris. This being disposed of, he then settled down for a good chance to practice his English, and asked me, to the girls' rather horrified amusement, if I was a "sporting woman." After one good gulp I got it, and said no, I didn't indulge much in sports except for tennis when I was younger, but now I mostly just sat around and listened.

Finally in Brussels Carol broke down and told me she did have an "understanding" with Ernst. But there was no question of marriage for a long time as he was just starting in with the Bank of America, we did not know his family, etc. But at least I could then go in for trousseau linen in a big way.

A stop in Rheims, and then to Paris where Mother left us, feeling she had been away from home long enough and should return. The first thing I did was to get a doctor, who agreed with the diagnosis, gave me the piqueurs, and told me to eat no fruit or fresh vegetables, and not to touch anything alcoholic! Paris, in May, with fresh asparagus, fraises de bois, and prohibition at home! I told him I'd rather itch, which I did, until one day he said there was only one thing left to do. Change the current of my blood stream. This he did by removing about half a pint of blood from my right arm, and shooting it back into my left hip! I have never found a doctor since who even believed this story. But it did the trick. Two days later I was a well woman.

After Mother left, we finished all our shopping and then took a motor trip through the Chateau country and to Mont St. Michel, returning just in time to pick up our clothes, pack our trunks and get ready to sail for home on the "Ile de France."

Meantime I had asked the doctor for his bill. I was sure it would be a big one because, aside from treating me, he had prescribed for Carol's dry skin and Edna's thyroid condition. He also had called every day for two weeks while he was giving me my piqueurs and changing my blood stream. I figured it would be well over $200, which I had put aside. The day before we left I picked up the bill at the office, but waited to open it until I had the girls to give me needed support. It was $65.00! I said, "Girls, here's your chance—it's our last afternoon, here's the balance I expected Dr. Schwartz to get, go out and buy whatever your little hearts desire."

Boris drove us to Le Havre to take the steamer and we parted from him practically with tears in our eyes. I paid his final bill, and gave him his final pourboire. He kissed my hand—and there was Carol holding out hers! He kissed hers too. When we got on the ship she said, "Mother, Boris and I both knew that European gentlemen don't kiss an unmarried girl's hand, but he knew I wanted him to, so he did."

5

DEBUTS, WEDDINGS AND GRANDCHILDREN
(1931—1936)

THE summer passed pleasantly as usual, but people had begun to wonder uneasily if the "recession" wasn't more serious than it had seemed at first. Hoover had been renominated for President. He had refused, however, excellent advice to come out strongly for Repeal, to put a very high excise tax on the manufacture and sale of liquor, and to apply the proceeds to farm relief. Roosevelt did come out for Repeal.

Roger, who had said he would vote for anyone black, yellow, red or white, who advocated Repeal, did so in the November elections. I voted for Hoover. Lewis voted for Norman Thomas. The Lapham family might just as well have stayed home from the polls.

Carol's engagement was announced in September and after that excitement had died down, next came preparations for Edna's debut. But 1931 was a different era than 1929. The debut just couldn't be as large nor as elaborate as Carol's. But it was pretty and gay, and we had no such casualities as had marred some of the previous debuts. (At one the liquor had been hijacked on the way to the hotel; at the second, the supply arrived so late that when it did get there a regular mob scene ensued.) Roger had made it very clear that no pocket flasks were to be brought, and we had no trouble.

One of out guests, a young naturalized Hollander named Jan van Oosten, told a friend that he had never seen anything prettier than the debutante, and that he would certainly try to see more of her. I could easily see why; even though she had lost a great deal of weight, she was blonde, blue-eyed, and nicely rounded, and I am sure looked more like a little Dutch maiden than anything he had ever seen in America.

Both for the nation in general and for the Lapham family in particular 1932 was quite a year. Lewis was living at home. He had gone to work for the San Francisco Examiner, first as a leg man, and later on as a waterfront reporter from which he eventually got his own column "On The Gangplank."

Jan van Oosten had kept his word. He called on Edna and was taking her out so frequently that finally I told Roger that I thought he had "intentions." Roger poohpoohed it. He claimed that every time a man looked twice at a daughter, mothers always thought the man was serious. I said that was not the answer—Jan was twelve years older than Edna, he had had a foreign up-bringing, and foreigners didn't monopolize very young girls unless they did have intentions. I asked Edna how she felt about going out with him; she said she guessed it was all right, but he talked so fast and spoke with such an accent she couldn't understand him half the time. I asked why they didn't speak French? She said they'd tried that, but then neither of them could understand each other.

In the spring Roger took Carol and me East with him to get a few extra things for her trousseau, for she was to be married in June. She went off on her own one day and came in with a hat for which she told me proudly she had paid only $5.95. I could readily believe it, but had the grace to hold my tongue. That evening Roger and a friend of his took us to dinner at his old family home at 15 West 56th Street, which had been turned into a speakeasy. As dinner progressed, the two gentlemen took a strong dislike to Carol's hat. They finally asked how much she had paid for it, and if they bought it from her, could they burn it? She started to tell them $5.95, but I kicked her firmly and said "$25!" She said "Oh! Mother!" But I stuck to it, they anteed up—and burned the hat on a plate then and there. The stink practically got us thrown out of the restaurant!

The next event was a letter from Edna saying that Jan had asked her to marry him; how did we feel about it? It was a real bombshell to Roger. We really knew very little about Jan except that he had a position with the Holland-America Steamship Company. Roger made what inquiries he could, and then we telephoned Edna to hold everything in abeyance until we got home.

The evening we arrived stands out in my mind as one of sheer horror. Carol and Ernst, Jan and Edna, Lewis and Roger Jr. were there for dinner—plus a couple from Santa Barbara and their teenage daughter, whom Roger Jr. had asked up to a school dance . . . which had been cancelled. She had gone to Los Angeles to get a new dress and came all the way to San Francisco for the party, only to find there wasn't one. On top of that, Ernst arose and made a speech to the newly-engaged couple before we had even had time to talk to Edna about it—let alone interviewing Jan. Roger, looking like a thunder-cloud practically left the table, and I wanted to crawl under it.

All I had had time to ask Edna was: Did she really want to marry him? And if she didn't understand a word he said, how did she know he had asked her? She replied with great dignity, "I asked him to repeat it, Mother." That was that. Roger had his interview with Jan and the engagement was recognized. Then we were told that they would like to be married in July, as Jan had to go to Holland on business; he thought it would be a good idea to make it a honeymoon trip, too.

1932 . . . two daughters' weddings seven weeks apart—and Lewis engaged to be married in October—situations that really gave one pause. Of course, everyone had a very simple solution: have a double wedding. But that was out of the question. Carol had been engaged for a year and a half, and wanted to be married in our garden at Atherton. She had waited patiently for it, and was surely entitled to have the kind of wedding she wanted. Edna wanted to be married in the little Episcopal Church in Menlo Park. Even if the two girls had wanted the same thing, I don't think it would have been possible because Carol and Ernst were both very tall and Edna and Jan both short; a double wedding would have looked like something out of the comic strips.

So Carol had her pretty outdoor wedding with Lewis' Jane coming out to be a bridesmaid. And no sooner had her wedding presents been packed away than Edna's presents started coming in. That was when Roger Sr., saved Roger Jr.'s life by taking him on a trip to Alaska—he had been so excited and "helpful" with the incoming gifts that he had mixed up the numbers to be pasted on them, and many no longer jibed with the cards enclosed by the donors. I wasn't on too even a keel myself, and if Roger Jr. had stayed home, I am afraid I might have resorted to violence.

I had told Edna that I had neither the time nor the money to fit her out with much of a trousseau, so why not wait until December? But no, then she wouldn't get the trip to Holland. So she and Jan were married on the 30th of July. I had had a little Dutch cap made for her from some of my own bridal lace to hold her short veil in place; Jan was so overcome I thought he was going to faint when he first looked at her. She carried gardenias and I had warned the florist not to make too large a bouquet as she was so short. But when the bouquet arrived it was the size of a dishpan. I gasped, "Oh! Eddie!", and he said, "I know, But Miss Edna told me she'd never in her whole life had all the gardenias she wanted and this time she was going to have them."

Jan and Edna were going to spend a few days at Del Monte before leaving for Holland. As the car was pulling away from the house, someone discovered that the best man, who was extremely absent-minded, had neglected to put any of their bags in the car. We caught them at the gate, and in the silence that followed, Roger Jr. dropped a classic remark: "Gee, Mom, if they hadn't had their bags, Jan wouldn't have had any pajamas."

By September the financial situation all over the country was desperate. I will never forget the night American-Hawaiian stock went to 4. Roger came home, and I didn't even speak to him, just put a highball into his hand which he accepted in silence. Roger Jr. always read the stock reports, and thought in terms of algebra, so his opening remarks was: "Gee, Dad, I see A-H went down to 4. What do you do if it goes below zero—put a minus sign in front of it?" I couldn't reach him to kick him, so I closed my eyes and waited for the deluge. But

Roger laughed! And all he said was, "Well, we hope it won't come to that, son."

The last of the month we went East to see Roger Jr. settled in Milton, Edna in Brookline, and stayed on for Lewis and Jane's wedding in Montclair on October 14th. Then we came back to San Francisco for our own 25th Anniversary which was only a small, almost all family dinner. Jane and Lewis had come out through the Panama Canal on their honeymoon, and had arrived just in time to celebrate with us; and both she and I wore our wedding gowns. Then we turned right around and went back to New York to celebrate the Laphams' 50th; by that time I thought if I ever heard the word "wedding" again, I'd go into hysterics.

As a matter of fact, I did burst into tears one night and told Roger that if I couldn't get away by myself, and not have to be pleasant to anyone, I thought I'd go crazy. He was duly concerned, and after several suggestions, it was finally decided that I would sail from New York through the Canal on one of the A-H freighters. They didn't take passengers. They didn't like women on board. But the President's word was law. So I sailed from Brooklyn on a stormy night late in November on the "American."

We picked up the tail end of a hurricane, the ship was light, and I never left the Captain's suite which he had turned over to me for the trip. On the second night out, the ship's safe, camouflaged as a chiffonier, wrenched loose and fell across my bed. Fortunately I had packed myself well with pillows, and though the huge, heavy mass fell across me, when the ship righted itself I was able to give a mighty heave and send it crashing to the floor; then for one of the first times in my life, I screamed and screamed and screamed. Someone shouted, "I'm coming!" But the door was locked, and I had to navigate from the bed to the door with that huge safe sliding back and forth. I finally got there, and sailors came in and lashed it fast. Although my right arm was black and blue from the shoulder to below the elbow, nothing, by the grace of God, was broken.

From then on it was smooth sailing, and I couldn't have enjoyed my trip more. No newspapers with "Jumped or Fell" in the headlines every morning; no more heart-rending stories of people who were down to their last yacht.

The Captain thought it would be a good idea to teach me navigation. I assured him that even simple arithmetic was practically beyond me. After a couple of attempts, he agreed with me. Then he decided I should learn something of astronomy, but soon gave that up as a bad job, too. In fact, when we reached San Pedro after a fine 18-day voyage, he said with a sigh, "Well I guess the trip has done you good—you've gained five pounds, and I've taught you to light a cigarette on one match."

Just before I left New York a San Francisco friend had dropped in to see me in our rooms at the Ritz, and said she had a very personal question to ask me: Was I taking this trip with the intention of committing suicide? I was so stunned that all I could say was, "What in the world ever put that idea into your head?" Her answer was that she simply couldn't conceive of anyone going off alone on a freighter with no other woman aboard for any other reason.

By that time I had recovered sufficiently to say something I deeply regretted afterward: I said most emphatically that it was the last thought I had in my mind, and if the "American" arrived in San Pedro with me missing, I hadn't jumped, I had been pushed! But I had never been on a 10,000-ton freighter before, and didn't realize how very easy it would be to accidentally slip overboard from the narrow, slippery deck with no protective guard rail.

I talked so much about my trip after I got home, that Roger said I had become more nautical in three weeks than he had in 27 years, and said as long as I knew so much, what was the "mean slip?" I knew the answer! It's one of the most common topics of discussion on board— namely, the difference between what the Chief said his engines would have done if the Captain had plotted the proper course, and what they actually did.

Aside from our own social activities and those of the children, the decade from the early twenties to the early thirties was a full one for me. I went on the Boards of the San Francisco Protestant Orphanage Society, and of the Francisca Club, about 1923, and in time became President of both. When I joined the Orphanage Board, I must have been the youngest member by at least twenty years. So when several years later they told me I could take my choice of being either President or Treasurer, I was slightly appalled. But I made my choice promptly. I felt that I might just be able to run all the old girls. But my mathematical knowledge going no further than the ability to balance my own check book, the Treasurership was out of my line, even with the advice of our male trustees and our financial advisor. I was duly elected President. After the meeting the outgoing President came to me and told me I shouldn't worry—just say to myself that I was President of a million dollar corporation (our endowment fund) and continue from there! Famous last words! I didn't close my eyes all night.

But the thing I enjoyed most (and which has been of enduring pleasure and benefit ever since), was a musical ensemble I belonged to—four women playing two pianos under the leadership of Miss Ada Clement, the head of the San Francisco School of Music. We met every Friday morning at eleven, and nothing but death or smallpox could keep us away. We sight-read all the symphonies which the Symphony orchestra was going to play—Beethoven, Brahms, Schumann, Tschaikovsky—and then worked on them for two weeks or more, until they really sounded like something.

I think that one of the greatest thrills of my life came one day when our group went over its allotted hour-and-a-half, to finish the Tschaikovsky Fifth. (Or is it the Sixth? At any rate it is that wonderful movement that I have always called the "Charge of the Cossacks.") The first violinist of the orchestra came in to give a lesson, closely followed by the first cellist. They both took out their instruments and joined us. We ended in a burst of glory, and simultaneously (which was rare). If I had had any voice at all I would have stood up and shouted the Valkyries' "Ho-Yo-To-HOY!" at the top of my lungs, for mere words couldn't possibly have expressed by excitement and exultation. Even to this day, when I hear one of those good old favorites, I can follow every note of the part I played in our quartet.

Edna and Jan spent part of the summer of 1933 with us in Atherton. Edna was pregnant and more than happy about it. She gave birth to the first grandchild, Jan Roger, in Boston on February 5, 1934. I went there to be with her, of course, and struck the coldest weather since the winter of 1917-1918—the thermometer read 18 below zero on the day Jannie was born.

Fortunately, Edna's doctor had insisted on putting her in the hospital a few days ahead of her time because the snow was so deep it was doubtful whether a car could get through in case of emergency. However, all went well, except that she was given so much anesthesia that nearly 24 hours elapsed before she was fully aware of having a fine boy. I stayed on for about two weeks, trimmed a lovely bassinet for her and saw her safely home with a nice little Boston-Irish trained nurse.

Then I got back to the Coast as quickly as possible to be on hand for Carol's first child—also a boy, who was born on the 17th of March. He was christened William. Because there were already a William Ophuls (the Doctor) and two William Deamers (Ernst's brother-in-law and his son) in the family, Carol's William was immediately nicknamed "Pat" for his Patron Saint. He has never been called anything else. In fact I doubt that as a child, he even knew his name wasn't really Pat; the first day he went to school, Carol asked him what it was like, he said, "All right, but the teacher didn't know much. She called me William."

Lewis and Jane's first, named Lewis Henry Lapham for his great-grandfather, was born January 8, 1935, and a hard time he had of it. He was breathing at birth but then stopped completely. It took an agonizing half hour to bring him back to life. I have always felt that Jane, too, was given too much anesthesia and that it affected the baby to such a degree that he almost didn't survive. I felt at the time, and still feel, that any normal, healthy young woman can and should go through the early part of the labor fully conscious, but aware that help will be given her when she really needs it.

41

Mother Lapham came out from New York the following week, and she and I sailed for Honolulu a few days later. She had never been there, in spite of the fact that her family's steamships had been connected with the Islands for so many years. We had an unusually rough trip down on the "Lurline," but soon revived in our lovely suite at the Royal Hawaiian.

Roger's older cousin, Henry Lapham, and his wife, Becca, from Boston were staying there too. Henry insisted that I should take either hula lessons or learn to ride a surf board. I chose the latter as the lesser of two evils. And once, just once, I came in standing up triumphantly—only to hear a man's voice behind me saying, "Get out of my way!" Get out of his way? It was all I could do to keep my balance because steering was out of my line. At that moment he ran into me. We both fell off and went under, but with great presence of mind I stood on his head, and surfaced quite easily. I didn't care at all that he seemed slightly annoyed when he finally came up for air.

A pleasant two weeks passed quickly. Mrs. Lapham was introduced to okulihau at a cocktail party, and almost told me to mind my own business when I prevented her from taking a second. She said it tasted just like lemonade. But I knew it has a delayed kick like a Government mule. After only one, she went to sleep going home in the car, slept for two hours more in the hotel, and then admitted that I was probably right.

We had a much better return trip, sitting at the Captain's table with delightful companions, Prince and Princess Orsini. I knew she was American, born in Los Angeles, but the Captain didn't. At dinner the night after they left the ship in Los Angeles, he was almost in tears when he discovered his lovely Princess wasn't a Princess at all—she had been born in Los Angeles, and her name was Schwartz! No proper ending for a fairy tale for him.

That June (1935), Father Lapham died after an operation. We all felt he could have lived had he really wanted to. He had been very distressed by the new tax structure instituted by the Roosevelt Administration. I think he really felt that life was not worth living, if all that you had achieved by your own honest efforts could not be passed on to your children intact; he considered that the inheritance taxes amounted to confiscation. Perhaps it is just as well he isn't alive to see what they are now!

One evening shortly after the funeral, Mother Lapham and I were sitting alone in the Great Hall in "Waveny"—the New Canaan estate—when all of a sudden the electric organ which Father had had installed and on which he loved to improvise, began to play of its own accord. My hair rose on end. And even Mother said, "My patience!" Had Father become a revenant? With great courage I got up to investigate. Running up and down the keys was a large mouse! A most welcome anti-climax.

For some time I had been planning to fix up a small gardener's cottage on our grounds as a place for Carol and Ernst to spend their summers. I talked it over with Carol, but she seemed a bit hesitant and finally burst out with, "Well, Mother, I don't think it will be big enough—I'm expecting a second baby in September." So an extra bedroom was added to the cottage and it all worked out beautifully.

Carol's second son, Ernst, was born the 10th of September. After that there was a lull in babies for almost a year, although by early spring both Jane and Edna were expecting their second infants late in the summer.

That May Mother Lapham came out again, and she, Carol, Edna and I drove up to the Yosemite for a weekend. It couldn't have been a lovelier time to see it: all the waterfalls were full, there was a light powdering of snow on the ground, but all the dogwood trees were in full bloom.

On my return to Atherton I found a message to call Lewis immediately. Fearful that something might have happened to Jane, I put in a call at once and asked, "Your wife, Lewis?" "No, Mother," said he, "your husband! Cap Rieber (a very old friend of ours) has asked him to fly to Europe on the German zeppelin, the 'Hindenberg,' and he wants to know how you feel about it."

I gulped once, and then wired Roger who was in New York to telephone me that evening. He did, about 10:30 and we had a long and beautiful talk: "Is it all right if I go, dear?" "Why yes, dear, if you want to. Do you want me to come on?" "No dear, I think perhaps you'd better not . . . etc." We were both just too noble!

Carol came up to the house the next morning and asked if I had talked with Pa? "Oh yes, such a satisfactory conversation!" At that moment the telephone rang—New York calling Mrs. Lapham, and Roger came on the phone: "I got your wire, dear, but I got in so late last night I thought I wouldn't call you until this morning . . . hello . . . hello, are you there?" My silence was nothing if not blank. But I finally found voice enough to say, "Well, I suspected you were a little high last night, but I didn't know you were that high. You did call me, and we talked for fifteen minutes . . ." "What?? . . . then shrieks of laughter, which I answered coldly: "Laugh on your own time. When you get your bill from the Ritz, you won't find it's anything to laugh about." Carol thought it was funny; I didn't.

6

AN INTERLUDE OF WORK, PEACE AND TRAVEL
(1936—1940)

S O Roger floated off on the "Hindenberg" to visit Portugal, Germany, Holland and England, and returned on the "Bremen" after a grand and glorious trip.

I was really glad he could have such a break. Since the spring of 1934 the shipping companies has been beset by labor troubles on the waterfront. That year there was a 100-day longshoremen's strike affecting all the Pacific ports—in San Francisco it culminated in a general strike. It was then that Roger had his first talk with Madam Secretary of Labor Perkins—a long distance phone call which lasted 45 minutes. The next day when the shipowners refused to discuss anything until the General Strike was called off, the Secretary classed both the shipowners and the strikers as a "group of naughty boys, quarreling."

From then on it was one strike after another, or as one of the shipping men said several years later, "I lost count after there were over 400." It was not too easy or comfortable a time for me. Roger had an easily identifiable light-colored car, a cream-colored Chrysler. He used to drive around the waterfront every day, going on board the A-H ships tied up in the harbor to talk with the various masters who had stayed by them. However, no violence was ever shown him and the longshoremen's attitude was demonstrated by an accident at one point. Roger's car was hit broadside by another car on his way home and turned upside down. He crawled out shaken and bruised but with his cigar still in his mouth, to find a man standing beside him who said, "Well, Mr. Lapham, I'm a longshoreman and I don't think you've ever been right before, but I'm willing to testify you were this time. I've measured the skid marks, and that other car skidded 65 feet after he hit you."

In August of 1936, Lewis and Jane's second son, Anthony Abbot, was born. And in September I went East for the birth of Edna's second child, a daughter, Helene, named more or less for me. I wanted her to be called "Helena," which was a good Dutch name, and I thought Helena van Oosten was both rhythmical and appropriate. But Jan had a French ancestor and preferred Helene, so that was that.

That fall, there was another Pacific Coast maritime strike which lasted another 100 days. And some time in November, Harry Bridges invited any member of the shipping fraternity who was willing to debate the issues with him in the Civic Auditorium. There was sheer horror on the part of the shipping companies—all except for Roger, who declared himself not only willing, but anxious to do it.

Everyone was opposed to the idea and no one would listen to Roger: Bridges would make a monkey of him and the companies would lose face. But Roger insisted that they would lose more face if they refused, and most unwilling consent was finally given. The date was set for early December.

No one who was there will ever forget that night. The Auditorium was jammed—17,000 or more; 98% labor, of course, but with a few of our friends on hand for moral support. My evening started off pleasantly with a friend asking me as I went in if Roger was wearing a bullet-proof vest! "For of course, my dear, it would only take one crazy person to take a shot at him and kill him." But Roger was sure that having invited him, they would listen to him, and they did. In fact, two men who gave a Bronx cheer at one statement he made were promptly hauled out by the unions' own MP's.

There was practically silence as Roger mounted the platform, but the house came down when Bridges entered shortly afterward. Bridges ranted at length to tumultuous applause about the ills the waterfront unions had suffered at the hands of the shipping companies; then Roger spoke and explained the position of the companies, caught between the unions, the Government, and the stockholders. He never spoke better, and got quite warm applause at the end. His family were so proud of him they almost burst, and I really think he should be credited with offering a wedge of reason for the end of the strike. However, it did last into January, and by that time many of the longshoremen were heartily sick of it (and I suspect their wives were even sicker). Many came up to Roger on the street asking if he couldn't do something to end it.

In the late winter of 1937 Roger had a bad case of 'flu, which his doctor told him was largely due to strain, stress and overwork. He warned Roger that he would have to take a real vacation, preferably a long trip which would take him clear away from his long struggles with the labor situation.

We discussed it at length and finally decided that a trip to the Orient was in order. We invited our dear friend Florence (Mrs. Charles) McCormick to go with us, and pored over travel folders and alternate routes for the next six weeks. And how well our itinerary (Japan, China, Hong Kong, Manila, Singapore, Java, Bali, Australia, New Zealand and home) turned out.

We sailed from San Francisco for Yokohama on the 20th of May. Because it was Florence's first long trip, and the first one Roger and I had taken together outside of the country in years, our friends arrived at the "Tatsuta" en masse to bid us God-speed, each bearing a gift. We had two good-sized staterooms with a bath between, but by the time the gifts were disposed of, there was no room left for us! We opened champagne, then kissed everyone goodbye and went up on the deck to sail. As we passed under the Golden Gate Bridge, Roger thumbed his nose at the city, and kissed us both.

Because Roger was President of the A-H, we were at Captain Ito's table, and nothing was omitted for our comfort. Capt. Ito, slightly under five feet tall, was the Commandant of the Fleet and a ranking Admiral in the Navy. He spoke very precise uninflected English, but with such an accent that he and Florence, who was no linguist, always seemed to be talking at cross purposes. At one meal the Captain asked her if she liked soya sauce, to which she answered, "Oh no, Captain, I really don't swim at all." Puzzled but pursuing, he repeated his question; she repeated her answer, but volunteered that she played very good bridge. At this point I stepped in and said the Captain wanted to know if she liked soya sauce. "Mercy," she said, "I thought he said water sports."

All kinds of entertainment were provided for the passengers. One, a dance on deck, turned out sadly for Roger. Doing a duty dance with a fat red-head, and trying to swing her, hefty as she was, his rubber-soled shoes didn't make the turn and he snapped his Achilles tendon, which deprived him of a great deal of pleasure and all sightseeing which involved much walking for the rest of the three-month trip.

We had long lazy mornings, generally breakfasting in Florence's room, after which I insisted on reading aloud from one of my gift books, "How to Win Friends and Influence People." I was rather insulted when it was given to me, but then decided to be amused, especially as the rest of my gift from the same person was a bottle of tasteless castor oil and a package of paper toilet seats. The last part of the gift proved to be such a boon, that I forgave her for the insult.

There were very few Americans on board, but many N.Y.K. agents, as well as a number of Japanese Consuls and their wives, being recalled to Japan for "consultation." However the atmosphere at that time was peaceful and pleasant; we were more or less being wooed. Many of the Japanese women were charming and we thoroughly enjoyed them.

As we approached Yokohama, Roger, who was on deck, spotted a queer-looking object sticking up out of the water and called a sailor's attention to it. Then the excitement started, with a great deal of running around and shouting, "Put camera away—no picture taking!" As we drew nearer, we saw it was a Japanese sea-plane nose down in the sea, with two aviators on the pontoons and one way up on the tail. They had been in the water for two hours, had no radio, and it was just their good luck that Roger's keen eyes had spotted them. We sent off a boat to pick up the men, and then stood by until a Japanese destroyer came along to salvage the plane.

Through friends we had engaged a guide named Martin, and he was a real character. Both of his legs had been broken in the terrible earthquake of '23, and set so badly that they formed a perfect arc—but how he could get around on them! He came out on the quarantine boat to meet us, accompanied by a representative of every Japanese shipping company, plus what seemed to be the entire Japanese Press. Those who couldn't get near Roger surrounded Florence, to her unutterable horror.

We went ashore, and the customs officials showed signs of making us open all our trunks. But fortunately the first bag he opened had my paper toilet seats on top. "Ah ha! Tracing paper for plans!" So I unfolded one, explained its use—and that was the end of our customs examination.

We fell in love with Frank Lloyd Wright's charming hotel, with the smiling, bowing little maids (I am such a mimic that I found myself returning the three ceremonial bows before I had been there three days); with its cleanliness, its fascinating arcade shops, and oh! the whole general atmosphere.

We were royally entertained in Tokyo, the shipping companies coming through in a big way. One of the men took us first to a theatre, and then to dinner in a small restaurant (which he had reserved for the evening, as his wife had agreed to be present, and of course he could not risk having her exposed to the stares of strangers). We sat at a semi-circular sort of a bar, behind which a perfectly enormous 300-pound ex-wrestler cooked and served us delicious sizzling small, hot fish of all kinds. I was a little leery of the raw eel, but it tasted better than it looked, especially if I just shut my eyes and opened my mouth. At the end of dinner we were offered delicious looking strawberries, against which we had been most carefully warned on account of the fertilizer used. Safety or politeness, which? The wife saw our hesitation, assured us that she had raised them herself, and they were absolutely safe. We ate them in fear and trembling, but she was right and we suffered no ill effects.

As the men had remained upstairs while we three women were eating our possibly lethal strawberries, Florence indicated how much she would love to see the inside of a Japanese home. Many giggles from the wife, who admitted it has been considered, but "she say cannot allow

American high heels on her beautiful thick straw matting, and husband say cannot ask American lady take off shoe," so it had to be a restaurant. "My shoes!" said Florence, "why I'd have taken off anything you wanted me to. Oh, how I wish you had told us!"

After several days in Tokyo we travelled to Miyanoshita and Lake Hakone, from where one was supposed to be able to see Fujiyama in all its snow-covered glory. But alas! it was veiled in clouds, and we never even got a glimpse of it, a great disappointment to me (it is the only mountain I ever knew the height of—12,365 feet—the easiest possible number to remember).

Back to Tokyo by way of Kamakura with its wonderful Buddha, and then a day or so later by motor to Nikko. Driving in Japan is something you never forget. The roads are narrow and high-crowned; jammed with people, dogs, babies and rattle-trap buses. Every driver heads straight for an approaching car, and the game is to see who will chicken out first. To add to the general confusion, driving was on the left-hand side of the road. I sat with my eyes closed so much of the time, not wishing to see when we hit, I really missed a great deal of the scenery. But not the last part—that twenty-mile approach to Nikko through that wonderful avenue of 1000-year-old cryptomeria trees.

The hotel, a fine combination of Japanese architecture and decor, and modern convenience, was a most comfortable one with a lovely view of a rushing stream spanned by the red lacquer "Sacred Bridge." The temples, the coloring and the trees were beyond description. They involved an enormous amount of walking and climbing, so poor Roger had to miss most of them, as his leg just wouldn't take it. He had seen a doctor as soon as we arrived in Tokyo, but when he heard the verdict —an immediate operation and two months to recover—he simply said, "To hell with it," and hobbled around on a cane as best he could.

We were to leave by train for Kyoto on the morning of June 9, and being uncertain of the toilet arrangements on Japanese trains, I decided that a last visit to the nice, clean hotel bathroom was in order. The doors were half-doors (like those in old-fashioned New York saloons), and once I was comfortably enthroned, imagine my surprise to see Martin's

50

head appearing over the door. I said "Martin, go away!", and he said, "Pardon, lady—no matter, I just want to see if lady leave her tooth-brush." I said no, I was leaving something else that was nobody's business but my own, so he withdrew with complete dignity.

Kyoto (which Florence insisted on calling "Coyote") was perfectly beautiful, although I didn't enjoy it as much as I might have, as one of my miserable teeth had started to ache and I was living on aspirin. The day after our arrival Martin said he thought we had seen enough temples, so we would not go to Nara and the Sacred Deer. Instead he had a little surprise for us. It turned out to be a six- or seven-mile drive to the Hozu River, where flat-bottomed boats met us, and we shot the rapids! It was really a thrilling trip with skilled boatmen steering us through very swift water with beautiful scenery on each side (when we stopped shrieking long enough to look at it).

On to Kobe the next day where I went to a Japanese dentist who took a look at my tooth, drew in a hissing breath, bowed low, and said "Oh! So sad. I fear abscess—please to spit." I bowed and spat. All went well until I unfortunately bowed and spat in the wrong direction; I followed this faux pas with an even worse one, when I asked how much I owed him. He shuddered with horror at my rudeness and said, "Please to ask lady nurse." I did; she figured for several minutes on an abacus, and finally came up with the charges—75¢!

We sailed the next day on the "Empress of Asia" for Shanghai, down the Inland Sea by full moon, but I was far too miserable to appreciate it because of the tooth. So loaded myself with aspirin and went to bed. We stopped at Nagasaki to coal the following day; all the coaling was done by women, the majority of whom had babies strapped to their backs!

We had the whole day ashore. Roger saw a ship model he could hardly resist—all tortoise- shell, an exquisite piece of work. But the price was $3000, and he didn't buy it, a fact I think he always regretted; after the bombing of Nagasaki, he said wistfully, "I do wish I had bought that ship model." (I thought of this many years later—I was looking at a fascinating old carved emerald pin in Cairo and hesitating on account of price, when an American I knew came up to me and said,

"Buy it, Mrs. Lapham. It's never our extravagances we regret, it's only the things we passed up.")

In Shanghai we were met by representatives of Caltex and the States Lines. They staged a pitched battle for us on the docks; so we had cocktails and dinner with one set, and went on to a night club with the other, getting back to the Cathay Hotel well towards morning, with me practically *non compos*.

The next day I saw an American dentist who said the tooth would have to come out, and recommended another American who would do it for me. In the dentist chair I warned the dentist that I was very susceptible to drugs or anesthetics, and to please give me not more than half of whatever it was he used. But he paid no attention and gave me a shot of Evipan; an opium derivative. It was three hours before I could get off of his operating table! He had gone out as soon as the tooth was extracted, leaving me with Florence and his little Chinese nurse, who didn't speak English. When Florence saw I couldn't breathe, she got hold of Roger and for three hours they watched me gasp for breath, my lungs completely paralyzed. They finally got me back to the hotel, almost carrying me between them. Going up in the elevator an American woman turned to her friend and said, "That nice-looking American woman—drunk at four o'clock in the afternoon!" I tried to say "Not drunk, drugged," but thought that would make the situation worse.

I fell into bed and slept the better part of 24 hours, to be awakened by the dentist who asked me why I hadn't told him I had heart trouble! I said I did not have heart trouble, just extreme susceptibility to drugs, which I had told him, and to which he had paid no attention. I guess I was lucky at that; when we were in Hong Kong shortly after, there was a small item in the paper that an American woman had died in a dentist's office in Shanghai of an overdose of Evipan. (Florence's comment on that was that she was awfully glad I hadn't died just at the start of our trip, as she wondered how people would have felt about it had she continued on with Roger, chaperoned only by my ashes!)

Shanghai was high, wide, and rather unhandsome in those days. Its Swan Song, if anybody had realized it. There was horse racing, jai alai with wild betting, and night clubs with White Russian "hostesses" —all of them, of course, of noble birth under the old Czarist regime—, but with very little nobility remaining in any of them. They were out for all the traffic would bear. Roger escaped from us one night and went to a club called the "Del Monte," chaperoned by a States Line man. He came back mad as a hornet, for after he had bought the hostesses champagne at something like $20 a bottle, they had then demanded an extra fee for "entertainment," which consisted of sitting at his table and dancing with him.

We dined one evening with a Chinese Harvard graduate who asked us to his home, which we expected to be furnished with such charming things that we would be green with envy. But no! It was all filled with the very worst of Grand Rapids furniture, and the china and table linen must have been bought from a Sears Roebuck catalogue, sight unseen. Mr. Tsaou's wife was one of the most beautiful women I have ever seen, and her hands were such a poem I could understand why so much Chinese poetry dwells on the loveliness of hands. We were asked not to try to talk to her, as she spoke no English; she did dine with us, safely seated between her husband and her brother, but did not accompany us to the night club with "taxi dancers," where we went after dinner.

After ten days in Shanghai we flew to Peking and my first sight of it was one of the great disappointments of my life. I had read so much about it—"Indiscreet Letters from Pekin," "Peking Picnic" and many other books—that I expected everything to be colorful and romantic. But of course you see nothing of the beauty of the houses, surrounded as they are by their high, mud-colored compound walls.

We had been entertained to such a degree in Shanghai that Roger said as we landed, "Well, thank God we don't know a soul here." We didn't—then. But just as we were comfortably settled in the roomy bus to the Hotel de Pekin, up came a man who said he had been sent down from Tientsin by the States Line to take care of us during the whole four-day stay.

He insisted on our leaving the bus and climbing into his old Ford jalopy with his wife and a Chinese driver, who simply reeked of garlic. It was terribly hot; Roger's leg was badly swollen again, and he was in such a temper he never spoke during the long drive. The poor States Line agent, who was only doing what he had been told to do, kept right on making Roger madder every time he opened his mouth. He advised that he had scheduled every moment of our precious four days, always in the company of him and his wife. We finally got to our hotel rooms alone, and Roger turned to the two of us and said, "Get rid of them! I'm not going to see or speak to either of them again!"

We finally persuaded him to lunch with them, and I explained as tactfully as possible that my husband was not up to the program they had planned. Far from being upset, I think they were rather relieved and said that as they had been told to stay in Peking for four days at States Line expense, that is what they would do, with pleasure.

The charm of Peking was insidious, and I could see why people who have lived there for any length of time never wanted to leave, and became like the repatriates in the South Sea Islands who "miss too many boats." We did a lot of sightseeing: the Temple of Heaven, indescribably beautiful; the Winter Palace; the Forbidden City, which entailed too much walking for Roger; then the Summer Palace which suited us all perfectly, as we were all carried around in sedan chairs. The shopping was out of this world, even though we didn't have time to do much.

The names of the streets themselves were fascinating—Jade Street, Silver Street, Gold Street, Silk Street, Lantern Street—all of them selling just the wares for which they were named. Then we were put in touch with an agent who brought men carrying brocades, furs and other treasures wrapped in blue cotton bundles which they dumped on the floor and opened for our inspection. I did buy a few things, and my *cumshaw* was an invitation to cocktails at the Danish Legation, a real thrill to get into the famous Legation Quarter.

We ran into some California friends of ours who had rented a house for a week, with all their food and five servants, for less than we were paying per day at the hotel. They asked us for lunch, and what a storybook place they had. Inside those dull compound walls was a feast of delight for the eyes; one courtyard opening onto another, with moon gates, lily ponds, the little tutelary gods perched on the corners of the Heaven-pointing tiled roofs; at last we could picture what the social life of the old days must have been, when Peking was the center of the diplomatic life of the country.

We left Peking sadly, just ten days before the July 7th "Incident" at the Marco Polo Bridge which precipitated the Chinese-Japanese War.

When we got back to the Cathay Hotel in Shanghai, we all noticed a strange change that had taken place. Before, the No. 2 Boy had always come to Roger or to me for orders; now he went to Florence. Previously, Roger and I had been carried first side by side in our rickshas with Florence behind; now, Florence was handed the menu, and driven beside Roger. Why? No use asking the boy. His English would have deserted him. I did ask several Chinese who either couldn't or wouldn't offer an explanation. So I made my own. Roger slept in my room, but generally had breakfast with Florence in the sitting room; I think that the boys had decided that she was the mother of his children—but I was his favorite concubine. It was an explanation Florence didn't like; after all there was only six months difference in our ages, and as she said, "That's too ridiculous; why I had my hair touched up just before I came on the trip!"

We sailed for Hong Kong June 29th on the "Empress of Canada," and the ship's doctor put me on a diet of tea because of an upset. I protested feebly that I was sure a little boiled rice and boiled milk would at least nourish me, but all I got was tea for three whole days.

Hong Kong was glamorous, even in my enfeebled condition. We stayed at the Repulse Bay Hotel, but spent our time wandering around the City. We dined with the head man from Standard Oil at his home on the Peak, being carried up the last quarter mile in sedan chairs, as the car could go no further. It was a memorable, if not an enjoyable, evening. I sat next to the host, who couldn't have been duller; there wasn't one single thing I could eat, everything was either fresh fruit or fried. Florence was seated by an awfully good-looking man. Apparently having taken to heart my advice about listening once in a while, she was hanging on every word he said. But when we left she said, "Well! Harry's nickname may be 'handsome,' but he's never had a well moment in his life, and he has taken me through every one of his ailments from the time he was three. I didn't even have time to tell him about the operation on my knee! Next time, I don't listen, I talk—and at least enjoy myself!"

Two days in Hong Kong, and then off to Manila on the Dollar Line "President Monroe," which was even worse than the old "Byron" of the South American trip. Someone in Hong Kong had given me a bottle of white medicine which she said was guaranteed to cure my complaint, but all the directions on the bottle said were, "Take one-third." One-third of what? A tablespoon? The bottle? So I just tipped it up, took a good swig and again slept for 24 hours. I found out in Manila that it was practically straight opium. If I had taken a third of the bottle, I would have gone to sleep for good.

We had only one day in Manila, but everything possible was packed into that 24 hours. We docked at 6 a.m., and were met by Roger's nephew, Johnny Lapham, who was with the Texas Company, his wife, and High Commissioner McNutt's Aide with an invitation to luncheon. The Johnny Laphams and their two children were afterwards interned in Santo Tomas for three years, but nothing could have seemed more unlikely at that time.

As soon as we had settled in our air-conditioned rooms in the Manila Hotel (at $50 a day), I went off to see an American doctor. He told me I looked like a famine victim, and to eat. I ate with alacrity on the delicious lunch cooked by the couple the McNutts had brought out with them.

Then sightseeing in the early afternoon, a large cocktail party at the Polo Club later, and finally some people at the hotel for dinner and dancing in which Roger indulged while Florence and I fell into bed. We felt more dead than alive, and were sailing again on the "President Monroe" the next morning at six.

We found the food, the insolent service of the stewards, and the whole devil-may-care atmosphere of the "Monroe" incredible. I wrote the following letter to Stanley in Roger's name, but Roger refused to let me send it:

Mr. Stanley Dollar,
President of the Dollar Lines
Dear Stanley:

Although I have known your father for many years and thought I knew the old Captain fairly well, I never before realized how profoundly his religious life influenced his ship-building; I refer particularly to the location, temperature and general characteristics of our bathroom. No one, I feel quite certain, has ever used it without being inspired to lead a better and purer life during the days he may have left on this earth. As a foretaste of the future of the damned, it is invaluable; for as one lowers oneself gingerly into the foot and a half of space between the tub and the wall, one is attacked in the rear (as if by one of Satan's minions armed with a red-hot poker) by a virile steam pipe, heated seven times hotter than the fiery furnace of Biblical times to which your father so often alluded.

Then too, it is almost impossible to rid oneself of earthly impurities, as the toilet lacks what the steam pipe possesses in virility, and definitely refuses to flush away that dross which even our sinful natures reject. The old Captain, Stanley, in just seven days on the "Monroe," has made a better man of me. My foretaste of Hell-fire has purified my nature, and in the sweat of my brow and all other parts of my anatomy, have I resolved to be a better and a wiser man—and never again to travel on another Dollar ship, so help me Robert. So here is a suggested slogan, just to show there's no hard feelings:

"Oh! a dollar a day on a Dollar ship
A dollar a day for a 'Round-the-World' trip;
A dollar a day, no less, no more

But—save your money and stay on shore."
Very sincerely and most cordially,
Roger D. Lapham

As bad as we thought everything about the ship was, we didn't know the half of it until Roger was presented with his bar bill—$128 for three days at sea from Manila to Hong Kong (and on account of my ailment I was drinking nothing but a small brandy after dinner). We began checking the items, and discovered that Roger and Florence were supposed to have consumed 80 quarts of liquid nourishment, including 48 highballs, mineral water, lemon squashes, and anything else the barkeeper could think of! Ten cartons of cigarettes, and six boxes of cigars were also on the bill, none of which we had.

Roger took it up with the Purser who said he knew the man was a crook, and just to pay what he liked; but to please wait until he got home before making an issue of it, otherwise the ship would be struck, and everyone held in Singapore indefinitely. As a shipping man Roger was sympathetic. He paid what he considered was an equitable amount, and let it go at that.

Our ship from Singapore to Java was the K. P. M. "Both," small, but immaculately clean and comfortable. Landing at Tandjoeng Priok, the port of Batavia, we were met by the guide we had engaged, Pulai, whom Florence with her usual linguistic disability immediately christened Boola. We stayed at the Hotel des Indes, and discovered lots of things we hadn't run into before: that the beds were hard as rocks and had the big bolsters called "Dutch wives"; that you must tuck your mosquito net in tight around you when you got into bed; that the bath water didn't run out through pipes but onto the bathroom floor, where it emptied through a hole in the corner. (Roger found that out when the last clean underwear he had left on the floor floated gently to meet him as he stepped out of the tub!)

And from there on we had a marvelous week's tour of Java which with its colorfulness, its cleanliness, and its greenness I felt must be the prototype of the Garden of Eden. The first night of four we spent at Bandung, a city of 400,000—of which I had never even heard! All our reservations had been made in advance, and after a bit we became accustomed to Pulai's method of claiming them. He would stalk importantly up to the registration desk proclaiming, "Important visitors arriving! The de luxe rooms reserved for My Lord and My Ladies!"

That evening there was a charming popular concert with an orchestra conducted by a Dutch woman. We sat comfortably at small tables on the terrace, drinking beer and eating popcorn. When it was over at 10 o'clock we entered the dining room for dinner. The Hungarian band leader bowed to us, and the band burst into "California, Here I Come!" It was too much, 7,000 miles away from home; Florence and I wept copiously, and I think even Roger was not completely dry-eyed.

As we climbed higher and higher towards Wonosobo, everything we saw fascinated us: the terraced rice fields, the miles of poinsetta hedges in bloom, the water buffaloes, and oh! above all, the ducks—flock after flock of them, driven by little boys who directed them with a long stick with a bit of rag on the end of it. As our car approached, he would point at them, shrill out a word or two, and every single duck would waddle to the side of the road and face inward! They were never permitted in the newly planted rice field, but could be turned loose in fields from which the rice had been harvested.

After Wanosobo came Jogjakarta, the center of the batik industry. There we bought a few rather stiff, garish new batiks, and two or three really lovely soft-toned old ones. Then on to Semarang and Surabaya. On the way we visited the famous ruined temple of Borobudur with its platform after platform lined with huge stupas, and its walls completely covered with carving depicting the life of Buddha. Pulai interpreted at great length, especially about Buddha's marriage to a wife who told him she preferred to remain a "Vir-geen." But one night she told my Lord Buddha that she had dreamed of an elephant. He said that meant she would have a son. She did, and all was well.

Another small K. P. M. ship, the "Merak" from Surabaya to Bali, and on to the Bali Hotel in Den Pasar, where we stayed three days, drove all over the Island and didn't miss a thing. The first day I must say we fairly goggled at the women—naked from the waist up. But as time went on, we became a little critical and decided that the older ones would look better with a bit of covering. Among the young girls, we learned that the real belles wrapped their upper bodies in large Turkish towels, on which were embroidered in large blue letters the words, "Matson Lines!"

We saw the charming little native dancing girls; the second largest banyan tree in the world; the temple dedicated to the Bandar Log; and monkeys so tame that grabbed at you so persistently to be fed, that even I, who love monkeys, fought a bit shy of them. We saw strange temples, all facade with nothing behind it; dreadful looking dogs; and even a cock fight.

The high point was the *Ketjak,* or monkey dance, which "portrayed two warring groups of monkeys, representing the forces of good and evil in mankind." It took place in an open, thatched roof marketplace in a small village in the evening, with a torrential rain pouring down outside. It was performed by men and boys, all done with gestures to a blood-tingling chant, and the pantomime is so expressive that you can follow the maze of the involved story. I have never seen anything more primitive nor more impressive; the only thing that even faintly resembles it to me is the funeral gathering in the second act of "Porgy and Bess." It was a marvellous climax to our tour.

The next day we sailed for Australia on the K. P. M. ship, "Nievw Holland." I asked the Captain immediately what "K. P. M." stood for. He said it was the name of the Dutch shipping line, but it was too long and difficult to remember, so he always said it stood for "Keep Pleasant Memories."

The 12-day trip to Sydney was delightful, especially as both Florence and I immediately fell in love with our Dutch Captain, Blaubooer. He took us down the Inside Passage of the Great Barrier Reef so that we might see as much of it as possible. On August 3rd we landed at Brisbane for the day, arriving as usual at 6:30 A.M. We were met, of course, and did the Grand Tour of the city, of which I have forgotten practically everything except the cuddly koala bears in the Zoo.

I had told Roger as we left the ship that I had to go to a chemist's for something I couldn't get on the ship—zinc and carbolic ointment for an open cut. We drove and we drove and we drove, ending up at a hotel for cocktails and lunch, both of which lasted indefinitely. The ship was scheduled to sail at three, and I still hadn't gotten to my chemist's. I finally found one and it took about twenty minutes for the chemist to understand what I wanted and put it up. We still had a five mile drive to the steamer, but we got there . . . just as the gangplank was going up, to Roger's wrath and rage. He said that all he had asked of us was to be on time for sailings. We could buy whatever we wanted. We could take as much luggage as we chose. But we were to be on time for sailings!

We were in the midst of a fine family row when word came down inviting the three of us up to the bridge to sail out of Brisbane harbor. "Well, Meester and Meeses Lapham, and Meeses McCormick, you were a little bit late in arriving." "Captain," said Florence, "don't even say it; I have just got the Laphams so they are speaking to each other!" "But why should Meester Lapham worry?" said he. "I would of course have waited for him"—and once again the fat was practically in the fire.

I think we were the only Americans on board. The rest were mostly Australians, including one woman who took the round trip to Singapore every year to throw a wreath on the spot where her husband had been buried at sea some years earlier. She considered Captain Blaubooer her private property, and bitterly resented Florence's and my attentions to him, as well as his evident pleasure in the same. Naturally that was just gravy for the two of us, and we didn't spare the horses.

There were also two nice sisters from Auckland with whom Florence struck up an acquaintance. She asked them where they came from, and when they said, "Auckland," she said, "Why that practically makes us neighbors! You're just across the Bay from us!" They looked a bit bewildered, thinking the Pacific was quite a Bay, so I stepped in and said, "Florence, they come from Auckland, New Zealand, not Oakland, California!" "Goodness," said Florence, "I never heard of it."

After 12 days of listening to Australian conversation and the accent, I wrote my impressions of them in the form of a supposititious chat overheard on deck entitled:

AN AUSTRALIAN WOMAN VISITS BALI

Well good morning, Miss MacCorquendaile: it's quaite naice to be back on the ship again, isn't it.—what? Of course travel is broadening and all that, but to be aboard the New Holland with all your friends is a little bit of all raight,—what? But I must say there seem to be a lot of Americans on board, and I rally believe one of them is a Yankee. Just let me tell you what happened to Cyril and me this morning. We went up to the Sports Deck to do a spot of cricket, and there was one of them stretched out in the middle of the cricket pitch! I said "Excuse me Miss, but you're in the middle of the cricket pitch." And she said "Gracious, do the British pitch crickets too? I've been hit by every kind of ball already, but I really didn't expect to be hit by a cricket. I thought they just came and sat on your hearth and chirped the way they do at home." Pulling my leg, Miss MacCorquendaile? Oh! no indeed,—the poor thing didn't know any better.

Well now and how did I laike Bali? Oh! I laiked it well enough, but it's not a bit laike Sydney,—what? Going ashore in those dinkies or whatever they call them, and no way to keep an eye to your luggage; and then the rooms at the hotel; no proper way to lock yourself in, no top sheet, and then when you tuck yourself into those mosquito net things, there's no way to get out in a hurry, no matter what for . . . Oh! excuse me, Miss MacCorquendaile, I forgot you wasn't married. Then there's those Dutch wives,—what a vulgar naime! Someone told Cyril about two men—Americans of course—and after his first night in Bali, one of them asked the other how he laiked his Dutch wife, and he said he didn't know she was Dutch. Oh! you're laughing too? So did Cyril, so I suppose it must be droll, but I confess I don't see much point to it.

What did we do the first day? Oh! they took us out to see the second largest banyan tree in the world; I hear the largest is in British India, though I wouldn't put it past the Americans to I did say to Cyril "A bit unrestrained, don't you think?" Then we went to the Monkey Temple, and if you'll believe it my dear, there was monkeys all over the place. Now don't get me wrong; I laike monkeys in their proper place, laike a pit in the Sydney Zoo, where you can throw them peanuts and no harm done; but monkeys hopping around under foot just don't seem natural, and some of them a bit too human, if you know what I mean . . . but there I go again, forgettin' that you ain't married.

The girls was a real disappointment to Cyril,—or so he said —but not to me, they wasn't. I didn't expect much, not after seeing our Mabel at 16. Yes, I know she's plumped up a bit now, but you know, that is you must have heard, what nursing twins does to the figger; and I've always said that an extra pound or two is better than being on the scraggy side; Oh! pardon me,— nothing personal of course—what?

Then the dogs; that is if they really was dogs; why even that sweet little setter bitch Rosie we had when she had pups by that Airedaile across the street—Excuse me, Miss MacCorquendaile, I think that American Yankee is going to sit down by Cyril, so I'll just tootle along and see to it. I have enjoyed our talk so much but Sydney Bridge'll be a sight for sore eyes. Cheerio!

We landed early in the morning and were met by several people— the Von Schillings of the Texas Company; the MacMurtries, old friends of Roger's; the Matson Line agent, etc. We went right to the Australia Hotel and lunched off of a dozen oysters apiece; Sydney oysters are the most delectable I have ever eaten. We made up our minds then and there that we would like to have them for every meal. But we had been invited out for a good many meals already, so how to solve our oyster problem? We managed it nicely. To each prospective hostess we raved about Sydney oysters; a far away "did-I-order-oysters" look would come into her eyes . . . and we never missed once!

The "Nieuw Holland" was in port only two days, so we went down to have a farewell drink with Captain Blaubooer. Roger had bought him a present—a first edition of Tasman's Journal. Blaubooer had shown it to Roger on board, and said how he longed to own it, but that it belonged to the ship. The Captain was so overcome that he promptly folded me to his bosom and kissed me good-bye. I thought Florence would cry until he opened his arms, said, "Meeses McCormick!" and she went into them like a homing pigeon!

We were royally entertained. We were taken to many beautiful but shark-infested beaches. Florence was horrified that anyone would swim when in danger of being taken by a shark, but our host said there were rarely more than eight or ten deaths a summer from sharks, and "no one expected to be taken any more than a Sunday driver in America expected to be killed!"

We had a day's drive out to the Blue Mountains, another to a sheep station and a day in town at the races (which we girls loved as we could bet $2.00 across the board; following MacMurtrie's tips, we won 20 shillings apiece, while he never took his own advice, and lost every race!).

We were given a charming dinner by the von Schillings. Mrs. von S. told me how valiantly she had striven to keep her two children, 8 and 10, from acquiring the Australian accent. But on their last home leave while visiting her mother in Virginia, they had walked into the living room where the children were lying on their stomachs examining the tiled fireplace representing hunting scenes, and overheard the following conversation. The 10-year-old girl: "Which tiles do you like the best, Tommy?" The 8-year-old boy: "I think I like the 'orses tiles!" Her mother, being an F. F. V., like Queen Victoria, was "not amused."

We were very much interested in the general Australian rejoicing that Edward VII had abdicated in favor of his brother George. Apparently the last time that Edward, as Prince of Wales, had been in Australia, he had consistently misbehaved and had offended practically everyone, including the members of the Order of the British Empire, who were giving him a large reception. When the head of the Order had called to escort him to the function, the Prince, a bit more than half seas over, had asked who he was. "The head of the O. B. E., Your Highness," was the reply. "Ah, yes!" said the Prince. "O. B. E.—Only Bastards Excepted." That remark dropped into a deep well of silence.

On Friday, August 13, we sailed for New Zealand on the "Awatea" — a beautiful ship, but what a roller! Even though the Tasman Sea was in one of its calmer moods, and the "Awatea" had just had stabilizers installed, we rolled and we rolled and we rolled. We were at the Captain's table along with three Australian wool exporters, and they razzed the poor Captain, who was a peppery little individual anyhow, to the point where I fully expected him to have a stroke. The climax was reached at Divine Service Sunday morning. We had prayed for the King and the Royal Family, and were just asking the Divine blessing "For those in peril on the sea," when the "Awatea" rolled practically over on her side. Every chair with its occupant slid into a confused heap in one corner of the saloon; even the Captain was not exempt. But as he slid by me, purple in the face, his lips were moving freely, and though I caught only one word, "——— landlubbers," I don't think that the word which preceded it came out of the Prayer Book.

We landed in Wellington Monday morning to be met by the Texaco people and entertained by them all day—a long drive, dinner, etc. We had hired a seven-passenger Buick for our tour of New Zealand, and left early Tuesday morning for Napier; a most interesting drive through country very reminiscent of various parts of California, with the exception of the vegetation—hedges of Scotch broom and heather eight to ten feet high, with enormous tree ferns growing right beside them.

We were fascinated by the hotel entrance in Napier. On each side of the front door was a brass plaque reading, "Destroyed by earthquake and fire 19—, rebuilt 19—"; and, "Destroyed by earthquake and fire 19—" (some 15 years later), "rebuilt 19—." "Goodness," said Florence, "we don't like people even to mention ours, and they boast about theirs!" After lunch we went out to shop for woolies, sox, pants, gloves and scarves, and in one shop found all the china and glass on the floor. "We keep it there you know," said the clerk, "so it won't get broken in our weekly earthquakes!"

The next day's drive took us over three mountain ranges and it couldn't have been more spectacular. We lunched at Waeraki, with its hot baths and geyser valley; saw the Huka Falls; drove around Lake Taupo; and at the end of a long afternoon, with snow-capped mountains in the distance all the way, arrived at the Chateau Tongariro. It couldn't have surprised us more—a Ritz-type hotel in the middle of a howling wilderness! And all the proper Britishers were gathered in the lounge in evening dress. I put Roger's out for him. He swore he wasn't going to wear it, but I, who had packed and unpacked it right from Java on, was equally determined that he was. I won my point; with true Machiavellian guile, as soon as he went in to take a bath, I sent both his other suits out to be pressed! What could the robin do then, poor thing? He wore his dinner clothes. We found out later that it was the finest hotel and the best ski resort in the Southern Hemisphere.

The next day we drove to Waitomo, a lovely spot with violets, daphne, camellias, daffodils and china lilies in full bloom, and hundreds of little lambs gamboling and bleating in the fields. That evening we visited the famous glow-worm cave, where you cross a small lake in a cave by boat in total silence, and suddenly the whole ceiling and walls are illuminated by the light of millions of tiny glow-worms. It is a really incredible sight.

Friday the 20th we arrived at the thermal region of Rotorua. It was a sunny cold day, and the thermometer in our rooms registered a snappy 59°. But by this time we had learned two things: one was that if you rushed right to the registration desk and said you had to have an electric heater (even though admonished that it would be three shilling a day extra), you generally got one before they were all bespoke; the other was that the cup of tea with which they woke you at seven in the morning was an absolute necessity—without it, you would never have had the courage to get up and face dressing in those icy rooms.

Rotorua is a spooky place, with its lake of boiling, bubbling mud (exported, incidentally, as the basis of facial mud packs); the jets of steam rising from the ground in all directions; the hot geysers; and the ground which trembles and quivers beneath your feet, giving you a very awe-inspiring sensation of the tremendous unleashed force beneath. We were guided through the Maori village by Rangi, the famous Maori Chieftainess, and saw the river where you catch a trout in the cold water on one side of a bridge and cook it by dropping it in the hot water on the other side. We saw the Maoris doing all their cooking over the capped steam vents, and ended at a place appropriately named "Hell's Mouth" where the guide cautioned me to walk carefully, as "only the week before the ground opened up under a lady, hot water came out, and she lost a foot." I didn't need a second warning. I moved. And I was ready to agree with what George Bernard Shaw had written in the register: "I would have given ten pounds not to have been here."

We left in good season the next morning, and after a picnic lunch on the banks of a lovely river, reached Auckland by half-past three. Florence agreed that it wasn't Oakland, and that she would never confuse them again. It's really rather a dull little place, especially on a Sunday.

We did a final bit of shopping the next morning—sox, sweaters, and a lovely thin wool blanket for Mother Lapham—and sailed that afternoon on the Matson liner "Monterey." We had a fine lanai suite and, Florence a good room close by, but, comfortable as we were, we really hated to feel our grand tour was so nearly over.

We were seated at Captain Johannson's table, with a most delightful Australian couple, Sir Philip and Lady Street, and their son, the Honorable Mr. Justice Kenneth Street. Sir Philip had been Governor-General of New South Wales and Chief Justice of the Supreme Court, and was a grand old boy in his middle-seventies, and Lady Street, Belinda, couldn't have been cuter or a better sport. She had never seen a slot machine before and, after winning the first time she played, she couldn't be torn away. Poor Kenneth used to come up on deck and say "Have you seen my mother? I'm a bit afraid she's back at those dreadful poker machines again." She was also fascinated by the food, and one day when I had ordered frog legs, she examined them with such interest I gave her one. "Simply delicious," she said. "Philip, you must order them." But Sir Philip would have none of it; saying he had lived 75 years without eating reptiles, and he wasn't giong to start poisoning himself now.

And so . . . home at last, after a truly grand three-month trip. All of us had lost weight in spite of the rich milk and cream in New Zealand; Roger's foot still bothered him although he had limped around a golf course on it in Sydney; but these drawbacks didn't seem to amount to much in view of the fun we had had.

One amusing thing happened as we began distributing our presents. Florence had bought a couple of pounds of tea from a factory in Java for a friend of ours who was a devoted tea drinker, but unfortunately it had been packed in the trunk we had filled with camphor so that all the linen we had bought wouldn't mildew. We never gave it a thought until the friend said the tea was delicious, but it had such a different flavor—almost like camphor. "How right you are!" said Florence. "The tea plants have to grow in the shade, so they are grown under camphor trees, and naturally they absorb a bit of that taste from the soil!" Nothing like being able to think fast, especially when you know you're in the wrong.

Around the first of October, Roger and I went East as we had done each fall for many years. I generally left him to go about his business in New York while I went up for a two-week visit with my mother in her charming little home in Washington, Connecticut, which had been built before my father's death. She had lived alone there for a long time, cared for by a devoted elderly Irish cook-maid-companion, and an equally devoted Swedish chauffeur-gardener. At first she had had an apartment in New York, going to Washington only in the summer. But when she grew older and my sister Dorothy married keeping up two places was too much for her.

After we moved back to San Francisco she visited us several times— the last time when she was 80, she was a bit hesitant about it, but when she asked her doctor's advice, he told her to go. She said suppose she got sick there, or even died; to which he replied that she had a return trip ticket, didn't she? She said she had, and he told her they could ship her back in a coffin at no extra charge. She was so mad she took off for the West the next day! Other winters she went to Camden, South Carolina.

But finally she decided she had had enough of travelling, and settled down in Washington for the rest of her life—and was at last accepted by the Connecticut Yankees as one of them, and not one of "them danged summer folks!"

She loved her garden, her radio and her independence. In fact, when one of her friends commiserated with her on being so distant from her daughters, she replied, "I love both of them dearly. Both visit me at intervals during the year. And I thank God on my knees every night that I don't have to live with either of them!" She added she was glad she didn't even live near enough for them to feel they had to run in and see "Poor Old Mother" every other day!

She was a marvellous letter-writer, and in other days her letters might have been as well known as Mme. de Sevigne's. After the stress and strain of her earlier life, filled as it was with illness and the death of her dear ones, she developed a truly wonderful philosophy of life. I asked her once what one should try to achieve within one's self, and she gave me a slip of paper on which she had written:

"Try to be: calm, content, courageous; faithful, fearless, helpful; joyful, peaceful, quiet; patient, reverent, thoughtful; tranquil and trustful."

And then she said, "Life is inward adjustment to outward circumstances, Helen, and the ones who refuse to adjust are the ones who crystallize in a mould and crack"; adding with a smile, "and it's not only the old ones, either; the young can be that way too."

I told her that she would never grow old, because she had lived up to everything she had just said. And while I would try to follow in her footsteps, I was afraid it was going to take me a very long time to attain the serenity that she had achieved.

Mother was a passionate letter-writer. She wrote to radio stations, approving or disapproving of their programs; to Walter Damrosh to thank him for her enjoyment of his concerts; to authors whose books she liked; and once to a company which manufactured something called Kutnow Powder, saying she had taken it for 43 years, and had noticed that while the price had risen, the content of the bottle had diminished. To that she got an answer from the President of the company, explaining that the content was better but more concentrated, and that he was sending her a two-pound bottle as a testimonial to her 43 years of faithfulness to his product. She wrote and thanked him, but said that as she was then 84, she doubted if she would live to finish it, and a pound would have been quite enough.

I always loved my two quiet weeks with her. She once said she supposed I found it boring, but that it wouldn't hurt me—she herself was quite often bored, especially after daylight saving went out in September and it was dark by half-past four. I was never bored; just being with her was a real inspiration.

Although I am not too clear as to the actual dates, it must also have been during the middle-thirties that Roger and I, through our friends the Fleishhackers, spent two long weekends at Wyntoon—the fantastic W. R. Hearst place on the McCloud River in Northern California. I was a bit hesitant about going, as Marion Davies was the chatelaine; but the invitation was put to me in such a way in the middle of a large dinner that I couldn't very well state my objection. Besides, it had been a liaison of such long standing that it had acquired the aura of respectability. So we went and I cannot conceive of anything further removed from what most of us consider as reality than the life that was led there.

Wyntoon was really a self-contained community. The main residence was an old two-story house bought from the previous owner, with several bedrooms, dining room, living room, etc., fronting on tennis courts and swimming pool. About a mile beyond it was the Tyrolean village which Hearst had built; three or four chalets on the river around a village green with a Nuremburg fountain in the center. The outside walls of the cottages had fairy-tale murals of Cinderella, Goldilocks and

Snow White done by Willy Pogany, using Marion as the model. They were furnished with the choicest antiques, heated by huge porcelain stoves and had such heavily embroidered sheets that your chin had scratches on it in the morning. There were also silver inkwells and silver cigarette boxes—but no ink and no cigarettes. There were only two bath towels in the luxurious bathroom and when we asked for another, we were told that the allowance was two a day per couple!

Luncheon was never before two, and dinner at 9:30, and no drinks were served before either meal except a very sweet sherry. But on request, you could get anything you asked for. The table was a long refectory one, with a procession of condiments—salt, pepper, catsup, pickles, oil, vinegar, etc.—up and down the center of the table; nothing but paper napkins were used, but you could name any vintage wine you could think of, and it would be forthcoming. Marion was an expert hostess, who very cleverly managed her invited guests and her many droppers-in, ranging from Hollywood big names to second- and third-raters. You were either above or below the salt, and there was no question about it.

Dinner was over, even including the coffee served afterward, by 10:30. Then the limousines pulled up at the door, and no matter how you felt about it, you went to the movies in another building a mile or so away. There were previews, reruns, newsreels; some of them good, one or two of Marion's old ones were pretty awful. But the movies didn't bother Roger much because the chairs were deep-cushioned and very comfortable; he usually went to sleep as soon as the lights went out.

Marion had shown signs of taking quite a fancy to Roger, and I warned him: "Watch your step; remember what happened to Ince" (who had been stabbed on a yacht some years before; the gossip being that it was because he had cast an eye in Marion's direction). One evening when the lights went on, Roger didn't wake up, and Marion leaned over the back of his chair and kissed him. He opened his eyes to look into her big blue ones, stared wildly around and said, "Oh! "Sport" (which he and he alone had called me for twenty-five years). I smilingly rescued him; no harm done, just a nice Sleeping Beauty kiss in reverse.

It was just as well that 1938 had proved to be a quiet year, for 1939 was something else again. Very shortly after the first of the year Jan was transferred from Boston to be the head of the Paris office of the Holland-America Line. Edna was five months pregnant, and it did not seem wise for her to go with him and try to find a house in Paris and get settled in the middle of winter. So they shipped all their household goods to Rotterdam by H-A, and she and the children came out to me to stay until after the baby was born.

Late in March Dorothy telephoned me that Mother had had a coronary and to come on as soon as possible. I flew East the next day and was met at Newark by Mother Lapham's car and driven up to Mother's. She was lying in bed with her eyes closed when I got there. She greeted me calmly: "It may interest you to know, Helen, that Roosevelt has killed me." I couldn't have been more horrified. I knew she'd had a heart attack, but no one had told me her mind wasn't clear. But then she continued, "I was a perfectly well woman until four o'clock Saturday afternoon, when I listened to one of his Fireside Chats—and had a coronary."

She had two excellent nurses most of the time, was not in pain, slept a good deal, and was her own serene self when she was awake. She had told both Dorothy and me over and over again that she never wanted anything done to keep her alive—no transfusions, no saline solutions. She wanted only to be allowed to die quietly and in peace. She had given full instructions for her funeral, in anything but a morbid way; she had first selected "Rejoice, Give Thanks and Sing" as the hymn, but on second thought had decided that people might think Dorothy and I had chosen it, and find it strange.

We had been there nearly five weeks when she called us in and said she wanted both of us to go home; she loved us both dearly, but everything had been said; she could make no further effort and just wanted to go to sleep. We left the next day, one of the most superb days I have ever seen. There had been a sleet storm during the night and every tree and shrub was sheathed in crystal when the sun came out that morning; you felt you have been given a foretaste of what Heaven might look like.

It was really time for me to go home, for I had developed another abscessed tooth which necessitated an extraction in the hospital. Mother died a week later, and the nurses told us that she had never really been conscious after we left. I still wasn't fit to turn around and go back to the funeral, but Dorothy told me it was just as simple and beautiful as Mother had planned. It was strange that my Father died in the spring of 1914 before the First World War, and Mother in the spring of 1939 just before the Second; perhaps just as well in a way, for it would have made both of them more than sad and unhappy at the loss of life and fearful destruction.

Edna's second daughter, Elinor, was born early in the morning of May 27th. Jan, who had called the sex of the other two children correctly, was quite certain this would be another boy, and had impressed it so firmly on Jan Roger that when I told him he had a baby sister, he said, "Oh! no. Grammie, it is a baby bruzzer, my fazzer told me so!" Edna burst into tears when I told her she had a little girl, so of course I judged she was equally disappointed. But when I tried to comfort her by saying that little daughters were pretty nice, she said, "Mother, you just don't understand; I'm so glad it's a girl! If it had been another boy like Jannie I couldn't have stood it."

Jannie wasn't a bad boy in any sense of the word, but he was the busiest little imp I ever had anything to do with. He was into everything all day long, and nothing held his attention for any length of time. If you read aloud to him, he wanted you to play the piano; if you played the piano, he preferred the radio. Edna had had her hands full just keeping him out of mischief as much as possible, and I perfectly understood her reaction to the thought of dealing with another like him.

On June 28 Roger had another first flight, again due to the good auspices of Captain Rieber. This one was the first commercial flight of the Pan American flying boat "Dixie Clipper." It took off from Port

Washington, stopped in the Azores to refuel, put down in Lisbon for the night, and landed safely in Marseille, 48 hours after the take-off! The passengers all broadcast by radio from the "Clipper," and Roger's closing sentence was, "What is going to happen in the development of air transportation, heavier-than-air or lighter-than-air, in the next 10, 15, or 50 years is beyond anyone's imagination today." (How far-sighted he was; in September 1960 my daughter-in-law and I flew from New York to Lisbon by jet in 5½ hours!)

He and Captain Rieber then went off on a rugged two-week trip which included stops in Paris, Rotterdam, the Hague, Berlin, Hamburg, Copenhagen, Oslo, Stockholm, London, Dublin and Limerick, finally leaving from Foynes on the sister ship, the "Yankee Clipper" for the return trip to Port Washington. He was more dead than alive when he got back, and spent the weekend at New Canaan to recuperate, even missing the first weekend of the Bohemian Grove. But it had been a wonderful experience, and he had enjoyed every minute of it.

Before he left, he had been convinced that a European war was inevitable; and after talking with many people of different nationalities and classes, he came home surer than ever that it was not only inevitable, but also imminent. But even as late as that, less than six weeks before Germany marched into Poland, very few people here saw the handwriting on the wall, or were particularly concerned about the menace which threatened them.

Early in August Edna left for Paris with the three children, Jan Roger, five, Helene, three, and Elinor, two months, plus a Dutch nurse and my faithful Christena Monahan to help with the children and deliver them all safely into Jan's hands.

On the 1st of September we went to a beautiful ball given by the Comte and Comtesse de Limur at her Crocker family estate in Burlingame. It couldn't have been gayer or lovelier, until midnight . . . then word was whispered around that France was at war. Such a pall of gloom descended that the guests felt it an intrusion to stay and witness the De Limurs' grief. They simply melted away, and I think that by

74

one o'clock only a handful of close friends and relatives was left.

Our chief concern at that time was, of course, for Edna and her brood; but a brief cable from Jan told us he had gotten them all off on the 2nd by train to Rotterdam, where his family lived. They stayed there over a month, until the worst of the rush of terrified tourists was over; then he got her on a New York-bound Holland-America ship, crowded to the rails with German Jewish refugees. She told me when she got home that the first lifeboat drill had resulted in such a frantic scramble and near panic, that she had made up her mind she wouldn't even try to get into a boat, but just gather the children together and sit quietly, ready for whatever might happen. When she was telling about it here, someone said to her, "Oh Edna! What a dreadful experience, to be mixed up with all those horrible people." But her answer was, "No, I was better off than any of them. I had people who loved me and a home to go to; they had no place to go, and no one who wanted them."

After ten days at New Canaan to rest and relax, she and the children came to us, and were with us for over a year in San Francisco and Atherton. Jan didn't get out of Paris until the following April, and then had no business and no other place to go himself. He was as truly a displaced person as hundreds and thousands of others. I can see the poor soul now as he sat on the porch in Atherton with his head in his hands, while the radio relentlessly poured out the details of the destruction of Rotterdam on that fatal day, May 10th, 1940.

The whole Lapham family was very airminded—all except me. Jack owned and flew his own plane; Edna had her pilot's license, and their four children gradually acquired theirs. I made my first flight in Jack's small plane, on a 20-mile round-trip flight from New Canaan over to Long Island and back. To my great surprise, I lived through it. Then early in the thirties, Roger insisted that I should fly across the country to San Francisco with him. I remembered it was the year "Gone With the Wind" was published and he sat and read while I sat bolt upright in the narrow seat of the Ford Tri-motor plane, clutching the seat arms

—afraid to move for fear I would upset the balance of the plane. In those days it was a long flight of 34 hours or more with ten or fifteen stops for refueling or food. One such stop I will never forget—it was at Cheyenne for a meal at 2 A.M., and even at that hour the arrival of a plane was such an event that there must have been a couple of hundred sightseers waiting for us to land.

By the time we got to Reno, I had had it. I stretched out on the couch in the waiting room and announced that I would take the nice, safe, comfortable train from there on to San Francisco. The stewardess was completely horrified: "Spend overnight on the train, when we'll be in San Francisco in only four or five hours?" Roger arrived on the scene at that moment and, anything but sympathetic, took me firmly by the arm and walked me back to the plane. We did get home safely —and I went to bed for two days to restore my shattered nervous system.

From then on we had all kinds of flights in all kinds of weather. On one trip we were grounded in Des Moines for the night, and of course by morning had come to know all the small group of co-passengers very well. One of them was a charming woman, who was Dr. Aurelia Reinhardt's sister. She lived in Zurich with her Swiss husband, and was making her first trip to the States in 20 years. She said she was entirely baffled by the changes she saw, and by the language used, especially by the young. "In my day," she said, "a pansy was a simple garden flower. But now I understand it has a totally different connotation."

The worst flight was one we had going East from Seattle in a small Lockheed. It was on my birthday, September 13, and it was supposed to be a celebration for me. But I stated emphatically if that was my husband's idea of a birthday present, he need never give me another. (After that, he stuck safely to orchids.) We started out in a driving rain, which rapidly turned to sleet and then to snow. The pilot lost his bearings going into Spokane, went up the wrong canyon, and, just as a mountain loomed up in front of us, banked and all but threw me out of my seat. Later, we landed on top of a sawed-off mountain in Helena; dove through cloud, rain and mist to come in under a 200-foot ceiling at Fargo; and when we finally reached Minneapolis, my mouth was set in a grim line. This time I was determined to take the train to Chicago, no matter who said what. At that moment the announcement came that all passengers would proceed to Chicago by train as the ceiling there was zero! But the next morning was bright and clear. We went on to New York by air.

Another flight I recall only too vividly is the one we made from Los Angeles after we heard of Father Lapham's death. We had been able to get on a chartered flight with Jack Frye at the controls. The passengers were all movie stars flying on to New York for personal appearances, except us—Roger, Lewis and myself. We landed at Albuquerque and passed through a line of eager beaver movie fans, and as I came along I heard one woman say, "Well—I don't know who that one is, but she certainly ain't Mae West!" Me? My eyes red from weeping, my hat over one eye, no makeup—I couldn't have agreed with her more.

Dorothy di Frasso was on board, armed with a quart of liquor and an outsized jewel case, both of which she passed around freely, one to be shared, and one for a look-see. We were invited one by one up to the cockpit, and by the time I got up there, the weather showed signs of rapid deterioration. Jack Frye told me there were two thunderstorms ahead—I could see them both—but he was going to fly between them. A perfect idea, except that we met where they did! A vivid flash of lightning revealed, directly below us, the largest cemetery I have ever seen. I thought this was simply a short cut to the end, returned to my seat and took St. Christopher out of my purse, intending to say one of my best prayers. But instead I found myself shaking my medal, and saying, "Look, St. Christopher, we're in a jam. If you're any good, now's the time to do your stuff!" I could have killed Roger; he was sound asleep and woke only when the rain turned to hail and beat against the windows, at which he decided he was in the First World War, sat up straight, and said, "Men—we're being strafed!" Seeing me shivering in the next seat, he pulled an emergency flask out of his brief case and handed it to me. While it took both my trembling hands to get it to my mouth, it did me a world of good.

Shortly afterwards the co-pilot came back and said, "Well, that wasn't too bad, was it Mrs. Lapham?" "No," I answered. "I had St. Christopher on the job, and he brought us through." "St. Christopher, hell!" he said. "We've got the best pilot there is up in the cockpit." But St. Christopher has flown with me ever since 1927. And even though he now has practically no features left from being rubbed so hard in times of emergency, my faith in him is untarnished. I would be very upset if I had to fly without him; in fact, probably due to that tremendous faith, by the time we were living in China, where you either had to fly or stay home, I had lost most of my terror. Today, it bores me to death to travel any other way.

Early in 1940 we joined a group of friends going down to Guaymas for deep-sea fishing and a stay at the Playa de Cortes, a most charming hotel. Roger needed a rest and change. As for me—my father-in-law once said, "Don't ask Helen to go anywhere with you unless you mean it, for she will say yes before she even asks where! So we flew down to San Diego, motored to Tiajuana, and took off from there in the early hours of the morning. We were greeted enthusiastically by the Witters, the Orrie Johnsons, the Spencer Grants, and Mrs. Bowles, a widow. (Mrs. Bowles had apparently had an unattached suitor named Galston, but the budding romance had been effectually broken up before we got there by the ribald group saying they could hardly wait for the wedding announcement of "Mr. Gallstones and Mrs. Bowels.")

Dean Witter was a more or less self-elected MC, who liked a definite program and a complete schedule of each day's events, which he proposed each morning. "We will leave for fishing at 9:30, returning at 12:30 for cocktails around the pool and lunch at 2:00, with time between to bathe and change. Nine holes of golf after luncheon, two rubbers of bridge from 6:00 to 7:00, a siesta until 8:30, cocktails in the bar, and dinner at 9:00. Does this suit everyone?" "No," from my husband. Loud and clear. Ever since he was in the Army, he never took kindly to being told what to do, and when. We were left more or less on our own.

We went fishing once or twice and one day ran into such a large school of mackerel that you could practically scoop them up with your hands; not very sporting fishing, but awfully good eating. It was really too early in the season for the big fish to be running, anyhow. We drove into the sleepy little town of Guaymas and wandered around the shops on the Plaza; mostly tourist stuff, but a few really nice old things. I bought a lovely old ivory prayer book (in Spanish, of course) and a rosary. I only wanted the rosary to take home to a friend who collected them; but the shopkeeper said they had been ordered from Spain 100 years ago for a bride who had died before they arrived, they had never been separated, and I must buy both or neither, so naturally I bought both, for the large sum of $10.

The time passed quickly, albeit somewhat lazily for us, and we decided to stay on for a few days after the others left. In the meantime a delightful young couple from San Francisco, John and Sugie Menzies, had come down on their honeymoon. They flew in about noon one day. We were all sitting around the pool, greeted them uproariously and invited them to have a drink. "Oh NO!" said Sugie. "After the night I've had, I've got to get some rest." Poor John, his face purple, and stuttering with embarrassment, explained that she didn't mean what we thought she did. They had been married at four, the reception had followed; they had flown to San Diego, driven to Tiajuana, sat up in the airport for two hours or more, and then flown in to Guaymas. The poor kid was really tired. When she recovered, we enjoyed them tremendously.

None of us who went down to the train to bid the three couples and Beatrice Bowles farewell will ever forget the historic Battle of Guaymas which ensued. John had bought a case of beer and hired two musicians to make it a gala occasion. The Witters had the drawing room on the train, no argument about that; but it appeared that both the Grants and the Johnsons were sure they had the only compartment, while Beatrice was in the first lower berth outside. The Grants, Orrie Johnson and the conductor came out on the platform, all talking at once; Beatrice came next, complaining that as she had reached over to put her things in the little hammock, a nasty man from the opposite lower had pinched her "you-know-where!" Meantime the beer was flowing freely, and the musicians were bellowing "La Paloma" at the top of their lungs (except when the little cross-eyed one stopped long enough to embrace John around the stomach, which was as far as he could reach, and address him at "Mi carissimo amigo" with the tears running down his face)! Katie Johnson, while all this was going on, had imitated Bre'er Rabbit, said nuffin', gone into the compartment, locked the door, and gone to bed. The train finally pulled out with the three women in the drawing room and the men in the lowers, but it almost broke up the 30-year friendship of the Grants and the Johnsons.

It was well after midnight by this time. Being far too early to go quietly back to the hotel, we progressed to a nearby cantina where Roger proceeded to pick up one of the taxi-dancers. She was dressed in royal purple, and he has always had a weakness for that particular color. He led her up to the bar for a drink, at which point John, the taxi driver, and one of the waiters from the hotel closed in on him, and eased him gently but most firmly out the door, under bitter protest. The waiter explained in no uncertain terms, and in quite understandable English, that she was the woman of the *Jefe,* and he did not wish to see his patron with a knife in his back, which he undoubtedly would have if by some mischance the *Jefe* happened to come in! Because he was not only the *Jefe,* but also the *Gobernador* of the Province, and had much, much power—in fact killing didn't bother him at all! Even my somewhat irrepressible husband seemed to take this seriously, and we returned quietly and peacefully to the Playa de Cortes.

Late in the spring we prepared to go East. Mother Lapham had planned a wonderful family reunion at Waveney in June, which worked out perfectly for us, as it was Roger Jr.'s graduation from Harvard, and both Roger's and my 35th college reunions. (Nothing is more over-rated than reunions. What is there to talk about to people you haven't seen for ten years, and never liked much in College anyway? Even though some of the "girls," who had not been outstanding during their four years in college proved to be by far the most interesting, Edna and I found it on the whole a rather depressing experience. We lasted only two and a half of the scheduled four days.)

In New Canaan the clan was gathering—forty-nine strong. Mother Lapham had been making preparations for the great "do" for two years. Her arrangements were perfection. She had said she would pay the way of every grandchild, great-grandchild, and one nurse for each family, but her four children could get there on their own. She had rented a small cottage for the young ones and their nurses, and the rest of us were parcelled out among the different members of the family.

Remarkably, with that number of people, everyone was able to come. And how we "Forty-niners" did enjoy ourselves! We had every possible kind of picture taken—stills, movies, the whole family, individual groups, outdoors for the baseball games, and indoors for the big dinner dance Mother gave. We had a fancy dress party and many parties at the swimming pool. The whole affair lasted for nearly two weeks. All went well, and even though Jane developed whooping cough on the way home, no one, not even her own two boys, caught it.

It was a happy time, but the last time we would all be together— Roger and I had been told that Jack and Edna were getting a divorce in the fall, after thirty-two years of married life. Jack insisted on the divorce, as he had found someone who "understood" him. Edna had fought it for three years, but finally gave in when she found the situation was hopeless. Knowing how dreadfully Mother Lapham would feel about it, nothing was said before the reunion, and Jack and Edna came there together and were able to put on a pretty convincing act.

Roger and I went back to San Francisco, but it was arranged for us to go East again in August, when the news of Jack and Edna's divorce would be broken to the family. So early that month I flew to Houston and met Edna, who had driven up from San Antonio, and we drove to New York by leisurely stages. It was not a cheerful trip. And we spent a sad week at New Canaan, trying to convince various members of the family that any attempts at reconciliation were hopeless. Edna returned to San Antonio, and, as a resident of Texas, got her divorce in three months. A week later Jack married his secretary who "understood" him.

After the reunion, I met Dorothy in Washington, Connecticut, and we broke up Mother's house. It was tiring work physically, but easy otherwise. Dorothy and I were in complete accord about what we wanted and what we didn't want. (She would hold out a bronze clock and a pair of matching candle-holders and say, "Do you want these?" I'd answer, "I wouldn't give them house room"—fortunately—for she, I would discover, really hankered after them.) We divided fifty or sixty sample plates, designed by Father but never put into production, and wrapped just as they came from the factory in Limoges some thirty years before. All the letters and papers were tied into neat bundles and carefully labelled: "These may be destroyed unread" or "Look these over, they may amuse you."

One thing I did take the lion's share of was a collection of period dresses and hats which she had saved for years. There was her wedding dress, a most beautiful silver-blue bocade that had been worn by her grandmother; my golf hat, cape and bright red jacket that I had had in my freshman year at college; my graduation dress, and Dorothy's. Most of them were in good condition, and later on I had a seamstress put them all in first class order. For years I myself had kept an outstanding dress—my gorgeous Worth evening gown from Paris in '23, one from the very long waist-very short skirt period—and a "Merry Widow" sailor I had the year I was married, so large it wouldn't go in the door of a Fifth Avenue bus without bending my head sideways.

Roger Jr. entered law school that fall, at Boalt Hall in Berkeley. While he lived there, he was home a good deal at weekends. He seemed to think he ought to get married, and asked me what kind of a girl I thought he should choose. I told him a girl like Nancy Scott, the daughter of a good friend of mine, because she was most attractive and had enough character to settle him when he needed it! I never suspected at the time that he was already seriously interested in her! It took the better part of another year to find that out.

After her divorce Edna had taken her daughter Jean, and gone down to Mexico City to spend the winter. In December Carol and I took a three-week vacation to join them. We sailed early in January on the "United States" for Acapulco where Edna and Jean would meet us. We had reserved a comfortable enough cabin, but when we got on board we were ushered into one of the de luxe suites by courtesy of the shipping company. Roger, who was seeing us off, was so overcome that all he could say was: "My God! Ken Dawson didn't have to do this. Sport, you will tip suitably, won't you?" I assured him I would, but made a mistake in not giving the steward $5.00 at once, because we really didn't get very good service—two women, alone, with nothing but suit-cases, only going as far as Acapulco . . . why bother with them? When I finally did suitably tip the steward—and everyone else in sight—at the end of the trip, they almost dropped dead.

Acapulco was nothing but a sleepy little Mexican fishing village then; a few hardy souls came there because the deep-sea fishing was good. There really wasn't much to do or see, except in the evenings when the young men and the girls paraded around the Plaza in clockwise and counter-clockwise circles, smashing eggs filled with confetti or horrible cheap perfume on each other's heads; the more you liked the girl, the more violently you bombarded her. We all joined in, and it took us days to get the confetti out of our hair, and the smell of that awful perfume out of our clothes.

After two nights, we motored on to Taxco, which we thought perfectly delightful. The wonderful Spratling silver works were there, and the goods on display just dragged your money right out of your pocket. It was fun just to sit on the hotel's upstairs verandah overlooking the Plaza at the cocktail hour, and watch the colorful crowds milling around below. The Cathedral was ornate beyond words; with so many gilded shrines, so many highly-colored plaster saints, so many splendidly dressed and bejeweled Virgins with myriads of candles burning before them, that they left me completely bewildered. I felt the appeal was entirely to the senses and not at all to the mind.

From there to Mexico City, where we stayed at the Hotel Geneve. We were there for two weeks, and didn't miss a thing. Jean spoke enough Spanish so that we didn't need a guide, and we went everywhere: to Xochimilco, for a Sunday of drifting around the lovely floating gardens, passing other boats filled to the brim with flowers, some with native singers and some with ordinary sightseers like ourselves; to the Pyramids, where we saw the famous Black Virgin of the Miracle; to two bullfights (half way through the first one, when one of the best known matadors had failed to kill his bull in a very bloody bout, Carol had turned pale green and said she was going to be sick at her stomach unless we left, so we did—precipitately. On the trip back I paid the taxi driver, and started to add his tip. To my surprise, he drew himself up and said "No, Senora, I am a man of honor. I have already charged you twice the regular fare as a *Yanqui,* and I can take no more." Jean and I went back to the bullfight alone the next Sunday, for we just had to see that matador kill his bull. He did, and was rewarded with both the ears and the tail.)

We had one unforgettable evening with the Witters, who had come down on the ship with us, and asked us to dinner. They left it up to Edna to choose the time and place. She said 9:30, at the best restaurant in Mexico, and told Dean to be sure to reserve a table. But Dean rather likes to run things his own way, and approved neither of the hour nor of having to make a reservation. They were to come to Edna's suite at 7:30 for cocktails and bridge. When the evening arrived Helen W. was laid up with the usual "Mexico tummy" and in bed on tea and toast, and Dean was left to escort four ladies.

By nine o'clock he began to get fidgety, and by 9:15 we were enroute, although Edna assured him we would be the only people in the place. We were, but when I stepped up to the maitre d' as Dean stopped to check his coat, and asked for "Senor Vittaire's table," he simply shrugged and said the Senor had no table. Great embarrassment on Dean's part, a good deal of hemming and hawing it really hadn't seemed necessary to him to reserve a table. A bit of money changed hands and we were finally seated in the darkest and most remote corner of the room.

All went well for a bit, then the room filled with diners and Dean began to swell up. He seemed to grow taller right before my eyes. At last he burst out, "I've never seen anything like the disgusting behavior of these Mexican men. Every one of them in this room has walked by this table just to ogle our two charming young girls."

"Dean," I said, "they have a much better reason than that. Look behind you!" Directly in back of his chair was a door marked in large letters *"Senores!"* We were all laughing hysterically, and even Dean had to join in.

7

POLITICS, WAR AND WASHINGTON
(1941 — 1942)

SHORTLY after my return from Mexico, Roger announced that he had heard that Madame Secretary of Labor Perkins was coming to the West Coast. He wired her an invitation to dinner on a date of her own choosing. That was the last I heard of it until one fine Sunday morning a friend called me up to ask what I was going to wear to dinner the following Sunday? Being slightly surprised, I hedged, and said I hadn't definitely made up my mind. She then asked should she wear long or short? I said I'd let her know, and hung up, wondering what in the world was going on. I attacked Roger as soon as he came in from golf, and his reply was, "Oh, didn't I tell you? We're giving a dinner for 16 Sunday night for the Secretary!" I was really just as glad to know a little in advance! Next day I telephoned my friend and said, "long."

The Secretary was an easy, gracious woman, and certainly knew her way around socially, even if she knew little or nothing about California. She candidly confessed the State had been nothing to her but a long pink strip on the map before she went into office. She had motored up from Los Angeles through the San Joaquin Valley and, as we had had a very wet winter, it couldn't have looked more lush. She was very much distressed over the conditions under which the "Okies" lived, and was outraged that the banks, which held so much of that beautiful, fertile land, wouldn't distribute some of it to "those poor itinerant workers, who wanted so little, and had never had anything done for them."

In vain did I try to convince her that the land wasn't fertile, that it got no rain for at least six months of the year, and that everything that grew there was grown with irrigation; that the owners of the vineyards and other ranches had tried in vain to do something for the Okies, but that they kept coal in the bathtubs, chopped up the furniture for kindling, didn't send their children to the schools provided for them, and as soon as they had exhausted the possibilities of one place, moved to the next. But she had "Grapes of Wrath" too firmly in her mind to really believe anything I said.

Then the men came in from the dining room and surrounded her —each primed to speak his piece on labor conditions on the Pacific Coast in general, and on the waterfront in particular. The male guests were a hand-picked group, and all set to go; but did they get a chance? Not for an hour. She never stopped telling them off herself. By the second hour they began to wear her down, and by the third hour, they had taken the floor.

At quarter of one, she rose and said that as her car had been waiting for three hours, perhaps she had better leave. I went over to say good-bye to her, and told her she must feel as Daniel did when he was in the lions' den. "Oh, but Mrs. Lapham," she said, "I knew they weren't going to eat me, and they all roared so charmingly, I assure you I really enjoyed it." Maybe she did and maybe she didn't. But she certainly left with a pretty clear picture of what strikes, slow-downs and work stoppages had cost the Pacific Coast ports, under the aegis of Harry Bridges.

Judging by results, Madame Secretary meant it when she said that her lions had roared so charmingly that she had really enjoyed it. About the middle of March she telephoned Roger to ask if he would be willing to serve as an industry member on the National Defense Mediation Board. The President was about to set up NDMB. It was to consist of three public, four industry and four labor members, with authority to hear and presumably to settle labor disputes. Roger said that if called upon he would be very willing to serve; that afternoon the President announced the creation of the Board. Roger flew to Washington, to be gone a week or ten days, to see the Secretary and try to learn a bit more about his new job.

The day after Roger left, Helen Witter saw me making a face as I tried to get up out of a chair after lunch and asked what the matter was. I said that, according to my sister's colored maid, I had "misery in the back." (She was the one who called Dorothy and told her she couldn't come to her one day. Dorothy asked what the trouble was, and she said there was nothing "pacifically wrong," but she just felt that "life was too daily.") Helen said, "Come with me, spend a week soaking in our hot sulphur pools, and you'll never know you've had a backache." Roger was away—why not?

So I went, and had a most interesting and worthwhile week with her at the Horseshoe Ranch, near Beowawe. The ranch was located on the old Overland Trail, and derived its name from a horseshoe-shaped ring of poplar trees planted, I should think from their size, by some of the early migrants. All sorts of things had been found in the surrounding pasture land—oxbows, old glass bottles purpled from exposure—and Helen had used them all in the simple house in one way or another. A cattle yoke was the mantle shelf, built into the field-stone fireplace, and the bottles were arranged on it. At one of the near-by towns she had bought an old square piano from the sale of the effects of a saloon.

I found it all fascinating, but best of all was being able to take a daily swim in the hot sulphur water. There were two pools, one small one with a temperature of over 100°, the other a much larger one with the water about 80°; and as they were both enclosed by a high corral fence, and no one used them but Helen and me, you could swim as the Lord made you. It didn't take a week; in two days my aches and pains were a thing of the past, even though one day we had snow. (It's quite an experience to swim in hot water with snowflakes pattering down on your head.)

I have hated walking for years, my feet aren't made for it, but Helen insisted I should walk every day, or no pre-dinner drink; as I did like my toddy I walked, willy-nilly.

One day she drove me in to Elko, about 50 miles away, for a bridge tournament which she said I must win, as all the Elko ladies fancied themselves the best players in the world. It was progressive bridge, starting before lunch and resuming for the rest of the afternoon, and was nothing if not a social event in a big way. Everyone was dressed in silks and satins except Helen and me. We were modestly clad in tailored suits. I started at table #14, and there I stayed all day long; they all progressed except me. I never held a card over a jack, and the only reason I didn't get the boobyprize was because they had a local rule that if you took a trick with a two-spot, you raised your hand, they rang a bell, and they added 100 to your score. I took four tricks with deuces, so ended up with 1700 total points, the lowest was 1300, and the highest 6600! Never in my card-playing career have I been more humiliated.

Roger and I arrived home almost simultaneously. He spent about a week in San Francisco settling up his affairs, and then early in April we returned to Washington together, bag and baggage, for an indefinite period of time. It turned out to be nearly three years.

We moved into a very small suite at the Carlton Hotel, 212-214 on the second floor. It was dark as pitch, and so congested with furniture that I at once christened it the "Igloo." It was impossible for both of us to dress at the same time, and I always felt I had to back out before he could get in.

We discovered as time went on that that small room had its advantages. Just as people seem to prefer a small crowded dance floor to a large ballroom, the different members of the Board formed the habit of dropping in to discuss the cases which they were going to hear, beforehand. If there weren't enough chairs, they just sat on the floor, and perhaps the very fact of its being so small gave it "homey" atmosphere in which they felt relaxed.

They were good enough to let me sit curled up in a corner of the sofa with my knitting and my cigarettes, and to serve as bartender— so long as I never spoke or, even more important, repeated what I had heard. It was truly a course in adult education. I enjoyed every minute of it, even thought it was quite a while before this situation developed.

We had probably been in Washington for about two weeks when the Secretary invited us to dinner at the swank and very attractive F Street Club. Of course, we accepted. Before dinner, as I stood talking to Chief Justice Harlan Stone and General Marshall, cocktails and tomato juice were passed. Both men refused either drink. I asked the Chief Justice if he never drank anything, and he said, "Ma dear lady, there is only one drink fitten for a gentleman, and that is straight Kentucky Bourbon whiskey. And ma doctors won't let me have it, and I wouldn't insult ma stomach by putting that red hogwash into it!"

At dinner two of us women were seated next to each other, while there were two men together on the other side of the table. I thought it a bit strange, but it was later explained to me as protocol. With a table of 16 and two ranking guests—in this case the Chief Justice and General Marshall—the Chief Justice sat at the hostess' right, and the General acted as host at the other end of the table; so two men and two women had to sit together somewhere. There is no other possible arrangement unless, as the State Department Book of Etiquette suggests, you never invite 16!

If I had been sitting next to the Chief Justice, I might have been tempted to remind him of an episode which had taken place a good many years before, and of which I am certain he never knew the inside story. He and Mrs. Stone had been visiting in California, and had been entertained at dinner by the McCormicks at their Atherton home.

A few days afterwards, Florence, who had just taken a bath and was relaxing on a chaise-loungue with her hair screwed up on the top of her head, heard a tremendous rumpus in the kitchen. She threw on an old cotton dress, ran downstairs, and found the Chinese laundry-boy, with a large carving knife in his hand, chasing the Chinese cook! She knew they belonged to different Tongs, but did not expect a China-town war to explode in her kitchen. She was so mad she grabbed the knife and said to the boy, "What you think you do?" He said, "Cook no good—I kill him." She yelled, "You no dare kill my cook; he good cook, I likee he; you go back to wash-tub," and he went obediently.

Just at that moment the doorbell rang. It was her maid's day out, so she went, and there to her horror were the Stones, immaculately dressed and holding out cards. Looking at the knife in her hand with equal horror, they asked feebly for Mrs. McCormick. Florence, as I have said before, was a quick thinker. She put out her hand for the cards, said, "She ain't home," and closed the door firmly in their faces.

By the time she got back to the kitchen the cook had departed for good, and the laundry boy said, "I don' know, Missy; wash clo' all month, get $50.00; kill a man Chinatown, fi' minute, get $300." Then she was sure the cook had been right to go. I was equally sure that the Chief Justice would have appreciated hearing the real story of his courtesy call on the McCormicks!

After dinner our hostess saw to it that we all played a sort of game of musical chairs, moving people around quietly so that everyone had a chance to talk to everyone else. Promptly at 10:30, the Stones rose to leave. That seemed very early to me, but I caught Roger's eye, he rose too, and we moved towards the door. But as I was thanking the Secretary, she whispered "Don't go," so we didn't. Again a question of Washington protocol; the ranking guest must leave on the dot of 10:30, and after that the rest may do as they please.

Several couples left, but quite a few of us remained, and Miss Perkins told us of the terrible gaffe she had made at her first Washington dinner. She was enjoying herself tremendously, didn't know the rule, and was stunned when at midnight her hostess came over and muttered in her ear "Go home!" She sprang to her feet, everyone else left precipitately, and it was explained to her the next day that no one could leave before she did, and no matter how much she was enjoying herself, 10:30 was the deadline.

That was a delightful evening, but how was I to fill my days? I had never before lived in a hotel for any length of time—after I had read the papers, dressed and picked up the rooms, what did I do next? I knew no one in Washington except Roger's sister, Elinor Ford. Although she was awfully good to me, she had lived there for years and had her own life to lead. She was an excellent artist and painting took up a great deal of her time. And I could hardly expect her to give up everything and devote herself to me.

Those first weeks I went to every movie in town, saw every art gallery, museum and historical monument and explored the shops thoroughly. My sister lived in Baltimore and she either came over to me or I went to her one day a week. The weekends were wonderful. The Board didn't meet on Saturdays and Roger had taken delivery of a new car in Washington. So we went off and explored the countryside . . . Richmond, Williamsburg, Charlottesville, Gettysburg. How beautiful that country is in the spring, with laurel, dogwood, redbud, rhododendrons and azaleas all in fullest bloom.

Roger developed a passion for battlefields, and I think that even today I could pass an examination on Antietam, where we spent the better part of a Sunday, or Gettysburg, where we spent a day.

But the weekend that stands out in my mind most clearly is one Fourth of July. We had expected to leave early Thursday afternoon, but Roger was kept late. Then a terrific thunderstorm burst just as he came in, so we decided to wait until the next morning. As we got into the car I said, "Where are we going?" Roger replied, "Well, we've never been to Kentucky. Let's go there!"

I had simply expected to cruise around a bit, stopping at any attractive motels we saw, so I had nothing but sports clothes with me. I thought Kentucky was quite a trek, but was willing to give it a try. We stopped for lunch at Martinsburg, not at the place recommended by Duncan Hines which didn't appeal to Roger, but at some little dump which looked so pecularily unattractive to me that I lunched chastely on a fried egg sandwich and a bottle of beer—feeling that neither of them could possibly poison me.

After lunch Roger said he was sleepy. He retired to the back seat to take a nap while I drove. "Just keep going on Route #19, and you'll be all right." I was for a while, and then it began to rain, and soon was pouring in torrents. I lost #19 once, because I couldn't even see through the windshield, but found it again and kept on going until

Roger woke up and asked where we were. "Twenty miles from Hot Springs," said I. "Fine," he said, "we'll go there!" We did, and sat in the Homestead for three days with the rain beating down on the windows, everyone but me dressed to the teeth for the big weekend doings, and not a soul we knew in the place!

A very sad piece of news greeted us on our return. Our beloved friend Florence McCormick had had a stroke; we were told there was no hope, and she died a few days later. She and I used to see each other almost daily in San Francisco—at our Monday luncheon-bridge club of eight, which was an institution of some thirty years standing; at long sessions of Mah Jongg; and in the earlier days when we were all going like mad socially, at least a biweekly visit to the stores, as shopping had been our passion. She was a gay and quick-witted companion, but her wit never had a sting; it was always directed towards some ridiculous thing she herself had done, and never, never in an unkind way towards others. I knew I should miss her sorely, and to this day I find myself smiling when I think what "Cormie" would have said under some given situation.

I wanted to get into some kind of war work, and had asked a San Francisco woman who lived in Washington, and whom I knew slightly, how to get into the Red Cross. She said "My dear, the only day you could possibly go would be Tuesday, but that is reserved for Senators' wives, so you are not eligible. All the other days are simply for the "hoi-polloi." Well, I wasn't so much daunted by the thought of the "hoi-polloi" as by the fact that, as I had never taken any of the courses, I would probably be set to rolling bandages or making laparotomy pads, both of which I had done before and despised.

So I decided I would be a Gray Lady. But not a prayer; I was over 50, and apparently after 49 you weren't attractive enough to titillate the spirits of the boys in hospital, although I really felt that a certain amount of maturity had its points too. Then a friend of Elinor's suggested Bundles for Britain where she worked. They accepted me with alacrity

—to do all the dirty jobs: reknitting other people's mismated socks, leaning over and packing huge cases with smelly, woolen sweaters and clothes that had been donated; not too pleasant, but somebody had to do it, and I supposed it might as well be me.

The woman in charge was a high-born Russian, a former lady-in-waiting of the Czarina. One day she announced that our unit was to be inspected by a Countess; we were all to line up when she arrived, and would be presented. I smiled when the Countess entered, for it was Ethel Crocker de Limur from San Francisco! I was about the middle of the line, and as our chief said, "And now may I present Mrs. Lapham," Ethel said "Helen! For heaven's sake, what are you doing here? Why didn't you let me know you were in Washington?" She asked why were we there, what was Roger doing, where were we staying, and said she would get in touch with us for dinner very soon. Say what you please about snobbery. It, like maturity, has its points for the underdog. Mrs. Lapham was promoted to a desk within the hour, and never packed another old clo'.

One thing I enjoyed tremendously was the Episcopal service in French at St. John's church (only a block from the Carlton) every Sunday afternoon at four. It lasted only an hour. The minister was a dynamic young Frenchman who always had something to say. We sang the Psalms in the old metrical Huguenot version. And even though I always finished the General Confession at least four words behind everyone else— it seemed so much longer than it does in English—I really loved and got a great deal out of the whole service.

We went up to New York or New Canaan for occasional weekends, and I stuck it out in Washington until the middle of July when the heat got me. Then I thought longingly of those damp, cold San Francisco fogs. Our house in Atherton was open and ready for me. I went back to California.

Roger returned later for his favorite vacation, the summer encampment at the Bohemian Grove. Lewis and Jane had taken a house just across Atherton Avenue from us. Carol and her family were in their own charming house. It was delightful to be back in the bosom of the family again.

Poor Lewis had been miserably ill for some months, crippled by sciatica, and suffering in addition from a chronic duodenal ulcer. He spent his time reading enormously, and had pursued a real course in tracing the history of Empire. One of his conclusions was that England was now reduced to a third-rate world power—a thought that really shocked me through and through. But how right he has proved to be!

Roger Jr. had decided that the law was not for him and seemed to be in somewhat of a quandary as to just what he was going to do. He was draft age. He had already signed up for the Navy if he were called. It was doubtful if he could get a job under the circumstances. And we thought he had something on his mind, though we couldn't discover just what. But it didn't come out until after Roger had gone back to Washington. He told me he had asked Nancy Scott to marry him and she had replied that she wouldn't marry anyone who didn't have a job. He was thinking seriously of going into the shipyards. I couldn't have asked for a more delightful prospective daughter-in-law. Her mother, Norma Bartlett, was one of my dear friends and I had already seen a good deal of Nancy and loved her for herself as well.

So Roger Jr. got a job in a small San Francisco shipyard and, of course, had to join a union—the Hook and Dillon outfit, one of the more unsavory ones with which the steamship companies had had quite a bit of trouble. When he went in to sign up, the agent asked if Roger were his father; Roger Jr. admitted he was, and the agent said, "Well, when your old man hears you've joined us, he's going to bust a gut!" At any rate, working the swing shift, midnight to 8 A.M., he got fantastic wages, besides being able to sleep all day and still take Nancy out in the evening.

They were married on October 4th in St. Catherine's Church in Burlingame with Lewis as best man. I may have been a bit emotionally inclined at my youngest son's wedding, but the thing that really set me off was seeing Lewis, who had hardly walked a step all summer except from his bed to his bath, able to walk beside his brother and down that long, long aisle.

Roger Jr. had taken from Friday morning at 8:00 until Monday midnight for the rehearsal, the wedding and his honeymoon. He had invited all the other workers on his shift to come to the wedding, but all he had gotten was jeers. "You getting married in Burlingame? Sure, sure—we'll all be there, just as likely as you are." But when he returned Monday, all the accounts from all the newspapers had been carefully cut out and pinned on the bulletin board, and the general reaction was "My God—he meant it!"

Roger had come out for the wedding but stayed only a few days and I went back with him. Marguerite Ecker, through whom I had gotten into Bundles for Britain, told me I should take a course of lectures on Civilian Defense with her, which I did, and some of the question-and-answer periods were most amusing. We were being told that in case of a bomb attack, we were to get to the nearest shelter at once, no matter at what time nor what condition we were in, when one old girl spoke up and said: "Well, young man, if you think that when I'm taking a bath I'm supposed to get out and go gallivanting around Washington in my skin at my age, why you've got another think coming."

I passed the very simple exam, was accepted as a member of the Civilian Defense Corps, and worked in rather a desultory way at various odd jobs all that fall. I didn't feel I accomplished very much, but then at that time I didn't think that anyone else did either.

The first weekend in December we went up to New York to see Mother Lapham. We had had lunch and she and I were sitting chatting. Roger had gone out to call on an old American-Hawaiian associate. Then Roger phoned me: "Sport, Sport—turn on the radio! The Japanese are attacking Pearl Harbor. Half of our Fleet is sunk and the rest in flames!"

The Japanese had made a more-than-successful sneak attack on Pearl Harbor while their envoys were still in Washington for discussion? It couldn't be true, the radio reports must be exaggerated. But as further details of the Day of Infamy leaked out, it proved not only true, but worse than we had dreamed of. As we learned when we returned to Washington the next day. Guam had been attacked, too, and our Air Force in the Philippines wiped out.

The President declared war on Japan on December 8th, 1941 and on Germany and Italy on the 11th, and within the next few days we could see signs of the madhouse which Washington would become for the next four years.

The services of the National Defense Mediation Board were ended. The President called together a 24-member Management-Labor Conference—12 members representing each side, with Roger as a member. They were told that we were at war, many decisions were pending, and those decisions must be made—quickly. They weren't; shortly afterwards this group was superseded by another new organization called the National War Labor Board. Roger was again asked to serve.

By this time Christmas was upon us—our first Christmas away from home and the family and I was as blue as the proverbial indigo. I bought a tiny tree, one string of lights, a few ornaments and trimmed it. I sat down and was about to burst into tears when Marguerite Ecker telephoned and suggested my coming over for a spot of Christmas cheer. Never did I need it more—I couldn't wait to get there!

When I got back, Roger told me that the Kirsteins (a younger couple, and he was staff secretary of the Board) had asked us out for dinner and to help them trim their tree. My indigo blue started to turn to rose color. The other guest was Governor Gruening of Alaska. The Kirsteins grilled steaks over the open fire in their living room, and it all couldn't have been pleasanter.

After dinner Jackie Kirstein was trying to get George to help her with the tree, but all he would say was, "In a little while, Jackie. I want to talk to the men now." The third repetition brought signs of annoyance on both sides, so I spoke up: "Listen, Jackie; some of the worst fights Roger and I have ever had have been on Christmas Eve, over trimming the tree. Now be honest—have you ever really liked what George did when he helped you? You and I can do it far better together. Let's just allow the men to enjoy themselves in their own way." She agreed that as a matter of fact, she never had liked the way George did it. So we trimmed it together, joined the men for a nightcap, and went home in a happy mood of relaxation.

Now we were at war, I felt I simply had to find something really worthwhile to do instead of the rather desultory, unsatisfying kind of thing I had been doing. At the back of my mind for some time had been the thought that if I could only type, my services might be really valuable somewhere. I was a prolific letter writer, but my handwriting was so bad that Carol said when she was at college she used to read my letters over several times, and get something quite different out of them at each perusal.

I asked Roger if he thought I was too old to learn to type. He said that was ridiculous. So I chose the Temple School, on K Street only four blocks from the Carlton, and went there to enroll. But I had great difficulty in persuading them to take me! "I didn't want to take the full course." (Shorthand and business arithmetic—certainly not!) "I wouldn't be faithful. They had too many young girls who needed the course for jobs as it was." But like General Grant, I was going to "sit it out on those lines if it took all summer." I finally got in and went for three hours every afternoon; and then on Saturday mornings, when there was no school, to practice.

They taught the touch system. I adored it from the first moment, except for one unfortunate day when I met my Waterloo. Our teacher put a record on the phonograph, turned it on, and told us we were to copy from our books in time to the music! Now if it had been "Pas-sen-gers will please re-frain from flush-ing toi-lets while the train is stand-ing in the sta-tion—I love you!" to the tune of Dvorak's "Humor-esque," I might have managed. But trying to write: "Next to sincerity, the trait that wins us and binds us most firmly to man is courage. Cour-age in the face of danger brings a glow to the heart, and wins respect of others," to the beat of "Stars and Stripes Forever" was completely beyond me. I don't wonder that my teacher sighed when she looked at the mess which was my paper, and said, "Oh dear, Mrs. Lapham. You really have no sense of rhythm at all, have you?"

Of course my burning desire now was to have a typewriter of my own, but it was impossible to buy one as they were all reserved for Government use. However, through the kind offices of a friend, I was able to get a fairly good used one at which I spent hours, feeling that I was really acquiring a new language. In time, I was even able to copy some of Roger's WLB dissenting opinions for him. He wrote so many— outstripped only by Wayne Morse, one of the public members—that I felt he should be called the modern "Great Dissenter." He said that when he first went on the Board, he felt like a freshman in a new school; but very soon discovered that he had had so much more actual experience in day-to-day, month-to-month labor negotiations, that he was appalled at some of the decisions reached, apparently in total ignorance of their far-reaching implications and results.

All sorts of things were happening. Roger Jr. had been called up by the Navy. Because he did not have 20/20 vision, he had been assigned to the School of Supply in, of all places, Cambridge, which he had left only a year and a half before. Nancy had written me that, come summer, the patter of baby feet would be heard in their menage.

Lewis, who had been rejected by all the services on account of his ulcer-cum-sciatica, was working for General Gilbraith, Commander of the Port of San Francisco. Lewis acted as liaison between the Army, the shipping companies, and the labor unions. "He is invaluable," said Gilbraith. "If everything goes right, the Army gets the credit; if it goes wrong—what could you expect of a civilian?"

The WLB began to hold open hearings to which I went whenever it was possible. John L. Lewis spoke on several occasions. He was a real spellbinder; I listened to him once for 45 minutes, and would have sworn at the end that he had not spoken for more than 15. Mrs. Lapham and her companion-friend Miss Carlson came down for some of these hearings. After one, around Easter time, I accompanied them down to Williamsburg for a week's holiday, for even my second Alma Mater, the Temple School, gave its students an Easter vacation.

Late in June I took my final typing exams—three sessions typing 35 words a minute for ten minutes, with only four mistakes! It was in the middle of an early heat wave. I wore pince-nez glasses which, between the heat and the excitement, kept slipping off my nose so that I came to the end of a page and typed a whole row of copy on the bare roller without even noticing it! The only person who was more nervous than I was my teacher. I know she didn't expect me to pass, but I did. When I went back a day or two later to hear the result, she handed me my little certificate most dramatically, and said, "Mrs. Lapham, here is your passport to the business world. You told me you were a good speller, and I have tried hard to get you a good job, but the best one I can find will pay only $125."

I was speechless, partly at the idea of anyone being willing to pay $125 for what I had to offer, and partly at having to confess that I didn't want a job at any price. I tried to soften it by telling her that my husband was working for the Government and I had really taken the course in order to be available when he needed me. But I am afraid she was disappointed in me, just the same. I only wish I could find means to tell her what my being able to type has meant to me, and how very grateful I am to her for all the effort she expended on me.

Early in July I went up to New Canaan for a weekend with Mother Lapham. Around noon on the 4th, she was called to the telephone, "Boston calling." Miss Carlson and I heard her say, "Oh Roger! No!" and burst into tears. We stared at each other in dismay. To which Roger was she talking? What had happened? But the next remark was, "It's just too wonderful. I can't believe it." She came back, still in tears, to tell us that Nancy had had a little girl, born that morning, and she was to be named Antoinette Dearborn Lapham, for her.

Miss Carlson disappeared, I thought to get smelling salts for Mother.

But she came back with a different kind of a restorative, an ice-cold bottle of champagne, which the three of us polished off in nice style.

I went back to Washington briefly, packed and left for California on Roger's assurance that he would be able to join me there later. Lewis, Jane and their boys were in the Big House on the place in Atherton that summer, so I moved into the little cottage that I had fixed up for Carol, with my faithful Christena to take care of me.

Ernst had gone into the Service, was stationed at Santa Ana, and Carol had taken a house at Newport Beach some 18 or 20 miles away. I waited around to hear when Roger was coming out, but when I heard that the Little Steel case was dragging on and on, and that he couldn't even get out for the Bohemian Grove, I gave up and went south for a week with Carol. She had a nice house, not on the ocean but on the lagoon. Both the little boys were regular water rats. Lots of her friends, whose husbands were also at Santa Ana, had houses nearby, and I had a delightful week with them all.

I had seen my new grandchild, of course, and approved of her. On my return from the south her grandmother, Norma Bartlett, and I went up to Lake Tahoe for another visit to some friends. It was a lovely informal home, right on the south shore of the lake. We had a most pleasant, relaxed time, with plenty of bridge and Mah Jongg, but with time out for a siesta in the afternoon, and an early bed hour.

Soon after our arrival we all developed "Tahoe tummy," which comes from some algae in the drinking water. Our hostess sent for a doctor, but it took him hours to arrive and his explanation was that he had been doing a really delicate operation on a small boy who had caught himself in the zipper of his bathing trunks, and he thought that to keep his manhood unimpaired was more important than to treat three females for stomach-ache and diarrhea.

By the time I got home, Roger Jr. had finished his course at the School of Supply and was in San Diego. Nancy was able to join him there for a couple of weeks before he was assigned to the "Bogue," one of the small escort aircraft carriers which was outfitting in Tacoma. He was there for some months. When he sailed it was "Destination Unknown," and everyone was betting on the Pacific area. But it turned out to be the North Atlantic, which they discovered when they reached Panama. To be based at Argentsia and do the run from there to Iceland was not what anyone would have chosen had they been given a voice in the matter.

I went back to Washington early in October. Then things began popping in a big way.

I registered with the head office of Civilian Defense as a semi-skilled typist and said I was willing to go wherever they sent me—as long as I got practice in typing. My first assignment was with some organization for the day-care of children of working mothers. What a piece of work they handed out to me! Page after page of figures and statistics to be copied which were supposed to be correct to the last decimal point. Try as hard as I might, I always seemed to end up with some ridiculous result, such as having it cost $50 to take care of one-third of a child for two-and-a-quarter days. I knew I was making a mess of it, even though I deserved E for effort. I was so relieved when, after I had thrown up my hands in despair, the head of the office told me not to worry; no one else had been willing to tackle it; they had all waited until some good-natured sucker of a volunteer put in an appearance!

My next job was at Headquarters, where I was asked to do a report for a peppery retired General, who had been in charge of a simulated bombing attack at a rendezvous outside of Washington the week before. The smart little redheaded secretary who gave me the assignment said, "I do hope you'll get along all right, Mrs. Lapham. He reduced the last two volunteers to tears in no time flat." I assured her I wasn't the weepy sort, and started to work. More statistics: "Time of assembly—1900 hours; proportion present .05259; 1900+1—.07632 arrive; 1900+2 —slight rain begins, not enough to keep people away"; etc., etc. ad lib. I spent hours on it, took the finished product in to him, and was amply rewarded with a grunt and "Not as bad as I expected."

Shortly before Christmas I was sent to Selective Board #6, housed in an old red brick building on the corner of Pennsylvania Avenue and H Street. I was given an enormous stack of folders, containing men's life histories, and an equal number of post cards to be filled in in eight different places with the man's former status, classification, serial number, and decision of the Board as to whether he should be continued in Class 1-A, B, or, perhaps, a permanent 4-F. I was a little appalled. There must have been 150 to 175 cards. As I introduced myself as the one semi-skilled typist instead of the five skilled ones they had asked for, I said I was afraid I would have to ask a good many questions. "Please do," she said. "The last volunteer we had left things in such a mess we had to get a trouble-shooter from Headquarters to straighten us out." Some 50 cards were missing, and she hunted for ten days before she found them—filed under D for "Don't know!"

The cards were so stiff that the typewriter bar wouldn't hold them in place, and the eight places left for the information to be filled in were such that you could neither single nor double space them, but had to hand-adjust for each one. Who said anything about Government efficiency? It took nearly five minutes to do each one, when it should have taken a minute and a half.

I was sure that each 4-F was a VD case, and felt I should handle the letters enclosed in the folders with gloves. But I soon discovered that most of them were permanent disabilities—missing fingers, flat feet, TB, heart trouble, and not a single VD case among them.

The prize was a letter from a man who didn't seem to have any address, just a number. It began: "Dear Selective Service Board #6: Nothing, I can assure you, would give me greater pleasure than to accept your invitation to report to Washington for induction into the Armed Services. Unfortunately the Warden and I do not see eye to eye on this matter. As I am in Sing Sing for six years for forgery, he seems to think I should remain in his keeping rather than in Uncle Sam's. So it is with real regret that I am forced to sign myself #80267, rather than Private ——————." I always felt that it was the Army's loss; I think

103

that anyone with such a sense of humor under such circumstances would have been a real asset and quite a morale builder, if they kept him away from the funds.

I finished the job by working on New Year's Day—thus earning about equal portions of admiration and disgust from the girls of the office force. Why on earth did I work on a holiday when I didn't have to? I said that I was a volunteer and didn't have to work at all if I didn't want to. My husband was in Government employ; he had gone to work, so why shouldn't I? And I really felt I had contributed my bit, for some of the decisions of Draft Board #6 had been made the previous May; many of those poor boys had been waiting for seven months to hear the results.

By this time I had accumulated enough hours to qualify for a uniform. So I took myself to Garfinkel's to buy one; horizon blue, with CD on the arm, and a little overseas cap with a Civilian button pinned on it. No ball gown that I could have worn would ever have created the sensation my uniform did when I appeared in it for the first time at the Carlton. Everyone from the cigarette girl to the Assistant Manager gathered in the lobby to admire me: "Turn around, Mrs. Lapham. Gee! Don't you look nice!" The coat had been a bit loose for me when I had started out, but swollen with pride, I filled it out to the farthest seam when I left the hotel!

A few days later, a sunny crisp January day, I reported to Headquarters for reassignment. The Colonel's secretary greeted me—the Colonel was the head of Civilian Defense—and asked how I was feeling. "Never better," said I. "Why?" "Because," she said, "I've got a lovely job for you. I will have to do it if you won't and, believe it or not, I have some really important things to do." I asked what it was, and she said it was to acknowledge the Colonel's Christmas cards! I said, "Who acknowledges Christmas cards?" And she said, smiling sweetly, "The Colonel! There are 65 of them and he wants an original and two carbons of each, all to begin 'Dear Johnnie, Tom, or what have you.'" I said feebly that I thought we had all been urged to save paper, but she said that only applied to underlings, not to the Colonel!

So I began. His acknowledgment was mercifully short, and I got along pretty well until I came to one which was signed by a Rabbi. I had never written to a Rabbi, so didn't know how to start, but found I should say "Dear Doctor." I finished and took them in for approval. The Colonel inspected them and said I would have to do about four over as I had "first-named" them, and he really didn't know himself who they were from! I did them, put on my coat and cap, and started for the door. "Where are you going?" said the secretary. "Home," said I, "to f'ow up!" "I don't blame you a bit," said she. "If I followed my inclination, I'd come along with you and f'ow up, too!"

That evening Roger and I went to a large dinner, and I talked, freely. While I cannot claim I was entirely responsible, I have always felt it was my greatest contribution to the war effort. Within a couple of weeks the Washington scene saw the Colonel no more. I heard afterward that he had been sent to a by-passed outpost in North Africa.

Early in February I went out to the Coast. I have never had a more gruesome trip. I had a long stop-over in Chicago. With the hundreds of service boys with duffle bags and other impedimenta piled on the pavement beside them, there was no chance of getting close to the gate, which was not opened, as usual, twenty minutes before train time. The hubbub was such that I didn't hear the Overland called until, "Last call for the San Francisco Overland" rang out loud and clear. Then I tried to get through the crush. I just squeezed through the gate when the announcer grabbed me, and said, "You're too late, Lady, the train is leaving." It was standing there, 50 feet in front of me! I tried to break away, but he was stronger than I was. And off it went, in front of my eyes, with everything I owned on it except my perfectly useless hatbox!

Then I made the biggest scene I have ever made in my life. I told him what I thought of the Chicago Northwestern in general, and of him in particular; that I had been in the station for two hours; that he had never called the train; and that it was up to him to get me to

San Francisco. I stamped my foot, I screamed, I cried. When he could finally get a word in, he said there was another train leaving in 15 minutes, and I could catch the Overland at Omaha. So I got aboard and was ushered to Lower 13 which I refused hysterically, as only the month before a woman had been murdered in Lower 13. So I was given my choice and took #11, my lucky number. I felt I was due for a bit of luck.

Omaha the next morning . . . and the Overland had left. I was one of seven who had missed it, but the only one who had any luggage. After the scene I had made, apparently someone had thought they had better do something about it, and put mine off. Then I was told that there was nothing out of Omaha for three days! And then I really went to town—with the result that I, with a typewriter, two large and one small suitcases, plus a fur coat and a hat box, got a lower berth; while two GI's with full equipment including tin hats, occupied the upper above me.

The endless day dragged on. I did get a cup of soup and an egg for dinner (our boys in uniform had good appetites). Early the next morning the conductor came back and said he thought I could catch the Overland at Ogden. It was being held for a delayed mail train, and he had wired ahead to hold it if possible for me. We got to Ogden—there was my train! I had subsidized my porter; he and I ran through the underground tunnel like a couple of milers, and I fell onto the Overland, all my luggage hurled after me, just as it pulled out. I felt that the gates of Heaven itself had opened to me. My own little compartment, drinks, food, no one pushing me around—it just seemed too good to be true. Home was even better—the very height of luxury, and I throughly enjoyed my short stay there.

Then back to Washington, and into a job with Recreation Services Inc., which proved to be a permanent one. It was an organization set up to provide boys who came in to Washington on leave with both housing and recreation of one sort or another—sightseeing, dances, movies, or entertainment in private homes, which many of them preferred above anything else.

The heads of it were two competent society women. And there was an excellent paid manager and an office staff of young women who couldn't have been nicer to me. They taught me how to cut stencils (and how to correct my mistakes, which was even more important); how to run the mimeograph machine; and even took me with them to their favorite cafeterias for lunch. I liked them because they were so good to me (they were all young enough to be my children), and they liked me because I amused them. All my old stories were new to them. Besides that, even though I never got there before ten o'clock in the morning, I was always willing to stay until five or six to finish up whatever was necessary, or even to come down Saturday mornings.

I worked on records in the office every day except Thursdays, when I substituted on the lower floor where the arrangements for the boys were made. It was very interesting to meet them as people and not as statistics. They were all so young and so sweet! One Navy kid came up to the desk one day, and I suggested all sorts of things for him to do, but nothing seemed to appeal. Finally he said, "Lady, if you've got time, could I just sit down and talk to you? You kind of remind me of my Gra- (gulp) . . . I mean my mother." Another one asked me if I could find him a sea book. We had only a tiny donated library, but I happened to find "Captains Courageous" which I gave him. Two weeks later he came back with it carefully wrapped in paper and said, "Gee, that was a swell book. I finished it last week, but you wasn't here when I come back, and I wouldn't give it to nobody else. You got any more by this same feller? Gee, he writes real good."

Two others came in one day, and all they wanted was a dinner in a home; they had been in Iceland for four months and wanted to see what the inside of a real home looked like. I called up one of the women on my list who had volunteered for this kind of thing. She said sure, she'd take them if they were decent; but she had two teenage daughters, and she had to be a little careful. I told them I had a place for them, but there were two girls there and maybe they wouldn't want to go under the circumstances. "Oh boy! Oh boy! Oh boy! lead us to it!"

I telephoned her the next day to find out if everything was all right. She answered, "More than all right. They were Navy cooks, turned us out of the kitchen, cooked the dinner and cleaned up afterward."

Meanwhile time was marching on. Food and gas rationing had come in. Nylons had disappeared from circulation (despite our Government's pledge, as we were asked not to buy more than we usually did or not to hoard, that there would always be plenty for everyone). You could buy them in the Black Market at $60 a dozen. But I refused and just wore those horrible rayons and saved my few remaining pairs of nylons as carefully as if they had been gold or diamonds.

Then came a tear-jerking appeal to donate whatever rubber we could—spare tires (what was the use of them now that gas was rationed and you couldn't drive?); the rubber mat from your car, which of course you really didn't need. I thought it a fairly reasonable request if the shortage of rubber was really as serious as depicted. Then one day I saw a dump heap outside of Silver Springs with odds and ends of donated rubber on it, piled six or eight feet high. In wrath and rage I went back to the hotel and wrote the following jingle:

The Grasshopper and the Ant.
1943 Edition.

When I was a child, I first learned my tables,
And was then taught to recite Father Aesop's old Fables.
The Ant and the Grasshopper you may recall
As the best, but most sorrowful one of them all.
Walt Disney has done it in gay technicolors.
But I still feel the Ant (tho' somewhat the duller)
Had a lot on his side; for why had he worked
Day in and day out, while the Grasshopper shirked,
But then sang his song (with one ear to the ground)
In that heart-melting voice that just twists one around,
"My Dearest—but almost forgotton Old Friend,
How noble the work you perform without end!
How quick your response to that erstwhile barrage

Of 'Two motor cars in each family garage!'
But now on your shoulder I've just come to blubber,
Because, my Dear Friend, I find we've no rubber!
The Ant was astonished—he couldn't believe it—
His poor average mind wasn't tuned to receive it.
"But I thought . . ." said the Ant. "Don't do that" said the other,
I will think for us both, my poor little brother."
He continued "You see . . . er . . . the fall of Malaya
Didn't make the U.S. any brighter or gayer;
Then Java went too . . . and with it our rubber . . .
Can't you understand facts, you poor stupid lubber?"
But I thought," said the Ant, who was truly perplexed,
(Though he saw that the 'Hopper was more and more vexed)
"Some inventor like me, just a diligent grubber,
Could supply us with plenty of synthetic rubber."
"Don't be dumb," said the 'Hopper, "You're really a bore;
Can't you realize we've got to get on with the WAR?
So come through with your rubber (I don't want to force it,)
But give up a tire or your wife's worn-out corset;
Take the ball from the baby, his bone from the dog,
The mat from the bath-tub, and don't be a hog!
Uncle Sam"—his voice quivered, tears came to his eyes,
"Needs your rubber for Army and Navy supplies."
"If you're right," sighed the Ant, his voice growing weaker,
"I'll give what I have; could you use an old sneaker?"

The moral, my friends, now my ditty is sung?
Just . . . don't be an Ant, . . . or you'll always be stung!"

I was so pleased with my production that I sent it to the Saturday Evening Post, which rejected it even faster than I had sent it.

Washington that spring was a veritable maëlstrom, and more closely resembled the Mad Hatter's tea party in "Alice in Wonderland" with "No room, no room" than anything else I can think of. All kinds of people were pouring into the city from all over the United States—

"Dollar-a-year" men who either had or were seeking Government contracts; and 'Experts' on every subject, from the production of synthetic rubber to ways and means of increasing the output of beet sugar. The hotels were jammed; the restaurants worse; you often waited an hour to get a table; taxis, except at the Carlton where you could usually get one, as scarce as hens' teeth; and everyone seemed to be living either in a complete state of frenzy, or one of equally complete frustration.

Our small rooms became a more popular rendezvous than ever, quite as much so with the Labor members of the WLB as with the others; we once even had a call from Louis Goldblatt, the Communist lawyer, and a current girlfriend.

Frequently we had phone calls such as the one from Alfred Swinerton, a good friend of ours from California: "Helen, I'm just off the train and downstairs in the lobby. Is Roger's bed empty? And if it is, can I come up and occupy it for a couple of hours? I want to get a bit of sleep, bathe and shave, and my room won't be ready until 6 P.M."

Roger and I were really the only permanent Washington residents, so to speak. We came from so far away that we couldn't go home weekends as did most of the other members of the Board, who lived in such places as New York, Chicago or Philadelphia. Few of the wives came for any length of time, so I began to feel like Little Mother in Israel to the various men. For example, Roger came in late one afternoon and said that Tod Horton, who lived in the hotel a floor or two above us, had a touch of ptomaine, and could I go up and do something about it? I went, armed with my entire pharmacopoeia—a bottle of castor oil, some aspirin, an electric pad, and a whodunit. Tod, chastely clad in a Sulka dressing gown, was sitting in a chair staring forlornly into space, feeling very sorry for himself.

He promised to take my medication, then asked me to stay and have dinner with him, as Roger was to be out. I said I would if he would eat what I ordered. He agreed. I rang for the waiter, who knew us all intimately by that time. He came in and took the order (a cup of consomme, two soft boiled eggs and a baked custard for Tod; some raw oysters and a nice steak for me) and then asked, "And what will

Mr. Lapham have?" I told him Mr. Lapham wouldn't be there, at which he raised an eyebrow, and went out, leaving the door open on white-haired Tod, and gray-haired Mrs. Lapham!

"Tod," I said, "this is one for the book, and probably the greatest compliment we've ever had in our lives." "Close the door," said Tod, "I'm in a draft." "Close the door nothing," said I, "unless you want the house detective up here, telling you either to get dressed, or me to leave the room." So eventually dinner was served. We ate it with the door still wide open to the public gaze.

I really think that those unique Washington characters, the taxi drivers, deserve a word of description. To say they were chatty doesn't begin to do the subject justice. They knew more about the political scene than the Members of Congress themselves, and imparted their information freely and to all comers. One day I hired one to take me to see the cherry blossoms, which were at their height. When we got to the Lagoon, I told him I would walk around and he could go. It was an unseasonably hot day in April, and he said, "Look, Lady, it's much too hot for you to walk. I'll turn off my meter, drive you around and just charge you for the time."

I agreed. When he took me back to the hotel, I gave him $2.00 and said, "Give me two-bits back." He swung around and said, "Gee, lady! Do you come from 'Frisco? Say, I hadn't ought to charge you nothing. I was born south of the Slot myself! How is the old town?"

I said the same thing ("Give me back two-bits") to a New York taxi driver some weeks later, and his reply was "How crude can you be!"

All during that winter of '42-'43 the industry members of the WLB had Wednesday night dinners in a private room at the Mayflower, generally with out-of-town guests who had come to Washington for the hearings. It worked out wonderfully for me, because that was the night of the Washington Symphony Orchestra concerts. I had been able to get a seat with Marguerite Ecker and her husband, and they took me; I couldn't have gone otherwise on account of the difficulties of transportation.

The composition of the Board had changed considerably from time to time. One of the public members was Frank Graham, President of the University of North Carolina, who Roger said was the only man he had ever met whom he was sure would go to the stake for his convictions. One night Roger didn't get back from one of the Panel meetings until 5 A.M. He came in laughing as he told me what had happened. The Panel had been endeavoring to mediate a dispute between a small textile mill in the south and a newly formed union since 9:00 that morning. It was still hopelessly deadlocked at 11 P.M. The members had not even left the room, but had had sandwiches and coffee sent in at intervals. Then Frank had taken over; he started to lecture on the rise of democracy, beginning with Magna Carta! It had nothing whatsover to do with the subject in hand, but he talked for nearly two hours. And everyone listened spellbound. When he finished, the Panel came to a unanimous decision.

One evening we went to dinner at the Eugene Meyers, one of the original members of the old Mediation Board. I sat next to Thurman Arnold, who was the trust-buster in the Attorney-General's office. I thought him a pretty sinister-looking gentleman; he had been in an automobile accident that afternoon and had a piece of sticking-plaster over one eye and a large purple bruise beneath it. He asked me where I came from. I said San Francisco. Glaring at me with his good eye, he said, "Oh—Lapham! Wasn't your husband one of the founders of the Employers' Council, that organization working hand-in-glove with the unions in restraint of trade?"

"He was one of the founders, yes," said I. "But otherwise you simply don't know what you are talking about!"

My voice rang out loud and clear, and Roger, who was sitting opposite to me, gave me a horrified look and said, "Sport! Don't you think it probable that Mr. Arnold knows more than you do?"

"Not in this case," I replied firmly. "He doesn't know the first thing about it."

Mrs. Meyer, at Arnold's right, intervened at this point. and the conversation was dropped. I apologized to her afterward, but she said not to give it a thought; the last time he had been there for dinner he had made himself so obnoxious that her son had hit him!

I related the whole thing to Roger on the way home. He exonerated me and told Al Roth, who was on the Board and the head of the Employers' Council at the time. Al was so worked up about it that he and Roger went to see Arnold some days later, to put him right on the aims and efforts of the Employers' Council.

April was terribly complicated for me by my teeth misbehaving in an even worse manner than usual. I had had trouble with them all over the world. Now the time had come, my excellent dentist told me, when I would have to part with some of my remaining treasures for good, and wear what he politely termed a "replacement"; in other words, a complete upper plate.

I had all the necessary ones out and the new gadget in in one morning, and then decided to retire from public communication until I could learn to talk without hissing. I shut myself in the bedroom. But did it do me any good? None whatsoever. Roger had invited four men for lunch upstairs in our sittingroom, and each walked unceremoniously into the bedroom to 'rest his hat,' asked what was the matter with me, and wasn't I going to have lunch with them?

I said I had a cold, and Roger thought it wiser for me not to mingle. (I had no desire to practice eating with my new teeth for the first time before a large audience!) Nothing did me any good. They dragged me in for a drink anyway. Then Henry Woodbridge, one of the younger Panel members, came in with an armful of spring flowers, saying: "Helen! You poor girl. I hear you've had all your teeth out!"

This I denied hotly, for it really wasn't true. But the cat was out of the bag. If I had ever been inclined to be sensitive about my *edentate* condition, I certainly had to get over it fast. Somehow or other the news got around the Carlton, and everyone from the elevator boys to the transportation man asked me about my teeth. It might just as well have been on the front page of the morning paper. But this I will say: after the six weeks it took me to adjust to them, they were so much better looking than the ones I had lost that I became quite proud of them.

Roger Dearborn Lapham and Helen Abbot Lapham in the year of their marriage, October 30, 1907.

The Laphams in the 1930's and 3680 Jackson Street in San Francisco's Pacific Heights, their home since June, 1929.

II

MAYORALTY PERIOD
(1943-1948)

1

CAMPAIGNING, THE ELECTION AND VICTORY
(1943)

LATE in May, Roger received a most astonishing invitation; to come out to San Francisco and run for Mayor! Rossi, the incumbent, had been in for 12 years. The other principal candidate was George Reilly, the head of the State Liquor Control Board, who had none too good a reputation.

Roger's first inclination was to say he wanted no part of it. But he was told that a group of good, solid citizens had chosen him unanimously to represent them. Wouldn't he at least give it serious consideration? He did agree to think about it, and talk it over with me.

I was dead against it, for many reasons. First of all, I thought he was too innately honest to be willing to slide gracefully round issues instead of insisting on meeting them head-on; in other words, he was not enough of a politician. In the second place, I couldn't see how he had a chance of winning if he did run. Rossi and Reilly were both native sons and Catholics; San Francisco has a huge Catholic vote. Roger had lived in the city only a little over 25 years. He had been President of the American-Hawaiian (or, as it was affectionately termed by the longshoremen's union, the "American-Highwayman") and had been involved in endless labor disputes; organized labor was practically sure to be against him. I just couldn't bear to think of all the planning and work involved in a campaign and the resulting disappointment if he lost.

That next week the telephone wires between our suite in the Carlton Hotel and San Francisco were surely kept busy. Roger finally agreed to go out to the Coast and hear what it was all about; but he told me that he still expected to turn the proposition down. So he left, and I heard very little from him except a phone call saying when he would be back. I met him at the airport. He put his arm around me, and said, "Sport, I've decided to do it."

I heard the details afterwards. How everyone had tried to convince him that the City needed a man of his caliber and standing; that it was his duty to do it; and that with a good campaign manager, a good financial committee, and with all the help they were willing to give him, he was sure to win. He listened, still unconvinced; then he went off into the wilds for a few days to thrash the matter out in his own mind. When he went back to San Francisco, he said "Yes."

I was sunk. I hated being "Gloomy Gus," but all I could see was trouble ahead. However, it was decided. There was nothing I could do about it, and that was that.

The next day, Sunday, I went to St. John's, hoping for guidance. As I have said before, I had always found the young French minister inspiring. But what he did for me that afternoon seemed almost beyond belief, he chose as his text, *"Ou il n'y a pas de vision, le peuple perit"*— "Where there is no vision the people perish" (Prov. 29, 18).

He began with a quotation from Joel: "Your old men shall dream dreams, but your young men shall see visions." He developed it, saying that if a man had a vision or an idea of being able to employ his talents for the welfare of others, or for the improvement of existing conditions, for anyone who placed obstacles in his way . . . "it were better for him that a millstone were hanged about his neck."

I sat spellbound . . . and shivering. I felt that a true message had been sent to me in my hour of need; that from now on, my path at least was clear—faith in my husband and in what he felt he could do, and all the encouragement I could give him. I went back to the hotel calm and relaxed, told Roger I knew now that he had made the right choice, and that I was with him one hundred percent.

The next day I wrote the minister telling him what he had done for me at a time of real crisis in my life, and offered him humble and hearty thanks. His reply almost moved me to tears. He wrote that it was rather for him to thank me; for the first time in five years he had been made to realize that he wasn't preaching to empty pews.

Those last days in Washington were hectic ones. We went down to Hot Springs for the spring meeting of the Business Advisory Council (to the Department of Commerce), of which Roger was a member. Cy Ching was there. We had seen a great deal of him and his attractive secretary, Mildred Verguesen—Vergie—who looked out for him as if he were a beloved, but slightly moronic child. He had been a widower for years, and she had done more for him than it would have been possible for any wife to do—seen to it that he knew what his appointments were, and kept them; bought his railroad or air reservations, and got him safely on board.

So . . . one by one different members of the WLB came to me, and told me it was up to me to have Cy and Vergie married! I said it was none of my business. But they all seemed so sure it was that I finally tackled Cy on the subject. He said he was too old. I told him Vergie would never look at another man as long as he lived, and that I thought she was entitled to the protection of his name. I didn't get anywhere at the time. But I had dropped the seed, and later it germinated.

One very nice thing happened to me during that last month. I had completed 600 hours of volunteer work, and the Washington Junior Chamber of Commerce gave me a luncheon of recognition as the "Volunteer of the Week" with an armful of flowers and a scroll. Of course, they did it for someone different each week, but at least the time I had put in, much as I had enjoyed it, had been recognized and appreciated.

Roger's candidacy was announced on June 23. He handed his letter of resignation from the WLB to President Roosevelt that same day. The President replied accepting his resignation "with great regret," and saying that in his various positions Roger had "served faithfully, and with rare judgment and discretion, discharged the multitudinous duties which fell to him." Roger read this letter to the Board the following day and received some very fine tributes, not only from Will Davis, who headed it, but even from Wayne Morse and some of the Public members.

Wayne Morse said, "I suppose there isn't a man in the country I enjoy quarreling with as much as I do with Roger Lapham, because he is a swell fighter. And I am sure I have never had an opponent on issues for whom I have had a greater respect—and in regard to whom I never made the mistake of underestimating the opposition! But with all these differences, I don't think I have to tell this Board that a pretty beautiful friendship has grown up between us."

John Brophy, one of the Labor boys, added his bit. He said that when he first saw Roger he had asked, "Who is that fellow there?", and had been told that he was one of the employer representatives. He asked, "How is he?" and was answered, "Pretty good as employers go." Roger said, "Well, John, if I enjoy a fight, I think you enjoy it twice as much." John allowed he was right, and the meeting broke up in laughter.

In the meantime Roger Jr.'s ship had put in to Norfolk for two weeks, and Nancy had flown there to be with him. Then I went up to New Canaan the first week in July for a short visit with Mother Lapham, leaving Roger to finish up the odds and ends in Washington. I was to meet him and Nancy in New York and all three of us would fly home together. The day came and I entered the suite at the Ritz to find the two of them sitting gazing at each other in total silence. Something was palpably very wrong; but what?

It soon came out—Nancy said she didn't know what was the matter with her, but she had never felt sicker; Roger had sent for Mother's doctor. He came in shortly after, took her temperature and said, "Into my car for you, my girl, and up to the hospital as soon as I can get you there. You have virus pneumonia." A bit of telephoning, and they were off. Naturally I couldn't leave under the circumstances, so Roger went to the desk and told them that I would have to keep the rooms. Because he knew the manager, and we had stayed at the Ritz for years, they waived the five-day occupancy law, and let me stay on.

Roger left that afternoon. And there I was for two weeks in boiling hot weather without the right clothes, and with nothing to do but make that long, long trek from East 47th Street to West 168th every day. I tried every form of transportation from a taxi to the subway, which I entered in mortal terror, always sure I'd end up in Brooklyn. I finally decided that the most comfortable and the coolest way was the top of a double-decker bus, and it didn't take much longer than either of the others.

One night I got back to the hotel to find a telephone message: "Call Mr. Lapham at such-and-such a number." I recognized the number—it was Stanford Hospital. That was the last twitch. I put in my call at once only to be told that "There-would-be-a-delay-of-from-two-to-four-hours-on-all-transcontinental-calls." I waited two hours and called again, to get the same word. In desperation I called the Supervisor and told her it was an emergency: that my husband was in the hospital and I didn't know what was the matter with him. She asked why hadn't I said so in the first place—and got me a connection within three minutes.

It was not too serious. Roger had gone in to have a small cyst removed from his inner eyelid and was temporarily blind; also, in view of the strenuous months ahead, he had decided to have a complete physical while he was there. But he thought I should come home. So I arranged to leave by train the next day. I couldn't do much more for Nancy anyhow; she was going up to New Canaan to recuperate within a few days.

It was another horrid trip and I never smelt anything as good as the San Francisco fog when I finally arrived.

I spent the next two days with Norma Bartlett in the City. By Saturday Roger was well enough to leave the hospital, so I drove him to Atherton, stopping on the way to register at the City Hall so I could vote for my Popper come November. As the Atherton house was in my name, I had always registered there by request of the other residents, so as to be able to vote on the various local issues, but as 3680 Jackson was our legal residence, I reregistered with that as my address.

I finally got the house cleaned and stocked, and we moved in towards the end of August. It looked so spacious and so luxurious after two-and-a-half years in the Igloo that Roger just went around patting the furniture and emptying ashtrays, which I had never seen him do before.

He had engaged a campaign manager, Don Nicholson, whose wife told me that Roger was sure to win, as Don never touched anything he didn't think would succeed. On Don's advice the campaign started off very slowly. He said you must work up to a climax and save your heavy artillery for the end. One of the first events was a tea given by the Ladies' Committee for Lapham at the Palace Hotel. To my great surprise I was called on to "say a few words." I said that I had certainly known my husband longer than anyone else there, had been married to him for 36 years and had no complaints; and was sure that the better everyone knew him, the more anxious they would be to work for his election. Rather a gracious little compliment, I thought. But it was repeated to him the next day as "Helen said that if she could take you for 36 years, the City of San Francisco could put up with you for four!"

Little by little the campaign began to gather momentum. Two men, Dan Gallagher of the Board of Supervisors, and Jimmy Sullivan, a real estate operator in one of the outlying districts, constituted themselves as Roger's political advisors, tour managers and bodyguards. They conducted him from one end of the City to the other to appear before Civic Improvement Clubs, church bazaars, Catholic card parties, the French, the Russians, the Chinese, etc. (Roger inadvertently called it the candidate's "Circus" one night, which really described it much better than the proper word "circuit" did.)

Dan, a Democrat, was in it because he was truly interested in Roger's election; but why Jimmy, a Republican, was, we never did know, except that he was Irish and had a natural love for a fight, even though it was a non-partisan election.

They took me along with them to a meeting one night and seemed to think I had made a good impression when, after being introduced,

I said we had been married for 36 years, had four children and 8 grandchildren. I was generally included from then on although I always felt that, as far as they were concerned, I was simply a part of the scenery —a pawn to be pushed here and there—and that as a person, didn't exist.

Early in September, Roger made his first 15-minute radio talk. I stayed home to listen. It came over well; the subject matter was good, and the voice well-pitched and pleasing. Of course he had done it often before, and really enjoyed speaking; but how he could do it four or five times a night as he did towards the end of the campaign, without being completely exhausted was beyond me.

I made very few public speeches, but I did talk to everyone I came in contact with. One was a taxi driver whom I told my husband was a candidate for Mayor. He said George Reilly was an old buddy of his, and was trying to get him to work for him, but he'd just told Reilly outright that he knew him too well to have any confidence in him. When I got out of his cab, he shook my hand and said, "Tell your husband good luck from me."

Towards the end of September the pace of the campaign began to step up enormously. We went to four or five meetings a night, and in a short time I could have closed my eyes and repeated all the other candidates' speeches (for a different position) by heart. One persistent heckler who followed Roger from place to place, came up to talk to him once. Roger said, "Well, Mr. Petre, I guess there's no use in any discussion, as we always seem bound to disagree about everything." "Oh! I don't know," said Petre, "I think your wife's all right, don't you?"

At another meeting a man came and introduced himself to Roger, saying he'd talked to me, but didn't know him. It turned out to be my taxi driver, who had only seen my eye in his glass, and whom I didn't recognize, because I had only seen the back of his head. But he had bypassed Reilly, and was working for Roger.

After one session in the Potrero, Roger said as we came out, "I didn't speak very well, did I?" Hesitantly, I said "N-n-o." He explained that just as he stood up, the Chairman told him it didn't make any difference what he said, as they were all Russians and didn't understand a word of English!

About this time Don Nicholson picked up an underground rumor which was being circulated freely that Roger was a Jew, whose name was really "Lapman," and that he was completely anti-Catholic. How to combat it, without bringing it out into the open?

Roger was to speak on the radio a night or two later, so a very clever speech was prepared. In it he said that one of the reasons he wanted to be elected Mayor was to rescue San Francisco from the stigma of being a Ghost Town, which had been said only too often in the East. He pointed out that the City was one of the two great and most important ports in the United States; and because he came from a long line of ancestors from the State of Maine, the Dearborns, all of whom had been sailing ship captains, he was naturally interested in the recognition of the real status of San Francisco. His Lapham forebears, said he, came from Vermont; but his father had been interested in shipping too, and had been one of the original founders of the American-Hawaiian Shipping Company in 1900. We heard no more of that particular rumor.

Everything began to look pretty rosy. A funny little man named Reichel, who apparently spent his life prognosticating the result of elections, called up almost daily to report greater and greater progress. The betting odds, which had started at 10-7 on Rossi, were dropping daily, although Rossi never allowed anything better than that to be published. Unofficially, they were 5-1, and then 3½-1. And then the roof fell in.

On a Friday afternoon just ten days before election, there was a tremendous and most enthusiastic rally for Roger at the Marina Theatre. Just as we left, all walking on air, we got word that a snide lawyer named Vincent Hallinan had filed a "taxpayer's" suit against Roger saying that as a non-resident of San Francisco, he was not eligible to run for Mayor!

The charge was presumably instituted by Reilly, and based on the fact that I had always voted in Atherton which was ridiculous because Roger had always voted in San Francisco. In any case, the husband determines the residence, not the wife. But it meant that he would have to cancel many of that last week's important appointments, engage lawyers, and give up his time preparing an answer.

Saturday we were supposed to go to the races at Bay Meadows, where Roger was to present a bond to the winning jockey of the Lapham-sponsored race. But he was so busy with our lawyer, Jack Neylan, he couldn't get away, and his flag-draped box remained empty all the afternoon. My host, Mr. Klein, the track owner, said someone had to present the bond, and he guessed it had better be me. So I betook myself to the Judges' stand, spoke very briefly over the loud-speaker, and handed the winning jockey the bond. I didn't kiss him, as I understand all the Hollywood girls do—I don't know who would have hated it worse, he or I, if I had attempted it.

I was driven home, and just as we drew up at 3680, Jane came tearing up in her car and said, "Don't go in, Mother! There's a process server waiting for you. Come right to my house and stay there until you find out what to do." So I fled to Jane's and got in touch with Jack Neylan, who told me to go home and accept the subpoena to appear as a witness at a court hearing Tuesday morning.

I made Jane go with me; the process server, who had been waiting for me for three hours, was even more embarrassed at serving the paper than I was at receiving it. He fell over his feet getting out of the room, muttering, "I had to do this Lady, but I'm goin' to vote for your husband anyhow."

Sunday, Roger spent in consultation with his lawyers, of whom he had six or seven—all volunteers, including Maurice Harrison. Monday I had lunch with Neylan to prepare answers for possible questions I might be asked the next day. His final piece of advice was, "Just remember, Helen, that you are a lady; that a lady is dignified under all circumstances, and never loses her temper in public. Don't wise-crack with Hallinan, he's smarter than you are; and take your time about answering questions. If you're not dead sure of what he is asking, have it repeated, because he is very apt to ask you a double-barrelled one, such as 'When did you stop beating your wife?'"

Tuesday morning Lewis drove me down to the City Hall a little before 10:00, only to find the hearing had been postponed until 10:45. The courtroom gradually filled up, until people were standing around the walls and they had to close the doors. The morning was taken up with a suit against the Registrar of Voters for certifying Roger illegally; then Jane and I went off and had lunch together; mine starting with a cocktail to pep me up, and ending with a bromide to calm me down.

After lunch an hour or so was taken up in demonstrating a voting machine. Then I was called to the witness stand. I wasn't particularly nervous, as Jack Neylan had told me that I would be "window-dressing" only, and probably would not be questioned for more than 15 minutes. But I was on the stand for two hours and a half, with only one five-minute recess ... and I don't see how anyone could have dreamed up the questions Hallinan asked me, beginning with our marriage in 1907! Where had we lived? The addresses of the different houses? Where had the children gone to school and college? (Then an aside to the audience: "Mr. Lapham wishes to be elected Mayor of San Francisco, but didn't consider either our schools or our colleges good enough for his children.")

When did we buy our Atherton "residence," a term he always used, and which I always had to remember to correct—"You mean our summer home, Mr. Hallinan." What month did we move there? How many servants did we keep? And what were their names in 1927? I said I couldn't possibly remember, except that the old Chinese cook was named Tim, and my maid who was still with me was Christena Monahan.

Then, how many rooms did we have in our Atherton residence? I said I was never sure just how you counted rooms, at which he commented very sarcastically, "Mrs. Lapham had so many rooms in her Atherton residence she couldn't even count them!" Followed by, "Just possibly you could tell us how many bedrooms you had?" "Oh, certainly! we had five." "Did you and Mr. Lapham occupy the same room?" I opened my mouth to say sweetly, "We have four children, Mr. Hallinan," when Jack Neylan objected and was sustained, to my great regret.

Then, consulting his notes, Hallinan said, "You were 60 in 1932, I believe, Mrs. Lapham?" At that I really bounced; I told him he must have added in the date, for I wasn't 60 yet! Jack said, "I don't think you are very gallant, Mr. Hallinan," to which he replied, "Oh! I don't object to women of 60; my mother is." I couldn't restrain myself, and snapped, "But I'm not your mother, Mr. Hallian," which got a laugh out of the crowd. The recess was called at this point. I had no idea how I was doing, so was very relieved when one of the reporters muttered "Keep it up!" as he went past me in the hall.

Hallinan slipped once when the session resumed. He asked was it not true that we had bought the house at 3680 Jackson Street the previous May, so as to have a San Francisco voting address. I answered that we had purchased our San Francisco residence in June, 1929; he would have known that had he consulted the real estate records. He dropped that subject like a hot potato.

Finally, he asked whether I had committed a conscious or unconscious fraud on the voters of San Francisco when I registered there the previous July. I saw Lewis and Jack both squirm in their chairs, so I knew that that was the loaded question. I asked him to repeat it. He did. I in turn asked him if he meant to imply that I intended to vote in two places. He replied, "I wouldn't put it past you!" I protested: "Why, Mr. Hallinan!" while everyone roared. Judge Meikle banged her gavel and adjourned the court until 7:30, for by that time it was half-past five.

Jane and I went to Nancy's for a drink and dinner, then back to the City Hall. I was recalled to the stand for another twenty minutes. Roger was called for half an hour only, and asked mostly factual stuff about car registration, utility bills paid from Atherton, etc., and the lawyers summed up. The decision was given in our favor, "on the merits of the case."

By that time it was after nine. I was so tired I could hardly stand up. It had been a real ordeal—I had had no idea how hard it would be to tell the truth about something you could hardly remember. But I realized I was too wrought-up to sleep, and was glad that quite a few friends came out to 3680 to have a drink, which we all needed, and to talk it over. Jack was most complimentary, and said that any time I was hard up, he would hire me as a professional witness! I said, "Never again, please God!" I meant it from the heart (even though as we left the courtroom, Hallinan had touched me on the arm said said, "Well, if it's any satisfaction to you, you lost my case for me").

Tired as I was the next day, I dragged myself out to hear Roger speak to one of the women's groups. I met him as he was going in, and he handed me the evening paper and said "Just read that!" It was an editorial on the front page, entitled "The Boomerang," about me! It practically reduced me to tears; I will never again have such a tribute paid to me. It commented: "On the stand Mr. Lapham handled himself with dignity and force, revealing anew the type of man it is the city's opportunity to have as Mayor."

And then it went on: "Every woman, every man should be proud of Helen Lapham, his wife. Under examination which lasted over two hours, she answered with patient courtesy every type of ruthless or trick question, endured every innuendo a resourceful legal foe could devise. She is a gallant, courageous woman, a fit mate for a man who showed himself to have the quality we need in a Chief Executive."

Apparently the editorial was justly named "The Boomerang"; the telephone rang constantly the next day, and congratulations on the outcome of the hearing poured in. One phone call was from a man who said he was a longshoreman and a union man, of course; that he had naturally never been in sympathy with Mr. Lapham's shipping policies; but he had been at the hearing and that he was, before anything else, an "American." He thought the way I had been treated on the stand was disgraceful. He hadn't sunk so low as to think that elections ought to be won by abusing women; so he was going to vote for Mr. Lapham, and so was his wife. What's more, she was going to work for him, too, and she was probably the best talker in San Francisco! I asked his name, which he refused to give, saying he was just one of the little fellows and his name wouldn't mean anything, but he thought he simply must tell me how he felt.

The day after that I went over to christen a ship at the Moore shipyards, taking Nancy, Jane and her two little boys with me. We had all sorts of pictures taken. Then promptly at 11:15, Mr. Moore let the boys pull the rope that launched the ship. I swung my gaily-decorated bottle of champagne with all my might. The sound of shattering glass was music in my ears as I had hardly slept all night thinking of how terrible it would be if I failed to break it, and the "Golden City" would have slid down the ways unnamed.

After the ceremony, we all went to the Administration Building for lunch. I was given a lovely oil painting of San Francisco, looking up from the waterfront, by Jules Pages. I thoroughly enjoyed the whole thing, as it was something I had always yearned to do.

Roger wasn't there because he had gone to meet Mother and Miss Carlson on the Streamliner and to get them settled in the Fairmont. I stopped in to see them on my way home, and they couldn't have been happier or more comfortable.

I had started to keep a scrapbook before we left Washington; in fact, as soon as Roger had made his decision. He only half approved, but agreed, only if all the unpleasant things said about him were also included. And as time went on there were plenty of them, principally from the "Daily Worker," the very leftist labor paper. But the most scurrilous attack came from the least expected source—Mayor Rossi's headquarters. It read in part:

RETAIN

MAYOR ANGELO J. ROSSI

WE WANT A MAYOR WHOSE HEART LIVES HERE!

WE WANT a Mayor who knows and loves every square inch of San Francisco and has never willfully harmed a fellow citizen in it.

WE DON'T WANT a Mayor who once urged bullets and now asks ballots.

WE WANT a Mayor who knows Bernal Heights from Bay View, the Potrero from Fort Point.

WE DON'T WANT a Mayor who could get lost in the Sunset and have to go to the nearest police station to find his way back to the Pacific Union Club.

WE WANT a Mayor who lives in San Francisco and here only.

WE DON'T WANT a Mayor who needed the courts to unscramble his legal voting residence and tell him where he lives.

Roger had taken most of the attacks in his stride, but this one really got under his skin. He had gotten up very early for years and cruised all over San Francisco, and was willing to back himself any time at knowing San Francisco, at least geographically, better than Rossi did.

The Friday night before election day there was a huge rally at the Scottish Rite Hall. Mother and I sat on the platform and heard Roger give an excellent talk, and his enthusiastic reception was heart-warming. Sunday we made a last whirlwind tour from one Catholic Bazaar to another. Monday Carol came up from Menlo, bringing Edna and Carol's two boys with her. That evening we all went to one of the radio studios to hear Roger's final radio talk, which was a corker. Lewis had written it for him, so the subject matter was presented a little differently, and Roger delivered it beautifully.

Tuesday was one of the longest days I have ever put in. Even though the bookmaker's odds were now 2-1 on Roger, and everyone said the election was in the bag, I guess that with my New England background I am just naturally a doubting Thomas. I was inclined to agree with a man who had said to me a day or two before, "Helen, it looks so good I've got my fingers crossed."

132

We voted early and had many pictures taken. It had been rumored that my vote would be challenged, but nothing of the sort happened; I imagine the Reilly-Hallinan outfit decided it would do more harm than good.

That afternoon, radio men came in to install a microphone, and telephone men to put in an extra phone which connected directly with one of the newspaper offices. I fussed with preparations for the buffet supper for 16 we were giving for the family and a few loyal supporters —the Jerd Sullivans, the Nicholsons, etc.

Early returns began to come in while we were still at the table. Roger was in the lead in almost every district right from the start. Reporters and photographers arrived, phones rang, two radios were going strong, everyone was milling around. Between the confusion and the excitement the four little boys got away with four plates of ice cream apiece.

After we left the dining room we had hundreds of pictures taken —on our lovely curving stairway in the hall, gathered around the radio in the living room, family groups, and Roger and me over and over again. It helped fill the time and deaden the suspense a bit. But the suspense fortunately didn't last too long. By 9:30 P.M. the different candidates began to concede Roger's election! Even though only about 50% of the votes were in, the experts told us that the pattern would hold true, and wanted Roger to broadcast at once, thanking people for electing him. He did, but I think he felt it was just as premature as I did.

About 10:30 we all tore off in a fleet of cars to the newspaper offices. First to the Chronicle, then to the Examiner, where, after Roger had spoken, they had me in front of the mike before I knew what was happening. I have no idea what I said, except it was along the lines of having been proud of my husband a good many times before, but never more so than at that moment. From there we progressed to campaign headquarters, and I have never been kissed by so many total strangers in my life. At that I was more kissed against than kissing! Home around midnight, with drinks set up for the chosen few who accompanied us. After everyone had left, Roger, Carol and I sat up talking until three!

133

What the next four years would bring was uppermost in my mind: all sorts of problems for Roger without any doubt, and all sorts of new experiences for me. I still couldn't visualize myself as First Lady of San Francisco. But after the two years and more of valuable experience in Washington, I thought we would both be able to cope as the various situations arose. Roger said he felt very humble at receiving such a tremendous vote of confidence; I knew he would do everything in his power to justify the trust the voters had placed in him.

A few days later Roger went East to attend two meetings: one of the Harvard Overseers, and the other at the American-Hawaiian. I didn't go with him, partly because travelling was really hard at that time and I was too tired to do the one- or two-night stands he had planned; and partly because I wanted a few quiet weeks in which to rest and relax, and be prepared for whatever the New Year might bring.

Shortly after his return, the Chings, whose marriage I had tried to promote before I left Washington, came out on their honeymoon. They had decided to take my advice, and had been married the month before. They seemed radiantly happy, and I was really very glad, for I couldn't have helped but feel responsible if they hadn't been.

I had a dinner for them in the midst of which my waitress, Catherine, slipped in the pantry and fractured her wrist. Fortunately, there was a young Navy doctor present, whom I had asked as an extra man for Carol. He got her to St. Luke's hospital for X-rays, and they confirmed his diagnosis. Her arm would be in a cast for weeks which was tough luck for both of us, although we were of course covered by insurance.

All that fall I had had domestic difficulties so I felt this was the last twitch. The first Chinese cook had asked Christena, who had come back to me, to marry him—or if not, to go to the movies. When she refused both invitations, he took after her with a carving knife. I had had to get rid of him. The next one spoke very little English, understood less, and wasn't a particularly good cook—but at least he was someone in the kitchen.

The first replacement I got to take Catherine's place confessed to being 65, but I think 75 would have been closer to it. She kept the house at an even temperature of 80° but still complained of the cold. She came to me after ten days and said she was leaving as she had no private bath, and wasn't accustomed to roughing it. The next one was slightly deaf and more than a little dumb, but was willing to stay until Catherine came back. A couple of days later she came and said the cook had tried to hit her, so that meant he would have to go.

I was in the Slough of Despond, when God tempered the wind to the shorn lamb. The doorbell rang that very day, and the nicest looking Chinese stood there. He said, "You want cook? You remember me? I Ming Lew. I work for you five years in Atherton when Old Tim there! How Louie? How little Loger?" I surely wanted a cook. He offered to stay then and there, but I thought I had better get rid of the one in the kitchen first. I told Ming Lew to come back two days later, then was ready to kick myself for letting him out of my sight. But he turned up at the appointed time and life went back to normal.

The fall seemed to pass very quickly and our two Thanksgivings— the next to last Thursday as declared by President Roosevelt, and the last Thursday which we all celebrated—were upon us before we knew it, swiftly followed by preparations for Christmas. I sent about 150 Christmas cards showing a picture of one of Roger's billboards with the two little Lapham boys pointing at Grandpa on it.

Carol and her boys came up a week or so beforehand. We were sitting one day trying to make plans for the Christmas dinner of 18 or 20, when the phone rang. It was Mr. Reichel, the forecaster of Roger's election, who said his wife was the best female Santa Claus impersonator of all time, and wouldn't I like her to come and entertain us? I hated to refuse, but I had already chosen Lewis as the MC for the party, so at least had a good out.

No paper hats or favors were available, so I suddenly bethought myself of all the old period hats I had stored away. We looked them over, and they were perfect. We chose an appropriate one for each person, and I wrote couplets to go with them. Mine was a tiny lavender ribbon and steel wing affair that my mother had worn to her brother's wedding in the late '80's. I wrote:

> *"A First Lady's hat should suit her demeanor, which I s'pose*
> *from now on ought to be more serener."*

Nancy's was my huge "Merry Widow" sailor, and I wrote:

> *"Any girl who can get away with a 'Merry Widow' sailor*
> *Should be written up by Columnist Arthur Caylor."*

Mrs. Ophuls, who hadn't changed her style since 1905 and still wore a boned, net guimpe in all her dresses and had a pompadour hairdo, got the pretty brown velvet I had the winter I came out with the following:

> *"This 1907 hat from Balch & Price's store*
> *Was palpably made to sit on a permanent pompador."*

All the hats were wrapped in red paper. Lewis stood on the steps leading into the living room and called each recipient's name. He read the verse, and then made everyone come up, unwrap the hats and put them on. They made a real hit, and strange to relate, most of them were quite becoming, even then.

We hadn't planned anything for New Year's Eve, just the Laphams and one other couple (friends of theirs) for dinner. But people began dropping in afterward. Two of them brought a bottle of Bourbon apiece which certainly started the New Year right; we welcomed 1944 eleven strong with quite a bit of good cheer and hilarity.

The next evening Mother was having a buffet supper at the Fairmont for the family. But then her party, too, began to grow. Lewis suggested asking Bill Kitchell, one of Admiral Halsey's aides. He accepted with pleasure, then said why not ask his side-kick, Moulton, the Admiral's other aide. So we asked Moulton. He said he'd love to come, but there was just one problem—it would leave the Admiral all alone. Chorus from all the Laps: "Bring the Admiral!" Which was just as well, as Roger Jr., who was home at the time, arrived to say he was bringing the Admiral's son.

So we ended up with one of the nicest and most unexpected parties in the world.

The next Saturday was Inauguration Day, or as Roger said, the day he was to climb into his cage for four years. He added that the thing he was going to miss most was the view of the Bay from his office window at 215 Market Street; all he would see looking out of the City Hall was those "G-D seagulls" in the Civic Center.

2

INAUGURATION AND FIRST DAYS
AS FIRST LADY

THE Great Day came. It was one of the most impressive ones of my whole life. I got to City Hall very early, hadn't any idea where to go, and finally threw myself on the mercy of a policeman, who escorted me to the Supervisors' chambers, where I understood Roger was to be sworn in.

That proved to be wrong. It was Dan Gallagher, who was being sworn in as President of the Board. But I was taken right to the rostrum anyway and introduced, interrupting all the proceedings to my un-mitigated embarrassment. It was a very short ceremony, and then Dan escorted me out to the head of the great marble staircase, where I met Roger and Mother. The three of us walked slowly down to the Rotunda, where a platform had been erected on a landing just above the first floor. The place was jam packed. Everyone stood as we came in. There was complete silence until the band struck up the "Star Spangled Banner"—and I thought I was going to disgrace myself by bursting into tears.

A telegram from Rossi was read (he was too ill to be there). Dan made a short introductory speech. Roger was sworn in, and made his Inaugural Address, which was perfectly splendid. In closing he said that in times like these he thought a spiritual note would not go amiss, so he would quote the last verse of "The Chambered Nautilis." He began, "Build thee more stately mansions, Oh, my soul!" You could have heard a pin drop. Friends who were listening to the radio told me afterward that they not only had tears in their eyes, but rolling down their cheeks, it was so seriously done, and so appropriate to the occasion.

After the ceremony we all trooped up to the Mayor's Office, a beautifully panelled room on the second floor. The room was filled, as the papers said the next day, with floral tributes, including a wonderful model ship, made of gardenias, red carnations and cornflowers, with a streamer that read "Skipper—Captain Roger D. Lapham," from Jimmy Sullivan.

We stood in line and "received" for about an hour, had many pictures taken, and listened with amusement to some of the comments the rest of the family had picked up from the crowd. "He's real cute, isn't he?" "She looks kind'a Spanish, don't you think?" "That's his mother, I guess; she's kind'a cute, too." "Don't you think he looks older than 60? Nearer 70 if you ask me." "Go on. The paper said his mother was 82 and she never had him when she was 12."

After a quiet dinner with just Carol, Roger and myself, Roger went to bed, but asked to be awakened at 10:30 so he could hear the rebroadcast of his speech. Lewis, Jane and Happy Neill, a young friend of theirs dropped in. We called Roger in time, and while he thought his speech sounded all right, he was crushed because they cut out his poetical quotation.

Then everyone sat around and made suggestions for an appropriate theme song. Lewis was all for "It's Going to be a Great Day." Carol's idea was "Hallelujah!" But Happy won when she said the only possible one to consider was "I'm Only a Bird in a Gilded Cage."

Busy days from then on. Roger had 89 appointments to make to the various City Commissions. He had been giving a great deal of thought to the kind of men he wanted to nominate. All of them were a very much better type than those with whom Rossi had surrounded himself. And most of them, I thought, would be willing to accept positions under Roger as Mayor which they wouldn't even have considered under Rossi.

Roger fully realized the tremendous problems ahead of him. With the war going on, San Francisco was getting more and more crowded all the time as more and more men and supplies were being shipped out to the Pacific area. Other problems: the outmoded city street cars, insufficient housing, no long-range planning for the absorption of returning servicemen into peace time economy; to say nothing of just familiarizing himself with the provisions of the City Charter (which he called his "Black Bible"). He felt that each day should be at least 36 hours long.

Several bits of family news about this time. Roger Jr. and Nancy had told us that they were "infanticipating." Norma said that they had been married on October 4th and Tonia was born on the following Fourth of July, so she supposed that as Roger Jr. got home November 8th, this child would arrive August 8th. (As a matter of fact, he was born on the 1st!)

Carol had gotten her boys into the Palo Alto Military Academy as boarders. Since they were near enough for me to take them for their one weekend off a month, she decided to go East to join Ernst in Charlottesville.

One of Roger's first problems was to find quarters for the Di-Dee Wash, which had been turned out of their laundry to make room for some government project! Nancy said that if he refused, she was going to take a bunch of diapers down to City Hall, dump them on his desk and say, "What are you going to do about it, Mr. Mayor?" So after consultation with the City Attorney, he was able to declare "An Emergency in the Interests of Public Welfare" and house them in an ex-garage.

Almost all the men he asked to serve on the Commissions accepted. The one which amused him most was the Recreation Commission to which he appointed: Mrs. Stern, a Jewish lady close to 70; a Catholic priest; a Chinese banker; and Mrs. Moore, a classmate of Carol's at Miss Burke's School, who was a former President of the Junior League! Every time he thought of that combination he chuckled, and said, "Who says I can't mix 'em up?" He also appointed a fine Negro, Dr. McKinley Thomas, to the Housing Commission. As it was the first time that either a Chinese or Negro had ever been asked to serve in such a capacity, both racial groups were more than pleased.

Roger, being not only very photogenic, but also so different from any of the former occupants of his position, was God's gift to the newspapers. They played up his getting to City Hall by 7:00 or 7:30 in the morning, not realizing that it was no stunt on his part, but a routine he had followed for years. And his neckties! For a long time he had bought them by the dozen from a woman in Hollywood, and each lot was gayer than the last. (He explained that it was a reaction from the colorless clothes his Quaker grandmother had always worn.) One columnist described them as "the invention of a surrealist with DT's"; another as "an explosion in a tomato canning plant," continuing "just as Mayor Rossi's trademark was the carnation he always wore in his buttonhole, so Mayor Lapham's ties would be known as the bright spots amid the gloomy reaches of City Hall."

On the last night of Chinese New Year we were invited to a ceremonial dinner in Chinatown, and I was glad of the experience I had had with chopsticks in the Orient in '37. After the ten course dinner we were taken into the holy of holies, the club room of the "Four Families," which we were told was the greatest honor which could have been accorded us. From there we went to the building where the "Six Companies" (the Association which governed Chinatown) had its meetings. They were in session, and Roger was a little embarrassed by our interrupting them; even more so when he was asked to speak. But he did, briefly and well, stressing the dignity and culture of the so much older Chinese civilization; and how much we, the younger nation, still had to learn from them in the art of living. It was a simple but very sincere talk, and they all seemed pleased.

The next excitement was a request from the State Department asking the City of San Francisco to give a reception for Princess Juliana, who was making a tour of the United States. Roger decided that the best place to give it would be at Bohemian Club, and that the guest list should not exceed 350. He suggested that I make a short list of personal friends we would like to invite, which I did. But by the time we had finished with the "musts"—the Army, Navy, Air Corps, church, banks, city officials, all the Consuls, the Dutch and the newspapers—I was down to eight members of the family.

When we had gotten this far, I learned that Miss Combs, the Civil Service Chief Clerk, whom the new administration had inherited, had her list of 600—all of whom had "always been invited to everything the City gave!" I looked it over and pointed out to her that the invitation to Archbishop and Mrs. Mitty really should be changed, as he was the Catholic Archbishop and unmarried. Also that at least six of the people on her list had been dead for years and I thought we had enough live ones to ask without going into the cemeteries! Her answer was, "But Mrs. Lapham, you must be wrong—they've always been asked!" I inquired mildly if they had ever accepted, and she was forced to admit that they hadn't. She turned up her nose at a few of the remnants from my list, and said she saw no need to ask them. She had never heard of them! Although we were hardly on speaking terms by the end of the day, we did get the list down to under 400.

We had a 20-minute audience with the Princess at the Fairmont the day before the reception. By the end of that time the conversation was wearing thin but she showed no signs of dismissing us. So Roger stood up, thanked her for receiving us, and said we would not trespass any longer on her time. I asked him if he thought he had done the right thing, and he said, "My dear, I don't know any more about royalty than you do!" But when I saw her at lunch in the hotel dining room a little later, she bowed and smiled at me most cordially, so I guess we didn't make too much of a gaffe.

We asked the van Oosten's up for the reception thinking that as our Dutch son-in-law wore the ribbon of the Order of the House of Orange, it was only fitting that he should be presented to his Princess. Everything went well. The rooms were beautifully decorated and never too crowded, because after being presented each person passed into the next room for the food and drinks. The Princess was most gracious, and we thought she really enjoyed herself.

142

The days seemed to fly by, each one filled to overflowing. Carol's boys came up from Palo Alto for their first weekend, looking as cute as could be in their military uniforms. Walter Garcia, the City driver, met them at the train. He was a special policeman, and with great presence of mind, he put them both in the front seat and handcuffed them together, which was the greatest thrill they had ever had in their lives. They were fine, appreciative boys, and everything—Children's Symphony, zoo or movies—all was fish that came to their net.

After Roger's inauguration, he had suggested having an unlisted telephone number, but I had said that as an elected official, people should be privileged to get in touch with him when they wanted to. But after a while I began to wonder, because I seemed to spend a large part of each day on the phone. Roger said I didn't have to do it, and that it was just curiosity that made me answer it every time it rang. However, I felt that it might help a bit just to let people blow off; I might even be able to give them some practical advice.

The range of calls was infinite; for instance, a man just in from the Pacific, whose wife was to meet him in San Francisco, wanted the Mayor to engage Suite #626 at the Mark Hopkins for him for a week, because that was where they had spent their honeymoon! At that time, most people were spending their night sitting up in the lobby!

Still another was from a man who wanted the Mayor to come out in person and remove a dead cat from his front lawn! He couldn't have been more annoyed when I said the Mayor wouldn't do it; then I told him Roger's secretary, Bob Letts, might come out, but why didn't he just bury the cat himself? He said it wasn't his cat, and besides it was very dead. Poor Bob did go out and remove the cat. I found out afterward that all I had to do was to call the City Reduction Works and the problem would have been solved.

The call I really think I helped most was from a girl who said she wanted to speak to the Mayor. When I said he was not home (it was Saturday afternoon when, as usual, most of the tough ones came, and he was at the golf club), she asked who I was. I told her I was the

Mayor's wife, whereupon she said, "Well, dearie, under the circumstances, maybe you'll do even better than him. I want to know is a marriage license I took out in San Diego Monday good in San Francisco Saturday?"

I said I was afraid it wasn't. She said, "Well I was going to be married in San Diego Monday night, see? And my boy friend—he's in the Navy—was sent up to 'Frisco that afternoon. He's shipping out tomorrow, and I got to get married today—if you know what I mean!"

I said I might make one guess. Her answer was, "And Baby, how right you'd be!"

So I gave her the number of the County Clerk and told her if he couldn't do anything for her to call me back and I'd do something, though I hadn't the faintest idea what. She thanked me, and then said, "Oh! My friend's willin'! I wouldn't want you to thing he ain't." I never heard from her again, so I guess the County Clerk was willing too.

Two women called in one day. One, who called me "darling," wanted me to do something about a man in the flat below them; he consistently beat up his wife every night when he came home, and she and her husband couldn't sleep on account of the noise the wife made. Answer: call the police and swear out a warrant against the other people for disturbing the peace.

The second one said that when she had gotten home that afternoon, her apartment was a mess, with glass and blood all over the kitchen floor. Her neighbors told her some man had tried to commit suicide by jumping through her glass skylight. She wanted to know what to do? Who was going to clean the place up? She said she was so nervous she was sure she was going to have a spell. I told her that I'd ask my husband about the clean-up job, and that she should go and spend the night with friends. She said she didn't have any. So I said to lock the kitchen door, take ten grains of aspirin and go to bed. "That," said she, "is good advice. I'll take it."

But the prize call came at one o'clock in the morning. My common sense told me not to answer the phone, but my curiosity got the better of me. Some man said he wanted to speak to the Mayor. I told him the Mayor was asleep, and he said "Wake him." I asked why, and he said he wanted him to have the sirens blown to announce the invasion. I told him the Mayor couldn't do it—the Army had ordered no sirens blown except in case of an actual air raid. At which point he said, "Well, who are you anyway?" I said "The Mayor's wife—who did you think I was at this hour of the morning? And incidentally, who are you?"

He told me he represented one of the radio stations, and he intended to speak to the Mayor! I simply said he hadn't a prayer and he might as well hang up, which he did, with a bang. At that moment Roger sat up in the other bed, and practically talking in his sleep said, "Who was it? What did they want? What goes on?" I told him it was one of the radio stations that wanted him to have the sirens blown to announce that the invasion had taken place. With every white hair standing on end and his eyes half open, he muttered, "You don't blow a siren —you sleep with one!" Clasping his pillow to his bosom, he relapsed into peaceful slumber.

We had no social life of our own at all. In time I did reserve Monday as my day off, unless of course there was something that it was really necessary for me to do, or an unusually interesting Supervisors' meeting. We did go to several official receptions. At one, I met General Simon Bolivar Butler, who had the Alaskan Command. I asked him if he could qualify as a sour-dough, and he said he could on two out of three counts. You had to have summered and wintered in Alaska, to have seen the ice come in and go out of the Yukon, and to have spent a six-month-long winter night with a squaw. On the third count, he hadn't made the grade.

Roger was given a dinner by the Norwegian Society and made an honorary member, a courtesy, I believe, extended to only five other men, two of whom were Nansen and Amundsen. I thought it very nice, but hoped he wouldn't feel it necessary to start off for the North Pole just because he had suddenly become an honorary Norwegian.

But he assured me he had plenty to keep him busy right here in San Francisco.

All sorts of family things began happening. Lewis and Jane bought a charming, semi-modernistic house on Fillmore Street. Shortly after they moved in, Lewis Henry unfortunately batted a neighbor's child over the eye in a school baseball game. The boy's father happened to be the most unpleasant editor on the "Examiner." He called Lewis and told him the child had a six-inch cut over his eye, a fractured skull, and was suffering from shock. Lewis frantically called up his own doctor to ask what to do, and was told to do nothing at all. How right he was. The next afternoon the boy dashed out of the house with an inch of adhesive over his eye—so we all felt the original report had been slightly exaggerated. The "Examiner" was pretty nasty to Roger for the next couple of days, but that was the extent of the damage.

Late in April was our first Policeman's Ball. I had been in doubt as to how I should dress for it, so asked the Chief of Police when he came out to the house to see Roger one day. He said, "Mrs. Lapham, you got a real good dress, with a train?"

I said I had; it was a green and silver lame Lanvin model that I had had for years, but as Lanvin's things are all good materials and good lines, they never go out of style. Then he asked if I had any jewelry. Again I said yes. He said, "Wear it all!" I protested feebly, "Oh, Chief Dullea! I'd look like a Christmas tree!" He replied, "Mrs. Lapham, those people who come to the ball have paid a dollar to see the show, and you're part of it. They want a Mayor's wife they can be proud of, and say, 'Gee!—don't she look grand!'"

So I had my answer. I got some jewelry out of safe deposit, wore my Lanvin dress, and long white gloves with my bracelets outside of them for the first time in my life. I not only looked like a Christmas tree, I felt like one. But all in all, it turned out to be quite a thrilling experience.

We had a good dinner beforehand. Then we all trooped down to the Civic Auditorium, and as we stepped on to the floor, I was handed an enormous bunch of red roses. Finally we made the Grand Entry, I was on Roger's arm, announced by trumpets, and with an escort of four of the tallest policemen I had ever seen. With the spotlights on us we walked the length of the floor, then we turned and went to our box.

A very good vaudeville entertainment was followed by the Grand March, led by Governor and Mrs. Warren, Roger and myself. We marched and countermarched, finally forming a line of sixteen in front of the stage, and held it while the Municipal Band played the "Star Spangled Banner." It couldn't have been more impressive. I hope the people who had paid a dollar felt they had gotten their money's worth.

The next and by far the most serious item on Roger's agenda was the proposition to purchase the Market Street Railway, which had been on the verge of insolvency for years.

San Francisco's transportation systems were really unique. There was the Market Street Railway which charged a 5¢ fare, the Municipal which charged 6¢, and the three cable lines which charged 7¢, and there were no transfers between any of them.

The purchase of the MSRY had been put up to the electorate four times in the form of bond issues and turned down by large majorities each time. But things had gone from bad to worse, and Roger decided something had to be done to remedy them. So against the advice of all the politicos, he announced that he was going to campaign for the purchase of what he quite frankly described as a bunch of junk under a different formula. The sale price having been fixed at $7,500,000, he wanted to submit to the voters in the May election a proposition to buy it for $2,000,000 down, the remaining $5,500,000 to be paid out of future earnings.

The newspapers supported him, but the "Argonaut," a weekly magazine which had been for him when he ran for Mayor now turned against him, and published a nasty lead article entitled "Why insult San Francisco intelligence a fifth time?"

The campaign really got under way in March. As time went on, Roger pulled off all sorts of unusual and colorful stunts. For instance, he picked names at random out of the telephone book, called the number and said when it was answered, "This is Mayor Lapham speaking. How do you feel about the purchase of the Market Street Railway?"

One woman's reply was, "Mayor Lapham? Sure! And I'm Cleopatra!"

He said, "But I really am Mayor Lapham." And he heard her say in an awestruck voice, "Girls—it is the Mayor! I recognize his voice."

Then a circus came to town and he decided to ride one of the elephants. But he told me when he got home that it looked "awful big," so he just stood between two of them and broadcast over a loud speaker: "This kind of transportation was all right for Hannibal, but is it the kind San Francisco wants today?"

On another day he drove an enormous pair of white brewery horses hitched to an old street car up Market Street, the idea being more or less the same—that what was good enough for the city in the eighties, wasn't good enough now. I had swung aboard en route, and Marshall Dill, President of the Public Utilities Commission who was acting as conductor, tried to collect a 7¢ fare from me. I had six pennies, and a ten dollar bill which he refused to change; on the other hand, he didn't like to throw the First Lady off. So he put up the extra penny himself, and promptly told the papers that I had short-changed him. I read it, of course, and the next day mailed him a bright penny very simply labeled "Conscience Money."

I accompanied Roger on most of his campaigning. Once I was speaking before a Pro America group of women and getting along pretty well with my factual, prepared speech, when I looked up and saw Marshall Dill grinning at me from the doorway. I departed hastily from my facts, and gave them a pep talk instead. I converted at least one woman, for she came up afterward and said that she had voted against the MSRY four times, but I had convinced her and this time she would vote for it.

I also broadcast one Sunday afternoon at a "Grandmothers' War Bond Drive." I had a prepared script handed me—fortunately some days beforehand—and it was so sick-making I said to count me out unless I could write my own. The original had begun "I am such a novice at being a grandmother" (I wasn't, to begin with, for I had eight grandchildren by then), "that all I do is worry over my little Sonny Baba, and wonder if my sweet daughter-in-law really knows anything about the care of babies. I feel so helpless. I can't even say 'Mummy will fix' as I could when my own precious ones were little." Of course the corollary to all this mush was that grandmothers could always buy War Bonds to be put away for Itsy Bitsy Totsie's college education.

The program was a honey all the way through. It started with transcribed messages from Mrs. Roosevelt, Mrs. Marshall, and Eddie Cantor (why I wouldn't know, as he certainly wasn't a grandmother). Then an 82-year-old GM with 89 grandchildren spoke; then a 34-year-old GM; then Mrs. Nimitz; and then I gave my version of a GM's role, which was to keep out of their children's hair. In fact, I said, the only time I ever remembered really interfering was when I discovered 20-months-old Ernie lying on the floor of his playpen and sucking the dachshund's tail, which he had pulled between the bars. My daughter told me a couple of days later that the child had a queer rash around his mouth, and she couldn't understand it.

On May Day we went out to Kezar Stadium for the children's festival. Roger crowned the 8-year-old May Queen, and as he placed the crown firmly on her head I heard a mutter from one of the City Hall officials behind me, "My God! it's on upside down again for the 13th time in succession. I did think that this year it might be different."

Toward the end of the campaign Roger went one night to address the Miraloma Park Improvement Club, which was located on the outskirts of the city. Shortly after we left the hall, we passed a young Ensign plodding down the road in the darkness, and asked him if he wanted a lift, which he accepted with alacrity.

He told us he came from Philadelphia, where he had been in the transportation business, and he had come out to hear the Mayor speak, but it had taken him so long to get there he had missed the speech. We said to come along with us, as the Mayor was going to speak again in town. So he did.

149

When Roger had finished he invited him to come out to 3680 and have a drink. While Bob Letts and Roger were out in the pantry fixing the drinks, the kid came into the living room. He just stood there, refusing either to take off his coat or to sit down. Roger came back and urged him to do both, but he said, "I just can't. I've never been in a house like this before, and I'm paralyzed with fright! I've seen the President, and I've spoken to La Guardia. But I never expected to end up in the Mayor of San Francisco's home with a drink in my hand."

Just at that moment he spotted a picture of Roger Jr. in uniform with his Ensign's insignia and said, "Oh! Have you got an Ensign in your family? That's different." I told him our youngest son was one. He changed completely, was at ease, drank his drink, and entered into the discussion of the transportation problem with real intelligence, saying as he left, "I can't bear to go to New Guinea and not hear whether Proposition #1 carried or not. If I give you my APO number, would someone let me know?" Bob Letts said sure he would.

The fatal day came, May 16th. Roger had done all he could. He had spoken to 70 different groups, the betting odds had gone to 2½-1 in favor of the purchase proposition passing, but we still had our fingers crossed. We voted early, and had many pictures taken. I had heard "Smile, Mrs. Lapham, show your teeth!" so often, that more than once I had been tempted to say, "They are mine—bought and paid for!"

It was another long, long day. We left for City Hall about 9:00 P.M. and got to the newspaper offices by 10:00, where we were told it was all over but the shouting. As a matter of fact we learned the next day that it had passed by 22,000, whereas the time before it had been rejected by 35,000. Of course there was one great difference to be considered: the former proposals had all been for bond issues, which required a two-thirds majority to pass, while this one required a simple majority only.

3

STORKS, CARS AND OTHER
WARTIME FAMILY EVENTS

S O the campaign was over and had been successful. But we were both exhausted, and hoped it would be a long time before it was necessary to engage in another. Roger decided to go down to Cypress Point for ten days of relaxation and golf. I was more than willing to stay quietly at home, and catch up on all the things I had neglected.

Telephone calls continued to come in daily, of all sorts and kinds—so many from drunks at night that I had told the household they need not answer the phone between 11 P.M. and 7 A.M. Roger had made arrangements with Chief Dullea to be able to get in touch with him in case of emergency.

On the 7th of July we had a large cocktail party for the Chinese Ambassador, Dr. Wei, to celebrate the Triple Seventh—the 7th day of the 7th month of the 7th year of the war. We had about 350 guests, but our living room, with some of the larger pieces of furniture removed, the entrance hall and dining room could take care of that number easily. It was a cold, windy day, with the fog so thick you couldn't see across the street. I apologized to the Ambassador for the weather. But he said, "Madame, you have been in Washington in July? Yes? Then you will know that this is the most beautiful day I have seen in a long time."

The house was filled with flowers and really looked lovely. When the receiving line broke up at six, I plucked up enough courage to ask Dr. Wei if I might be permitted to present a very fine young Chinese to him—my cook Ming Lew. He smilingly agreed so I extracted Ming from the kitchen, and I am sure it gave him real "face" in Chinatown.

151

From time to time we had to attend banquets given by some AFL or CIO organization, and I was always in a quandry as to how I should dress. I certainly didn't want to overdress and have people feel I was showing off. On the other hand, if I wore one of the little safe black lace numbers, the chances were 10-1 that all the labor ladies would be in white satin. One affair, the Plumbers' and Steamfitters' dinner dance in the Civic Auditorium, was such a dignified gathering that Roger didn't even fancy-dance! It was given for the Montie Durkins, he being one of the former Labor members of the WLB. And I felt that no matter what stratum of society you were in, there was no such thing as democracy or equality—we were asked to come to the rear entrance and join the various heads of the union in one of those small back rooms, where we had drinks served for at least 40 minutes, while the 1,000-odd people gathered at the tables in the great hall just waited patiently and were served ice water!

But I thoroughly enjoyed myself. I had been taking Spanish lessons with Jane Swinerton at the Berlitz School, so when I was introduced to a man who said he "regretted to only speaking Spanish," he got no further—I backed him into a corner and started trying out my Spanish on him, for free. Just before we went out to join the crowd, he told me that if I came to Mexico and lived for three months in a Spanish family, I would speak very well indeed. I replied that I had been married for 37 years, and I thought it far more important to stay home and keep an eye on my husband than to speak good Spanish. He laughed heartily, kissed my hand, and said, "Senora, you sound just like a Mexican wife!"

Roger Jr., on shore duty at Alameda since November, was due to be shipped out at any time, but hoped it wouldn't be before the baby was born. The baby—a fine little boy—proved most cooperative, and appeared on August 1st at four o'clock in the morning. Norma, Roger Jr. and I were at the hospital, and as Nancy was wheeled out of the delivery room, she raised her head from the stretcher and said, "Did you ever see a homelier baby? But it's a boy, so it won't make any difference what the next one is!" Pretty spunky of our redhead, I thought.

The following week Norma and I drove up to Lake Tahoe to visit some friends for a ten-day stay. We had a delightful, relaxed time and I found the change of altitude, from sea level to 6,000 very stimulating. We had daily sessions of bridge and mah jongg, with plenty of time to read and rest in between. Even better, we got home just in time to see Roger Jr. before he left to join his ship, the "Manila Bay," in San Diego. She was being refitted for her voyage to the South Pacific, where she would probably join either Admiral Mitscher's or Admiral Halsey's outfit.

In the meantime, Carol had come back to me, leaving the boys in the cottage at Atherton with Esther Flynn to take care of them. Dr. Traut, who lived only three doors away, came in to see her every day, and bent all his efforts to have her carry the child at least through the eighth month. She had had a mean pregnancy, on the verge of a miscarriage almost from the start, and from then on really spent most of her time in bed.

The baby was due the second week in October. But on the 18th of September, in the middle of dinner, she said she didn't feel very well and I had better call the doctor, which I did, pronto. He said to get her right over to the hospital and he would be there to meet us. Just as I hung up, she called from upstairs: "Mother, I've had three bad pains —let's get going!"

I threw on a dirty old coat, and we got her into the back seat of Roger's car. And oh! How I wished he had been willing to have a siren put on it! That drive across town to the University of California was nerve-wracking, with Carol saying, "I'll never make it. And oh, I don't want my baby born in an automobile!"

We got to the hospital . . . only to find the ambulance entrance locked. Roger rushed off to get it opened. No sooner had he left than a streetcar came along—we were across the tracks, and I had to get out and back the car off. Poor Roger! He had gotten the entrance opened, but could get no one to listen to him except a very bland nurse—she patted him on the arm and told him there was plenty of time, and there were three people ahead of him! He backed the car in. Carol said, "Get someone—the baby's coming any minute!" So off he rushed again. Carol exclaimed, "Mother, it's up to you!" I stepped back into the car, held out my hands—and within ten seconds had a baby in them!

I slapped her on the back (it was a little girl, for which Carol had longed) and no symphony that I will ever hear could be sweeter music than that first cry. It was a cold foggy evening. We had collected a large and interested audience, which bothered neither of us. But there I stood, paralyzed with terror, feeling I had life and death in my hands, and having no idea how long a baby could live before the cord was cut. Carol, calm as a summer sea, said, "Mother, I think it would be better if you stopped beating my child and wrapped her in your coat."

Roger came back for the second time, still alone. He almost fainted when he saw me holding the baby. Back to the office for the third time. Grabbing the nurse by the arm he said, "I hope you're satisfied with your 'plenty of time' stuff. The baby has been born in my car!"

And then he really got action. An intern, a nurse, and then a second nurse appeared. The intern cut the cord. Between them they got Carol on to a stretcher and took her up to the delivery room where Dr. Traut was waiting. One nurse took the baby to a private room, as she was BOA (born out of asepsis), so could not be allowed to contaminate the other babies. And then I had hysterics—I laughed and cried until the second nurse gave me a whack on the back and said, "That's enough. Now we'll go up and see how your daughter is."

Roger said feebly that he thought if she could get us a drink we'd both feel better. She said it was all locked up, but she guessed she could borrow a bottle from a patient. She did, and it helped during the hour we sat and waited for Carol to be brought down to her room. They kept her there that long in case of a chill or after-shock, gave her a whiff of anesthetic, and sewed up a tiny tear. In the meantime they sent down to tell us that everything was all right with both mother and child.

We waited until Carol was brought down, gay and giggling from the gas they had given her, and addressing me as her "Little Midwife." Dr. Traut appeared and gave me a large sleeping pill. He told me not to worry about what might have happened—it didn't—and to go home and have a good night's rest. He said the baby weighed 5 lbs. 10 oz., she was not considered premature, and would not have to be put in an incubator. So home we went, and telephoned everyone we could think of! How I got to bed I could not recall the next day, for between the whiskey and the pill I was out like a light.

Well, when a woman has a baby in a taxi it's news. But when the Mayor's daughter has a baby in his car, delivered by his wife, it's big news. All the newshounds flocked to City Hall the next morning, and from then on it was headlines such as, "Stork Stalks Mayor—And Wins!" or "Stork Outraces Mayor's Automobile." My phone rang ceaselessly; one of the spectators even called to say she just had to ask if everything was all right. I was pretty shaky and on the verge of tears all day, until Lewis said very philosophically, "Never mind how you feel now, Mother. It will be your best story for the rest of your life."

The next day I had to go to a luncheon given by the Native Daughters of the Golden West. I was introduced as "the charming wife of our Mayor, competent and imperturbable, who met and conquered the stork single-handed." To which I replied that while neither of my daughters were Native Daughters, my latest granddaughter had been in such haste to become one that she had not only rushed into the world almost a month early, but couldn't even wait for a doctor to help her into it! And all I could hope for her was that she would carry on the fine traditions of all the Native Daughters present.

All sorts of unusual questions and comments arose out of Maria's debut into the world. The universal interest was in the cord—what did it look like? How long was it? Why hadn't I bitten it? To which I replied, "Definitely not with my teeth. I'd probably have left them in the cord, and given Carol rabies to boot." Every man I talked to seemed to think the only topic I was interested in was obstetrics. I heard more about their wives' various accouchements that I had heard in all the years I had lived in San Francisco.

155

Now I had a real problem of my own—gasoline rationing. I had driven my own car for years. In view of the fact that we were at war when Roger took office as Mayor, and that his predecessor, his wife and his daughter had all had City cars operated at City expense, Roger had been very against allowing me the same privilege (although he said I could always have the use of a City car when on City business). I had managed to do my marketing and my social engagements in town on my 16 gallons a month. But my daily visits to the hospital had begun to put a crimp in my ration.

In addition, Roger called me up more than once to say that he was entertaining a foreign VIP—once it was Hore-Belisha—and would I mind entertaining his wife at lunch and showing her the City? Sorry, but no City car available. I always did it. But then, no more gas. He finally let me have another 16-gallon ration book, and from then on I was all right.

But I began to agree with my sister-in-law when she said now she understood why women of former generations accomplished so much in their homes—they had no means of getting away from them! I did things around the house I hadn't done for years! Handing over to the children some of their wedding presents which I was still harboring; bringing up to date the scrapbook I had started just before we left Washington; clearing out accumulated rubbish; and coming to the conclusion that the greatest mistake in the world was to have a large storeroom.

After a while Carol and I began to think it strange that she had had no bill from Dr. Traut. When she called his office, she was told that there would be no bill since the doctor had not delivered the baby. That, of course, did not satisfy either of us; without his constant and meticulous prenatal care, there mightn't have been any baby. She wrote him to that effect. He replied by sending a bill for $125.00 with a charming note saying that he always made a special rate for women whose husbands were in the Service. If she thought it too high, she should pay what she wished. And although he did not believe in fee-splitting, perhaps in this case a portion of it should go to me as "Associate Midwife!"

156

The days went on. Jerd Abbot Lapham was christened in my christening dress, which was over a yard long. It had been the last thing my Grandmother Abbot made for me before she went blind. Tonia enlivened the event by talking right through the ceremony, ending up with "Daadla-da." This was freely interpreted as meaning "I want to go some place—quick!" She was removed before she could profane the church.

Election Day came around, and Roger won another signal victory —a $1,200,000 sewer bond issue, and the appropriation for a new Juvenile Home of over $1,000,000 both passed, although, as one paper put it, "San Francisco is notably allergic to bond issues."

Shortly after this the Saturday Evening Post had a lead article about Roger of which I didn't approve at all. I considered the pictures most undignified, and that some of the anecdotes, while true, could easily have been omitted. But when I found the general reaction was favorable and that Mother Lapham was not in the least upset, I calmed down.

December was ushered in with a birthday party for Roger on the 6th. I had been deputized by his office staff to keep him there until five, as they had an entertainment planned for him. I told them it would be easy. I was going to meet Mrs. Warren at the annual Salvation Army Bazaar, and would bring her over to City Hall afterwards. I was sure Roger would be on hand to greet the Governor's wife. It all worked out beautifully. We got there a bit before five and the girls followed us in to Roger's office. They sang a wonderful song one of them had written for him, entitled "He's only a Mayor in a Gilded Cage." Then they produced a bottle, and everyone had one drink, the first in those sacred precincts during Roger's administration.

A day or two later we went to a cocktail party at the St. Francis, given by the Petri wine company for Basil Rathbone and Nigel Bruce (famous everywhere at that time for their weekly appearance on radio as Sherlock Holmes and Dr. Watson). Bruce, with his charming English accent, told me about stopping for gas at a small station in Northern California, asking the attendant to fill up the car, and being answered, "Coming up, Dr. Watson." He said, "Just fawncy! How could that chappie possibly have known me?" Roger was having his picture taken with Basil Rathbone when a short, plump, blonde woman, very strikingly dressed in a gold-embroidered scarlet jacket and a tall Cossack hat, entered the room.

"Gee!" said Roger, "look at the Russian countess!" "The 'Russian countess' is my wife Ouida," said Rathbone. "Oh!" said Roger feebly. "She's very stunning looking, isn't she? I'd like to meet her." He did, and had his picture taken with her, although she said that she always photographed like a cross between Elsa Maxwell and Kate Smith.

As usual Christmas started to catch up with me before I was quite ready for it. Carol's boys came up from the Palo Alto Military Academy for their vacation. They thought little or nothing of Maria; were disgusted with her spitting up; and horrified at her "doing things in her pants" and said they never heard of such a thing. Ernie asked Carol if she was sure Maria was a girl? And if she really was, how did she know? Which I thought was pretty sweet for an almost-nine-year-old.

I bought my two Christmas trees—a small white one to stand on the table in the stairwell with the crèche beneath it and a tall green one between the windows in the living room. Carol and I cut cartoons suitable for our 17 Christmas dinner guests from various magazines, and pasted them on red cardboard. The Christmas cards and gifts began to pour in, the cards ranging from one from Secretary of State Stettinius to Oleta O'Connor, a leading left-winger. Gifts ranged from a beautiful jade statue of Kwan Yin from the Chinese, and gorgeous poinsettias from the Park Commission, to a case of champagne from the Scavengers' Protective Association. The latter infuriated my husband to such a degree that he was all set to return it until he examined it, decided it was worth about $12.50 a case, and not even worth sending back. So at Christmas dinner after good champagne, we ended up with the Scavengers', and by that time no one knew the difference.

Christmas Day started delightfully for me, when I opened my sister's gift—a most charming portrait of my mother as a child, painted by an Eastern artist, Jack Folinsbee, from an old daguerrotype. The oval frame was an old one which Dorothy had removed from a steel engraving of Benjamin Franklin. I felt sure my mother's face graced it far better than Ben's ever had. Some choirboys dropped in during the morning to sing carols to the Mayor. After that, when the children had finished looking at their presents, we went down to Nancy's to see how her little family was faring. Norma was there, and the Jerd Sullivans. We all had a bit of Christmas cheer while watching Tonia who was completely absorbed in her presents. But, childlike, she left the room after a few minutes and dragged in a dirty old dog I had given her two years before to give one of her new dolls a ride on it!

The only sour note of the day was the announcement in the morning papers that all ration points, which were supposed to be good indefinitely, were cancelled until after the first of the year. Everyone without exception had been saving them all through the month for the holidays, and for the boys who were coming home on leave. I just couldn't see how Chester Bowles, who was head of the OPA, had had the heartlessness to do it. And felt it was just another instance of the Government undermining the peoples' faith in its given word.

The afternoon passed quietly, with Roger working on his annual report, and a little before seven our dinner guests began to arrive. From the time our children and grandchildren had been little bits of things, they had always had a sip of champagne at Christmas dinner, and had then been required to stand up and make a speech, even if it was only to say "Thank you." This time Ernie carried off the palm; he first recited the story of the Nativity according to St. Luke, and then the whole of the school play in which he had taken part. Once started nothing could stop him. But as he went on and on, we were all so convulsed that no one wanted to. It was a gay, merry party, and I enjoyed it. But I did wish I didn't have to face the preparations for the big New Year's Eve party which Mother Lapham had asked to give at the house.

It had started out to be only 25, which was simple enough; but the guest list now stood at 65, which was a different proposition. It meant that all the ornaments in the living room would have to be put away, all the furniture removed by van, all the food and music ordered, and I just didn't feel I had the strength to cope with it. But Mother said she didn't want to give her last San Francisco party in a hotel, so how could I refuse? (Incidentally, she gave her last big party herself, some five years later.)

My next production was an open letter to the San Francisco Chronicle's "Safety Valve," again written at Roger's suggestion after I had aired my mind violently and often on the subject of the cancellation of the ration points. I wrote the letter, in which I turned myself loose, and gave it to Roger. And what did he do with it? Showed it to Mr. Cahill, the head of Public Utilities, who said, "My wife feels the same way, and I think you should give it to all four papers." Roger did with the result that on the morning of the 31st I was awakened by having the Examiner flapped in my face with the screaming headline *"Mayor's Wife Scores OPA For Dishonesty!"* One of the other papers headed their article *"OPA 'Gyp' Raked By Mrs. Lapham."* I had written a fairly long letter, of which I will quote only a portion:

"Editors: Keenly as I felt over the Christmas present received be the housewives of America from the OPA, it was nothing to my reaction when I read their explanation in the morning papers stating that 'Old coupons in the hands of the few *who apparently did not need them during 1944* (the italics were mine) would have put a critical drain on already low food stocks.' It insults the hundreds and thousands of patriotic, decent American housewives who, guided by their patriotism and their conscience, have tried to expend their coupons as wisely, as thriftily, and as slowly as possible. . . . We had been asked not to hoard but to buy as necessity demanded, and we had complied upon the assurance of our Federal Government that our points were good indefinitely

—and what is the result? Those of us who have been decent, honest and law-abiding are now heavily penalized for that very decency. So it is the fundamental dishonesty of the OPA statement to which I so violently object. . . . According to the Bible, it is better to build upon a rock than upon shifting sand; but it says nothing about what happens to you when you build upon what you think is a rock—and are left there, high and dry.

"I would suggest that the OPA might take a tip from the railroads, and adopt as its slogan for the coming year the little note we see on all timetables—'Subject to change without notice,' or the housewife, now forewarned, might possibly adopt as hers 'The early bird catches the worm.' "

All this before I was even awake, and I still had the New Year's Eve party to face! But the party must have been a great success, for it lasted until nearly three o'clock in the morning. I must have talked to my dinner partners, and I must have danced; but I was too weary to be anything but vague. The only two things that stood out in my mind after it was over were what a truly beautiful "Great Lady" Mother Lapham was, sitting in the center of a long table in the living room under her father's portrait (she stayed until the party broke up); and the fact that a little after midnight a group of three walked in, one of whom announced that he was an Apache Chief who had sung in everything from opera to vaudeville, and who would like to sing for the Mayor! So sing he did, with me playing his accompaniments. And as a matter of fact, he had a very good voice; but I agreed with one guest who said "You just never know what is going to happen at the Lapham's." For that matter, neither did we.

Within a few days the house was in order again, and I took to my bed with the worst strep throat I had had since I was a girl (when it was called "quinsey"). I alternated between there and my chaise-longue for the next two weeks. My doctor was anything but helpful, first asking me if I thought I had cancer of the throat which I indignantly denied, and then saying he could suggest nothing but to rest, keep warm and drink fluids, as "these infections were really sometimes very obstinate."

The only rather surprising amusement I had was the flood of letters which poured in in response to my OPA diatribe. I received between 30 and 40, all but two sympathetic. One began: "God bless you for your courageous stand against the Gestapo methods of the OPA"; another, "Amen, Mrs. Lapham, amen"; a third invited me to head a committee to oust Chester Bowles. The two condemning me were both vituperative, and both unsigned. I answered all but those two, and then devoted myself to getting well quickly because Roger had asked me to go to Washington with him on the 20th.

He was going on to Washington to submit to Secretary of the Interior Ickes proposals by which the City of San Francisco would be able to sell its surplus electrical power generated at Hetch Hetchy, and still be in "substantial compliance" with the Raker Act. The City got its water supply from Hetch Hetchy, a lake formed by the damming of the Tuolumne River in the mountains back of the Yosemite Valley. Under the terms of the Raker Act, passed in the early 1900's, it was forbidden to sell power to a private corporation such as the Pacific Gas & Electric Company, but allowed sale to any municipality, municipal district or irrigation district.

Conditions had changed so tremendously in the years since the Raker Act was passed, that the City had for a long time been trying to find a solution for the disposal of its excess power which would still be in conformity with the terms of the Act. The latest proposition was to sell it to the Turlock-Modesto Irrigation District, and let them in turn sell their excess to the P. G. & E.

The subject had been widely discussed, and was now immortalized in a hand-painted necktie presented to Roger by Benny Bufano, the erratic sculptor, whom he had appointed to the Art Commission. The tie had everything: transmission lines to represent Hetch Hetchy, a trolley car, an early bird catching a worm (possibly symbolic of Roger's habit of getting down to City Hall by 7 A.M.), $1,200,000 for the sewer bonds, an enormous Seeing Eye, and a reproduction of Bufano's statue of St. Francis (with "arms upraised as if reaching for Lapham's Adam's apple," according to the "Examiner").

We left on the 20th, though I was still feeling pretty poorly, and was looking forward to four nice quiet days, safely shut in our drawing room on the San Francisco Streamliner. Roger needed the time to relax just as much as I did, for he was tired too. Dion Holm, the Assistant City Attorney, was on the train, as were Jim Turner, the head of Public Utilities, and Perrin, his assistant.

I realized there would have to be discussions among the men. But I did not count on being joined by an old Harvard classmate of Roger's as soon as we had disposed of our eight pieces of luggage. Nor, shortly afterward, by George Creel, who was at that time doing a series of pro-Administration articles for Collier's. The old classmate immediately explained that he had expected to have his daughter-in-law with him, but she had just had a miscarriage (which I figured was my good luck, or else I might have found myself officiating when my medical lore had only reached "B" for birth, and not "M" for miscarriage). He belonged to the "Do you remember?" school. George Creel muttered in my ear, "Get rid of this Perpetual Sophomore, and I'll take you both to dinner." But there wasn't a prayer. He had apparently taken as his motto: "I'll never desert Mr. Macawber." He stayed on and on, even though Roger didn't remember any of the 40-year-ago college events that he did. The three City men came in to discuss how best to present their case, and after that the only remark the old classmate got in was: "Would anyone mind telling me what a Hetch Hetchy is?"

I don't believe that even the Prodigal Son had a warmer welcome than we did when we got back to the Carlton. All the old bellboys and waiters fell on our necks. We had the same suite, 212-214—the "Igloo." My Fatted Calf took the form of a carton of Chesterfields presented to me by the girl at the newsstand, although she warned me that if I told anyone she had given them to me, she would say I lied.

Roger found a message that Assistant Secretary Abe Fortas would see them the next morning at 11:00. Dion Holm seemed to think I could go and listen in, saying that after all the worst they could do would be to throw me out. I got in, but was sure it was bad for my blood pressure; no matter what our men said, Fortas had only one answer: "Gentlemen, do you really feel that the proposition you are submitting is in 'reasonable and substantial compliance' with the terms of the Raker Act?" He sounded like a phonograph record with the needle stuck.

All sorts of people dropped into our rooms the next day, including Louis Goldblatt and his girl friend. That night we dined with Secretary and Mrs. Forrestal. Saturday morning I took to my bed with either a very bad bronchitis or a light pneumonia, and a temperature of 102°. It was very upsetting as I was ordered not to get out of bed under any circumstances. I had to leave the door on the latch so that the droppers-in—whose name was legion—could have free entry. It was good of them to keep me advised of what was going on, and I appreciated the spirit in which they did it. But by the end of the day I was exhausted, dripping with perspiration and close to tears. Roger told me he had been given 48 hours in which to present a final report to Fortas. So the next day, still with a high temperature, I hoisted my faithful typewriter on my lap and wrote the following:

"In summing up the week we have been in conference with the Department of the Interior, Mr. Fortas, I would like to submit these conclusions: namely, that the City of San Francisco, after months of honest study, has placed before you two contracts which we believe are in 'reasonable and substantial compliance' with the Raker Act.

But there's something about that smile of yours, Mr. Abe-for-short-Fortas,

That anticipatory, chop-licking, cat-at-the-mousehole, waiting until you've caught us,

That makes us feel you prefer the Proverb that says

'As the wringing of the nose bringeth forth blood,

So the forcing of wrath bringeth forth strife,'

To the better-known Biblical quotation 'The letter killeth, but
    the Spirit giveth Life.'
It's wonderful to be policeman, jury, judge and executioner all
    in one, isn't it, Mr. Fortas?
For you never have to stop and ask yourself 'What has life taught
    us?'
You don't have to stop and analyze 'reasonable and substantial
    compliance,'
You can just close your eyes, look down your nose, and say, 'This
    smells to me like defiance.'
Why do certain letter combinations such as T.V.A. and C.V.A.
    ring in your ears like the march of Caesar and his legions,
While certain others like S.F. and P. G. & E. sound to you like
    something out of the Infernal Regions?
Could it be that some shred of power, even 'dump' or 'inferior'
Might go to some other place but the Department of Interior?
If it's your will to try to force San Francisco to 'do as I say—or
    else' why that's your privilege, Mr. Fortas;
And we'll admit we're beaten, but never that you outfought us.
We've come a long way believing that this time the game was
    square;
But we find the cards still stacked against us.
                    Respectfully submitted,
                        Roger D. Lapham, Mayor."

Roger came in and I showed it to him. He picked it up without a word, which was a bit disappointing as I thought it was pretty good. But how did I know that he was going to take it down the hall to where the others were in conference, and tell them he was ready with his report? He told me on his return that it had been received in stony silence; then Dion had said, "It's all true, but you can't do it, Mr. Mayor!" (As if he had ever intended to!)

The next morning Mr. Fortas came up with a counter-proposal: that the City of San Francisco should buy out the P. G. & E. Then, of course, with that company under public ownership, all problems would

be solved. Roger said he thought there were only two objections to it
—one being that the P. G. & E. had no thought of selling; the other
that he was quite sure that the City of San Francisco would not even
consider putting up the X million dollars necessary to consummate
such a purchase. So there seemed to be a complete impasse, and I felt
(rightly or wrongly) that we left Washington without a dish being
washed, and with both sides dissatisfied with the outcome.

We had a quiet trip back on the train, and after ten days of con-
valescence my cough left me. The City had been alerted to the fact that
a World Conference, to be called the "United Nations," would probably be held here in April, and I knew I would have to be in the pink
for all the official doings.

I asked Norma if she could possibly go down to Santa Barbara with
me for a couple of weeks of real rest and freedom from all responsibility.
She said she could, so we planned to leave the first of March.

In the meantime, much to our surprise, Roger Jr. came home on
leave. He was thin, but didn't seem too jumpy, although from what
he was able to tell us, he had plenty of reason to be. He was much hurt
that Tonia didn't remember him. She kept asking in tones of dark
suspicion, "Who dat man?" An attitude which intensified to positive
dislike when she found him in her mother's bed his first morning home.
He had 21 days leave, and was then to report to San Diego where his
ship was undergoing repairs. But Nancy would be able to be with him
there while the other half of the ship's personnel had their leave.

February 20 produced our next excitement. My phone rang just
after lunch and a woman's voice said, "This is the Palo Alto Military
Academy speaking. And I am awfully sorry to have to tell you that
Ernst Ophuls is missing, and we think he has run away from school."

Apparently he had been in a spot of trouble that morning for rough-
housing, was to be sent to the dormitory for the younger children as
punishment, and had not been seen since roll-call at nine. I got hold
of Roger right away, who said that after getting all the facts from the

school he would send a special police officer down to see if he could pick up any clues.

I called my gardener at Atherton and told him to take the station wagon and scout around. When Carol came in, of course, I had to tell her. The gardener called back at the end of an hour to say "'e couldn't find 'ide nor 'air of 'im." Carol and I put in a pretty anxious couple of hours, until the door bell rang at four, and Ernie walked in.

He had left school right after roll call, walked (or mostly run) the five miles to the Redwood City railway station, seen a freight train standing there, and asked the brakeman to give him a ride to San Francisco! The man asked him why he wasn't at school, and he said he had the Washington's Birthday weekend off. So the brakeman told him to go ask the boys in the caboose, and if it was okay with them, it was with him. They took him in. He promptly told them he was on his way to visit his grandfather, the Mayor of San Francisco. When he got to town, he picked up a truckman who gave him a ride to the California Street cable car, as well as 7¢ for carfare.

As he unfolded his tale, he became a bit cocky, saying he was the only boy who had run away from the Academy and gotten away with it, etc. So Carol decided to leave it to Roger to deal with him when he got home—which he did in no uncertain terms. He told Ernie it was a Military School and he was AWOL. Was he prepared to go back and apologize to everyone, and take whatever punishment was meted out to him? *If* the school would take him back. Ernie ended up in a very chastened frame of mind. He agreed to everything, his only worry by then being that the school wouldn't take him back.

Norma and I left for Santa Barbara, stopping at Cypress Point Club for a few days en route. The first week at Santa Barbara, while Norma was there, was pleasant as she knew lots of people and we had a little social life. But after she had to leave, I decided I might as well stay on for another week, and that was pretty dull. The weather was overcast. I had been moved to a smaller room which was so dark I might as well have stayed at home, sat in the broom closet, and saved $14.00 a day!

I found a lending library where they rented jigsaw puzzles as well as books, so was able to indulge my passion for them without undue strain on my arm. Also amused myself by answering a letter from the Smith College Quarterly. They asked me to write a 1,000-word article on the "Preparations of a Mayor's Wife for a World Conference," as Smith "liked to be tied in with world affairs whenever possible." I wrote them that this Mayor's wife had spent two weeks getting away from it all before it started. But I had purchased two pairs of half-size-larger-than-normal shoes and three new hats. I figured that I was sure to do so much standing around that I might as well be comfortable; and that the crowds at the different receptions would be so large that no one would see anything but my hat anyhow! I concluded by saying, however, that I would be glad to write them my impressions of the Conference after it was over. And did I get a chilly letter in reply! They regretted that what I had written was not what they had had in mind, and they thought it would be quite unnecessary to trouble me further . . . Smith must have changed since my day.

One of my last days there I was interviewed by a lady reporter for the local newspaper. She brought a photographer along, whom she told to take a picture of me doing a puzzle for "color" and "interest." The interview was pretty blah-blah, but not too bad. But oh, the photograph! I looked like "Polycarp, that feeble old Bishop of 90 who died in a dungeon," which my mother used to quote as all she remembered of her history lessons as a child.

Aside from looking old in the photo, I looked unutterably startled. I can only account for that by the fact that the puzzle I was doing was entitled "Magic of the Orient." But there was a note in the box saying that the title was really "Street Scene in Holland," and that there were two pieces missing. And while I had been searching for either Oriental splendor or a canal or two, I had put together two ladies in hoop-skirts entering different Colonial houses, one of them carrying a baby; and from the expression of the other one, I thought the name should have been "More to be Pitied than Scorned" or "Maid, Wife or Widow?"

4

WAR'S END AND THE
UNITED NATIONS

O NE wonderful piece of news reached me the day before I left
Santa Barbara. Edna's eldest son, John, his wife, Marion, and
their little ten-year-old girl, Joy, all who had been interned in Santo
Tomás for three years, were safe. And they were pretty sure that their
seven-year-old Jackie, who had been allowed to live with a Spanish doctor during that time, was all right, too, and would be able to join them
shortly. Johnnie had had beri-beri and had lost 40 pounds. Marion
had had a stillborn baby girl. But when you heard they had been living
on 750 calories a day for months, you wondered how any of them
had managed to survive.

Edna had planned to come out to San Francisco to meet them whenever they arrived. To my great surprise, she and Roger met me at the
train, and I heard what a perfectly incredible thing had happened.
Immediately after the liberation Roger had been asked to broadcast a
welcome to the internees, proffering all the hospitality that San Francisco could give them.

Without mentioning any names, he had said that he had a very
personal interest in those who had been in Santo Tomás, his nephew
and his family being among them. One of the old American-Hawaiian
captains, then in command of a Liberty ship, the "Gershwin," had happened to pick up the broadcast while his ship was anchored in Subic
Bay off Manila. He had decided to make a few inquiries, and found
the family was still there (Jackie had been returned to them). After
cutting a tremendous amount of red tape, he was able to get them
aboard his ship and was bringing them back to San Francisco in peace

and comfort, instead of their being packed in on board some Army transport.

It was impossible to find out just when the "Gershwin" was due, but, of course, Edna would stay with us until she arrived.

A day or two later Roger received a most informal wire from Secretary of State Stettinius, whom he had known for years, reading: "Dear Roger: Quote—'California here we come'—unquote. Counting upon you to make arrangements for good weather during May. Asking Joe Grew (Assistant Secretary of State) to get in touch with you to start the ball rolling regarding all other arrangements. Affectionate regards, Ed."

This was a bit cryptic, but a wire from Secretary Grew followed immediately: "It is my great pleasure to inform you that San Francisco has been selected as the site of the United Nations Conference to take place beginning about April 25, 1945, for the purpose of preparing a charter for a United Nations Organization for the maintenance of international peace and security."

Roger of course wired back that he was very happy that San Francisco had been so honored, and assured the Secretary of all possible assistance and cooperation. And then the ball really started rolling. Wires poured in from all directions, asking all sorts of questions: What about security measures? Transportation? Hotel reservations? Business offices? A place large enough and safe enough for the open sessions? All of these inquiries or demands had one thing in common: each delegation wished assurance that it would have preferential treatment, and the best suites in the best hotels.

Roger finally telephoned Secretary Stettinius that he would have to have someone here from the State Department through whom all these requests could be channeled, and who would act as a liaison between the City and the Department. A most charming young man, John Peurifoy, was sent out. We took to him on sight and he later became one of our dearest friends. He was a South Carolinian and a

West Pointer, fine looking, tactful beyond words, and oh! so able. His wife, Betty Jane, joined him during the latter part of the conference, and she was just as charming as he was. She is between my two daughters in age, and I have ever since felt as close to her as if she were one of my own children.

And then, on Friday April 13, the bombshell—President Roosevelt's death in Georgia from a cerebral hemorrhage. I had not been listening to the radio, so the first I heard of it was when Jane telephoned me just as I came into the house that afternoon. From the pictures of him taken at the Yalta Conference, no one should have been surprised. Even so it was a very real shock. And it raised some puzzling questions: How would it affect the U.N. Conference? How long would the period of mourning be? Certainly all plans for the entertainment of delegates would be cancelled for the time being. The next day at the City Hall memorial services were held which were both dignified and impressive. Roger spoke briefly and well.

On arrival home we learned the "Gershwin" was due in the next day, but might arrive too late for the Health authorities to clear the four passengers. We hung around all the afternoon at City Hall, waiting and hoping. At 7:00 we were told we could go down to the dock at 8:30, and at least talk to Johnnie and Marion, even if they were not allowed off the ship. But in view of all the circumstances, the Health authorities examined them after hours, and they could leave as soon as the ship docked. All four of them were hanging over the rail as she came up to the pier. It was a thrilling moment, and everyone had a lump in their throat.

We swept them off and out to the house. At first they all looked better than we had expected, but we soon began to realize that Marion was all eyes, and Johnnie too fat; he had gained too much weight too quickly, and it made him look soft and pudgy. Jackie seemed by far the most nervous of any of them and tried to crawl under something every time an airplane went over the house, convinced it was a bomber.

Joy went right to my heart. She had all the charm in the world, and all the poise of an adult, but she wanted to be considered as a little girl, and not to be told how grown she was. After asking her mother if she wanted any washing done, she asked me if she could have a hot shower, and I said she could get right into the tub if she preferred it. When I went upstairs a bit later I found her sitting in a tub with two inches of water in it. I suggested she run some more, and her answer was, "But Aunt Helen, it's hot water!" She said she was just as glad the baby had died at birth, for if she had had a baby sister to care for even for a little while and then lost it, that she couldn't have borne. Reporters and photographers came out the next day, and one of them asked Joy what was the best thing about Santo Tomás? She replied in two short words: "Leaving it!"

Edna had fitted them all out with clothes, because they had practically nothing except what the Red Cross had supplied them with before they left. When they went off for Texas a few days later, they were a happier, healthier-looking foursome than when they had arrived.

Be degrees the Conference problems were being ironed out. The Opera House was to be the scene of the opening session, and after that of the plenary ones. The Veterans' Memorial building would be available for offices. And the 3,000 people who were to attend (instead of the 2,000 expected) would all be housed somehow. Stettinius arrived on the 24th. The Conference opened the next day, an historic and memorable occasion, and one which no one who was there will ever forget.

Lewis, Jane, Carol and I went together. We had excellent seats in the orchestra, and didn't miss one of the principals as they came down our aisle: Eden, Lord Halifax, Soong, and Molotov, who came in with an armed guard of six men looking like East Side gangsters. (Overheard as they came in: "Oh! there goes Eden! Isn't he dreamy? Now which one do you suppose is Molyneux?")

The stage setting was right out of Maxfield Parish—a sky blue background, with four huge golden pillars connected by garlands, and the colorful flags of the 46 nations in front of them. There was an honor guard of WACS, WAVES, SPARS, young soldiers, sailors and marines; and on the rostrum sat Governor Warren, Secretary Stettinius, Roger, and Alger Hiss, the Permanent Secretary of the Conference.

The proceedings opened with a radio address by President Truman from Washington, followed by a speech by each of the four men at the rostrum. Of course we all thought Roger's speech the best, though perhaps Lewis and I were slightly prejudiced as we had both had a hand in writing it. His secretary Bob Letts had done the first draft, which Roger had brought home Sunday night, tossed in my lap and said: "You do it, Sport. It doesn't sound a bit like me."

So I did another version. I didn't think it was long enough, and called up Lewis. He gave me fine suggestions which I incorporated into still another draft. When Roger went over it he approved of most of it, but cut out a sentence or two here and there, and added quite a bit of his own.

To quote one of the newspaper comments the following day: "The President made an honest speech. The Governor made a worthy speech. Secretary Stettinius made a friendly and moving speech. Mayor Lapham made the best speech of any, I thought."

Even a London reporter said, "I say—what about this Mayor of yours? Quite stole the show, didn't he?" This seemed to be the general consensus.

Mrs. Warren and two of her daughters were sitting next to me. Her 13-year-old was doing a report for a school paper. She asked me the significance of the four columns, and I said possibly the Four Freedoms, or even the Big Four—America, England, France and Russia. Then she wanted to know what the garlands meant. She was so wide-eyed I couldn't resist, but told her we had been very lucky, as a python we had been watching for some time had shed its skin just in time for it to be stuffed and draped between the columns, and of course everyone knew that anything to do with snakes always brought good luck to conferences! She was so fascinated and taking notes so fast, I finally had to admit that I was drawing on my imagination; I guessed the garlands really were supposed to represent the ties of friendship between the different nations.

The only sour note of the day was that unfortunately the flag of one of the Middle Eastern nations had been carefully hung upside down.

The next two weeks were a foretaste of what to expect when the month of official mourning was over and the real entertaining began, for as it was we went to a luncheon, cocktail party or dinner every day, without even beginning to accept all our invitations. There were several open Conference sessions, most of which I went to, taking different people with me. The first person I invited was Norma, as she was the only person of my acquaintance who had not asked me for a ticket.

One evening Roger and I went to a "World Labor for Peace" meeting at the Civic Auditorium, at Harry Bridges' invitation. He had asked Roger to make the opening address of welcome to the foreign delegates. He introduced him with one of the most beautiful speeches I have ever heard, starting with "Our beloved Mayor needs no introduction." Roger arose, welcomed the crowd, and then turned to Harry and said, "I would be less than human if I failed to refer to the last time Mr. Bridges and I were on this same platform together, just eight-and-a-half years ago." Everyone in the 100% labor audience roared with laughter and gave him a big hand. It proved, to me at least, that the wheel of things had come full turn, and that it did pay to have courage and be true to oneself as Roger had been when he had accepted Bridges' challenge to a public debate.

Of course the big news early in May was V-E day, very soberly celebrated here; we were too near the Orient to feel the war was more than partially over, particularly with Roger Jr. "somewhere in the Pacific." I was reminded of Armistice Day, November 11, 1918, and the hysterical excitement in New York as I drove the children up and down Fifth Avenue to see the crowds, just a few hours before Roger Jr. was born.

The following Sunday we took the Walter Lippmanns up to the Valley of the Moon for a picnic lunch. We decided to drive back to

San Francisco by the coast road. When we were still a good 40 miles from the city, and it was then four o'clock, Lippmann casually remarked that he had to be at the Palace Hotel by five for a broadcast! Sunday traffic on a twisty, turny road . . . and a deadline to meet. We made it, with three minutes to spare. But it was a drive I doubted if any of us would ever forget.

The next Friday Lewis and Jane had a cocktail party for the Belts (of Cuba) and the Martins (of Brazil), two perfectly charming couples. Roger took us all down to John's Rendezvous for dinner. Toward the end of the evening, he went over to one of the other tables and asked a pretty blond to dance with him. She accepted, and then dressed him down for action unbecoming to a Mayor! He told her he had always done this sort of thing, and he had to be natural. She countered that it was his privilege to be natural if he were a private citizen, but as the Mayor, he had to be dignified. No one had expected anything of Mayor Rossi, but everybody loved Roger, and he had to live up to it! He was so staggered he told me all about it on the way home.

By then the formal invitations had begun to pour in for three or four functions a day. We realized we would have to ask Jack Peurifoy's advice as to which ones were "musts," for it would have been a sheer physical impossibility to have accepted them all.

The first formal reception was given in a private home. Mrs. Warren and I received, she in a green gown and I in dark red, with a background of tall scarlet rhododendron trees. I had tied a chiffon scarf around my right wrist, and shook hands with my left—I knew that 500 firm handshakes would put my right arm, barely recovered from bursitis, back where it had been before I went to Santa Barbara. Many celebrities were there. Lord and Lady Halifax, Andre Kostelanetz and Lily Pons, Jim Farley, Eric Sevareid, Vincent Sheehan, and all kinds of foreign delegates, of black, white, yellow and coffee color.

As one woman came through the line and was introduced as Mrs. Street, I realized she was a woman from Australia whom I had entertained in San Francisco several years before. I didn't have time to speak

175

to her then, but when the line broke up I went over and introduced myself only to hear, "Mrs. Lapham! Really! You've aged so I wouldn't have known you!" I was tempted to say "Well, you're no rose your-self!"

The whole of the next month was a kaleidscope of entertainment, some of it amusingly and delightfully done, and some boring. But one pay-as-you-enter tea given at the St. Francis Hotel by the Federated Women's Clubs, was one of the most disgraceful exhibitions of bad manners by American women that I had ever seen. Mrs. Warren, Lady Halifax, Dr. Wu and I were in the receiving line, and as the hordes of women stormed in, we felt as though we had been caught in a stampede. Twice I pulled Dr. Wu out of a large flower pot she had been knocked into. You really felt that if you lost your footing, you would be trampled to death.

More than one woman dashed up to me with outstretched hand, grasped mine, and said, "Who are you? Oh! the Mayor's wife? Good-night! I expected to meet someone famous and foreign."

If I had thought the first ten days of official doings were heavy ones, I was soon disillusioned; in a short time we were going to no less than four, five or six functions a day. They usually started with a ladies' luncheon for me, and a stag one for Roger; then about four he would send the car for me, and we would start on our round of receptions.

One charming luncheon was given by Dr. Wu in Chinatown for Mrs. Vandenberg, Mrs. Connally, Ruth Bryan Rohde, Mrs. Stassen and me, during which Mrs. Stassen made what I considered a real diplomatic gaffe. She was young and pretty, but certainly not very smart. In a momentary silence she said, "Dr. Wu, how do you tell a Chinese from a Japanese? I've never been able to do it!" Dr. Wu was Chinese, and we were at war with Japan! But being the great lady she was, she just smiled, and answered, "Do not look at their faces, Mrs. Stassen, look at their feet. The Japanese toe in."

As a matter of fact, I didn't think either of the Stassens were too smart. When you were speaking to him, he never looked directly at you, but always over your head to see if he were missing someone important. For a man with his political aspirations, I thought this was rather stupid.

At another luncheon I sat next to Ruth Bryan Rohde. She asked me to compliment Roger on his speech the opening day of the Conference, and said to tell him that he had set such a high standard of excellence, both in content and delivery, that it had been difficult for the others to live up to it. Coming from the daughter of the Silver-tongued Orator, I knew how much he would appreciate her praise.

One typical afternoon started with Russian War Relief at the St. Francis. We refused to stand in a receiving line, but we did stand at attention when we heard the Star Spangled Banner played on the bala-laika (when we recognized it, which was after the orchestra was about half way through). From there we progressed to the Panamanians at the other end of town. Back to the University Club for the Netherlands. Then to Berkeley for the Czechs. We arrived home at 8:45 without having seen the Russian or Panamanian Ambassadors, the Dutch Minister or Masaryk, for whom the receptions were given; they were all tied up in Committee meetings, and hadn't arrived before we left.

We saw the same people day after day and felt we knew some of them very well—Lord and Lady Halifax, Viscount and Lady Cranborne, Nelson Rockefeller, and Alger Hiss, of whom we thought very highly at the time. All the Central and South American delegates flocked around Rockefeller, as he spoke really beautiful Spanish. I asked him where he had learned it, and he told me he was the prize graduate of the Berlitz school, where he had studied it 8 hours a day for three months!

Berenson, the New Zealand Minister to America, was a real diamond in the rough, but we got along beautifully; especially after he had asked if he should call me "Mayoress," to which I said no, it made me feel as if I were being put out to stud. He said "Ow! Mrs. Lapham, what a dreadful thing to s'y!" but laughed like a banshee and called me Mrs. Lapham from then on. For all their socialist government, the New Zealanders were the only ones who had fresh caviar at their reception, and how I appreciated it after the same tired canapes we had been served day after day, many of them I am sure making their second or third appearance.

There were not so many dinners given, principally because no one ever knew how long the Conference sessions would last. One quite small one was given by Lord and Lady Halifax. I sat next to His Lordship, and said I had a conundrum to ask him. "What is the difference between a diplomat and a lady?" He said he could see there was a difference, but would prefer to have me tell him what it was. So I said: "If a diplomat says 'yes,' he means 'perhaps.' If he says 'perhaps,' he means 'no.' If he says 'no,' he's no diplomat. Whereas if a lady says 'no,' she means 'perhaps.' If she says 'perhaps,' she means 'yes.' If she says 'yes,' she's no lady." He didn't even smile, but just said, "My dear that's no conundrum, that's the truth."

There were two enormous dinners with no expense spared. One was given by Skouras, the movie magnate, with orchids flown in from Honolulu for all the ladies, and filet mignon for everyone, when most of us didn't have enough red points even for hamburger. The other was hosted by the Arabians at the Legion of Honor Museum, with a whole gold service, and champagne flowing far more freely than water.

The Arabians had aroused a tremendous amount of interest from the first: the supply of goats that had to be on hand for their food; their purchases, they practically bought out the San Francisco stores; and their fascination with American gadgets, especially plumbing. On one occasion, at a reception in a private apartment, they retired one by one to the bathroom, but none of them came back. On investigation, they were discovered flushing the toilet with a foot-pedal, one by one, and then standing back and saying "ah-ah-ah!" The host then showed them the garbage disposal unit. After that, everyone's plate that had food on it was snatched away from him, in order for the Arabians to dispose of it.

One story about Prince Feisal (who presented Roger with a complete Arabian costume) was that as he walked through the lobby of the Mark Hopkins in his snow-white flowing robes one morning, a woman in the crowd gasped and said, "Isn't he dreamy?" Whereupon he winked at her, and said in perfect English, "But you ought to see me on a horse!"

The dinner given by the Filipinos for General Romulo was very stirring. He is a great orator and made a very fine speech, ending with the analogy of the American eagle pushing the eaglets out of the nest when they were ready to fly, but flying below them with outspread wings until they were able to soar alone. This America had done, granting independence to the Philippines, but remaining in the background in case of necessity. He then described the lowering of the American flag on Corregidor—defeat; the raising of it again at Corregidor by Mac-Arthur—victory; the final lowering of the flag on the day of Philippine independence—reverence; and the raising of the Philippine flag in its place—consecration. It couldn't have been more moving, or a greater tribute.

At the dinner given by the Uruguayans for the French delegate, Joseph Paul-Boncour, I started with not three but four strikes against me. To begin with it was an unusually hot night, and we were in an inside private dining room on the mezzanine of the Palace Hotel. I sat next to Paul-Boncour, who was not only stone-deaf, but spoke nothing but French; and in addition to that had his very chic, very blonde "secretary" on his left. I finally managed to attract his attention, and asked the most banal questions possible: "Have you ever been to San Francisco before?" "Did you fly?" etc. But his answers were memorable. "No, Madame, I have never been to America before; the French are not great travellers. I did not fly, I came by train. And I am glad that I did, for I now realize why America did not rush to the defense of 'La Belle France' when she was so foully attacked. I now know that America is not one continent, but five: the financial center in the East; the industrial center a bit further west; the great granary in the Middle West; the mining country beyond; and then, mon Dieu, Madame! California. A continent in itself." He went on to say that foreign wars were so far away from most of us, that it had taken a long and careful education to make us see that our involvement might be a matter of our own safety. And I really felt that my struggle against odds had been rewarded.

My French, which was fluent, had been of great help to me during the various dinners. So had a little book I had run across called "Fractured French," from which I had copied some of the juicier items and used them with great success at some of the more difficult dinners. They were free translations, or the average American's understanding of spoken French; for instance:

> *Mal de Mer*—Mother's trunk.
> *Montparnasse*—My father's seat.
> *Avant-garde*—Birth control.
> *Femme de menage*—A woman of my age.
> *Faux pas*—Step-father.
> *Entre chat*—Between us girls.
> *Grace a Dieu*—Good-bye Grace.

They were a great hit, and I must have made 15 or 20 copies of them to give to those who asked for them.

The dinner for Gromyko was really something. I sat between him and Governor Warren. Gromyko ate well, and devoted himself entirely to his food. But having been brought up to feel you must talk to your dinner partner, I finally said, "Mr. Ambassador, it has been a matter of real regret to me during the Conference that I speak no other language but French."

Looking me up and down with his cold black eyes, he said "I am not surprised—none of you Ama-r-r-icans spik anything but Ang-lish. It is always we who must spik Ang-lish. It is all a part of your isolationism."

I felt as if I had been slapped in the face, but I gathered myself together and replied that I did not think isolationism had anything to do with it. That in Europe it was an aboslute necessity to speak several languages, but that here, while we may learn them, we had little or no occasion to use them. Without a change of expression he said, "I was making a jo-o-ke."

I murmured I was sorry I hadn't recognized it, and turned with relief to Governor Warren, while he, with equal relief, turned to Mrs. Warren.

The next time I had to talk to him, I said that I had always wanted to go to Russia, which brought forth "Why? Vary few peeples go to Russia."

By that time I was mad and said my son had been, and had had a most interesting trip down the Volga to the Black Sea.

"The Volga flows into the Caspian," said my grim friend.

"It was probably some ather river."

"It was the Volga," I countered. At which point he pushed back his chair, and stated, "I go home now."

I was horror-struck. My husband was the Mayor, and I had offended the Russian Ambassador! I felt better when his Aide whispered would I excuse, please—the Ambassador was already two hours late for a meeting. I told my son Lewis about it the next day and he said, "Mother, how could you have been so stupid? When he said it probably was some other river, all you had to say was 'I was making a joke!'"

The last dinner was given by Nelson Rockefeller at the San Francisco Yacht Club. It was a night in a thousand to anyone who knows San Francisco summer weather. Not only was it warm enough to have cocktails out-of-doors, but there wasn't a breath of wind, and there was a full moon, turning the waters of the Bay to silver.

After dinner Nelson gave us the works, with Carmen Miranda and her sister to dance for us. Roger had always had a passion for fancy dancing. In no time flat he was on the floor, dancing with—or possibly at—Carmen, without having the faintest idea that she was probably the best-known exotic dancer in the country. She didn't seem to mind, until he took one of her maraccas, waved it around, and broke it. A sigh of horror went up. Jane grabbed him and told him he might just as well have injured a Stradivarius. He was so convinced he had committed an unpardonable sin, that he sent Carmen an armful of roses the next day, with an abject note of apology.

Then came the last days of the conference. We were all in the Opera House Monday evening when the vote was taken on the adoption of the Charter. There were few dry eyes as the chairmen of the different delegations rose to signify their assent and Lord Halifax, who was presiding, said "I declare the Charter ratified unanimously."

Tuesday afternoon was the final session. President Truman had arrived. I thought him the prototype of the 100 per cent American. As I said to Roger, he reminded me of all the Sunday School super-intendents I had had as a child. His speech was much too long, and his delivery left something to be desired. But he was obviously sincere, and you could understand how he had said, on becoming President, "Pray for me, boys. I'm going to need it."

The other speeches were in seven languages—English, Chinese, French, Spanish, Portuguese, Russian and Arabic. I thought Masaryk's the best, with Lord Halifax a close second. It was thrilling to hear how much had been accomplished; to realize that the United Nations was now a permanent organization; and to wish it every success as a court for the discussion of world problems in the hopes of peaceful settlement.

Well, it was over. We had met people from all over the globe, and felt we had gotten to know some of them very well. Betty Jane Peurifoy had come out for the closing days, and we had fallen in love with her on sight. We counted the official functions we had been to; between us, they totalled 81, and we had accepted no private invitations what-soever. We were both weary, and a day or so later took off in different directions, Roger going north to the woods, and I south to the little cottage at Atherton. The night before he left Roger came home with a gift from Stettinius—the largest redwood bowl in captivity, which we heard he had presented to all the delegates, the President and the Governor, as well as the Mayor. We conjured up a picture of their transportation to the different homelands—Dr. Wu's on a camel, Prince Feisal's on an Arab steed, the Peruvians to Lima on a llama—Helen Hokinson should have done it for the "New Yorker."

After ten quiet days away I returned to town to attend a dinner and a play called "The Forgotten Factor" put on by the Moral Re-armament group. The dinner was at the St. Francis, and I sat next to the founder, to whom I took an instant dislike for I thought he was both unctuous and a would-be pincher. The menu couldn't have been more elaborate —guinea hen under glass, Baked Alaska, etc. My impressions were confirmed that their supposed "plain thinking" came second to their "high living." I saw why they never bothered with people except those capable of making substantial contributions to the cause.

The play was supposed to shock me, as it advocated close management-labor relations. As this was what Roger had been working on over a period of years, I simply felt it was a bit behind the times. After it was over, I was invited to come up on the stage and meet the "delightful cast of young people." But I saw a photographer lurking in the background and realized that I was to be used as the Mayor's wife endorsing Moral Re-armament. So I politely declined and said if it was not convenient for them to take me home, I would call a taxi. A bit more urging, a bit more sales resistance, and then the young couple who had brought me took me home.

En route the wife told me a dramatic story of the way MRA worked. She and her husband, who was a Czech, had been in Paris when war broke out, but their two boys were in Czechoslovakia. She knew her husband couldn't go back for them, and even though she was seven months pregnant, she felt she had to be the one to do it.

"So," she said, "first I tried the American Embassy, who refused me a visa. Then I went to the American Express, who said they couldn't help me either. And then, Mrs. Lapham, I tried . . . God! And the very next day I got my visa, went in, and got my boys."

I merely said it was too bad she hadn't tried God first. Neither of them spoke to me again, even to say goodnight.

On the 14th of August came the news of the Japanese surrender. I listened to it on the radio with tears running down my cheeks, though for me it wouldn't be really over until I heard from Roger Jr. We went down to Lewis and Jane's to celebrate. By seven o'clock I began to realize that if anyone was going to get anything to eat, it was up to me to provide it. So I telephoned home to say we would be 12 for dinner instead of four, and left it up to my household to cope! They did, carving and serving my five-pound leg of lamb from the kitchen. As everything went round and round, I felt it was a second miracle of the loaves and the fishes; only this time there wasn't enough left over to feed a small size dog.

While we were still at dinner the phone rang, and a group of American-Hawaiian shipping girls said they would like to come out to congratulate their old chief. So they arrived, ten strong, and my always hospitable husband asked them if they had had dinner. The answer was no, so Roger said sweetly, "Well, nothing simpler! We can feed them, can't we, Sport?" As far as I knew, there wasn't a thing in the house. But I said yes in a die-away voice, Lewis betook himself to the kitchen, and scrambled two dozen eggs for them. We eked this out with the rest of the Scavengers' Association champagne, plus an enormous bottle of brandy Jan had brought us from France in 1940—we had been saving it for an occasion, and this was definitely it.

The next day Norma and I drove up to Lake Tahoe to visit the Spencer Grants. We had been literally hoarding our gas coupons in order to make the trip, so had a dreadful shock at Sacramento when we presented them at a gas station and said, "Six gallons, please." The attendant said, "Save them for your scrapbooks, ladies. They're no good!" We both shrieked at the outrage until the attendant smiled and added, "Didn't you know gas rationing went off this morning?" We had left so early that neither of us had read the papers! Sighing with relief, we said those beautiful words, unheard for years, "Fill 'er up!"

We had a quiet, pleasant ten days. The wonderful news came from Nancy that she had heard from Roger Jr., and he was on his way home. So for me, the war was really over. But what would peace bring? How long would it be before we went back to our easy, rather unthinking way of life again? We in America had been absolutely free from actual, material hardship. We had had our driving cut to a minimum. We hadn't been able to buy nylons, much meat, butter or cigarettes. And we had done a good deal of standing in line for what we had bought. The ration points, especially in units of 16, had been a nuisance to cope with, but some such system was an absolute necessity, or no one would have been able to buy anything. My prayer was that we wouldn't forget how little we had really been inconvenienced; that we would approach the future with at least a humble, if not contrite heart.

When I got back to town, it didn't seem that my prayer was to be answered. The papers were full of the shambles that had been made of the city in celebration of peace. For some unknown reason the Navy had turned thousands of young recruits from boot camp loose in town, without warning the local police, or supplying adequate Shore Patrol. They had torn the place to pieces. Many injuries; much looting—all the bars and liquor shops were closed, but they simply smashed the windows and helped themselves; many cases of rape; and ten deaths, before the Navy threw in the sponge and called on the city police. It seemed incredible that any Navy officer in command could have been so short-sighted. In looking for a scapegoat, there were those who picked the Mayor for not stopping the rioting sooner; but the City was powerless until the Navy asked for aid.

The first week in September Roger and I drove up to Hamilton Field to welcome the first of the Generals who had been prisoners-of-war in Japan since the fall of Corregidor. And an affecting sight they were as they debarked from the planes. The Air Force had set up an elaborate buffet-bar, but not one of them touched a drop of liquor. All they wanted was milk—they had had none in four years—or coffee with loads of sugar. I was standing next to one of them when he asked for coffee. The pretty girl who was serving asked him if he wanted sugar, and how many lumps? He asked, "Can I have all I want?" She said "Of course." Beaming all over he said, "Then I'll take six lumps— I haven't tasted anything sweet for four years." They were all so thin and drawn, and their teeth were in such dreadful shape; it made your heart ache to think of what they had endured.

A few days later we drove up there again to meet General Wainwright. He certainly deserved the nickname of "Skinny" for he was a walking skeleton, all except his face which was terribly swollen from an abscessed tooth. He was kindly and charming, and seemed very much touched that his sister had flown "all the way from Seattle" to greet him!

The next day was official V-J Day. There was a huge parade in honor of the General, starting at the Ferry Building and ending at the reviewing stand in front of City Hall. I had taken Pat and Ernie and we sat on the second floor balcony. I really choked up when the first car drove up with Roger and General Wainwright in it. Roger looked so dignified and so handsome, I thought for the thousandth time how lucky the City was to have such a wonderful representative during this important period of its history.

The poor suffering General stuck it out in the reviewing stand for half an hour, and then went up to Roger's office, where a chosen few were presented to him, among them Pat and Ernie, by invitation of his Aide.

Roger told me afterward that the General had seemed so nervous while they were waiting for the parade to start, that Roger had assumed that he was in great pain. But little by little it came out that he was afraid he would be hissed by the people en route for having surrendered the greatest body of American troops in history. Instead of which, he was cheered to the skies. He kept saying, "But I just don't understand it. Are all these people really cheering me—a defeated General?"

Roger's answer was, "Why General, don't you realize you stand as the symbol of sportsmanship that all Americans admire above everything else? You obeyed orders to do one of the hardest things anyone has ever been called on to do. If you think this is an ovation, just wait until you get to New York and Washington!"

Roger Jr. arrived home about the middle of October, having left his ship, the "Manila Bay," in Honolulu and gotten in a week ahead of her. But when she got in, he took us down and showed us his stateroom which had been demolished by a kamikaze, while he most fortunately was at battle stations. He said he saw it coming, and never felt his 6 ft. 4 in. height so keenly in his life, as he didn't see how it could miss him. It hit at the foot of the control tower, and he found himself curled into a two by three foot space under an iron step. He had no idea how he had gotten there. All he knew was that it took him ten minutes to get out. The only injury he sustained was a skinned nose which he had tried to press even further into the solid plates of the deck.

Even with all the conference activities behind us, the days continued to be busy ones; various luncheons, meetings, and one dinner here which I have never forgotten. Roger had invited a group of Pacific Coast mayors, but said he didn't know just how many would be here. I told him the table seated sixteen—and sixteen there turned out to be. I had saved up my ration points for weeks in order to buy a five-rib roast. Though I was to have dinner upstairs, my mouth was watering for a nice slice of rare beef. What did I get? A poached egg on a saucer of spinach! I almost burst into tears, but the maid said she didn't think the beef would even go around—as the first man had taken five slices, the second four, and by the time it got to the 16th, there was just one slice left, and not enough left on the bones to scrape off some bits for me.

The next excitement was Admiral Halsey's arrival. Roger, General Pratt (the Commanding Officer at the Presidio), Archbishop Mitty and several other officials had been invited to board the "South Dakota" from the Marina, and proceed to anchorage with her while the Admiral reviewed the fleet. Mrs. Pratt had invited a large group to see the spectacle from her house in the Presidio. And what happened? The worst fog we had had in months. We could just make out the "South Dakota" as she passed under the Golden Gate Bridge, and the other ships were mere wraiths. The City tried to make up for it by giving Admiral Halsey a banquet at the Palace Hotel (at $10 a plate, pay-as-you-enter) a night or two later. I could only hope he enjoyed it, as he was surrounded by Laphams—Roger on one side, and me on the other.

187

Shortly after this Roger was advised by the State Department that President Rios of Chile was to visit San Francisco, and the Department would like him "suitably entertained." Roger asked just what that meant. He was told that Rios had had his fill of cultural entertainment, but was very fond of dancing. How about a dinner dance? Nothing could have been more acceptable to Roger. I was asked to prepare a social list, but as usual—with only 200 invitations—by the time the consular corps and their wives, Army and Navy brass, City officials, and San Franciscans of Chilean extraction or connection were included, my list consisted of six members of the family and four friends! Incidentally there were some 20-odd in the Presidential entourage, and it made the table seating a bit difficult, as no one knew whether they were young or old, short or tall, or even if they spoke English.

One thing I had definitely made up my mind to—I was going to mix people up, and rise above protocol. Apparently I managed it very successfully. I put all the wives of the ranking service officers at the head table and then seated all the husbands at different small tables on the floor and gave each of them an attractive young woman as a dinner partner. I wanted to mix up the consular corps, too, for like the animals going into the ark, they march in to every party, husband and wife arm-in-arm, always sit next to each other, and always look unutterably bored. But the Dean of the corps pleaded with me to leave well enough alone. He said that no matter how bored they were, they were used to it. That each one, fiercely conscious of his rank, was sure to feel slighted no matter where he was placed. And that some of them might even refuse to sit down at all. He would get all the repercussions. So I took his advice, and let them all sit in solemn silence as usual.

President Rios sat between Mrs. Warren and me on the raised platform. We found him pretty tough going as he spoke nothing but Spanish, and neither of us spoke any. The minute dinner was over I asked Mrs. Warren if she minded being demoted, to let the President have two Spanish-speaking young women. "Oh, no!", said she. "I have to go to a funeral tomorrow, and even that can't be any worse than this."

So we moved and joined the others on the dance floor. When I asked one of the women I had promoted how she got along, even she had found him a bit heavy going, although when he heard her husband was East, he had said it was pretty lonely in his big double bed at the Mark. She was smart enough to refuse his suggestion gracefully, and he must not have minded too much, as he absolutely refused to go home at 11:30 as tactfully advised by his guardian from the State Department.

My next assignment was quite different. Roger rang me up one morning and said there was to be a big stag dinner that night for the head of the Utilities Commission who was retiring, and he wanted me to write a jingle which was to be both rough, and amusingly insulting! I told him first of all that I was giving a luncheon so had very little time, and second that I did not have the vocabulary of a muleskinner. In fact the only two words I could think of off-hand were "bitch" and "bastard." He said, "Use 'em both," and hung up.

I did the best I could with my somewhat limited knowledge of the terms he wished used and took it down to him. He said it was neither rough nor insulting enough, but he'd fix it. Whereupon I said, "In that case, please Roger, do not announce when you read it that your wife wrote it. I am the Mayor's wife and a lady. This is not my regular line, and I do not wish to be connected with it in any way." I got no answer but a wave of the hand, but I heard no repercussions, so I guess he obeyed my request.

I had learned my lesson a couple of months before. He was to introduce Henry Kaiser at a luncheon which was being given for him, and had come home the night before casually mentioning that he had no idea what he was going to say. I said "Why that's a cinch! 'Kaiser' is a corruption of 'Caesar,' whose motto was 'I came, I saw, I conquered.' Just enlarge on that and you've got a natural!"

I listened to the broadcast the next noon. To my horror I heard Roger say that he had asked his wife what his theme should be, and she had told him it should be the easiest speech he had ever had to make. So he had adopted her suggestion—and that Kaiser was certainly a Caesar in his own right!

From November 1945 on, all sorts of things happened. I have pictures of Roger doing practically everything from leaving a Good Friday mass with Archbishop Mitty, to eating a Victory Garden carrot; to flying an Ercoup airplane as a publicity stunt to promote the passage of the $20,000,000 bond issue for the enlargement of the airport, which was to be on the ballot that fall.

I wasn't too keen about his flight after only ten minutes of instruction even though the Ercoup had dual controls. I didn't think some of the pilots were too keen either, because just as he was about to take off, the crowd was urged to move back, "as the Mayor was a City official, and really didn't want to kill anyone." There were about 40,000 people there, lured by the promise of free rides for the holders of the lucky gate tickets, and they all moved without any further urging. He taxied to the end of the strip, took off almost vertically, landed, took off again, circled once more, and then came in for good, greatly to my relief.

The bond issue was passed by a 5-1 majority to our great surprise, as so many others had failed in the past. It was, I felt sure, a tribute to the people's belief in Roger's integrity, and their assurance that the monies would be spent for the purpose intended, and not diverted into other channels.

Two suggestions came up shortly after this: one that Roger should go to Berlin as Civilian Governor, which he refused because he had been elected in good faith to serve four years and felt committed to do so; and the other to go to London to work for the choice of San Francisco as the permanent seat of the United Nations Organization. This suggestion had been made some time before, but he had been waiting word from the State Department as to whether it would be advisable or not. About the middle of the month he got the "Go" sign from Jack Peurifoy, so left on the 22nd. I had hoped to go with him but he thought I might have a hard time getting back from England. As a consolation he said he would take me as far as Washington and New York, which I knew would do me good as it meant getting away from points and rationing for a bit.

Going back to the Carlton after having spent nearly three years there, was like going to a second home. This time we were not in the igloo, but in a suite on the 6th floor. It had a huge sitting room, but such a small bedroom that the first night Roger kicked me twice when he turned over, and knocked a glass of water off the table once! But as it was only for three nights we decided we could stand it.

We really had quite a gay time for between Roger's briefing for the role he was to play in London, the telephone rang constantly. We were invited hither and yon for lunch and dinner, and I saw many of the friends I had made while I was there. One of them was a doctor's wife, who asked four of us for lunch and bridge. Over cocktails she read two short articles from the American Journal of Medicine.

The first reported that, among other surplus items, the Army had 1,000,000 tons of contraceptive jelly for all the women of the Armed Forces. Commented the Journal: "The Army must have been expecting a long war!"

The second told of a woman, who had been told to bring a specimen to her doctor's office, and arrived carrying it in a pie plate. "How did you ever get that here without spilling it in your car?" asked the doctor. "Oh! I didn't come in my car, Doctor, I came on the bus!"

That Sunday was a comparatively peaceful day. We slept late, went to Harvey's for a lunch of steamed clams and broiled live lobster, to the Walter Lippmans for cocktails and to the Eugene Meyers for dinner. That was quite a party; the guests included the Joe Davies, the Robert Lovetts (he was Under-Secretary of some Department), the William Mitchells (ex-Attorney-General, and then in charge of the Pearl Harbor investigation), and British Field-Marshal Sir Henry Maitland Wilson and Mrs. Wilson. He looked every inch the typical John Bull, but she looked as if she had been sired by a tired mouse on a rainy afternoon.

I sat next to Sir Henry, and told him my story of the search for a slogan to be used in the campaign following Ramsey MacDonald's defeat; the best one submitted was "Nine months of Labour produces only a miscarriage of justice," which the Conservative Party didn't feel they could use. But it amused Sir Henry who said, "Awfully cle-vah, what? Must remember to tell it to the wife."

As we left the dining room I heard Mrs. Davies say "Oh yes, my dear. She wore her decorations on her nose, and her ribbons on her bridge." Being very conscious of my own bridge-work, I was simply fascinated as I had never considered wearing either ribbons or decorations on it. "She" turned out to be the Davies' yacht which had been turned over to the Government during the war!

During the after-dinner session with the ladies, my stream of consciousness became definitely audible, and I regaled them with the story of Maria's birth, and some of my better telephone conversations during Roger's incumbency. I had a fresh, and I must say a most appreciative, audience. It inspired Mrs. Davies to tell me of the birth of her six daughters, plus her miscarriage in a fishing boat off the coast of Florida, attended only by a very nervous husband. She was a very pretty woman, simply dripping with pink coral and diamonds, and remarkably young looking to have an 18-year-old grandson.

Just as the men came in, Mrs. Mitchell asked me if I wrote, and told me I certainly should. When her husband joined us she said, "Sit right here by Mrs. Lapham, dear; she is so witty it will do you good and take your mind off everything." So of course he and I just sat and glared at each other, both of us completely speechless.

Roger took off for London Thanksgiving afternoon, accompanied by Don Cleary, a former newspaper man but then in the employ of the City, and two members of the Board of Supervisors. I went over to Ruxton to spend a few days with my sister before going up to New York to await his return. I heard of his safe arrival twenty-four hours later. I hoped all would go well with his mission, although I thought he had a very up-hill job before him.

I heard very little from Roger, except various cables telling of delays in any decision on the permanent site of the U. N. Finally one said that if I wanted to be home for Christmas, I had better leave as he had no idea of when he would be able to get away. So I made my reservations on the "Wolverine."

Home again, I had little enthusiasm for holiday planning. I didn't feel at all in a truly Christmas mood—especially with Roger away. And his news was not good. England didn't want the site anywhere in America; if in America, Russia didn't want it anywhere except in New York; our own delegate from the State Department leaned so far over backward to be neutral that he was a hindrance rather than a help. No decision seemed likely to be taken, and Roger left, feeling he had done all he could. But while he was still at the airport, he got word that the Council had voted to exclude from consideration any site west of the Mississippi! He felt there had been dirty work at the crossroads somewhere, and his remark to the reporters was "That's a hell of a note!"; while our Chinese cook's was equally terse and to the point: "Boss, he get lef'."

Roger was terribly disappointed, as well as being exhausted. He spent a day or two in New York to rest up a bit on his return, but he still looked tired when I met him at the airport. He brought home lots of things for my scrapbook—including invitations for luncheon with the Prime Minister at #10 Downing Street with the Lord Mayor, and for dinner with Lord and Lady Cranbourne, and Ambassador Koo. He had had an interesting, even though a frustrating, experience. When he had ordered flowers for his dinner hostesses, he had almost dropped dead when the bill for two dozen Chrysanthemums was $65.00! "Why in San Francisco," he said, "I could have sent ten dozen roses for the same amount!"

By the end of the first week in January I had recovered my health and my spirits, and had sufficient energy to acknowledge the gifts which had poured in on us at Christmas: Among them plants and flowers from all the City Commissions, and another case of champagne from the Scavengers' Protective Association.

Meanwhile, I was asking everyone I knew to tell me a good story about gardens. I had been invited to be the guest of honor at the annual luncheon of the San Francisco Garden Club in these words: "Dear, will you be the guest of honor at our luncheon, and will you please be very witty? We will have two speakers who will address us on 'The Effects of Garden Pests on Roses' and 'Can We Exclude the Japanese Beetle?' and you will be the one light spot on the program."

I thought that being asked to be witty on a specified date three weeks ahead was a bit of a job. But I said I accepted on one condition—that I would not be introduced as "Our Mayor's charming wife, who has a message for us" (as I had been introduced so many times before at large civic luncheons), inasmuch as I had never had a message for anyone, not even Garcia. The President promised. I unearthed a story. The day came and I spoke more or less as follows:

"Ladies and Gentlemen: I cannot think of anyone less qualified to address the members of the San Francisco Garden Club than myself, as I know so little about gardens that I have been consistently turned down for membership even in all of the smaller Country ones. The nearest I have ever come to participation was when I was asked to be co-hostess with an Atherton friend of mine to entertain some twenty members of the American Garden Club who were en route to Japan. I had the President of a Connecticut Club assigned to me. I learned the names of a few of the choicest flowers and rattled off my glib little spiel, only to realize she was paying no attention, probably having discovered how little I really knew. There was a momentary pause, and then she said, 'I hope you won't think it impertinent of me considering that we have just met, but do you mind telling me where you got your hat?' 'In Honolulu,' said I, sighing with relief. 'I will give you the address and you can get one just like it on your way through.' The entente was so cordiale from then on, that I ended up by telling her my best garden story—of a New England spinster who told her local club that she had a problem for them to solve: They knew how she loved roses, and also that her garden space was very limited; so under those conditions, did they think it would be all right if she put the Rev. Page Roberts and Dorothy Perkins in the same bed?"

With which I thanked them for their indulgence in listening to me, and sat down, always mindful of my father's dictum, "Helen, if you are ever called on to talk, stand up; if you want to be heard, speak up; but if you want to be popular—sit down."

Shortly after this Roger and I went down to Pasadena for a long weekend. He was to be the guest of honor at a Harvard Club dinner; we wanted to see the van Oostens; and of course have one session at Santa Anita. The weather was perfect. We should have spent all our time out of doors, but we couldn't as Roger was composing a letter to Chester Bowles (head of the OPA), who had issued an injunction to prevent the City from raising the carfare from 7 to 10 cents "in order to prevent inflation."

Roger worked over the letter but was dissatisfied with what he had written. He handed it to me for criticism. I said it sounded more like one of President Truman's productions than his. That put the quietus on it; he did it over, and it was a masterpiece. He read it to Dion Holm, the City Attorney, over the telephone, got his approval and released it to the press. I thought his neck was out a mile, but then decided it was time for someone to speak up before all our civic liberties were swallowed up by bureaucracy. Roger was one of the few men who had both the ability and the courage to do it. In spite of the fact that Judge Goodman upheld the injunction, the editorial comment was universally good. Roger was tickled to pieces with himself. (He had just thought what OPA really stood for—Order of Piss-Ants!)

Chinese New Year came along early in February, and we were invited to a luncheon at the best restaurant in Chinatown by the Woos. The luncheon was given for Mme. T. V. Soong, who was en route to China. It was quite a party, in spite of the fact that Mme. Soong, who was flying out, was held up by weather. She never arrived.

We had what my host described as "just a simple little luncheon, not a banquet." It consisted of course after course—melon soup, squab and Chinese peas, quail soup, chicken and walnuts, shark's fin soup, more chicken, duck, chicken with garlic, all washed down with cup after cup of delicious green tea, and finally, by the time I felt like the old hill-billy who said "Ah kin chaw, but Ah cain't swaller," we ended with hot rice soup flavored with almonds. I didn't want anything else to eat for the next twenty-four hours. How Mme. Woo and her daughters could eat as they do, still weigh not more than one hundred pounds, and have such divine figures, I will never know.

One memorable event was a beautiful dinner given for us by Mariategui, the Dean of the Latin-American consular corps. He told Roger he wanted to honor him with a dinner in recognition of all he had done for Latin America. And a beautiful function it was.

Mariategui arose and said how wonderful Roger was. Roger arose and said how wonderful all the Latin-Americans were. Then he suggested that his wife should second the motion! So I stood up, not having an idea of what I was going to say, but determined to work in my 20 Spanish nouns and four verbs—all in the present tense!

I started by saying that although my Spanish was very limited, there was one phrase that was applicable to every country south of the border that I had ever visited—"Que linda!"

At this point the fresh Cuban Consul chipped in and asked what I had said when I was in Cuba? A Heaven-sent opportunity to get in my second phrase: "Oh! In Cuba, I never said anything but 'mas despacio!' "

It must have been the right thing to say, for everyone laughed—and I was able to use the third, "Que simpatico, ustedes," and sit down. The Panamanian Consul who sat next to me patted me on the arm, and said, "But you don' know how you are fonny! You giv' that fresh one a hit in his eye!" I heard afterward that the Cuban Consul was renowned as a wolf if ever there was one, so I guess it was all right to tell him to "go slow!"

5

THE RECALL FIGHT
(1946)

E ARLY in April a movement was started by a man named Budde
(the owner and distributor of one of the neighborhood "throw-
away" papers) to recall Roger for his insistence on the necessity for
the increase in carfare. Budde claimed Roger was not only "bored with
his job, and arrogant, but considered only the downtown group who
elected him, and completely ignored the 'little man,' whom this 18¢
a week increase would ruin."

Budde was not influential, but the question was what groups were
behind him? The waterfront unions? The political "outs" who would
like to see a man in City Hall whom they could control? We just
didn't know. Budde had had it in for Roger ever since Roger had failed
to reappoint him to one of the City Commissions, but how serious was
this? And how far would it go? One of the newspaper columnists
wrote that the Mayor's theme song should be "I'm no-Budde's Sweet-
heart Now" which was almost too true to be funny.

Budde's next step was to circulate a petition, simply asking people
to sign it if they were in favor of a five cent instead of a seven or ten
cent fare—no mention of recall. He obtained 42,000 signatures, but
when the Registrar of Voters checked them, there were not enough
registered voters' signatures to qualify the issue on the June ballot.
Budde then legally had 15 more days to procure the necessary number
of signatures. It would then have to go to a special election called in
July at a time when Budde figured that most of Roger's supporters
would be out of town, and wouldn't take the trouble to vote by absentee
ballot.

Up to this time Roger had taken no action. But when one of the
newspapers telephoned the house and asked if it was true that the

197

Mayor had died of a heart attack during the night, he thought that things had gone far enough. He went on the radio to say that if Budde couldn't get enough signatures to qualify for the June election, he would circulate the petition himself in order to save the City the price of two streetcars. He then followed up by stopping by an old woman who was circulating the petition on Market Street, and signing for his own recall! She recognized him, of course, and said, "My God! If it ain't the Mayor! I feel like I could drop dead."

Budde was caught off base. First he said he would accept Roger's proposition; then he refused it, accusing Roger of insincerity and saying that if he was so anxious to save the City money, all he had to do was resign! By that time it began to look as if we were up against something that might really be put up to the electorate. Roger's backers, who had worked to elect him, told him he had to take this situation seriously; that they had expected him to be in office for four years; and with his approval, they would like to engage a campaign manager to plan the overall strategy.

Our activities were nothing if not varied. One Saturday night we went to the ILWU Ball at the Auditorium where I danced with San Francisco's leading leftist lawyer, Paul Schnur. Roger tried to dance with the lush blonde Harry Bridges had brought with him, but he didn't have a prayer. Harry guarded her as if the gold of her hair was real. I met two of the CIO wives who said they were glad to meet me. They had read of my delivering my daughter's baby in the Mayor's automobile and wanted to see what I looked like! Obstetrics is certainly a great Common Denominator.

One Sunday saw us at the very beautiful William Crocker home in Burlingame at a luncheon given in honor of Viscount Lascelles, the Princess Mary's 23-year-old son. He was a fine-looking young Englishman who seemed to be enjoying himself hugely as the party consisted mostly of his own age group.

The following Saturday was the Policeman's Ball, and after having been told before that I was part of the show that people had put up a dollar to see, I decided to glitter. So I wore a gold lace dress trimmed with mink. I had bought it in New York years before, but had hardly ever worn it. I always felt overdressed in it. Every other woman in the official party was in black, and I felt I stuck out like a sore thumb until Maud (Fay) Symington—a former star of grand opera—stopped at our box. She said "Dramatic, my dear, positively dramatic! Black satin! Black satin—for an affair of this kind! No sense of theatre at all! Pah!" So I felt much, much better.

My daughter, Edna van Oosten, called me up a few days later to tell me that the incredible had happened. The events had started seven years earlier. She and her husband had been living in Boston, where he was local head of the Holland-America Line and Consul-General for The Netherlands. Then he was promoted to Paris in January, 1939. Their possessions had been shipped to Rotterdam in three vans on a Holland-America ship, to be stored until the van Oostens had found a house in Paris. With the bombing of Rotterdam and the complete destruction of the docks, they naturally might never have expected to see their goods and chattels again. But Jan did because he had consulted two fortune-tellers, and each had told him the same thing: "It will take seven years, but everything you own will be restored to you." And now, just as the seven years were up, he received word that the vans had been found—apparently intact!

He had had them shipped to Pasadena, and aside from the fact that all the china and glass had been smashed, nothing was missing except one rug and all the table linen. Even the awesome portrait of Jan's grandfather (that scared Edna to death as he glared down at her from the wall of their apartment in Brookline where she went as a bride) was uninjured except for a slight crack in the frame. I lost five dollars on the deal, because I had bet Jan that the fortune tellers just told him what they thought he wanted to hear.

Early in May we went up to Hetch Hetchy, which I was more than glad to see—I had heard so much about it in connection with the Raker Act that I was sure that if I had died at that time, they would have found not "Calais" but "Hetch Hetchy" written on my heart.

We took Carol with us, and had a most happy weekend. It is the most beautiful spot imaginable, situated back of the Yosemite Valley, with the small City-owned Lodge built on enormous rocks above the man-made lake formed by damming the Tuolumne River. We looked out over pines and oaks, growing wherever they could find a scrap of soil, to two superb waterfalls on the other side of the lake, magnificent spectacles at that time of year when water is plentiful.

Friday morning we went for a boat ride on the lake with a Mr. Gray, who had been in charge of the dam for ten years. He was pushing 70, and had been struck by lightning the year before and given up for dead. But he fooled everybody by recovering, and was now as "pert" as could be—though he had a hole in his head and blacked out at times.

Saturday morning Roger, Carol and Walter drove over to Lake Eleanor, another source of our water supply. It was only about 10 miles away, but I could see the narrow road with nothing but hairpin turns on the other side of the Lake. Mr. Gray was going to drive and I didn't want any part of it. I pleaded with Roger to let Walter drive, but he said he didn't like to hurt Mr. Gray's feelings, although he knew Mr. Gray had been expressly forbidden to drive.

As they drove off, Mrs. Orth, who was taking care of us, said, "Say your prayers, it'll only be by God's mercy that they come back alive." She was right. Mr. Gray had a momentary blackout when they stopped on the way over to fish. And coming down the grade on the way home they would all have gone over had not Mr. Gray run into the only tree on the off side of the road and brought the car to an abrupt halt! Roger admitted when he got back that he had very definite qualms about getting back into the car again. I felt that Mr. Gray's "Thank you, Mr. Mayor, for letting me drive" was a most inaedquate compensation for almost killing them.

Home the next day in time to go to a dance at the Auditorium given by the sailors from one of the smaller carriers, the "Puget Sound," which was just in from Japan. Before the ship had left Japan, the crew had elected a "Queen" from photographs of their wives or sweethearts. When their lovely pin-up "girl" arrived, imagine their horror to discover that she was not only married, but very, very pregnant. No one was more horrified than the poor husband. He spent his time explaining to anyone who would listen that he hadn't known it when he entered her in the contest. And when he did find out, he was sure they'd be home before she showed it. They weren't . . . not by about five months. But she was pretty and suitably dressed. By the time the men had gotten used to the idea, they were rather proud of themselves for having chosen such a very different type of Glamor Queen.

Roger came home one night, laughing at himself. He had just turned in his old car (to Carol's horror—"You've junked Maria's birthplace!"). While he was driving home that evening, some kid had cut in ahead of him, and speeded on down Clay Street at 45 miles an hour, leaning on his horn. Roger was so enraged that he took off after him. Roger forced him to the curb, got out and walked over to the other car. Whereupon the kid stuck his head out of the window and said, "Who the hell do you think you are?" Which by no means improved the situation. Roger yelled, "I know who I am! I'm the Mayor of San Francisco, and a Special Police Officer as well." With that he pulled back his coat and displayed the gold police badge which he always wore on his suspenders. The kid wilted.

Roger gave him a tongue-lashing and got back into his own car. But he was still so mad he snapped the ignition on too fast, broke the key—and had to get the kid to push him far enough to get his car started by gravity! I said "Temper! Temper!"

By this time "busy-Budde," as one of the papers had nicknamed him, had filed the necessary number of signatures for Roger's recall, but too late to qualify for the June election. This meant a costly special election in July, and Roger would have to campaign again to retain the office to which he had been elected.

In spite of the fact that two of Budde's firmest supporters had resigned and urged him to drop the whole thing, his poisonous attacks continued in his throw-away paper. He even went so far as to offer Roger's signature on the petition he had signed to an autograph collector in Philadelphia! So it was abundantly clear that counter measures would have to be taken very promptly.

Clem Whittaker, the campaign manager who had been engaged, came out for dinner one night to discuss the policy to be employed. He had a dynamic personality, and his wife told me all would be well as Clem never went into a campaign he didn't expect to win. All he asked Roger to do was not to make statements unnecessarily on controversial subjects without first clearing them with him. He swung into action immediately with a series of newspaper cartoons depicting a huge question mark with "Whosit for Mayor?" stuck on its side. Then a pamphlet was sent out entitled "An Open Letter to San Francisco Voters—Who Don't Like Dictators—Who Won't be Rubber Stamps—Who Demand Fair Play." It continued:

The Issue

Mayor Lapham is the target, BUT HE IS NOT THE ISSUE! The ISSUE is whether the City Hall and the city government are to be turned over to an unholy alliance fronted by a puppet Mayor picked out of a grab-bag. Make no mistake about it, there is more—much more—behind this recall drive than appears on the surface."

Day after day this theme was stressed: the "Straw man"; "The Faceless Man"; "Do you want to turn your city over to boss rule with the powers behind the throne pulling the strings of the puppet in the Mayor's seat?"

One thing particularly upset me. The question on the ballot was so phrased that you had to vote "No," if you meant "Yes." In a simplified form it read, "Do you wish to have Mayor recalled?" But Clem said not to worry, it would all work out for the best, because the average voter always voted "No" whenever he was uncertain of what a proposition meant.

In the midst of all this, Carol was preparing to move to London, where Ernst had been sent as representative of the Bank of Manhattan. I provided all the packing trunks, had a cocktail-buffet farewell party for her, and saw her and the children off on the train from Oakland. I realized for the first time that Pat was older than I thought he was. When I offered to let him buy whatever comic books he wanted for the trip, he replied, "Thank you, Ma, but I'd rather have some science ones if you don't mind." I didn't.

This was also the year of the centennial of the Bear Flag incident in California's history. We managed to raise the Bear Flag three times in ten days—at Sonoma, Monterey and Portsmouth Square in San Francisco.

What historically took place seems to depend on the point of view of the historian. A band of either "patriots" or "hoodlums" decided that California had been under Mexican dominance long enough. They seized General Vallejo, proclaimed California a Republic, and raised the Bear Flag in the Sonoma Plaza on June 14, 1846. The Flag is described as a "piece of unbleached cotton cloth, five feet long by three feet wide, with a red five-pointed star in one corner and a crude grizzly bear in the center." One of the bystanders at the time wrote, "A bear stands his ground always, and as long as the stars shine, we stand for our cause." But most of the inhabitants laughed and said it looked more like a pig, which the various replicas certainly did—and a powerfully homely pig at that.

We arrived at Sonoma in time for a revolting barbecue lunch which I could hardly look at, let alone eat. I wished I had had a nice raven to feed me as one did Elijah. After the lunch period the ceremonies commenced—addresses by General "Hap" Arnold, Governor Warren, and a very brief one by Roger. The three of them were then initiated into a "Band of Wildmen" from Oregon, who presented each of them with the jawbone of some supposedly prehistoric animal—presumably to slay their thousands with, even if it wasn't the jawbone of an ass. The Flag was raised, and the serious part of the day was over.

Then we drove about four miles to the charming home of a Mr. and Mrs. Coblentz, he the managing editor of the San Francisco "Examiner," where we were treated to drinks and real food. The house was built in 1858 by General Swift, one of the original members of the Bear Flag party. Mrs. Coblentz had furnished it as nearly as possible with things of the period, almost all mid-Victorian: rosewood furniture, wax flowers under glass, very beruffled lampshades, and pictures of droopy ladies leaning over tombstones protected by even droopier weeping willows.

From there we called on the "Hap" Arnolds. Then to dinner with some friends nearby, where Roger distinguished himself by falling off the porch railing on which he was sitting and landing in the shrubbery 15 feet below—on his feet! No damage was done except that he lost his glasses, which were found a day or two later.

The Republic of California lasted from June 14 to July 9 when the American flag was raised in Monterey. We had been invited to go down for the Centennial, but it did not look as though we would be able to make it. A new and most unpleasant situation had developed—a strike for higher wages threatened by the city carmen. It was a wage raise that Roger could not grant them under the terms of the City Charter. We thought it might have been a move by the CIO to cloud the recall issue and prove to the "little people" that Roger had no regard for their needs. On the other hand, it might prove to be a double-barrelled gun. If the carmen struck they lost their civil service status, and risked the wrath and rage of an aroused citizenry at having all public transportation tied up.

Roger spent hours explaining his position to the unions. He talked to Clem Whittaker, who then wrote a speech for him which he delivered on radio at 11:00 Saturday morning. From the moment he went off the air my telephone started to ring. It never stopped day or night until Tuesday morning when I could stand it no longer, and changed to an unlisted phone number. We didn't even answer it after the first few calls, all of which were either denunciatory or threatening: "Your husband's going to tell the unions what he ain't goin' to do tonight, dearie? Well I hope he don't come home to you feet first—if he gets home at all."

He did speak that night, to both the CIO and AFL groups, and he did get home safely. But the men went on strike at midnight just the same. Sunday, of course, was a quiet day downtown. Monday the traffic jam was terrific. By Tuesday automobiles were parked four deep on the empty car tracks on Market Street.

Roger had been invited to address an AFL strikers' meeting on Tuesday night, and while we were at dinner an invitation came to appear at the CIO meeting afterwards. He had a respectful hearing at both meetings. He told them that, under the City Charter, he could not use his emergency powers to get them an immediate raise. But he said he would back a Charter Amendment, to be placed before the people at the November elections, granting a raise in pay, retroactive to July 1. The meeting went on a long time after he left, we heard later, until a war veteran rose and said, "Boys, I think the Mayor's an honest man and means what he says. I move we call the whole thing off." The strike was over by the next afternoon.

Thus we were able to get off for a long weekend in the Carmel Valley with our friend Mrs. Henry Russell. We were not able to leave until after dinner, so when we reached Salinas at 11:30 P.M., we still had a long drive ahead of us to get 23 miles up the Carmel Valley. But Roger stopped abruptly at a little side road, and said, "Sport, this is a wonderful short cut if it's still open. I haven't been over it for six or seven years, but let's try it." I was not over-enthusiastic—especially when I saw the name of the road, El Canyon de Los Animas Perdidas—but we took it. We climbed slowly up a mountain side with wisps of fog drifting around our heads, not a house nor a car in sight and Roger was none too sure of where he was going! As Lewis Carroll described: "The valley grew narrower and narrower still, The evening grew darker and colder." Finally I saw a light in the dim distance and shrieked "Land!" to which Roger replied: "Yes, Columbus." We did reach the Russell house by 12:30, and found her house guests waiting up to cheer us with warming drinks beside a beautiful big fire in the huge living room.

The next four days were delightfully relaxed ones—golf for Roger, swimming and sun-bathing beside the pool for me, dinner with various friends, the ceremonies and parade on Saturday and a ball that night. I had been told that everyone was to be in Spanish costume. So I unearthed a long scarlet lace dress with a high comb and a scarlet mantilla, which I had had for a former fancy dress ball, and wore it— only to find that I was one of not more than a dozen women who were in costume. A bit upsetting, but it was a becoming outfit, so I didn't care too much.

Home on Sunday, and then the last days of hectic preparation before the election on the 16th. Last meetings, last broadcasts, and for me, the planning of a supper party for 37 (City Hall, family, and, of course, the Whittakers) on election night. I had invited a young cousin from the East to join us. She was a social welfare worker, rather other-worldly, and I thought it would be a new experience for her and might do her good.

We left for Clem Whittaker's headquarters shortly after nine. By the time we got there Budde had conceded the election, and everyone could broadcast their thanks, including Mother Lapham and me. She had never done it before, but of course did it as she did everything else, marvellously. But me? All I can say is that the next day my faithful Christena said I "did real good, except for sounding so nervous."

We went on to the two newspapers and did it all over again, then repaired to 3680 Jackson Street for much needed refreshments. Gradually nearly everyone went home, Roger went to bed, and I was left with my cousin, Dora, and three men from City Hall, all of them very high. At 2 o'clock one of them said, "Mrs. L., the whisky's given out. I know where it's kept, I'll get another bottle." From me: "You haven't a prayer! I'm tired enough to die, and you can all go home." Which, like good little boys who know when they're licked, they did. Dora's horror was unbounded. "Cousin Helen," she said, "I don't believe my mother has ever told people to go home." "Then," I replied, "she hasn't dealt with as many people who don't know enough to as I have. They were all tight. I was sick of the sight of them. And it was high time they went home anyhow."

The vote for retaining the Mayor was 73,000 out of 105,742 people voting; but the absentee ballots had not been counted, and the expectation was that out of some 4800 cast, Roger would have about 4000 more. He was a bit disappointed, but I thought it just showed what 14 years of the New Deal had done to people's thinking. They now seemed to expect better transportation, better housing, more parks and all sorts of civic improvements without any increases either in carfare or taxes. "The world owes me a living," had certainly become a creed.

6

THE U. N. SITE STRUGGLE AND THE LAST YEAR AS SAN FRANCISCO'S FIRST LADY

A DAY or so later the excitement died down, and Norma and I took off again for our annual visit to Blanche Grant at Tahoe. We had a delightful ten days with plenty of bridge and mah jongg, but also time out for relaxing in between. While I was there I had a fine letter from Carol telling of her house-hunting—far more places to see than she had expected, although most of them were impossible; about the Scottish nannie she had engaged for Maria; and the ten days she and Ernst had spent in Scotland, during which it had rained eight (she said she didn't blame Mary Queen of Scots for saying "I t'ank I go home now"). She had also entertained the wives of three Scottish bankers while Ernst was talking business with their husbands, and said she reminded herself of a long-playing record. None of the three said anything but "Fancy that!" or "Quite, quite." But she must have been successful, for each of the men told Ernst the next day how charming their wives had thought his wife was.

For the first time a real lull in Civic activities during the early part of September, but we had one private celebration—a birthday dinner for Jane and me (mine on the 13th, Jane's the 14th) which Mother L. gave at Trader Vic's. We started with cocktails at Jane's, then gimlets at Trader Vic's, champagne at dinner, and Mother ate freely of the hors d'oeuvres, spareribs and fried shrimp, then had curried chicken and rice, and ended with fruit over ice-cream—not so bad for 85, especially as she slept like a child all night afterward. Nothing like that Dearborn State of Maine constitution!

The last of the month we went down to San Diego for the convention of the League of California Cities.

At the official dinner I sat next to Mayor Bowron of Los Angeles, who would look exactly like Buster Brown if he wore a sailor hat, a turned down collar and a Windsor tie. The next day we attended a cocktail party for Governor Warren in Mayor Knox's room; and then to the banquet, without which no convention would be complete. The Knoxes led off with the Governor, telling the Bowrons and us to follow them to the head table which was on a raised platform. We marched up. And then like the Good Old King of France, the four of us marched down again—there were only eight places for the supposedly official family of 12. I thought it was awfully funny, but not Buster Bowron, who swept in to the bar as pouty as he could be, and announced that as we palpably were not wanted, we would go elsewhere for dinner. He was also annoyed because he couldn't get the kind of Bourbon he wanted. While he was in the midst of telling the bartender what he thought of the whole set-up, Mrs. Bowron turned to me and made the only remark I heard her make all the evening: "Mrs. Lapham, have you got corns?" I said I hadn't, which was a boon as it gave her a chance to have something I didn't have.

Meantime, Ruby Carlson and I had been making plans for a vacation in Honolulu, and were all set to sail Friday the 27th on the "Matsonia," unless the ship was tied up by a strike. Indications were that we would sail, so we went on board, due to leave at 5:00. We didn't actually get off until 2:00 A.M., and then slipped out so quietly we didn't realize we were moving.

We were asked to sit with our friends the Jerd Sullivans. We did, managing to skip the Captain's table. The trip was really very pleasant, although slightly rolly because the ship was going out light. Ruby won $18.50 on the ship's pool the first day, so was able to play the slot machines on velvet for the rest of the trip. But her ardor didn't touch that of a friend of the Sullivans, whom everybody calley "Jonesy." He'd never been on a ship before. Complaining bitterly that there was nothing to do except play the machines, he announced that he was going to play until he hit the jackpot. He did one day. It cost him $15. He won $30 and came to lunch with his arm in a sling, sure that he had ruined it for life.

Our days were comfortably filled with swimming, touring around, being entertained by friends and friends of friends, and we enjoyed every moment of it, including a sukiyaki dinner that "Jonesy" gave at a Japanese restaurant. The guests of honor were a couple named Cobb; he had been Aide to General Emmons, and she was a dainty, charming little thing who could not have weighed over 100 lbs. But how that gal could eat! Cobb started in with 22 pieces of raw fish dipped in soya sauce, and followed it with crab salad, fried shrimps, broiled lobster stuffed with curried rice, meat, vegetables and chicken. And she kept right up with him. The two of them ended up with a second broiled lobster. Where she put it all, I will never know; we couldn't believe our eyes as she kept on and on. Toward the end, when Ruby stretched out one of her long legs—we were all sitting on the floor—I said, "For heaven's sake, Ruby, don't put your foot on the table. Mrs. Cobb will dip it in soya sauce and eat it!"

After Kona, we spent one night in Hilo, flew back to Oahu for two more days in Honolulu, and then headed for home on a Matson Company airliner captained by Ernie Gann. He had just had his first book, "Island in the Sky," accepted for the movies, had been paid $30,000, bought a house in San Francisco, and decided there was more money in writing than there was in flying. He was charming to us. And even though we were warned that we were encountering head winds, and might have to turn back before we reached the point of no return, we were not unduly alarmed; especially as the wind changed in time, and we didn't have to.

One really amusing incident had occurred the night before we left Honolulu. We were at the Alfred Castle's for cocktails (he was a classmate of Roger's), and I saw a beautiful Chinese painting on the wall. "What an exquisite painting of the Wheel of Life—Tibetan, I presume," said I, my knowledge drawn entirely from "Kim."

My host said that the experts were not quite certain. It was presumably the Wheel of Life, but it came from Jehol which was a bit far to the north for that sort of thing. Why was I so sure it was Tibetan? I murmured that a cocktail might help me to think, and disappeared as rapidly as possible when he went to get me one. The next morning Mrs. Castle wrote me a note saying that she had no idea I was a connoisseur of Chinese Art, and was sending me a delightful book to read on the plane. I opened it with horror, feeling I had gotten into very deep water, indeed. But it was a delightful novel called "Great Lady." I am sure Mrs. Castle had my number, even if her husband didn't.

I was home for five days, and then off to Hot Springs, Virginia, for the regular fall meeting of the Business Advisory Council, of which Roger was a member. Then to New York where it looked as if the question of the permanent site of the U. N. was to be opened up again. Roger wanted to be on hand to put in another plea for San Francisco. My traveling bags were so well trained by then that when I whistled, they came out of the closet and whinnied, even if they didn't sit up and beg.

The week that followed beggared description. Our rooms at the Ritz were the headquarters for everything and everybody, to the extent that I had to lock myself in the bathroom if I even wanted to change my mind. Governor Warren was in and out; so was the whole San Francisco delegation; Jack Peurifoy and Jack Ross (Senator Austin's right-hand man) as an unofficial steering committee; two influential men from Los Angeles; and the Press at all times. The Governor had a press conference at which I was allowed to sit in and pass drinks and cigarettes, if I never spoke. I sat curled up in a corner of the sofa most of the time. When Roger had a conference three days later, I was still right in my little corner, and one of the reporters said, "My God, Mrs. Lapham. Have you been there ever since Saturday afternoon?"

We entertained various delegates. A Mme. Mora from Uruguay called up and said, "You will remember me, Madame, I sat in front of you at the U. N. sessions in your Opera House last year, and you admired my hats." I did remember her, and asked her and her husband for cocktails at once, because Roger had said "The Uruguayans are doubtful—pet them!" They in turn took us for dinner at the St. Regis with the Martins from Brazil and the Belts from Cuba. They were two charming couples whom we had seen a great deal the year before. Roger turned himself loose, and out-tangoed, out-rhumbaed and out-sambaed them all. His finishing touch came when at five minutes past twelve he had our waiter hand me orchids—it was October 30th, our 39th wedding anniversary. There wasn't a dry eye in the house, the emotional Latins saying: "After 39 years! Que simpatico!"

The sessions at Lake Success started on the 5th. The first one lasted from 2:00 until 7:00, the first two hours being taken up with discussion of a motion made by the delegate from Lebanon in the floweriest possible French. The motion proposed that all the classics of all time be translated into all languages, so that the underprivileged of all nations might be able to become acquainted with the beauties of thought through the ages. The Lebanese delegate finally sat down and Gromyko arose to ask in English, "I vould like to ask thrr-ee qvestions: Vat classics? Vat languidges? Who pays?" Manuilsky from the Ukraine then asked. "Vat is a glassik?" The questions started a long and lively discussion. They spent half an hour, for instance, on whether Rabelais was "classic" and if so, just what could an Arab get out of it?

Then Senator Austin introduced an amendment to reopen the question of a permanent site. It was accepted at 7:00 with much less opposition than we had expected; it would then be placed on the agenda for acceptance or rejection by the Plenary Session on Saturday. On Saturday, unfortunately, Senator Austin had gone to the Army-Notre Dame game, leaving the amendment to be introduced and read by Sol Bloom (proving that it isn't true when they say he can't read). However, he allowed the British to add their amendment to throw the site open not only to the New York and San Francisco areas, but also to "other sites in the United States which may be offered at reasonable or no cost." Austin would have certainly side-tracked that one!

By the time of the next meeting on Tuesday, 57 cities had thrown their hats in the ring! Austin finally limited it to four areas—Boston, New York (Westchester at that time), Philadelphia and San Francisco. The voting took ages and was very tense, as none of us was sure who was for what; the South African, Bolivian and Russian delegates took up a great deal of time trying to add phrases which would have nullified the whole procedure.

At last the Indian delegate rose and said, "The Indian delegation votes for San Francisco for a reason that no one has brought up. In ho-ot countrr-ies tem-perrs are ho-ot, as I am sure my British frr-iends will agree. Differ-rent in San Fr-rancisco; it is co-ol, and our heads are co-ol to do our worrk." The amendment was passed 35-2, followed by the appointment of a sub-committee to come out and look us over. We had precious little time to prepare for them, really only three days after we got home.

We flew out the next night, arriving five hours late due to head winds and a long delay at Reno. Roger spent the next day at City Hall getting out invitations for the dinner-dance the City was giving for the sub-committee members at the San Francisco Golf Club on Friday night. Invitations were sent to all those we knew would be there, plus all the glamor-girl friends that Jane and Nancy could think of for the 22 extra men we had to do something about. Josephine Sullivan and I were to have the happy job of seating the tables.

The following day was one that might have killed anyone but my husband. He left for the airport at 8:00 A.M. to fly to Los Angeles to see W. R. Hearst. Because the Hearst papers had consistently played down San Francisco's bid for the U. N. site. The airport was fogged in so he didn't get off until 11:00. He saw W. R. at 2:30 and told him what an asset he thought the U. N. would be. When he finished, Hearst who had been listening intently said, "I don't agree with you Mr. Mayor —I think it would be a liability. But I'll keep my trap shut." Roger got back to the house at one A.M. after having left it 19 hours earlier. Fortunately the next day was Thanksgiving and he spent most of it in sleep.

The committee arrived and were shown the Presidio as a possibility.

Then there was a large cocktail party at the Pacific Union Club. Next stop was the Roth place at "Filoli" for lunch and to view it as a possible site. But as the rain was pouring down in torrents, and they discovered it was right on the San Andreas (earthquake) Fault, their enthusiasm was visibly lacking.

I spent the afternoon at City Hall with Josephine working on the seating for our party. It was a job I wouldn't have wished on my worst enemy! We had expected about 70 and had 105; the tables were for six, eight, and ten. Of course, we had no idea whether the committee members were young or old, or even what languages they spoke. Josephine had to go to a wedding at 4:30, so I drove myself out to the golf club with place cards for six extra men clutched in my little cold hand and no possible place to put them. I finally just put them all together at one table and drew a long sigh of relief. Then I realized there was no master seating chart and that the confusion would be indescribable. I made one out and started for home at 6:30—being due back at 7:30—through the pelting rain. I arrived at 3680 as close to hysterics as I had ever been in my life. Roger fed me a drink, patted me on the back, practically poured me into a hot bath, and assured me that no matter how the party went, I was not responsible!

As a matter of fact, it went very well. My six extra men were apparently all "outlanders" who wouldn't have talked to anyone but each other anyhow; all my glamor-girls spoke French, and even though a couple of them were so glamorous I am sure the visiting firemen thought they were "B" girls, they made a great hit.

I sat next to Zuleta (Colombia), the head of the committee and asked him if he preferred good English or bad French. He chose the latter. At the end of the dinner he told me pointedly that Mme Haas (his other dinner partner), *"parle mag-ni-fiquement le Francais."* I was too far gone from my efforts to care.

A few short speeches, dancing until one, then it was all over. And I agreed with Roger's secretary, Bob Letts: "For a party that was put together with spit and string in three days, it was a humdinger!" (Especially as the City Controller, who had a nice shine on, had agreed to take care of all the expenses without a single question!)

Saturday was a glorious day and in the morning the committee was driven out to inspect the Presidio again. It had appealed to them tremendously. Of course, only the President could give permission for it to be relinquished as an Army Post, but as it was no longer needed as a defense area, that was well within the bounds of possibility. That afternoon some of the committee went to the Stanford-Cal game and others to City Hall to look at maps and talk things over with Roger and various city officials. They left Sunday afternoon. Roger came home singing "Now let Thy servant depart in peace" . . . which wouldn't be very long-lasting since he told me we were off to New York again at the end of the week to play the string out.

We were back in our suite at the Ritz-Carlton by Tuesday. A most disillusioning, even mortifying, week followed—due entirely to Senator Austin's unaccountably spineless performance. We went to the long sessions at Lake Success every day. By Thursday we felt that we had a majority for the Presidio which had been made available by the Government at no cost. There had been a most insulting speech by Saksin, the principal Russian delegate. He accused Austin of lobbying, favortism, and endeavoring to coerce a decision for the Pacific Coast. In conclusion he said that if the Headquarters chose a site so far from the capitals of Europe, no self-respecting delegate would attend, and the Russians would walk out of the U. N. rather than go there! We could hardly believe our ears; the whole speech was not only a threat and an insult to Senator Austin, but to the United States as well.

Austin was the first speaker on Friday afternoon. We all sat breathless, waiting for him to blast Saksin off the map. But he never even referred to him or to his speech! He began with a lot of flowery guff about being in the position of a mother having to say which one of her children she loved best, and while San Francisco was the home of his soul (at which point I leaned over to Roger and said, "We're going to get the axe") the time had come for the United States to declare its position. The U.S. was in favor of a site on the Eastern seaboard. Disappointed as we were, we felt he must have been acting under direct orders from the President, or else there had been dirty work at the

215

crossroads somewhere along the line.

Saturday and Sunday we had time to lick our wounds. We lunched with Mrs. Lapham and dined with the head of one of the Hearst magazine publications and his wife at the Stork Club, preceded by cocktails at their Fifth Avenue maisonette. The wife, who was at least 20 years younger than her husband, looked to me as if she could step on any stage in a black lace bra and a diamond G-string. She told Roger three times that she was "just a country girl at heart." The statement, I felt, was open to doubt—especially after I saw her bedroom. The two principal pieces of furniture were a double bed (so large that all I could think of was the guide's description at Chantilly of the bed there belonging to Napoleon Third and Eugenie: *"On dirait, Madame, un veritable champ de bataille, n'est ce pas?"*) and a semi-circular dressing table with at least 75 bottles of perfume on it—about $1500 worth at a guess. I asked which was her favorite, and she said that was just her collection; the ones she used were in her bathroom.

Back to the mines on Monday. Makin, the Australian Ambassador, led off with a scorching blast at Austin for not answering Saksin. He expressed himself as amazed and bewildered by Austin's actions, and came very close to accusing him of double-dealing. Austin's reply couldn't have been weaker or more inept; all he said was that he declined to answer such accusations, or in other words was "too proud to fight." But he followed this up with a new proposition: other sites in the New York area had suddenly become available, and he proposed to postpone all decision for a year while these sites were inspected!

For a confusion of tongues, the Towel of Babel would have run a poor second to what ensued. Everyone got into the game. But the delegate from Iraq got in the best crack when he said: "Every time the distinguished delegate of the United States speaks and says he is endeavoring to help us, our confusion becomes deeper. Either he needs our help to clarify his own thinking, or something lies behind this of which we know nothing."

Austin spoke again that evening and amended his resolution to include the Boston and San Francisco areas, because the feeling against postponement was practically unanimous. But as General Romulo said with a sigh, "San Francisco is like a girl, who has grown so tall you cannot reach up to kiss her!"

I got a real compliment from one of the reporters that evening when he said "Mrs. Lapham, you are like the 'Enterprise'—a Gallant Lady —and a glutton for punishment! I've seen you here at every session. I know your presence has been a help to your husband, and all of us reporters hand it to you." I thanked him and told him I felt like Caesar and his Gallic Wars: "part of which I was, and all of which I saw."

Wednesday morning Austin took the floor at once. In a manner befitting the Marines, who had just landed and had the situation well in hand, or the 7th Cavalry repelling the attack of the wild Indians from the open spaces of San Francisco, he announced dramatically that John D. Rockefeller—that great-hearted philanthropist—was ready to present to the U. N. six square city blocks in New York City for their permanent home! Seventeen acres and the first *sine qua non* had been 36 square miles!

There was quite a bit of discussion, and then a vote to adjourn for 24 hours to inspect the site was taken and passed. We adjourned, too— to the delegates' bar. There, Secretary-General Trygve Lie came up to me and asked how I felt now, to which I replied: *"Plus ca change, plus c'est la même chose."* He was followed by Gromyko, who said, "Your 'usband is a vairy pairsistent man, Mrs. Lapham." I looked him firmly in the eye and with my best mother-of-four expression answered, "But aren't we all, Mr. Ambassador?" I think he got my message, for he said "Ya-as" rather feebly and walked away.

The final vote was taken after the 24 hours of inspection had elapsed. It was a foregone conclusion from the beginning of Austin's spread-eagle, for-the-record speech in which he thanked God for all the blessings that He and the Rockefellers (he did put God first) had seen fit to bestow on New York. He went into such paeans of praise that the "Sun" the next day suggested two possible names for the site—"Hooray-dio City" or "Socker-feller Center!" As the vote was taken, both Major Younger (Great Britain) and Zuleta paid Roger high compliments for his sportsmanship, his efforts for his city, and his dignity under defeat.

217

After it was all over we were standing outside the room receiving condolences and sympathy, when the Senator bore down on me. Knowing how I felt about him, the San Francisco delegation watched with bated breath. But I shook hands with him, smiled sweetly when he said he knew how disappointed I must be. I replied that all my husband had wanted was for the U. N. to settle where it would have the best chance of success; and that it now looked as if that success was his entire responsibility as he was the sponsor if not the author of the decision made in only 24 hours, casting aside a whole year's work of really serious consideration. And that was the last I saw of him.

On the way home, Bob Letts commented, "Well, I really feel better now that we're buried than I have for the last four days when we've just been dead."

Roger's annual message was due the last of the month. In it he advocated scrapping all the cable cars as being both obsolete and dangerous. The youngest car was 40 years old. Jim Turner said he crossed himself every time he saw one start up the Powell Street hill, and gave thanks in prayer each day that went by without an accident.

Nothing Roger had done to date aroused such a storm! He got about 1,000 letters of protest from all over the world. Obviously, the cable cars were an undeniable tourist attraction, and the local inhabitants were very sentimental about them as well. Even his daughter-in-law, Jane, objected! "Life" had just run an article about them, headed by a picture of Roger that looked as if he could bite a nail in two. When one of my friends said it was a pity they hadn't used a better picture as Roger was so photogenic, another of my dear friends said, "Oh! do you think so? Why I always think his pictures make him look even older than he really is!" Meow! P.S.: The Cable cars are still with us.

Shortly after our return we had a dinner for General Romulo, who had supported us so vigorously in New York. I greeted him in my best Spanish, *"Bien venido a nuestra casa, General Romulo."* His eyes twinkled, but he replied gravely in Spanish. Then switching to English, he amused everyone by telling them that I was the "pin-up" girl of the United Nations and he was going to get me a Filipino decoration as the winner in an endurance contest, for sitting hour after hour at Lake Success.

On a Monday a week or so later, I entertained my luncheon-bridge club of eight, which had been going on since the twenties or before. I told them there would be no bridge that day. At Roger's suggestion, I was taking them all to the Supervisors' regular Monday session at City Hall. None of them was overly enthusiastic, but they couldn't have enjoyed it more after they got there. It turned out to be a good stormy show. Roger attacked two of the Supervisors for putting their own personal and political desires ahead of what was best for the city. They stood up and yelled back at him. The ladies all thought Roger had staged it for their benefit and were simply delighted; but said that if they had ever seen those two men before, they would never have voted for them. I suggested that they might go to the meetings more often, but they seemed to think that they couldn't get in without my special influence. I explained to no avail that it was the Board which they had helped elect and they could go any Monday they wished.

Nancy and I went to another meeting a couple of weeks afterward when another controversial topic—the location of a second Bay bridge —was to be discussed. We both had our knitting and a photographer took a picture of us, unbeknownst to us. When he asked our names, we replied, "Two Mrs. Lapham's, Senior and Junior." The picture was published the next day in the sports section of the "Call-Bulletin," captioned "Knitting for the Future." It displeased Mrs. Lapham Jr. highly. She said it was bad enough to be announced as "infanticipating" in the society page, but she definitely objected to its being entered as a sporting event!

The days passed quickly with no major crises, although I did have one rather ridiculous, small experience. I tried to take two visiting friends for a drive through the Presidio and was stopped by a sentry who asked for my official papers. Needless to say, I did not have any. I gave him the slight argument that: "I've always driven through, ever since the war was over. Why can't I do it now?" But he pointed a finger at me and said "Out!" Out I went with no further ado.

A few days later Roger and I went to a tea at the Officers' Club in the Presidio given by General Hays, the Commanding General. So I asked our host if I could get a permit to drive through the Presidio. He seemed surprised, said none was necessary, and asked why? I told him of my experience. With a certain amount of embarrassment, he said two office safes had been stolen recently, and he supposed that the sentries were overdoing their orders not to admit suspicious-looking strangers! I assured him I did not have either safe. Shortly after I received an abject note of apology from the Colonel in charge of the sentries!

Early in March we went to the opening of the Tanforan race track. My dear husband, who was no race fan, habitually picked one number and played it across the board in every race. This day he picked #4. In the second race, #4 came in to win at 93-1! I lost $10 during the day, but really couldn't begrudge it under the circumstances.

Then there was St. Patrick's Day parade. I took some of the grand-children and Christena, who was fascinated but outraged by Supervisor Christopher. He rode alone in an open car, tossing out brown derby hats tastefully decorated with large green shamrocks. "That big Greek!" said she, "pretending to be Irish!" I had a chance to talk to him afterward, and said: "Why, Mr. Supervisor, I am so surprised to find that you are Greek. After seeing you throw out those hats on the 17th, I thought of course you were Irish." "And so I am," said he, "or Scandinavian or Dutch, or anything else I think will help me." I thought his comments as candid a declaration of political principle as I had ever heard.

The Policeman's Ball came as usual toward the end of April. As I was dressing in a white crepe dress with half-moons of silver spangles, and all the jewerly I thought was suitable, Roger said, "Well, my dear, this is the last time you will have to go through this." "Go through it, nothing!" I said. "When again in life will I have the chance to dress up in my best clothes, wear all the jewerly I can get on, and enter the Auditorium to music, with a police escort, and 10,000 people looking at me? Don't be silly! I adore it!"

The first week in May we flew up to Seattle to attend a meeting of the Junior Chamber of Commerce for which Roger was to make the principal address on the last night. We were there for three days, and except for the pleasure of seeing Seattle again after 16 years, neither of us enjoyed it too much. The Junior ladies were so very junior that they made me feel like everyone's great-grandmother. The hen dinner they gave with simply poisonous nonalcoholic drinks couldn't have been duller. And Roger left the men's stag party right after a strip-tease performer removed all her clothes and sat down on his lap.

Roger made the closing address at the banquet on the last night. It was not one of his best, but by that time everyone was so high that even if he had given them the silver-tongued oratory of William Jennings Bryan, no one would have appreciated it.

Shortly after our return from Seattle, I put the Atherton house on the market. It had served us well for 25 years but I had not been able to run two houses in wartime with Roger as Mayor, gasoline rationing and the servant problem. Now the fact was that nobody wanted it any longer. The Lewis Laphams had had it for one summer, and the Roger Jr.'s for another, but its usefulness was over.

So I went down to the little cottage on the place, taking Christena and Ming Lew. We spent a week clearing out the accumulation of nearly 25 years. It was hard—almost everything was of sentimental, not real value. The furniture I gave freely to any of the children who wanted it. Jane and Nancy came down, looked everything else over and said: "Give it to the rummage sale!" "Give it to the Salvation Army!" "Throw it away!"

As the week wore on, I got pretty ruthless myself and threw away things I have since regretted. One was a personal letter from Ben

Ames Williams in answer to one I had written him after reading his
"House Divided." In his book he blamed Lee for the loss of Gettysburg,
instead of Longstreet, who is generally held responsible. It was a long
reply, quoting source material, paragraph and page. But his P.S. contained the punchline: "General Longstreet was my great-uncle!"

June 6th was Christena's 30th anniversary with us, so Roger gave
her a pearl ring. I gave her a check and a dinner for her relatives and
the rest of the fine Irish girls, who had been a part of our household
over long periods of time. We were just ready to sit down, 18-strong,
when the telephone rang. Christena answered it and came back with
her eyes blazing and her "Irish" up. I asked her what it was and she
said some woman had said the flag on City Hall was at half-mast, and
had asked was the Mayor dead? When Christena said he wasn't, the
woman replied, "What a pity!" At which Christena had snapped: "And
the same to you!" and hung up. After that slight contretemps, everything passed off pleasantly.

Early in June, Roger took off in his car for parts unknown, or as
he always put it (for he had done it many times before) "to follow
front wheels." He did call his office at intervals, but it always made
me a little uneasy as we had absolutely no way of getting in touch with
him in case of an emergency. However, once he called in just in time
to hear that Juan Trippe had invited him to go on the Pre-Inaugural
Round-the-World flight of Pan-American Airways. Of course, nothing
could have appealed to him more. So he came home pronto to get his
shots, his passport renewed, and to take care of all the other details.

The flight, supposedly a stag affair of high-ranking newspaper men,
had had its complexion changed when Mrs. Ogden Reid of the New
York Herald Tribune had decided that she would be the one to accept.
So then they had decided to ask another woman and picked Mrs. Oveta
Culp Hobby, the owner of the biggest Houston newspaper. Three
mayors—Bowron of Los Angeles, Lapham of San Francisco and
O'Dwyer of New York—had also been invited. Roger was the only

one who could accept. Thus he found en route that he, as the only politico, was elected to make the principal speeches at all the various stops.

He took off on a Sunday to join the rest of the group in New York. He was to be gone just two weeks—four days in the air, and ten on the ground.

Of course, I did not hear the complete account of the trip until he got home, although the newspapers here were full of it (so much so that the head man at Pan-Am asked rather pathetically if it wasn't possible for them to mention Juan Trippe's name just once; and that is was a Pan-American flight, instead of giving the impression that it was a private jaunt of the Mayor's!). Betty Trippe flew out from New York to meet the plane on its arrival. We went down to the airport; it was scheduled to arrive at one P.M., and when it appeared 20 minutes early, coming in over the coastal hills, there wasn't a dry eye in the house! Roger and Juan stood together in the open doorway, the flags flew, the band played, and due honor was paid in the welcoming speeches to a really great achievement.

That evening Roger's mother entertained them all in the beautiful house in Burlingame she had rented for the summer. Naturally they had been feted magnificently everywhere on the whole trip; and they had all tried to pin Roger down as to the kind of a party he, the Mayor of San Francisco, was planning to give them there. His answer had always been, "Oh! I'm not going to do a thing. My Mother is going to entertain you!" General consternation—the 64-year-old, white-haired Mayor's Mother? What kind of a party would that be? The reason for doing it that way was that it was a private party; if he had given it, it would have been official and all the regular "musts" would have had to be invited.

As a matter of fact, it couldn't have been gayer or a greater success. My beloved mother-in-law was a truly "Great Lady" in every sense of the word, with the gift of real hospitality. Outside of the members of the tour, the guest list was hand-picked and everyone, who was asked, came—even one woman on crutches! Mrs. Lapham sat between Governor Warren and General Mark Clark, who was then in command at the Presidio. As she said afterwards, "I don't know who seated the tables, but I do know I had the two tallest and best looking men in the room."

Little by little—after Roger had made up his sleep—the details of the trip began to emerge. The first stop had been Shannon, where the Postmaster had welcomed them at the airport. He had said, rather belligerently, that the Irish would be found at every port they called at, and no matter where it was, they would always have an influence on politics there. Roger was asked to respond; he said he didn't have to travel around the world to know that: In his home City of San Francisco, he had a Police Commissioner, a Fire Commissioner, a Fire Chief, and two members of the Board of Supervisors—all named Sullivan!

He spoke again in London at a dinner given for them by Lord Beaverbrook. In Istanbul he was warned, by an Army General, through an interpreter, as he was handed a glass of raki: "That one drink will make you an antelope, two will make you a lion—but three will make you an ass." Roger stopped with one.

He was asked to address the Congress in Calcutta. And to his great embarrassment, as he stepped to the podium a shower of rose petals descended on his head, and then a decoration was placed about his neck. It was all gold thread and simulated jewels, terminating in a heart that hit him in such a vital spot that the minute I saw it, I christened it his Chastity Belt.

In Manila, he and Roy Howard slept in the Presidential Palace. In China, they flew up to Nanking and had an interview with Chiang Kai-Shek; and in Tokyo a long and fascinating one with General Mac-Arthur, with whom Roger was more than impressed. Engine trouble developed after leaving Wake, so they had to return to the island. They got in to Honolulu so late that they missed all the doings that had been planned for them. But not so late that Roger didn't get a swim, and a chance to try out his hula steps with some of the dancing girls.

My sister Dorothy Loomis and her husband Dana were to come out from Baltimore and visit us early in July. The day they were due to leave I had rather an upsetting experience. The telephone rang, and the operator said that Baltimore was calling, and wanted to speak to Mayor Lapham; Mrs. Lapham would not do. Of course all I could think of was that something had happened to Dorothy, and Dana was going to break it to me through Roger. So I insisted on speaking to whoever was calling. Finally a man came on, and in very blurred accents wanted to know the exact distance between Alcatraz and the Golden Gate Bridge—to settle a bet! I was so up in the air by this time that I almost hit the ceiling. Without a moment's hesitation, and knowing nothing at all about it, I said, "A mile and a half." He asked if I was sure. I said I lived here, didn't I—I certainly ought to know what I was talking about. As he was palpably very tight, I couldn't see that it made any difference if he lost his bet—in fact I hoped he would.

The Loomises arrived in due time, quite safely. Our first activity was for me to christen an American Airlines flagship. The wind at the airport was so strong that Mr. Damon, the President, had to clasp me firmly around the waist to keep me from being blown off the little platform. Between trying to hold on to a large hat, manage an armful of roses, and still have a hand free to swing the bottle of champagne, I was so confused that in the middle of saying "I christen thee Golden . . . ," I couldn't for the life of me think whether it was Gate or State! Mr. Damon muttered Gate in my ear; and I repaid him for his courtesy by taking such a mighty swing with the bottle that I almost brained him. But the bottle broke, so that particular bit of tension was over.

Then we all had a grand flight in the plane, a DC-6—up as far as Napa, down to San Jose and back at an altitude of 15,000 feet, and all in 45 minutes. No sooner had we gotten on the plane when Roger said to me "Sport, tell Mr. Damon the story of the woman who christened the ship in Seattle." I said I didn't know him well enough. But Roger said, "Go ahead." So I did with this story: A woman, who had been asked to christen a ship had asked if she might bring her 9-year-old son with her, which of course was granted. She broke the bottle, the champagne flew in all directions, and as the ship went down the ways, she raised her hand and said "God speed." Whereupon Sonny-boy said, wiping the champagne from his eyes, "He's pee-ed on me, too, Mom—my."

My brother-in-law is an architect, so of course we took him on a guided tour of the city to show him all the different types of architecture: the General Grant era houses, unfortunately not destroyed by the 1906 fire; the beautiful modern houses and apartments which are going up so rapidly; down the Lombard Street hill—"the crookedest street in the world"—and he was tremendously impressed with everything, particularly the cleanliness and "whiteness" of San Francisco—a sharp contrast to the dingy sootiness of Baltimore.

He enjoyed the weekend we spent on the Monterey Peninsula with its old adobes, the Carmel Mission, the 17-mile-drive with the sea lions barking at us from the rocks. And he couldn't get over the new picture-window type house, so functional for California, and so completely impossible for the East.

But the high point of their visit was an afternoon spent in Belvedere, where Roger was invested with the Order of the House of Orange-Nassau, with the rank of Commander. After cocktails on the patio of Mr. van Woerden, the Dutch Consul-General's house, we all went indoors. Mr. van Woerden stood on one side of the large living room, the guests lined up on the other, and he made an excellent speech explaining why the honor was being conferred on the eight recipients. Roger's was for "Unexampled services to the Dutch Government during the War." I was a bit baffled, wondering what he had done and kept from me all those years, but he looked equally baffled. After the reception was over, we could think of nothing except the reception the City had given for Princess Juliana.

Roger was the only Commander, a rank I understood was conferred only on Ambassadors as a rule; the next was dubbed an Official, there were several Knights, and the rest were Orders of Merit. Mr. van Woerden was so serious and impressive as he tied the blue and orange ribbon with the lovely blue and gold enamel star around Roger's neck, that I choked up. I couldn't but feel it was a great honor, and one not lightly bestowed.

226

We had all been given champagne glasses to hold, and after the ceremony they were filled. Mr. van Woerden proposed a toast to the President of the United States; Roger responded with one to the health of the Queen of The Netherlands. We all drank in complete silence. In spite of the solemnity of the occasion, all I could think of was the little boy who was asked to correct the sentence "The toast was drunk in silense," and his correction was "The toast was eaten in silense."

Nancy's second son was born July 23rd, with husband and both grandmothers in attendance. He weighed 8 lbs. 9 oz., was a better looking baby than the other had been, and was named Nicholas Scott Lapham. My Chinese cook Ming Lew thought little or nothing of the name. He said "Twenty year flom now no one know who is Nicky Lapham; should name him Loger T'lee, then evelyone say 'Sure— him Mayor's glandson.'"

Several amusing incidents occurred about this time. One was a tea party given by the Ladies' Auxiliary to the Merchant Marine which Roger seemed to think I should attend. I did, but I not only did not know a soul, but I didn't even have a match to light my cigarette. I saw a woman lighting hers, so I stepped up to her and said, "I am Mrs. Roger Lapham, the Mayor's wife, and I wonder if you could give me a light?" "*Certainly not!*" she snapped. "I am Mayor Rossi's daughter!" I said, "Well, how do you do, just the same," and passed on. But considering that Roger had been Mayor for nearly four years and that her father, the former Mayor Rossi, was dead, I thought her attitude was a bit far-fetched, even if Roger had won the election over Rossi.

On my way home I saw a little elderly lady standing on Jackson Street, palpably waiting for a bus—and busses, alas, in those days were few and far between. It was a hot day, she was leaning on a cane, so I drove up to the curb and asked if I could give her a lift. She seemed completely taken aback, hemmed and hawed, said she'd never done such a thing before, but finally got in. As I dropped her at her house, she asked if she might know to whom she was indebted for the kindness. With a smile which was really a simper, I said, "To your Mayor's wife." To which she replied, "Thank you so much, dear Mrs. Rossi!" And my chest went down like a deflated balloon.

I got a note from her the next day saying that her husband knew Roger (I had broken down and told her who I was), and he was ashamed of her for being so stupid. But she had never gotten into a stranger's car before, and was a bit nervous about it, until one look at my sweet, kindly face had shown her I meant her no harm. So would I wave ceremony, and come to tea that day? I went—in between the ceremonies for the arrival of the first war dead at the Marina in the morning, and "Pelleas and Melisande" in the evening.

October 30th was to be our 40th wedding anniversary, and we were planning to give our first private party in four years. The invitations were sent out for a dinner dance at the San Francisco Golf Club. I had a beautiful new white satin brocade dress made for the occasion, and was really getting pretty excited about it as the acceptances began coming in. It was to be on a Saturday night; the Monday before Roger came home and asked if he had told me we were to go to the Fireman's Ball that Saturday! I said flatly that I wouldn't go. I didn't intend to trail my brand new white dress across the dirty floor of the Auditorium. I'd been for three years. We were giving our own party, and that was *that!* He said everything was arranged—we would make the grand entree into the Auditorium on the dot of eight, go to our box, and the minute the spotlight was off us, we would slip out the side entrance, and be at the Golf Club in 15 minutes. So I had to agree.

Everything went according to schedule. The Lewis Laphams and the Roger Jrs. had been receiving for us, and as far as I could see, no one had even noticed we weren't there! When all the guests were assembled (about 185) C. O. G. Miller presented us with the gift all our friends had joined together to give us: a most beautiful and complete set of ruby Venetian glass—a lovely centerpiece for the table, two exquisite figurines, and 18 of every possible kind of glass imaginable. Chris Miller made a truly heart-warming presentation speech. Roger replied briefly, and then as usual said his wife would take over. I was pretty *emotionée,* but found enough voice to thank them all, and then said I wanted to tell them what had happened earlier at the Auditorium. That just as we started to leave, a young Frenchman in the next box had touched my arm, and said, "But Madame, you have just come. Why do you leave so early?" I explained that we were celebrating our Ruby Anniversary, had guests awaiting us elsewhere, and had to go. He asked me what it was, the R-ruby Anniversary? So putting my hand on Roger's shoulder, I said, "Why it means that this dear man and I have lived together for 40 years." A great light dawned, and with a beaming smile, he exclaimed: "Ah! ... And so now tonight you marry!"

It was a story I had heard so many years ago, that I expected at most a polite ripple of mirth, instead of which I got an absolute roar. And to my intense surprise, practically everyone believed it! One of our guests, André de Limur, came up and said he knew it was true, as that was precisely the way a Frenchman's mind would have worked; and what was his name, he would like to meet him! Even Roger said I told it so convincingly that he himself would have believed it, if he hadn't known I wasn't at the ball long enough to speak to a soul.

The party went like a breeze, with people coming from all over, even our dear friends "Cap" and Ruth Rieber from New York; he bringing Roger a paid of gold cuff-links with tiny rubies in them, and me a gold compact. He said that while he knew that gold was for the 50th, he might not be around by then. (Incidentally he was, and came out for that one too.)

Seating the tables, which were in two rooms, had presented a certain amount of difficulty. There were several divorced and remarried couples whom I had invited to help "Roger and Helen Lapham celebrate the 40th Anniversary of their Double Parking" as our invitations had read. I didn't like to put them in the same room on account of their possible embarrassment. I needn't have worried, though—four of them came up to say goodnight to me arm-in-arm, happy as clams at high tide, and apparently entirely unconscious of having swapped horses in midstream.

Election night the next week was another happy occasion, because all the bond issues, $87,000,000 worth of them, carried by big margins of from 2½-1 to 4½-1. This was unparalleled in the history of San Francisco, and due mostly, I was sure, to the peoples' belief in Roger's integrity. The retention of the cable cars was a foregone conclusion, a triumph of sentiment over cold fact; Robinson was elected mayor as everyone expected; and I had only two more months to go as First Lady of San Francisco.

We dined with some friends that night, and among their guests was Sir Winston Churchill's son, Randolph, who said he had never seen a voting machine and would like to if it would be possible. Our voting booth was only a block away, so Roger took him down there just before the polls closed at eight. Only one man was waiting to vote. Roger introduced Churchill to everyone and the man cordially invited him to step into the booth with him, which, with no objections from anyone, he did. There must have been at least 20 State and City propositions to vote on. Randy emerged mopping his brow, and saying that the American voter must be frightfully intelligent; he had read all 20, and hadn't the vaguest notion what any one of them was about.

After dinner and the tour of the newspaper offices, a small group came back to our house. As he entered our really beautiful panelled living room, Churchill said, "I say! The City of San Francisco does well by its mayor, doesn't it?" "City of San Francisco, my eye!" said Roger. "This is our house, and we have lived in it since 1929."

The next occasion was a large Smith College tea which I had wished on me. It was to start at 3:30 P.M. and continue, with no speaker and no sort of entertainment arranged, until it was time to eat at 5:00. I could think of nothing duller so I suggested having a fashion show of dresses which I would provide, modeled by the younger members of the group. I must possess the instincts of a pack-rat, for I had saved one good dress of each period since I had been married—in addition to a few treasures from the college years. I had found them all when clearing out my mother's house.

It was really a great success. The clothes ranged from the ubiquitous golf cape and skirt of 1901-1905, through a beautiful Worth evening dress of the early twenties, to the atrocious long-waisted, extremely short-skirted fashion of the early thirties. And there were hats to go with all of them. There is a small platform with an overhead light at the entrance to our living room which made a wonderful stage. One of the girls played popular tunes of the different periods on the piano. I had a photographer on hand, and the afternoon couldn't have passed more quickly or pleasantly. One of the women said, "How did our husbands ever put up with us when we looked like that?" I answered that it was because they had no choice—everyone looked the same!

Mother Lapham had been renting an apartment in town for several months. But after seeing a "dream house" in Burlingame she suddenly made up her mind that she would buy it, sell her apartment in New York, and take up permanent residence in California. Her lawyer was a bit perturbed by the speed of her decision—she saw the house on a Thursday, put down a deposit on Friday, and signed the papers on Saturday, as he said "without even knowing if the roof leaked!" He called Roger about it. But Roger said there were at least two things his mother knew—her own mind, and houses. And he was so right. She had lived in 26 at one time or another. But she did ask Roger if he thought it was foolish of her to do it at 86. She named her new house "Trail's End" and lived in it until her death ten years later.

Sunday the 4th we had a reception at the house to introduce the consular corps to Mayor and Mrs. Robinson. To say "introduce" is an exaggeration. As hard as I tried, standing next to Mayor Robinson, before I could get the name out of my mouth, his hand was outstretched, and he was announcing "The name is Robinson!" Mrs. R. arrived in a silver lamé outfit, and a hat like a Greek Orthodox Bishop's, with a silver flowered veil hanging almost to her waist. The Park Commission had supplied us with flowers for the last time. The rooms looked lovely, and although there were probably about 90 here at one time, they never seemed overcrowded. There was always room for me to corral one of the Latins and practice my Spanish on him!

The following Monday was the meeting of the Board of Supervisors at which Roger was to present his last report. Mother and I went, of course, but I was totally unprepared for one of the real thrills of my life.

The first business before the Board was a eulogy of Jesse Colman, who was retiring after 25 years of service. Then came Roger's very well-delivered and meaty message, followed by a fine eulogy of him. And then Jesse Colman said, "I have one more resolution to offer, Mr. President, if it may please the Board." It was sent up to the clerk's desk to be read, and the next thing I heard was:

"WHEREAS Mrs. Helen A. Lapham had added dignity and honor to the position of First Lady of San Francisco, WHEREAS the gracious presence of Mrs. Helen A. Lapham has won for her the staunch friendship and avowed admiration and respect of all those who have been fortunate enough to know her; now therefore be it resolved (etc.) . . . that a suitably engrossed copy of this resolution be perpared for presentation to Mrs. Helen A. Lapham."

It was passed unanimously.

By this time I was weeping copiously. The President of the Board said "Is Mrs. Helen A. Lapham present?" And a chorus of voices said "Yes!" He asked me to come up to the rostrum. My eyes were so red, my handkerchief so wet, and my knees so trembly, I didn't think I was going to make it. Then one of the Board members suggested that they suspend the rules, and hear a few words from Mrs. Lapham. Emotional as I was, I managed to say how surprised and overcome I was by the great compliment that had just been paid me, that my four years as First Lady had been very happy ones, and that I was indeed proud to have had even a small share in my husband's task of working for the City we both loved so deeply.

Then Mother Lapham was asked to come to the rostrum. Lewis, who was sitting in the back of the room, told me afterwards that by this time there wasn't a woman who wasn't mopping her eyes freely.

We stayed for half an hour, then shook hands with everyone in sight and departed—having completely disrupted all the proceedings of the Board for the afternoon.

Thursday the 8th, Mother and I met Roger in the Mayor's office (still his for the next half hour) to be on hand for Robinson's inauguration. Mrs. Robinson arrived wearing the thickest black veil over her face I had even seen. I promptly advised her to take it off so people could see her pretty, if somewhat fat, face. She said she couldn't possibly do so, as she had slipped in the bathtub and had a terrible black eye (a variant of "I ran into a door in the dark" which I had never heard before). I told her it didn't make any difference—she could powder it, and she would be on a platform above and away from the crowd. But she simply had to take off that veil; she looked as if she were in heavy mourning, and it wouldn't make a hit. So she acceded and no one even noticed the black eye. Robinson was inaugurated with the usual ceremonies. And we were free to be ourselves for the first time in four years.

There were some fine editorials written about Roger's term in office: what an honest administration he had given the City; how hard he had worked (at his office by seven every morning, instead of the customary ten o'clock appearance of his predecessor); how much he had accomplished in the passage of the enormous bond issues; and general regret that he had refused to run for a second term.

7

HOLIDAY INTERLUDES—
MEXICO AND EUROPE

A FEW days later Roger went East to attend a Harvard Overseers meeting, and to take care of some business in New York. He told me that on his return he planned to disappear again for a while, and "follow front wheels" in any direction they happened to turn. It seemed a good time for me to take off, too. Ruby Carlson and I decided to go to Guaymas for two weeks. We had talked rather indefinitely about going somewhere, but were still undecided when an advertisement came in from the Hotel Playa de Cortes, where Roger and I had stayed nine years before. That settled it and we made our reservations. Only then did we find that it took quite a bit of doing to get there—a tourist card for entrance into Mexico, a vaccination certificate for re-entrance into the USA, a flight to San Diego, taxi to Tijuana where we had to spend the night, and an early morning departure by Reforma Airlines to Guaymas.

The hotel was just as attractive as I remembered it and Mrs. Tanner, the manager, still a most cordial hostess. It was a quiet place, and though too cold to swim, the weather was perfect for sitting out of doors in the sun and relaxing.

We had been in Guaymas only a few days when a man came up to us at dinner one evening, and said, "Well Mrs. Lapham and Miss Carlson! This is a far cry from Honolulu, isn't it?" Sure enough, he was someone we had met there the year before. He invited us to come over after dinner and have a drink with him and his wife. He turned out to be a real friend, as he introduced us to a nice young crowd who took us right in with them from then on. One of the friends was a man from San Francisco named George Knoll; another was Gil Kuhn, half-German, half-Mexican, born and raised in San Diego, a former Lt.-Colonel in the Air Force, and at that time with a shrimp importing company in San Diego. We spent the better half of our evenings with them drinking Scotch at $1.25 per drink as long as our money held out—with only half a jigger of Scotch in each drink, no amount of it could affect you. Gil had a fund of slightly off-color but very amusing stories with which he regaled us. And Ruby always heightened the effect by looking at him round-eyed, and saying, "I don't get it!" He never explained.

The next two months seemed calm. And Roger had promised to take me to Europe to spend ten days or so in London where Ernst and Carol were living—Ernst was the Foreign Representative of the Bank of Manhattan—and then to tour the Continent with them for a month while he was making his annual business calls.

We left San Francisco in April to attend a Business Advisory Council meeting in White Sulphur, Virginia. I was deliriously happy at the thought of what lay before us. How little did I know what the day would bring forth! It was the second day, to be exact. Paul Hoffman, who had just been appointed head of the newly created agency, the Economic Co-operation Administration (an off-shoot of the Marshall Plan), came up to Roger, took him by the arm, and said "Roger, I want you on my team." "Don't talk to me about it now," said Roger. "I'm enjoying myself, I don't want to think. But I'll be in Washington on Monday, and I'll see you then."

Monday, he did see Paul, and Averell Harriman, and came back to the Carlton to report that he had been appointed the first chief of one of the Economic Missions, either to London or to China. London! With Carol there—what could be more marvellous!

Tuesday, I went to a cocktail party alone, after Roger had telephoned and said he would join me later. He did, shoved a highball into my hand, and said "Sit down. It's China." And to this day I am still ashamed of my behavior, for I nearly wept. No London, no tour of the Continent; just Shanghai, in midsummer. But the skies brightened for me a bit when I heard the whole story. He would fly to England

235

with me, spend a week there, fly back to Washington for briefing, and to China early in June. I could take my trip with the children, and join him in Shanghai in August when the worst of the heat would be over.

So we flew to London a few days later, and stayed at Claridge's while he was there. When he left I moved into Carol's charming house in Upper Cheney Row, Chelsea.

We had a real contretemps on our arrival at Claridge's. We had taken a taxi from the airport but had no English money to tip the driver. Roger rushed into the hotel to get some, but was told that he would have to show his passport and register first. He was given a form to fill out as long as your arm. So without waiting for formalities, he tore out again, borrowed a couple of shillings from the chasseur, looked the luggage over hastily, decided it was all there, and the taxi drove off. Then I discovered his one and only bag was missing, and he was left without so much as a clean handkerchief to his name! The chasseur, risking his life in traffic, managed to get the license number of the car. The hotel management telephoned the airport, and assured us that all would be well—a sentiment which I felt was very much open to doubt, considering the scarcity of coupons and the high price of men's clothing in England.

When we returned from cocktails with Carol, there was the bag! It had been beautifully unpacked, and dinner clothes laid out. A hovering valet informed us with an apologetic cough, that unless the gentleman was "properly" dressed, we would not be permitted in the main dining room, but would have to eat behind a curtain with the hoi-polloi. (He couldn't possibly have meant other Americans. Or could he?)

The next day, Sunday, we drove down to Harrow to see Carol and Ernst's eldest son Pat, aged 14. He was dressed in the traditional formal attire. As all clothing was rationed and so scarce you couldn't buy it even if you had the coupons, which you generally didn't, the incoming Harrovians rented from the outgoing ones the garments which came closest to fitting them. Pat's coat sleeves were too short, the trousers well above the ankle, the wing collar too large, and the black string tie had certainly been through the wars! Ernst said he looked like a third-class Italian waiter, of which he seemed to be completely unconscious. In fact he was very self-possessed, and even knew what to do with his hands.

He said he hated Harrow, and after I had seen his room I wasn't surprised. It was smaller and grimmer than the only prison cell I had ever seen. Aside from that, during the really dreadful winter, all the pipes had frozen, and there had been no hot water for a couple of weeks. When they had finally thawed out, a notice had been posted that baths would be available that Saturday night. There was only one bathtub to a floor, and poor Pat, unaware of the facts of life, had no idea that everyone bathed in turn in the one tub of hot water. So he was the last one in, and was sure he was dirtier when he got out than when he went in. The other reason for his hatred was that the matron charged them tuppence for a trunk call to London, whereas you could get it at the corner box for a penny-ha'penny!

A day or so later we ordered a hire-car to drive down to see 12-year-old Ernie at his school, Forest Row, in the south of England. Much to our surprise, the doorman ushered us into a 1948 Packard limousine. But we stepped in gaily and had a fine day with Ernie. On our return, Roger said, as he tipped the driver, "Just charge it to Claridge's." The driver said rather reproachfully, "There's no charge, sir, for an American Embassy car . . . my God, sir! Ain't you Ambassador Garrett? I'll lose my job for sure if you ain't."

Doubled up with laughter, Roger had to admit that he wasn't, but that he knew the Ambassador and would straighten it out with him in the morning. He did, and George Garrett called him every name in the book, from just a plain robber to a no-good-horse-thief; but finally told him he had gotten square with him, for he had taken the hire-car, and charged it to Roger!

When I moved in with Carol after Roger left, I started exploring London by bus. I had not been there since 1919, and the changes, of course, beggared description. The bomb damage had been cleared away, leaving many empty areas, some of them all to the good, such as the space around St. Paul's, which you could really see for the first time in all of its beautiful perspective. But the thing that impressed me most was the enormous number of five- and six-story vacant houses; all had a sign "To be let" on them. Carol told me there were two reasons for this. One, although the exterior might look undamaged, the cost of repairing the interior would be far beyond the ten pounds allowed by the Government; and two, because servants, who would carry up coals and hot water and then sleep in an unheated garret at ten or fifteen pounds a year, were no longer procurable.

Food was in short supply, strictly rationed and very expensive. You were not permitted to shop around, but had to trade only with the shops in the district in which you were registered. Even there they had to get used to you before they were willing to sell you anything. It took Carol a month before her butcher would sell her a bit of meat! Except for Harrod's, I thought the unsanitary conditions under which everything was sold were simply appalling. There was no refrigeration, and everything was covered with flies. But the British still clung to their traditions, and didn't approve of "mucking about with all that plumbing."

I had another amusing example of clinging to traditions when I saw a small piece of pink and white flannel in a draper's window. It was just what I wanted to trim a baby wrapper with. I went it to buy it, but the clerk said he was so sorry, but it was an "oddment," and they didn't sell "oddments." Translating this to a "remnant," I asked what was done with them? He really couldn't say, Madame. In spite of the fact that I should have known it wasn't done, I persisted. If I wanted it, and he didn't, why couldn't I buy it? As if speaking to a moronic child, he repeated in a slightly louder tone of voice, that "They did not sell oddments." I suggested that he consult some superior. He disappeared most reluctantly and returned with a small, neatly wrapped package. I thanked him and asked how much I owed him. To which he made his final, triumphant reply: "Nothing, Madame. As I believe I have mentioned before, we do not sell oddments!"

A good story I heard one day was somewhat along those same lines. A constable went to see Churchill about a Peer who had been charged with conduct unbecoming to a gentleman with a WAAC on a bench in Hyde Park; this was the reported interview:

CHURCHILL: You say Lord _____ was 60?

Constable: Yes, M'Lord.

CHURCHILL: You say the WAAC was 20?

Constable: Yes. M'Lord.

CHURCHILL: You say the temperature was 40?

Constable: Yes, M'Lord.

CHURCHILL: By Jove—makes one proud to be an Englishman, doesn't it?

My morning's chief occupation was reading the "London Times," of which a devoured every word, except the reports of the cricket matches. I allowed myself an hour a day on the crossword puzzles, and never finished one, but the Personals and the Society News were my special delights. The account of a very, very stylish wedding in St. Margaret's is tops in my book: "The bridegroom was Lord _____ aged 70, the bride Lady Moira _____, one of the season's debutantes, aged 18. The bridesmaids were all The Honorable Lady So-and-So. And . . . the wedding gifts were unusually tasteful and numerous, including a silver tea service from Their Majesties. The bridegroom's gift to the bride was an antique pendant. . . ." Interpret that any way you like.

Paris was lovely as always, but seemed a little *triste* to me, partly because of the weather, as it rained off and on during the four days we were there. But mostly I think because it was so quiet—so little motor traffic, and so few of the funny old taxis with their cheerful honking horns. We did get out to Versailles one day between showers —and saw the gardens only; the palace was closed for repairs—and to St. Germain for lunch another. Carol joined us as planned, and we left the next day for Brussels, spending one night there, and simply gorging ourselves on the delectable pastries. Rising above the scorn of my children, I bought a plentiful supply to take with us on our trip. And no one ate more of them than they did. One piece was left by the end of the second day, and they insisted that, like Gaul, it should be divided into three parts.

The next night we spent in a clean but rather grim little inn in Holland, as close to the German border as we could get, in order to make an early start on our 300-mile drive through the British-Occupied Zone of Germany the next day. All sorts of permits had to be procured. You had to be in and out between 6 A.M. and 6 P.M., and carry extra gas, food, and anything else you might need with you, as you were not allowed to buy anything.

Our route took us through Bremen, Hamburg and Kiel. The results of the pinpoint bombing of those cities was incredible—both what had been destroyed (all docks, military installations, etc.) and what had been left standing in the residential areas. The streets had been cleared and mountains of rubble were piled high at the sides. But many buildings had been eviscerated and still had pipes, girders, and dingy curtains hanging out of them; a really worse sight, to me, than the areas of total destruction.

It was an intensely interesting day, but a very depressing one to me. The country looked so much more flourishing, the people so much better dressed, and the children so much healthier and huskier than they were in England. And what masses of them there were; all dressed in their best—it was a Sunday—with white smocked silk dresses and white shoes (looted from Paris, according to Ernst). It got me down when I thought of the underfed children and the barely-decent poverty in which they lived in England.

The fields were filled with fat cattle and fine looking horses. The roads were filled with hundreds of bicycles. It gave one the feeling that the people were just as cocky as ever, with absolutely no awareness of defeat. We had an instance of this during the day. We had pulled off the main road to eat our picnic lunch in a small grove. The car happened to be parked across a narrow footpath. When a German couple rode up on bicycles and had to detour, they not only glared at us, but spit out some evidently most insulting remarks, never dreaming

240

that they could be understood by Americans. Ernst, who is bilingual, was on his feet in one bound and the German remarks he spat back must have been even pithier, for they pedalled away at top speed.

We reached the Danish border just before six, and were directed to a charming summer hotel on a nearby lake. At least it must have been charming in summer, but it blew a gale and poured in torrents all night. I spent the whole night trying to cope with my *plumeau,* a down comforter firmly buttoned into a linen sheet. If you wrapped it around you, you smothered. If you didn't, it slid off onto the floor. So I spent my time trying to keep my chin warm with my knees and felt like the woman who had a band of fur around the hem of her nightgown to keep her neck warm.

We arrived in Copenhagen at four, after a pleasant day's drive through rich farming country, plus an hour and a half trip by ferry. Denmark looked spotlessly clean and tidy to us after the untidy, rambling villages of France and Belgium. It was remarkable to note how the architecture, animals, and even flowers changed from country to country. I never saw such rhododendrons anywhere as there were in Holland where they grow wild for mile after mile, all purplish-pink —my least favorite color—and the combination of masses of them against red brick houses with orange-tiled roofs set my teeth on edge. All the cows in Germany had been Holsteins, but in Denmark your first remark was "How now, brown cow?" for every single cow was dark brown instead of black and white.

We found Copenhagen a delightful city, and the Hotel d' Angleterre very comfortable (especially after I got a sheet and blanket instead of a *plumeau*). But the service was rather surly and grudging, possibly a hangover from the German occupation. We explored the Tivoli Gardens, which had everything from excellent restaurants to amusing sideshows and the best was a one-ring indoor circus, which we chose in lieu of a symphony concert. We attended some dinners given us by Ernst's banking associates—and what a different impression of a city it always gives one to be entertained in private homes.

On our last day we made a trip to Frederiksborg Castle, which Ernst said was a "must." Little did we know what he had let us in for! The castle had 67 rooms dedicated to the history of Denmark from prehistoric times. We lasted through the 15th century and then tried to get out, but not a prayer! Firmly shooed onward and upward by Danish-only-speaking guards, by the time we caught up with the 20th century on the fifth floor, I felt like a doomed soul sentenced to wander through endless rooms and corridors for all eternity. We emerged exhausted, really too tired to battle Ernst's insistence that we then see Elsinore. But our luck was in. We got there too late to enter, and too early to see the Ghost of Hamlet's father.

The next day we left for Sweden, a ferry trip of about two hours across the Cattegat to Malmö, and there we ran into trouble. All sorts of officials surrounded us at once demanding every possible kind of paper in connection with the car because Ernst had lost his "GB" license plate. He was told to buy a new one on the spot (10 kroner) and to take out insurance against killing Swedes (6 kroner). What with the language barrier—even German didn't avail—Ernst was finally taken into the police station. He was there so long we were sure he had been taken into protective custody, especially as after half an hour a very large and important official appeared and was ushered in. Of course, aside from everything else, we had no Swedish money and Danish kroner were not acceptable.

At last Ernst emerged, shaking hands with everyone. The Big Boy climbed into our car, tried to talk to us in some language but finally just pointed to his car ahead and said with a beaming smile "Going my way?" But we were all set; Ernst had been provided with all the necessary permits, Swedish money and gas and food coupons.

Malmö was a gay, charming little town of many canals. Carol and I took a boat tour that afternoon, accompanied by a band which played "Hard Luck for Poor Old Eli," which did seem odd, especially when followed by "Way Down Upon the Swanee River!" Perhaps it was in honor of two visiting Americans.

We drove on to Götenberg the next day and were sorry we hadn't stayed on in Malmö for the weekend. Götenberg was rather a drab city, and the Grand Hotel grander in name than in actuality. It was the pottie-under-the-bed variety with only one bath and three toilets to a floor and all of them constantly in use with a long queue outside.

Monday morning we were to separate, Ernst motoring to Stockholm by himself, while Carol and I were to get there by a three-day trip on the Göta Canal. We left the hotel in plenty of time, but nearly missed our boat as we had been misdirected. It took the fifth man we asked to understand our pronunciation and say with a bright light dawning, "Ah! Götakanal!" and point right around the corner.

Very shortly after we got under way, a most attractive young American came up and said, "Mrs. Lapham, I am Fred Murphy of San Francisco and I met you in Paris. Do you remember me?" I did, and from then on he was with us a good part of the time on the trip, and certainly made it much pleasanter for both of us. Out tablemates at meals were two distinctly middle-class English couples, which meant we never spoke for the first 24 hours. But after they had gotten used to our faces, they were friendly enough, although we never did know their names. But for that matter, they may not have known ours; we were down on the passenger list as Latham and Othuls, so perhaps there isn't any "P" in Swedish.

Ernst met us on our arrival in Stockholm, and drove us out to Saltsjöbaden, a delightful hotel about 12 miles out in the middle of a pine forest and on a fiord. He took the tram to town every day, leaving us the car, so we were able to follow in our own good time, and sightsee to our hearts' content. The high point to us was the Town Hall, the most magnificent piece of modern architecture I had even seen. We spent over an hour going through it, much to our guide's delight, as he said he had shown it to two American ladies the day before, who had "done" it in 11 minutes flat! One room had huge murals with scenes from all over the world, including mining in California. I said "Oh! Car, look at the little burro!" At which the guide beamed and said, "Ah! the ladies are from California; all the other ladies call it a donkey."

Ernst rented a sailboat one day, and we sailed all around the fiord. And what was the first sight that greeted our astonished eyes? Mixed bathing in the nude! True, a low wire fence separated the sexes, but it was the only sop to propriety, as the visibility was 100%, even from our boat. All of us were too staggered to speak until Ernst finally found his voice and said, "Well! Now I've seen everything!"—a very pertinent comment under the circumstances.

Ernst finished his business in Stockholm sooner than he expected, so we had two nights en route to Oslo instead of one. We spent them at a charming hotel in Karlstad, Sweden. It poured in torrents all during the first day's drive. But the next day was sunny, and almost warm, so we drove 50 miles into the country for lunch at a little place called Sunne, visiting Selma Lagerlof's house on the way back. She still commands the greatest love and reverence, and her house is treated as a shrine. Ernst rushed through it in two ticks, and signed the visitors book as proof. He then betook himself to the garden and ordered something called a Godsaker because the name intrigued him, only to find out it was nothing but an Eskimo pie.

Just across the border, we came close to our first accident. In those days you drove to the left in Sweden and to the right in Norway, which we had not been told. So we were tooling gaily along on the left when we saw a car headed straight for us. Ernst pulled over as far as he could. Fortunately for us the oncoming driver recognized the situation, stopped, got out, and called our attention to a huge sign right overhead which explained the Norwegian rules of the road in several languages.

The Grand Hotel in Oslo had to be seen to be believed. It was something right out of a mid-Victorian photograph album: all the furniture heavy, dark carved wood upholstered in red plush; every woolen table cover embroidered in bright colors and fringed; and every lampshade dripping with beads. The only thing I missed were wax flowers under glass.

There was also a most remarkable inter-com telephone system. I was trying to get Carol, for which I dialed 101 to get 401—I wouldn't know why. A man's very Swedish voice said, "No, this is not 410, this is 201; but I am all alone and have two beds. Why don't you come down and join me?" Even though I thought it might be Ernst being playful, I decided not to take a chance, so I laughed and said I couldn't, I was too busy. He said I had a charming voice and that he was tall ... so I finished: " ... and blonde and handsome, I am sure." He replied: "Well, as a matter of fact, I am! How did you know it? What nationality are you?" Putting on my best accent, I said, "I ban Svede." At which he said, "Not really? Why I'm a Scandinavian too. Think it over!" ... and hung up. Whereupon I walked down to Carol's room. It seemed safer.

Carol and I did quite a bit of sightseeing: an Old Viking ship which had been unearthed some years ago in a remarkable state of preservation; the ultra-modernistic, enormous, amorphous statuary in the big park; and the site of the most famous ski-jump in Norway. We went to one movie, "Murder, My Sweet." American movies in foreign countries always make me shudder, as I am sure people take them as a serious representation of our way of life instead of Hollywood bunk.

We left the car in Oslo to be sent back to the Continent by boat and flew to London. It was really a most unpleasant flight as it was bumpy all the way. Then we had to circle over London for a long time as it had been terribly foggy and many planes were stacked up overhead. I didn't realize we were circling until I said to Ernst that cricket was certainly the national game, as I had seen eleven matches in progress below us in the last half hour. He burst out laughing and agreed but pointed out that we had been circling and I had seen the same game eleven times!

I went back to Claridge's for the few days I had left in London. Ambassador Douglas' Garden Party on the 4th of July was the high point. There must have been at least 3,000 guests, milling in and out under a huge marquee on the lawn of the Embassy residence. Unfortunately, the refreshments consisted of rather revolting fish-paste sandwiches and lukewarm drinks. Even though it looked as if it might pour rain at any minute, all the Britishers were dressed in their best. They must have been very natty in the reign of Edward VII—all the women's skirts down to the ankles, and generally dragging a bit in the rear, ostrich feather hats, feather boas, and sealskin coats—simply unbelievable.

245

I sailed on the "Queen Elizabeth" from Southhampton, and arrived in New York on a boiling hot day. I was met by Dorothy and Dana, and Lewis and Jane. One of my bags was lost—it took two hours to locate it—and then I had a horrid time with the Customs Inspector who was not only disagreeable, but positively insulting. He looked over my declaration which was under the $400 limit, then said, "Well how much are you wearing that you haven't declared?" I said, "Nothing. I have declared everything I have bought with the price I paid for it." He then ordered me to open all three of my bags and take everything out of them. He questioned a hat I had bought in San Francisco, insisting that I knew as well as he did that it came from Paris. He finally passed me, grudgingly. I couldn't imagine why he acted as he did. I had never traveled with less impedimenta, nor made a more completely honest declaration. The woman who stood next to me had five trunks, and her Inspector made her open only one, and pull out one drawer. All I could think of was that the name "Lapham" rang a bell in his mind connected with the waterfront troubles here, and he was determined to get even with at least one of the hateful family!

I had three days in New York, and then a peaceful trip home by train, which I needed, in preparation for the work that lay ahead of me in getting ready to take off for China in August.

As Mayor of San Francisco in 1944-48, Roger Lapham was hailed nationwide by the press for attaining new highs in vigor and honesty for metropolitan government of the period. This Time Magazine cover story was typical of many feature articles lauding him in major publications of the era.

TIME

THE WEEKLY NEWSMAGAZINE

SAN FRANCISCO'S MAYOR LAPHAM
In his cosmopolis, fog, cable cars and amiability.

FINAL ELECTION EXTRA

San Francisco Chronicle
The City's Only Home-Owned Newspaper

FOUNDED 1865—VOL. CLVII., NO. 111   CCCCAAAB   SAN FRANCISCO, WEDNESDAY, NOVEMBER 3, 1943   ⬥ DAILY 5 CENTS, SUNDAY 15 CENTS; PER MONTH, $1.50

COMPARATIVE TEMPERATURES

	High	Low		High	Low
San Francisco		68	Denver	41	20
Oakland	69	42	Fort Worth	80	43
Sacramento	70	40	Kansas City	56	36
Atlanta	78	57	New York	58	51
Chicago	58	39	Tampa	83	64

Forecast: Fair

LAPHAM LANDSLIDE BROWN IS ELECTED!

The Election

Doyle, Rossi Man, Rejected; One-Man Cars Defeated; Sheriff Murphy Is Winner

Two New Supervisors Elected;
Judges Michelsen, Dunn Are In;
Reilly Runs Second, Rossi Third

By EARL C. BEHRENS

Roger D. Lapham is San Francisco's new Mayor.

Edmund Gerald Brown upset the veteran Matthew Brady to become the new District Attorney.

These were the two outstanding results of yesterday's municipal election.

Lapham's victory ended the 12 year old regime of Mayor Angelo J. Rossi.

Brady will step out of office after 24 years of occupancy in one of the biggest upsets in many a bitter one, the election yesterday passed off without incident.

Mayor-elect Lapham rolled up a The total vote cast exceeded the margin of more than 30,000 votes estimates of the City Hall experts.

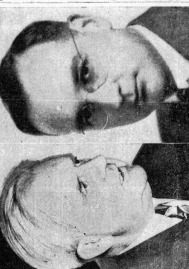

Final Returns

Complete semi-official returns from all of San Francisco's 1180 precincts were as follows:

MAYOR	Vote	District Attorney	Vote
Roger D. Lapham	90,646	Edmund G. Brown	97,229
George R. Reilly	57,741	Matthew Brady	90,127
Angelo J. Rossi	47,626	Howard C. Ellis	7,029
Chester R. MacPhee	20,346	Thomas W. Forsyth	3,633
Donald G. Ferguson	632		
Normand W. Mohr	443	SHERIFF	Vote
Richard Romo	349	Daniel C. Murphy	98,730
		Peter R. Maloney	63,987
		Leo Bunner	21,880
		Ray Conley	6,969

SUPERVISORS	Vote	
Dewey Mead	118,967	
Fred W. Meyer	110,606	
Arthur M. Brown Jr.	101,993	Judge of Municipal Court, Office No. 1
Jesse C. Colman	101,647	
Edw. T. Mancuso	94,036	George B. Harris
John J. Sullivan	90,381	
Alfred Roncovieri	80,989	Judge of Municipal Court, Office No. 2
Francis McCarty	71,013	
John M. Ratto	49,950	Frank W. Dunn	122,443
Clara Yates	29,935	Sylvin D. Lainie	27,132

ABOVE — Mrs. Lapham with characteristic enthusiasm christens a World War II cargoliner built for the U.S. Maritime Commission at Oakland, California.

BELOW — In a reproduction of a news magazine clipping, Mayor Lapham (right) participates in the 1945 San Francisco Conference organizing the United Nations. Left to right are Conference Secretary-General Alger Hiss, California Governor Earl Warren and U.S. Secretary of State E. R. Stettinius, Jr.

*In San Francisco Press Club "Black Cat" ceremonies,
Roger Lapham performs with Bennie Bufano (right),
internationally famed sculptor, a close friend and art-
ist-perpetrator of the Mayor's most outrageous hand-
painted neckties — also internationally renowned.*

III

ECA—CHINA AND GREECE
(1948-1952)

1

SHANGHAI HOUSEKEEPING AND
TRAVELS IN CHINA

AFTER a few days of relaxation at home in San Francisco, many problems began in preparing for China arose: (1) I hadn't heard from Roger whether we had a house; (2) I didn't have a Diplomatic passport; (3) the cleaners were on strike, and I had no idea when all the clothes I had worn abroad and sent out to be cleaned would be ready; (4) I could hardly raise my arms from the extra inoculations I had had to take; (5) how could I pack trunks intelligently, until I knew where we would live, and what I needed to take? It was all "very difficult."

Then the tide turned. My passport came "Diplomatic"; Roger wrote saying that the Bank of China had provided us with a "fully furnished" house; the cleaners returned my clothes; my arms stopped aching; I got my Pan-Am reservation and was told I would be taken good care of; I had a permanent and got my American Express checks. Life seemed inexpressibly brighter.

Before I left I had two luncheons given for me which will never be forgotten: the first by a friend in Burlingame, who added to it "just a little remembrance." Although I had said I was flying, and my baggage was overweight already, the "little remembrance" turned out to be six bottles of various kinds of vinegar and eight bottles of spices—total weight, 18 pounds!

The second luncheon was with Charlie Stillman, who had gone out with Roger and was on his way back to Washington via San Francisco to report. Roger had asked him to get in touch with me, so he called and invited me to lunch at the Mark Hopkins. I accepted, got there on time, and a few minutes later a very serious-looking gentleman emerged from the elevator and said, "Mrs. Lapham, I presume?" I resisted the temptation to reply, "Yes, Mr. Stanley."

Then we went in to lunch. He asked what I would like first. He looked pained when I said "A dry martini," but he did order another for himself. I asked how Roger was, and he said "Well." End of subject. From then on I tried all conversation gambits including questions and answers. His silence was broken only by his asking if I minded if he had a second tomato salad because he was very fond of tomatoes and one could not eat them safely in China. The only information I elicited was that it was hot in Shanghai, and that he was glad I was coming out because Roger was working too hard and I might be able to slow him down. If anyone was ever appropriately named "Stillman," he was. He was the stillest man I ever met. At the end of lunch he warned me that everything he had said was completely confidential.

The night I left, August 25th, Mother L. had a little dinner for me with a couple of rubbers of bridge before my 11:30 p.m. departure. The Swinertons were there, and just as we were leaving, I said to Jane "I'd like to snatch that dress you are wearing right off your back! It's the kind I have been looking all over for, and could never find." "Take it," said Jane. "I've had it for two years, I'm sick of it, and I have another dress in my car." So she peeled it off, and I went off with it hanging over my arm!

Everyone escorted me to the airport. I had my picture taken, smiling, as the newspaper photographers always demanded, with Roger Jr. kissing me a fond farewell on the nose. Then I was off. Pan-Am certainly did well by me, as I had a double seat with curtains round it, so I could get out of my dress and into a wrapper. I didn't sleep too much; even so it seemed no time at all before we reached Honolulu at 8:30 the next morning.

I was met by friends who covered me with my favorite pikaki leis, and took me up to the Royal Hawaiian. Steve Royce had placed a suite at my disposal, so I had a refreshing bath, and a delicious breakfast of

Kona coffee and sugar-sweet fingers of pineapple. Then off again at noon.

Shortly after lunch the Captain came back and asked me if I would like to come up to the cockpit at 4 P.M., when we crossed the International Dateline, and Thursday became Friday. Of course I said yes, although he warned me with a distinct twinkle in his eye that there was always quite a drop when we crossed, and I must be prepared to hold fast when he told me to. I agreed, and held on for dear life when he gave the word. Just as well. That miserable pilot deliberately dropped the plane at least 100 feet. But what did I care? The sight from the cockpit was incredible—seven separate little showers visible, each with its own rainbow, and our plane's shadow outlined below us on a cloud in its own perfect rainbow circle.

Tokyo at 7:30 the next morning after a fine night's sleep, in spite of what the stewardess described as "considerable turbulence," of which I was blissfully unaware. A Pan-Am agent met me there with coffee, orange juice and an orchid.

We were due in Shanghai at 2:30 P.M. Shortly before landing I retired, put on the black and white silk suit I had had hanging up all the way across, pinned on the orchid, hung the leis around my neck, and prepared byself to fall trimuphantly into my husband's arms. Little did I know how triumphal it was going to be! As the plane landed in Shanghai, the door opened, the Pan-Am man came in and said, "Everyone please keep your seats. Mrs. Lapham, come with me. Leave everything—it will be taken care of." He then handed me a sheaf of roses so large it would have done nicely on my coffin, and ushered me out to my waiting Roger, with photographers on hand to snap our enthusiastic kiss (repeated by request, as one of them missed it). Quite a crowd was on hand as well, including both American and Chinese members of ECA. After meeting them all we drove in to Grosvenor House where Roger had been able to sublet an apartment. He left Ed Bodman, his young American Chinese-speaking aide to deal with the luggage. By this time I felt so like a queen that I practically bowed to the populace all the way in.

On arrival, I was introduced to Ea Te, our #1 boy and his wife, our Amah. I was kowtowed and called "Missy," and first given a present by each of them, then handed the longest, most luscious gin fizz I ever tasted—the weather was not only awfully hot, but with all the excitement, I was dripping at every pore.

Ed appeared shortly afterwards with the bags. But one of them wasn't mine, and the missing one had all my dresses in it! I was almost in tears. Roger simply told Ed to go back to the airport and find it—which he did. The man who had taken mine was probably just as relieved as I was when he retrieved his own.

Roger and I had dinner alone, and talked our heads off after nearly three months of separation.

The next morning, though half dreading what I might be going to see, I was taken out to our house, 1803 Avenue Joffre. How pleasantly surprised I was! It was charmingly situated in its own compound with a watchman at the gate, a beautiful lawn stretching out in back, and many big trees. The house itself was just the right size: an adequate living room, smallish dining room, three bedrooms with baths (master bedroom with a large dressing room); and though there was still a lot of work to be done on it, and an appalling amount of stuff to be bought, I had enough imagination to see how livable and charming it could be made.

Dear Roger, always the optimist, asked if I thought we could move in the following week. My private opinion was that if we got in within six, we would be lucky—after my talk with Mr. Burton, the ECA procurement officer. He told me that he had run into such unexpected difficulties as (1) all the electric wiring had had to be redone; (2) they had discovered that the hot water piping did not extend to the second floor, and (3) the entire septic tank system had had to be replaced. As he said, mopping his dripping brow, "It all took much more time than we anticipated, although we have a force of 25 men on the job at all times!"

I then went on a tour of inspection to see what a "fully furnished" house in Shanghai was. And I found out: four bedsteads with woven rope "springs" and 3-inch cotton mattresses; seven overstuffed arm-chairs and 30 straight chairs to match, all covered with a hideous brown and white cretonne; four huge desks; ten small tables; two sofas; two amorphous pieces of furniture, the bottoms of which fitted over a radiator with shelves above; eight comforters varying in color from lavendar to scarlet—and 12 spittoons! No dining room furniture, rugs, draperies, silver, china, glass or kitchen equipment, and not a single bureau, chiffonier or commode.

To be truthful, my heart rather dropped when I thought of all I would have to buy in a strange city, with no command of the language except for my very limited pidgin-English. But Roger patted me on the back and said to cheer up; he would let me have a Chinese girl from the office to shop with me. He thought Ea Te and Amah would also come with us. Ea Te would engage the rest of the staff—#2 boy, cook, gardener and coolie—whose combined wages would come to a little under $100 a month! So I cheered up, went out to the Columbia Country Club with him for a drink, lunch and a swim, and could hardly wait to get things going.

The people with whom we were most closely associated during the months which followed included:

Colonel R. Allen Griffin: He had come out as Roger's Deputy Administrator. His advice and cooperation were invaluable. He and Roger made a splendid working team. Allen had served in both World Wars, lived in Pebble Beach, California, and owned and edited the "Monterey Peninsula Herald."

Hester Griffin: Allen's wife; a person of great charm, a lovely voice, exquisite taste, and a passion for shopping. I could never have furnished 1803 Avenue Joffre without her aid.

Peter Hately: Hester's son, a delightfully irresponsible, happy-go-lucky youth in his early twenties, who spent most of his time in the Language School in Peking.

Charles Stillman: Executive Vice-President and Treasurer of Time, Inc. He had gone to China with Roger to inspect various long-range projects for which the Chinese Government wished American loans.

Edward Bodman: A young American who had majored in Chinese at Harvard, and had been in China before with UNRRA. He had importuned Roger to take him back there again to "live dangerously," but ended up instead living quietly with us at 1803 where he dealt with Ea Te and his complicated accounts, with the Chinese on the telephone, and became—according to his views—"nothing but a G—— D—— housekeeper."

Jimmy Grant and his wife Ethel: Both of them had been born in China of missionary parents and spoke fluent Chinese. Jimmy was on a year's leave from Harvard Law School and due to return to the States shortly. Roger found him so invaluable as an interpreter, that he was able to have his leave extended for another year.

Dr. John Sumner: Head of the Economics Department of the University of Buffalo, and Economic Advisor to the Mission.

After the initial shock of discovering how much would be needed to make 1803 habitable, I got down to brass tacks. I had a long talk with Mr. Burton, whose fear was that as everything was to be done at government expense, I would go hog-wild. But when I told him that I was a good thrifty Yankee, he swung to the other extreme. He said I should remember that the house was being furnished as the permanent ECA residence—not just for ourselves but for whoever succeeded us —and that our position demanded a certain standard of excellence. Unless that standard was reached, the Mission would lose "face."

Would I buy solid silver? No, I wouldn't. It cost $2500 for a set of only 12 of everything, whereas I planned to buy a set of 18, plated, for $250; if anyone wanted to turn a fork over and see if it was sterling, I didn't care at all! Would I buy imported china? No. Why pay $600 for imported china that wasn't even very good when I could get it in the Chinese City for $60. He threw up his hands, gave up in despair, and let me "gang my own gait."

Then I had got my second wind. I hadn't furnished a house in 20 years and found it extremely exciting—especially as everything was unbelievably inexpensive. Miss Hardoon, the Chinese secretary helped me with the necessities (coat-hangers, soap, ink, toilet paper, Kleenex, carafes for the boiled water kept in each bathroom, and all the other 1001 items one always takes for granted at home). Hester helped me choose the furnishings and draperies. I ordered a dining room table, beds, mattresses, bureaus, rugs, new covering for most of the furniture and curtains for the whole house; all of it to be done in two weeks and at an incredibly low cost! In fact, except for the things I bought and paid for myself (lamps, rugs, and a few other things I wanted to keep), I furnished the whole house for about $6,000! The currency had just been revalued from 13,000,000—1 American dollar, and a new unit, the gold yuan, issued at 4-1. That ratio lasted for only a month, but in the meantime everything I had ordered was delivered and paid for.

Shanghai had changed greatly since we had seen it the first time in 1937. Then it was probably the gayest and the naughtiest city in the Orient. But since austerity had been decreed by the Gimo, there were no more night clubs with White Russian hostesses, no more jai-alai with frenzied betting, and even the sale of playing cards was forbidden!

The greatest physical change was the enormous increase in population. It had grown to 6,000,000 before we left. The streets swarmed with such mobs of people that trying to walk among them almost gave one a feeling of claustrophobia. Hordes of coolies, carrying everything from feather dusters to a grand piano on their backs. They wove in and out of traffic with that funny little dog-trot of theirs. Completely oblivious of automobiles or the hundreds of pedicabs—bicycle-propelled rickshas which had been substituted for the man-drawn ones—they would hold out one hand shouting "Wah!" and turned directly in front of your automobile. Why quantities of them weren't killed every day, I couldn't see. I finally came to the conclusion that it took a Chinese driver to know what a Chinese pedestrian was going to do!

Along with all the business connected with furnishing the house, there was a good bit of social life. The first big dinner we went to was given by two ECA men. We were invited for 8:30—and sat down to dinner at half-past ten! Fortunately I had been forewarned and had had a snack before I left home.

The dinner broke up at midnight then someone said, "Let's go out to Van Street's—he has a swimming pool." So five miles out into the country we drove, ten strong. The house was pitch dark, our involuntary host sound asleep in bed. But that bothered no one, and Van (ECA) appeared fully dressed a few minutes later, followed by an immaculate #1 boy bearing bathing suits and drinks. We had a lovely cool swim, which almost ended in tragedy. Charlie Stillman's secretary, who couldn't swim, got into the deep end of the pool by mistake. Someone missed her and said "Where's Claire?" Just in time, for she was almost unconscious by the time she was discovered and pulled out.

The following Monday, September 6th, we were supposed to move to an apartment in Cathay Mansions. The American from whom we had sublet at Grosvenor House was returning, and 1803 was still far from ready for occupancy. So early that morning I made the sortie with all my impedimenta only to be told "So very sorry. Rooms not ready until Tuesday. Tuesday we repeated the process in the midst of typhoon Hazel—all typhoons are named for women because they are so unpredictable! I never saw such rain. The water was knee-deep in the streets and the only way to get into the Mansions was to walk a duck board from the car to the steps, which were raised several feet above the lobby. Now I understand why.

That Wednesday, the 8th, we and the Griffins left for Nanking by train—a five-hour trip. We went directly to the official residence of our Ambassador, Dr. Leighton-Stuart, where we were to stay. He was a charming, other-worldly man, a scholar and a gentleman in every sense of the word, with a touch of St. Francis thrown in. He had been President of Yenching University for many years, and had been held under house-arrest during the four years of the Japanese occupation of Peking*. He was a widower and definitely above mundane things. But his house-keeper should have taken better care of him—blistering hot as it was, she served us a lunch of hot cream soup, hot dogs and sauerkraut, the butt ends of asparagus, and a puree of canned apricots and whipped cream in pie shells. And it turned out in the course of conversation that he was suffering from my complaint, delicately known as "Shanghai tummy."

Hester and I were taken on a sightseeing tour out to the Purple Hills and Sun Yat Sen's tomb that afternoon. We came to the conclusion that Nanking was a pretty appalling place. A few of the main streets are very broad and paved, but lined with dreadful looking shacks and swarming with such poverty-stricken mobs that you felt whatever you touched could give you anything from tuberculosis to leprosy. We never stirred out of the car. It was terribly hot, even though nearly the middle of September. I could see why August, when the heat was much more intense, was appropriately named "The Month of the Tiger."

A reception for Admiral Olds that afternoon; dinner at the Lewis Clark's (Minister to the Embassy) that evening; luncheon the next day at the Livingston Merchant's (Counsellor to the Embassy); dinner and dancing at the Officers' Club that evening; and back to Shanghai in an Army B-17 the next morning. Mrs. Clark and several others were with us. It took 20 minutes to warm up the engines and she said rather nervously that she did hope nothing was wrong: the pilot had only flown a B-17 once before and never made very good landings anyhow. Where-upon we both reached for our St. Christophers, who took such good care of us that we had a fine, short flight down and a perfect three-point landing.

At 1803 we found great progress had been made—including a re-paired and repainted dining room ceiling which had been badly dam-

---

* Chinese for "Northern Capital" and name of China's capital under the Imperial and Republican Governments until 1928. Changed to "Peiping" by the Nationalist Government and reverted to "Peking" at the Communist takeover in 1949.

aged the week before. One of the workmen, ignoring the fact that the plumbing had not been connected, had turned the water on full force in the bathroom above. The water went the only place it could go—the dining room below.

The Saturday night after our return from Nanking, Roger gave a large "Meet Mrs. Lapham" party for the entire ECA staff of about 130 Americans and 30 Chinese. I knew people were curious to meet me. I had gained the impression that they thought no one could be as genial as Roger, and that I might turn out to be some sort of a species of she-dragon. So I put on my best dress and my prettiest smile, and hoped everyone would be pleasantly surprised.

It was a cocktail-buffet-supper affair, given at the Omea Hostel, a very large house formerly owned by a German. There was dancing indoors on a marble-floored room, and outdoors on the porch. Roger's "fancy dancing" was the hit of the evening and the little Chinese girls almost mobbed him clamoring for dances. It was so hot I mostly sat, but did try to sort people out so I would recognize at least a few of them the next time we met.

September 13 was my birthday. I got four cables and five letters, plus the news that we could move into 1803 by the first of October. For a happy ending to the day, Roger took me to dinner at a charming little French restaurant nearby and truly French it was with only ten tables, checked tablecloths and the menu written on a blackboard. The food was delicious and cheap; we had pheasant, Crepes Suzette and a bottle of good wine for a total of $5.00

The next day Roger came home and said, "I hope you have no engagement for tomorrow as we have an invitation to lunch with Mme. Chiang." I hadn't, but I would have broken anything to lunch with that fabulous woman, whom Roger had already met several times in Nanking.

We arrived at her house on the dot of one. We had to pass the guards on foot (we were not allowed to drive in). We were then ushered into an enormous living-room, probably 40 x 60, and had time to take it all in before the Madame came down. It was entirely Chinese and very beautiful. All the furniture was heavy teak wood, the chairs upholstered in old rose satin brocade and arranged in a formal circle; a few fine scrolls on the walls and vases of flowers everywhere; but no rugs, either because the floors of dark hardwood inlaid in a diamond pattern were too beautiful to cover, or because it was still summer.

Mme. Chiang came down in about five minutes, accompanied by a huge police dog which she addressed in German. She was truly a dynamic-looking woman with a completely unlined face. She was very simply dressed in a Chinese costume, of course, and wearing no jewelry except for a large gold ring with earrings to match.

Luncheon was announced at once. She said she hoped we didn't mind being alone with her; she had asked no other guest in order to have the opportunity to becoming better acquainted with me! Never have I felt so dumbfounded, or so just plain dumb! I couldn't go into a list of the few accomplishments I had. In fact, I couldn't think of even one that would interest her. And like the *Pius Aeneas,* my *Vox hausit* and I hardly spoke during lunch but just listened to Roger and the Mme. discussing the problems and needs of Shanghai.

The lunch itself was a bitter disappointment to me. My mouth had been watering in anticipation of delicious Chinese food. Instead, it was as American as Kansas in August: lamb chops, baked potatoes and ice cream. It was just as well we had knives and forks; I couldn't have coped with that food with chopsticks.

On the way home Roger asked me what I thought of Mme. Chiang. After a bit of consideration, I said there was no denying her charm or the force of her personality, but that I wouldn't trust her any farther than I could throw a grand piano; I thought she was avid for power and would feel that any means were justified to obtain it. Of course, with the tremendous amount of relief work she did among the refugee women and children, particularly in Chungking, she was practically worshipped at the time; but now I felt that people were not too sure of her motives or of how far she would go to keep the Gimo and herself in power.

I never saw her again, but I have never forgotten the impression she made on me.

Friday the 17th turned out to be quite a day. We were called at 5 A.M., breakfasted at the Griffin's apartment and went from there to the airport, where we took off at 7:20 in a CNAC DC-4 for Hong Kong. We made unusually good time, as we picked up a tail wind from the outer perimeter of a typhoon which blew us in to Hong Kong in 3 hours and 15 minutes. But oh, that airport! By far the most dangerous one I had ever seen, with the island-studded harbor on one side and jagged mountains on the other. You had to come in dodging both as you lost altitude and flying speed, then make a steep bank over the water to land on a very short runway which ended in a moat and a Chinese village! Hester, on the harbor side, kept saying it was the most beautiful sight she had ever seen, while I, on the mountain side, felt it was just a question of which crag would take off my face first.

We were met by Vice-Consul Hill, who drove us from the Kai Tak airport in Kowloon (on the mainland) across by ferry to Hongkong and then out to Repulse Bay Hotel for lunch. We returned to the airport for a 4 o'clock, 45-minute flight to Canton. The plane followed the Pearl River all the way and flew low enough for us to see the crowded water traffic of junks and sampans as clearly as if we had been on a train.

Consul-General Ludden, the Mayor of Canton, T. V. Soong's representative, and Chinese photographers and newspapermen met us. We were driven in to Mr. Ludden's home on Shameen Island, where we were going to stay. The Griffins and Ed Bodman were parked at other houses nearby because the best hotel in Canton, the Oikwan, was so overrun with rats that no foreigners dared to stay there.

Shameen Island had been developed by the British for some 60 years and still remained true to British tradition. No cars nor even rikshas were allowed on the island. So no matter what the weather, you had to take at least a ten-minute walk from the bridge, where your automobile dropped you, to your house, with coolies trotting along behind you, carrying your luggage on a tote pole.

The Luddens couldn't have been nicer or more hospitable. He had been stationed in Chungking during the war and she didn't see him for five years. "And that," said she, "is why we now have only one child."

Their solidly-built stone house had four huge rooms on each floor, all with 16 foot ceilings, a boon in this climate. It faced on a combination park-playing field with the Pearl River beyond, always a colorful, constantly shifting scene to watch.

After delicious iced tea and "small chow" (assorted hors d'oeuvres) we were told we had been invited for dinner at Mr. Cochran's apartment (USIS man in Canton) at eight, but we could rest until nine, as we probably would not eat before ten. We didn't, and by eleven I felt as though it were the day after tomorrow! So Roger took me back to the Luddens where I collapsed into bed, but not to sleep; it was the first night of the Chinese Moon Festival and the park was filled to overflowing with Chinese paying honor to the full moon. They were divided into two groups, one chanting "BO-ca BO-ca!" at the top of their lungs, to which the other responded with a thunderous shout of "WAH!" Fire-crackers popped in all directions, river boats whistled, and the clanging went on and on. Because of my complete exhaustion, the din soon began to sound like a lullaby and I dropped off for a good ten-hour sleep.

I went on a short shopping expedition with Mrs. Ludden the next day but no buying. Even with smelling salts, a handkerchief over my nose and a fan, the assorted stinks in the little shops were such I couldn't stay in them long enough even to see if there might be anything I wanted to buy. *"Defense d'uriner"* signs would have made no difference, and the French *"Stations d'aisement"* smelt like roses compared to these Chinese shops.

That evening we all went to T. V. Soong's for dinner. Fortunately it was good weather for I would have hated to take that ten-minute walk in full evening regalia and high-heeled slippers in the pouring rain. T. V. lived on the far side of Canton. There were two armed sentries at the gate, and he received us with his bodyguard, a Colonel in the Chinese Army, one step behind him, a position he never left during the entire evening. We had group pictures taken, one gimlet apiece, and then went in to a 14-course dinner. (The prescribed etiquette is for the number of courses to equal the number of guests. We were 12. The almond-flavored rice soup and fruit served at the end apparently did not count.)

I sat next to T. V., who complimented me on my handling of chopsticks, a compliment I really didn't deserve as I only attempted to eat what I was sure I could handle. I was also very careful about my choices as I was having another slight go of intestinal trouble. T. V. didn't eat any more than I did, and hardly talked at all. He did tell me that he had both a touch of my complaint and an abscessed tooth. Under those circumstances, I wouldn't have talked either. We stayed only about 20 minutes after dinner, which is an excellent feature of those long Chinese meals—they often last two hours, but as soon as they are over, you go home.

We were sorry not so see Mme. Soong, whom we heard was one of the most beautiful women in China. She was in America putting one daughter in Wellesley and the other in Dana Hall.

On Monday I managed to hold my nose long enough to buy a beautifully embroidered linen and lace table cloth in the morning; had buffet lunch at "Sammy" Sampson's (ECA representative in Canton); took the afternoon off to do some typing; and went to a banquet that evening given for us by Mayor Auyang.

I sat next to the Mayor. He spoke slow but perfectly understandable English, to which I replied in kind. I asked him if he had ever been to America, and he said no, but his grandfather had been there in 1848. I said, "What a coincidence, for my grandfather was in Canton in 1846!" My grandfather, Thomas Wade Abbot, had signed on as a ship's clerk at the age of 19, and had sailed to China. He was gone almost a year and had kept a diary that I still possessed. His description of Canton 100 years earlier was, with the exceptions of such modernities as automobiles and electric lights, an exact picture of Canton in 1948! There were fine map drawings and a couple of rice paper pictures in the diary. But only one entry on one page shortly after leaving New York: "Seasick 17 days."

With this entente established between us, the Mayor and I got along famously—especially after I confessed to my inner disturbance. He said he had the same trouble, so we would both eat carefully. We held out very well on the different varieties of soups, chicken with marrow balls, that delicate winter melon soup, and some sort of a noodle concoction. But when the little roast pig appeared, he said, "Very bad for both of us—we eat." It was so crisp, so brown and so shiny, and so perfectly carved in chopstick-size pieces but still looking as if a knife had never been near it, that I knew I couldn't resist. Roger was given the choicest tidbit: the tail, and of course had to take it. When my turn came next, I was offered the ears or the hole under the tail. I thought fast and followed the example of the American woman who was offered a sheep's eye in North China. She said her status was too lowly to accept such a delicacy and she would waive it in favor of a higher ranking guest. So . . . I got a piece of the lovely crisp back and a rib instead.

There was a great deal of *"Gambei-ing"*—emptying your fortunately small cup of rice wine when someone extended his cup towards you at arm's length and said *"Gambei!"*. Whereupon, you had to drink and invert your cup to show that you had complied with his invitation. The Chinese drink very sparingly themselves, but the idea is to get the American men under the table if possible.

Roger was called on for a speech but said he preferred to sing. So he arose and rendered "Oh! you *push* the damper in, and you *pull* the damper out, and the smoke goes up the chimney just the same." After the third repetition, every Chinese in the room was on his feet singing with him, and a good time was had by all. This inspired the Mayor to sing a selection from a Chinese opera in a high falsetto. An Australian sang "Waltzing Matilda." Ludden, who sat on my other side, said the Chinese loved to laugh, and Roger had made a much greater hit than he would have with a long, beautiful speech. But a bit later and several drinks further on, my dear husband did arise and gazing soulfully at Auyang said, "We may not speak each other's language. We may not always understand each other. But when eye looks into eye— heart speaks to heart." At which point he collapsed into his chair showing strong signs of going to sleep. Ludden allowed that the evening was over.

We all flew down to Hong Kong the next morning, the Griffins going on to Shanghai, and Roger, Ed and I to the Repulse Bay Hotel for a few days. Our flight landed just in time because as our wheels touched down, the heavens opened; we were driven out to the hotel in a cloudburst. Between two and three that afternoon it rained 3.3 inches, and 5.9 inches in the next 24-hour period. The paper the next morning said how welcome the rain was as Hong Kong was quite a bit below average with only 76 inches to date as against a normal of 88! Needless to say we didn't leave the hotel for the rest of the day, nor until nearly noon on the day following, when the storm had subsided sufficiently to allow us out under the safety of our oiled paper umbrellas.

It had cleared by the time we went for lunch at Government House with Governor-General Sir Alexander Grantham and his charming wife. As I was introduced to her she floored me by saying, "I am a Californian, Mrs. Lapham, and met you at the United Nations Conference. But of course you wouldn't remember me as I was only the wife of a humble delegate, and you were the wife of the mayor." Whereupon Sir Alexander said, "She's only been a Britisher for 27 years, and she doesn't even say 'I'm an American,' she always says 'I'm a Californian!'"

We were ten for lunch. Roger sat next to Lady Grantham's sister, and asked her if she was here on a visit to her sister. "Oh no!" said she. "They are newcomers. My husband and I lived her for 15 years before he lost his head." Roger dropped the subject like a hot potato, not knowing whether her husband was in an asylum, or had eloped with his secretary. He made it a point to ask one of the aides after lunch how the husband had "lost his head?" The aide said, "Oh! Quite simply. He was decapitated by the Japanese, you know." Roger was aghast, and felt that the statement "until my husband lost his head" was an awfully casual way of referring to such a tragedy.

Long before this I should have said something about the varied and tremendous activities in which Roger was engaged. Aside from the organization of the Shanghai office, he had flown to Nanking almost every week for consultation with Dr. Leighton-Stuart; had been several times to Tsingtao to inspect the projects started by UNRRA there; for talks with Admiral Badger, and once with the Griffins and others; had had a fascinating but rather hazardous trip to North China—Tientsin, Peking, Communist-surrounded Taiyuan, Mukden and Kalgan; meeting and talking with our Army and Navy Chiefs, and many important Chinese such as the Generalissimo and Madame Chiang, Dr. Hu-Shih, a former Ambassador to the United States, Vice-President Li Tsung-Jen, and one of the most competent Chinese Generals, Fu Tso-yi.

Roger had sat in conferences that lasted for hours and had been wined and dined almost *ad nauseam* on the northern trip. But he had survived; and his conclusions were that he was most thankful for all the experience he had had in labor relations and for his four years as mayor, even though he had always called himself a non-political one. When to all this was added the organization of the Mission from scratch with only rather vague directives from Washington at the start (they came thick and fast later on), plus the intense heat of the summer months in China, I felt he had something else to be thankful for—his hardy State of Maine Dearborn constitution! One thing he did find amusing: he didn't get his security clearance until he had been in China for nearly three months. And if there was anything Washington was fussy about, it was security.

He was completely absorbed in his work. He felt that much could be accomplished, even though the Ambassador had told him at their first meeting that it was already too late to expect any really effective results.

My eagerness to get into our house stemmed largely from the fact that I thought it would be better for Roger to be in a comfortable home, where he could find true relaxation rather than camping out in small apartments and living out of suitcases. We moved into 1803 Avenue Joffre on October 2nd. We loved it from the start, and I could feel his tensions lessening little by little.

To this day, fifteen years later, I become both nostalgic and lyrical when I look back on those months in 1803. Quite a bit was still lacking when we moved in. Rugs, for instance, as I had had to order them from Tientsin—tawny ones for downstairs and off-white with a raised design for the three bedrooms. I had shopped everywhere for them in Shanghai, but they came only in stock sizes, there were never two alike, and the designs were either fiercesome dragons, or some sort of a horrendous horned creature such as I had had to call Ea Te to chase out of my bathtub one day.

My stock of china was 18 Minton salad plates and a tea set. The new dining room table was so high and the old chairs so low, that one's mouth practically rested in one's plate. But to offset these deficiencies, the soft green and gold bamboo patterned draperies and the chairs reupholstered in a heavier material of the same design were charming. Most of the furniture had been delivered and my two men—for Ed Bodman had come with us—were most enthusiastic. In fact I was pretty pleased with myself! To have accomplished so much in the five weeks I had been there (really three, for I had been away from Shanghai for almost two) I felt was a real achievement. At that, I didn't know how fortunate I had been, for the rate of the gold yuan began slipping almost at once. Very stringent government regulations were passed to prevent mass buying or hoarding. And by the end of September the purchase of silk materials was limited to three yards per person per month! But all of mine was bought, paid for and in place.

Our household staff fascinated me. I really had no idea how many I had. There were Ea Te and Amah, his wife, #2 boy, cook, coolie and either one or two gardeners. I never was sure how many because I kept seeing new faces—probably belonging to "f'lens" enjoying the hospitality of the servants' quarters over the garage. But as the combined wages of the whole crew amounted to $116 a month, the number didn't make too much difference.

Ea Te was, of course, the boss. He had engaged the entire staff, all of whom naturally were his relatives. He was a character, talked very fast, and while I generally understood his pidgin English, there were times when I was really baffled. For instance, he asked me to buy him a "rec eyo" and an "eyo bo." With the gestures that he made, I finally understood that he wanted an electric iron and an ironing board. After that a "big, big kettu" translated into "kettle" quite simply.

I had no objection to his bossing the servants. But I soon found out that he had every intention of bossing me, too. For who was I? Only "Missy." Roger, "Big Master," and Ed, "Little Master," were obeyed instantly; but every order I gave was immediately countered by "Missy, I think more better. . . ." So I realized I would have to assert myself quickly and forcibly to have him understand once and for all who ran the house. One day, when we had been in the house for about a week, I had the opportunity of a lifetime.

The drawback about the house was the lack of closet space. I had had a linen closet built on the second floor, and had naturally put all my linen, blankets, extra pillows, etc., into it as I unpacked them. For myself, I had one none-too-large closet for everything—dresses, hats, shoes and coats. But one fine day I opened the door and found it closely resembled Fibber McGee's closet. Ea Te had stacked every last thing from the linen closet on the floor of my closet; put all my lingerie, bags and whatever else I owned on top of the pile; and had carried all his tinned goods up from the huge closet downstairs, and put them in the linen closet! I yelled for Ea Te. I told him that my closet was for my clothes. The linen closet was for the linen. The hot water pipes went through the linen closet and all the canned stuff would blow up and to move it back downstairs where it belonged now! I listened to a few rather feeble "More betters," but simply said, "Put all rest of my things you take out back in master's drawer and take your stuff out tikki-tikki."

(I was pretty sure that that was not Chinese and found out afterwards I should have said "chop-chop." But it worked.) Everything was sweetness and light after that. Except that I was constantly losing "face" by picking up my clothes as I undressed and not calling Amah to do it, by not allowing her to give me my bath, and by drawing the curtains across a window directly behind me instead of walking across the room to ring for a boy to do it.

We had two most interesting social evenings during the next week. One, a dinner with the Whiting Willauers (he was an associate of General Chennault in CNAC), in honor of the General and his comparatively new Chinese wife. She was a tiny, attractive woman, who had spent most of her girlhood in San Francisco, where her father had been in the Consulate. She spoke perfect English. General Chennault certainly showed what he had been through while he had been in command of the Flying Tigers. He was very deaf and his face was so lined it looked almost scarred. I had a very interesting talk with him during the cocktail hour, asking how he felt about the importance of holding North China, which Roger was sure was a prime necessity. He was in absolute agreement and no one could know more about past and present conditions in China than he.

The second evening was a dinner with the Hampsens. He was the AP Shanghai correspondent. Their guests were the Archibald Steeles, he the Far Eastern roving reporter for the New York Herald Tribune; Brines, the AP man from Tokyo; the Griffins and ourselves.

After dinner Roger asked the hostess to give us all pencils and paper and he posed this question: "What are the five most important cities in the world today?" Everyone tried to pin him down as to what he meant by "important"—whether geographically, politically, physically or historically. But he said it was up to each one to make that decision for himself and defend the reason for his choice—particularly as to the order in which they were named.

When the papers were read after much pencil-chewing, Moscow

was the first on four out of five; Washington had a majority for second place; New York, Berlin, Paris and London were pretty well split between third and fourth place. The fifth ranged from Shanghai to Buenos Aires! No actual violence ensued; but it was a real free-for-all with everyone defending his choice with passion. It ended with all of them turning on Roger for not specifying exactly what he meant by "important."

Roger was flying Stateside the next day, October 10th, to report to Washington. He would probably be gone about three weeks. So that night we had dinner and a small conference at the house with the Griffins, Charley Stillman, John Sumner and a few other staff members present. Charley had gotten used to me by this time, and after the business matters were disposed of, in a moment of rare enthusiasm, he proposed that Hester and I should accompany him on a trip he was taking to Northwest China in a few days to inspect some projects (railroads, power plants, coal and tin mines, etc.) for which the Chinese wanted long-term American loans. Roger said "Girls, you're crazy if you don't go." But having learned quite a bit from long and sad experience about Saturday night invitations, I said, "Charley, if you remember and confirm this tomorrow morning, we accept with pleasure."

We all went out to the airport to see Roger off. Charley remembered his invitation, but seemed to think there were lions in the way—the principal lion being whether Hester and I could be comfortably lodged. There were to be six men in the party: Charley, Jimmy Grant, Ed Bodman, and three Chinese, Messrs. Yen, Chen and Wang of CUSA, a China-U.S.A. group working together for their common interests.

Hester and I sat on pins and needles for the next three days. But we were at last told that as the #1 and #2 ladies of ECA, we would be taken along to add "face" to the tour. So the following Saturday we took off for Chungking for what proved to be the most incredible and memorable trip of our lives.

In our long association, I had but one criticism of Hester, and that was that she never seemed to realize on our long flights that she had to "go some place" until the sign "Fasten your seat belts" went on. Then it was too late. This time there was again no exception to the rule. When we landed at the Chungking airport and found it was nothing but a palm-thatched shed. There was no "convenience" in sight and we had to motor 30 miles to the hotel where we were to have lunch. She was desperate. So I approached the young American representative of USIS and presented our problem. "Easy," said he. And he escorted us across a field in the rain to a most ramshackle, very far outhouse. He gave us a nice little roll of toilet paper, which he produced from his pocket, and stood guard outside until we were ready to return to the waiting cars.

We were driven to a place called P'ei Pai (Bay Pay), lunched with some of the local officials and the resident missionaries, taken on a tour of the city—Child Welfare Center, Hospital, Museum, etc.—then returned to the hotel for a little rest before going on to a place called Warm Springs, where we were to spend the night. By that time Hester and I thought a little drink wouldn't do us any harm. So we asked one of the lady missionaries for some water. Which she brought us—boiling hot! But she very tactfully left us, so we just took our liquor straight.

The men in the meantime had been out to look at a coal mine. Ed told me that one of the younger missionaries had said to him that his one desire in life was to read the Gospel in the market place in Lhassa! Mine wasn't nearly so exalted. It was just to be given the health and strength to keep up with my husband and go with him wherever he went for whatever space of time might be allotted to us.

After a fairly lengthy and rather boring dinner we were driven to Warm Springs, a rather primitive Chinese summer resort. It was most beautifully situated on the Chialing River, which cut a deep gorge right below the hotel verandah. The moon was full. The mists were rising from the river. For the first time we had a bit of understanding of the landscape as depicted on Chinese scrolls.

Ed had warned us that the toilet arrangements would not be what we were accustomed to. A large jar with a cover in an otherwise empty room was most generally used. But he thought that there was a real flush toilet here, so we investigated, making our way down a little path through a crowd of fascinated coolies. The door fell off its hinges as we opened it. The seat fell off at a touch. There was neither a top nor a handle to the tank and no water inside! But there were several large sticks of incense burning—no imagination was needed to tell why.

The beds were boards with inch thick pads on them. The electric lights failed as we started to undress, but a candle apiece and matches, which seemed to be as scarce as hens' teeth and worth their weight in gold, were finally produced. As hard as the beds were, we both slept the sleep of the just.

The next day began with a delicious dip in the hot natural spring water followed by a breakfast I found a little hard to take: noodles, heavy steamed bread, cold pork and tea. Not the food I would have chosen for that hour of the morning.

After breakfast we inspected a temple famed for its possession of a very old bronze bowl. When half-filled with water and rubbed by a Chinese priest with bare, scrubbed hands, this bowl vibrated so that the water boiled up from all four sides. Charley was induced to try it. But either his hands weren't clean enough, or he was lacking in the necessary animal magnetism. Nothing happened.

Back to P'ei Pai, and then off on a two-hour trip down the Chialing River on a small steamer. It was a fascinating experience. We became a part of the crowded river scene: junks; sampans being hauled upstream by gangs of chanting coolies; villages that had probably been there a thousand years; pagoda-crowned hills; distant cloud-capped mountains. The further we went, the better we understood the consistently low tones of the scrolls.

Just before the Chialing joined the Yangtze, we landed to inspect an arsenal, then went on to a cotton mill where we were to lunch. Our hostesses were the Mmes. Chi and Liu. The former was French, and spoke French and Chinese; the latter spoke Chinese and English. So we had a three-way conversation—Hester and I speaking French to Chi and English to Liu, Chi and Liu talking to each other in Chinese. The simple little 12-course lunch lasted until four.

Then we were driven in to Chungking where we were to stay at the Omea Hostel. We shared a comfortable room, and there was a real bathroom. The only problem with it was that it had three doors, none of which locked. So all you could do when you wished to use it was to go in, shout at the top of your lungs "I'm here!"—and hope for the best.

We were hardly settled when Charley came in and said it was time to dress for the mayor's banquet. I told him I was still so full of lunch I'd thought I'd skip it. But I didn't have a prayer. I was #1 Missy. I had been brought along to make "face" and I was to go. What's more I was to eat at least a little of everything. I went. I ate. This was the menu written out for me by Mr. Yen, who sat next to me:

Bear's paws—complete ones, even to the huge claws.
Gelatinous noodle and chicken with tomato sauce.
Soup of Chinese cabbage, carrot, melon, lettuce and white lichens.
Frogs legs.
Fish with bean curd.
Soup with pig's lung.
Pekin duck and steamed bread.
Sweet potato balls with sweet sauce.
Rice, with all sorts of pickled condiments.
Szechuan pears.
Tea.

Most of the ceremonial banquets at which we were entertained from then on more or less followed this pattern, except, thankfully, we never again met up with Bears' paws although the sea slugs we had later on were almost as repulsive. Sometimes women appeared at these dinners, and if they were present Hester and I were always tucked between them while all the men sat on the opposite side of the table. However, there were no other women at this particular dinner. It was explained to us afterward that it was no lack of courtesy towards us, but simply the fact that the mayor had eight wives; it was impossible to bring them all and equally impossible to choose one or two without raising merry hell with all the others! So he brought none.

We drove around the city by moonlight after dinner, ending up at General Stillwell's old headquarters above the junction of the two rivers. Here we listened to a half-hour talk on the proposed Chungking-Chentu railroad. And then we were offered more food! But it was only fruit and tea, so we managed, although I felt if I didn't see food again for a week it would be soon enough.

As banquets bulked so largely in our lives from then on—I attended eleven of them in six days—it might be well to describe the etiquette and procedure.

As soon as you entered the house where you were to be entertained, you were handed a small cup of green tea. When that was disposed of, you went immediately to the dining room where the tables were always round and spread with a white cloth (plain damask, not the lovely embroidered ones which we bought so eagerly). This rapidly became anything but white as the meal progressed—a great compliment to the host, because the more spotted the cloth, the greater the appreciation of his dinner.

Placed in front of each guest were a small bowl, a small plate, two tiny saucers—one with soya sauce and one half tomato and half mustard arranged in the pattern of the Ying-Yang symbol, a cup for rice wine and a pair of chopsticks. Instead of napkins, scalding hot towels were passed frequently. No water, which was considered, probably rightly so, too dangerous to drink. And you were never to touch your rice wine until your host held out his cup and *Gambei-ed* you. You did have one out at that point; you were allowed to smile sweetly and reply something that sounded like "Sway Bien," which meant "At my discretion." If he replied in kind, you took a sip; but if he repeated *Gambei,* you drank it all and it was immediately refilled. It tasted a bit like warm sherry and fortunately was not too strong.

All the 12 or 14 courses were placed, one after the other, in the center of the table. You held out your little bowl and the host filled it for you. You were supposed to eat a little of everything except the rice toward the end of the meal. This you could refuse if you were too full for utterance, which I always was. The last three courses were usually almond-flavored rice soup, fruit and hot tea.

Most of the food was deliciously flavored and I thoroughly enjoyed it. But some I could hardly look at without shuddering. I really envied Hester who ate everything, saying "Mmm—delicious" in that enchanting voice of hers that melted every Chinese heart.

The next day, Monday, we first made a short inspection tour of the docks and the site of the proposed railway terminal. I felt that while Chungking by moonlight appeared like something out of the Arabian Nights, by day it was a pretty dirty, repulsive looking city. Then we were ferried part way across the Yangtze to an island airport strip, which seemed terribly short in view of the tremendous amount of river around it. I was more than inclined to be nervous until I met the captain of our chartered plane, Captain Haley. He had flown the Hump all during the war, had just returned from flying Cardinal Spellman all around China, and I felt that if anyone could get us safely off of that tiny island, he could. And he did.

It was only an hour and a quarter flight to Chentu, of which I had never heard before. To my amazement, it turned out to be a city of 400,000, and the center of the largest medical missions in China, operated by American and Canadian missionaries.

Hester and I were most comfortably housed with Dr. and Mrs. Kilbourne, who lived just off the campus. There was no running water, but the bathroom was equipped with an enormous jar of boiling hot water to be hand-dipped and poured over you for a delightful bath.

We had luncheon at a restaurant, where I made my first acquaintance with sea slugs. They were described to me as marine vegetables, but I thought them horrid crawling little animals and couldn't face them. My favorite dishes were birds' nest soup, sharks' fins, Pekin duck and roast piglet. But they were all the most expensive of delicacies, and we had them only at very formal banquets. My feeling was that if just once I could eat all of the things I really liked—usually at the beginning of a meal—and not have to hold back for the next ten courses, I could thoroughly enjoy myself. But Hester and I both made great "face" at that luncheon by conveying a soft-poached pigeon's egg from the center dish to our mouth with chopsticks without breaking it.

After lunch out to inspect the Mission Girls' School, where we addressed the student body. Hester was magnificent. But all I heard when it was my turn was a babble of inanities, which I could only hope sounded better in Chinese than it did in English.

Back in time for a short rest and a bath, and then to the Governor's banquet, of which I won't give the menu, but will simply say it outdid all the others so far!

We left early on Tuesday to drive to Kuan Shien to see a power plant and irrigation system. The latter had been in operation for over 2,000 years, thanks to a far-sighted Emperor who had cut through a mountain and diverted a swift, wide river. No unions or 48-hour week in those days!

It was only 50 kms. from Chentu, but it took two hours to get there. The road was indescribably bad, mostly consisting of sharp, upended stones with a little dirt between them. But as motor traffic was practically nonexistent, and the human-borne traffic used to it and completely indifferent, who cared?

Luncheon at the power plant immediately on arrival. And I almost lost mine through choking on a tiny fish bone which stuck in my throat. Hester saved my life by feeding me dry rice until it went down, although the boy behind my chair claimed all the credit because he had turned my plate at a 180° angle and that had made it disappear!

A marvelous ride after lunch in what they called a mountain chair —a sort of bamboo hammock slung between two poles with a bar for the feet and carried by three men who relayed each other. Charley led, sitting on a tiger skin; I came next on a red blanket; Hester third on a green one; all the rest of the party had to be content to sit on plain bamboo. We were carried a mile or more through village streets not more than 12 ft. wide, up hill and down, to see a very famous old bridge built entirely of bamboo. We were invited to walk across the bridge, but the floor boards were so far apart, the sway so great, and the river below so swift, that when we reached the half-way point, I asked what you did when you got to the end. When the answer was "turn around and walk back," I stayed not upon the order of my going, but turned and went back then and there.

When we had been carried back to our cars, after about a two-hour trip, I asked what our bearers were paid. The answer was what amounted to 20¢ apiece, which our Chinese hosts said was sheer robbery because we were rich Americans; for them, it would have been 10¢!

We had a blow-out on the way back to Chentu—our only one, though we were told the average was two or three for that trip. In spite of the fact that it occurred in absolutely open country with not a soul in sight, within five minutes there must have been fifty or sixty people around us. They had the time of their lives. Jimmy Grant entertained them all in his perfect Mandarin—the high point being when he asked a 12- or 13-year-old girl if the baby she had slung on her back was her little brother. This elicited shrieks of laughter. It was her own baby boy!

This had delayed us so long we had no time to change for the dinner we had been invited to, so went right to our host's house. We were promptly ushered into a beautiful bathroom with very elegant colored plumbing—but no water! It was situated between the dining room and the kitchen and all the dinner service was routed through it!

On Wednesday, a never-to-be-forgotten day, and a flight from Chentu to Kunming. The weather was so crystal clear that one of the Chinese had asked Captain Haley if he couldn't fly us down to the west of the mountains, instead of by the customary valley route to the east. After checking the weather and asking if any of us had heart trouble— we would be flying at 14,000 ft. with no oxygen—and being assured that we were all sound in wind and limb, he said he would do it. We saw Mt. Minyatonka—all 24,000 feet of it. We saw the Pass over the Hump he had flown so many times and where 39 planes were lost one stormy night. We saw toy villages and rivers so far below us that they looked like little white threads at the base of the snow-covered mountains.

Captain Haley invited us up to the cockpit one by one, telling us to count five between each step on account of the attitude. When it was my turn he said, "Mrs. Lapham, do you realize that you are probably one out of the 10,000 foreigners in China ever to fly over Siking?" To which I replied that I was afraid it was one boast which wouldn't do me much good, as I doubted if one out of 1,000,000 Americans had ever heard of Siking, any more than I had. The flight took only an hour and a quarter, but we all arrived in Kunming just drunk with sheer beauty.

We lunched at the Bank of China guest house, were taken on a tour of the city, and then driven 20 miles out the Burma Road to a wonderfully modern hotel built by the Japanese at a resort noted for its hot springs. And hot indeed they were, as I found out shortly after arrival. I discovered a real flush toilet which I flushed with great pleasure—until the almost-boiling water hit me. Like the old monk of Siberia, I "burst from the cell with the hell of a yell" and rushed in to warn Hester to avoid a similar experience.

After still another banquet, the others motored back to Kunming. But Hester and I spent the night and luxuriated with breakfast in bed the next morning—with ham and eggs, and real coffee! Then a bath in a family-style bathroom, a small, sunken-tiled room, where each of us sat back-to-back on low porcelain stools in three feet of such scalding water that both of us were lobster red by the time we got out. A notice was posted saying you could have two baths a day for free, but would have to pay 10¢ for a third.

Back to Kunming in time to lunch at the American Consulate, where we were to spend the night with Consul McGeary and his wife. Then out for some shopping and to inspect a very semi-completed hospital. And then to the Governor's banquet. By this time I felt I could have written George Chappell's book "Through the Alimentary Canal with Gun and Camera." I had always had a small appetite and some of those banquets had been real ordeals—grateful though we were for the kindness and appreciation.

We took off for Shanghai at 9 o'clock, arriving at 7:15, a long and rather dull flight. Just before we reached Shanghai, Mr. Chen said to me, "Madam, you must have been a very powerful woman when you were young." To which I replied: "No, I have become stronger with every grandchild. I now have eleven." It had been a strenuous trip, and I was tired. But it had been one of the greatest privileges I had ever had. Except for a few minor items such as sea slugs and feeling like a boa-constrictor, who had just swallowed his semi-annual meal for at least part of the time every day, I had enjoyed each and every moment of it.

I found a letter from Roger awaiting me on my return. It was more or less in the form of a journal listing all his day-to-day activities in Washington. I didn't see how any human being could possibly do all that he was doing and live to tell the tale. His schedule included not only lunch and dinner meetings, but also breakfast conferences. He had met and talked to practically every important person interested in China, including a half hour with the President. Others were Paul Hoffman, Jack Peurifoy, Walton Butterworth, head of the Far Eastern Department of the State Department, Jim Forrestal, Eugene Meyer, Joseph Alsop, Ambassador Koo, and many, many more. He had held a press conference for twenty at which he "got by without being asked too many embarrassing questions." He had addressed the combined Intelligence Service Group of some forty-odd. He had even gotten in 18 holes of golf!

Hester and I took off for Peking at 5:30 A.M., completely rested after our two quiet days at home. We had a smooth, four and one-half hour flight, and were met my Bob Drummond—ECA and an "old China hand" who had lived in Peking for 30 years—and driven to the Wagon Lits Hotel.

He asked if there was anything we particularly wanted to do. I said, "Yes—go on a Peking picnic." After reading Ann Bridges' book "Peking Picnic," I wanted to see the temples in the Western Hills. He said, "Can do—if the weather warms up." It was then 36° and even with fur coats over our suits we were freezing. But I hoped for the best.

He put a car at our disposal which we used for sightseeing. We took pedicabs for shopping—the little lanes were too narrow for a car to get through.

What an enchanting, satisifying city Peking was! Its sheer beauty was both breathtaking and uplifting. On a more material plane, the shopping was so incredibly cheap with the GY at 10-1 instead of 4-1 as in Shanghai that we both went quite wild.

The day after we arrived was cold, but gloriously clear and sunny. We took a guide and went through the greater part of the Forbidden City. All I wished was that I could print every bit of it on my mind forever: the sunlight pouring down on the frost-covered golden-tiled roofs, the white pines soaring up into the pale blue sky, the perfect symmetry and balance of the buildings, the carved marble staircases and balustrades with the huge bronze incense burners as a note of contrast— all formed the most divine whole imaginable.

And yet, with all its beauty, I found it a bit *triste*. It was so vast and so dead. You felt that those vast courtyards and the miles of low buildings where the soldiers and eunuchs were housed must have been vacant for a thousand years instead of just since the fall of the Empire in 1911. I closed my eyes and tried to picture it in its heyday—all the little concubines fluttering around like butterflies in their colorful dresses; the Emperor and the "Old Buddha" climbing up to the enchanting little Summerhouse to drink their tea in silence while watching all the gay activity below. But I couldn't do it. The silence and the emptiness were too great. I let the dead past go and thoroughly enjoyed the living present.

Shopping anywhere in China was a real experience, to which the enormous curiosity of the Chinese added a great deal of spice. Entering a totally empty shop, you would be offered tea at once. By the time it arrived, the shop would be filled with kibitzers, panting to take part in the bargaining which ensued. You knew at once by the tone of the long drawn-out "Ah-ah-ah's" whether you had offered the shopkeeper so little that you had grossly insulted both him and his product; or whether, if you had offered him a price which he accepted at once (probably half his asking price) you had been a sucker and had deprived the audience of their afternoon's fun. Your pedicab driver always accompanied you. If he thought that you had paid more than you should have, even allowing for his *cumshaw,* a violent altercation took place.

I didn't know what happened when Greek met Greek, but I soon learned that when Chinese tangled with Chinese, it closely resembled the fight between the two cats of Kilkenny. Also that it never did any good, except perhaps to give the crowd their money's worth.

Allen and Hester went into really serious shopping and picked up some real treasures. Hester, with her flair, could look at a dilapidated old altar table, know it was Ming and repairable, and buy it. The same way with scrolls, of which she got a marvelous example of the Ming period. My cautious New England training, plus the fact that my house was fully furnished, rather restrained me. I contented myself with two charming 18th century rosewood cabinets, two inlaid coffee table tops from Jehol, a few modest but interesting scrolls, and some gay brocade jackets lined with unborn lamb for evening wear and for gifts. One could have bought almost anything at that time at any price in Peking.

There was a much greater feeling of uneasiness as to the future there than in Shanghai and with good reason. Rumors were rife, but it was fact that the Communists could walk in any time they wanted to. What was the wisest course of action to take, particularly for the younger members of the diplomatic staff, who had wives and children with them? If the wives left, when would they ever see their husbands again? If they stayed, they might be facing the possibility of open warfare, or a siege, with all utilities cut off and no food or heat for the children. Would Peking be declared an Open City? Would the Generalissimo feel there was nothing left for him to do but try to set up a coalition government with the Communists?

I had just reread Putnam Weale's "Indiscreet Letters from Peking," written shortly after the Boxer Rebellion and the siege of the Legations in 1900 and I felt that the tense atmosphere of those days was again being experienced 48 years later.

Allen Griffin and John Sumner had flown in a few days before. We entertained them at cocktails in my bedroom as neither of us had a sitting room. I really didn't know John very well at the time. He was very quiet, never spoke unless he really had something to say and then he was worth listening to. However, sitting beside me on the bed, and under the influence of a couple of martinis, he suddenly said: "Mrs. Lapham, I do wish you would not call me Dr. Sumner." I had my mouth half open to say I would be very pleased to call him John—when he completed his sentence: "I wish you would call me Mr. Sumner!" I reminded him of it frequently after I got to know him better and told him I preferred to call him John—unless I was angry with him, then I would go right back to Dr. Sumner.

A day or so later it was warm enough for our Peking picnic. We set off about noon on a beautiful fall day for the Western Hills. Bob Drummond, Mr. Sumner, the Griffins and I were in one car; Drummond's "boys" with the food and all the other appurtenances in another. But about half way to the temples, we were stopped in our tracks by a steamroller that had gone through a very narrow bridge, leaving no possible room to pass. I was ready to cry with disappointment. But Bob, who knew every inch of the countryside, said we couldn't have a better spot for our luncheon. It was called the Jade Fountain and was noted for its beauty. So we scrambled past the obstruction, walked a short distance up hill, and came out on a little plateau in sight of a small but exquisite white marble pagoda with two tiny streams from the Fountain purling around us on each side.

We sat on stone slabs carefully covered with laprobes, around a stone table spread with a white cloth, silver, china and glass. We had our choice of gimlets, martinis or scotch. The sun was warm, the view divine, the "boys" had lighted a fire in a small brazier and were cooking our eggs and cutlets. We had fruit, coffee and liqueurs to follow. All in all, I was sure we were better off than in a chilly temple courtyard.

We finished at 3 P.M. and found the cars, which had made a long detour, waiting for us on the far side of the bridge. We drove to the foot of the Hills, and walked a mile or so from there straight up hill on cobble stones to two beautiful temples to find tea all ready for us in the second one. It would have been impossible for us to go any farther in any case. It would have brought us too close to Communist-held territory. In a way, it was my good luck, for I was no walker; already, in spite of my low-heeled hiking shoes, I had walked a hole in each heel. We started back just at sunset, reaching the hotel at 7 o'clock after a never-to-be-forgotten day.

But "into each life some rain must fall"—the next evening we got ours at a dinner given by some man who thought he had to entertain us. He had a wall eye (so you were never sure whether he was talking to you or the person next to you), and a Chinese wife who didn't speak English. Allen had a cold. Hester had a cold. Her son Peter was just getting over the dysentery. Dr. Sumner never spoke. So all I heard during the long pauses of that dreadful dinner was the sound of my own voice ringing out loud and clear with one total inanity after another. Far from blaming Allen, I could have fallen on his neck in gratitude when at 9:30 he muttered "For God's sake, let's go home." And back to the hotel we went to fall into bed suffering from the kind of exhaustion that only comes from unutterable boredom to which we were anything but accustomed.

The men went back to Shanghai, but Hester and I planned to stay on for another week. We still had shopping to do and were being delightfully entertained: lunch with Bob Drummond once in his charming Chinese house with its courtyards, its lotus pool, its moon gate, and all the treasures he had collected over the years; dinner with Peter and his friend, Captain Lucky, who had taken a small house together. Peter had filled it with pots of chrysanthemums and cages of canaries! As Peter was in a constant state of financial liability, Hester was amazed. His explanation didn't help much: "But, Mother, they were so cheap you couldn't afford not to buy them!"

2

THE RISING STORM

THE next day was Election Day in the States. Everyone had taken Dewey's election as a foregone conclusion. But when we came down stairs in the morning the manager of the Wagon Lits greeted us practically in tears: "Ladies, ladies—Truman, he is ahead." We assured him that those were only the early returns, and just to wait until the later ones came in. Of course Dewey would win. He was the Chinese "White Hope"; everyone was sure that as soon as he was in office, the heavens would open and rain down gold on poor China. By afternoon the worst was known. The manager was in hysterics. Even Hester and I were a bit gloomy ourselves. We needed the marvelous item we read in the local evening paper to cheer us up; it ran as follows: "All unmarried women have been required to register with the Central City Council. To date 405 have registered—45 nuns and 360 prostitutes. They will be instructed in home-making, detection of sabotage, and loyalty to the Nationalist Government. Classes will be held separately."

We were to leave the next day. I had had a cable from Roger on the 30th, our 41st wedding anniversary, saying he was returning earlier than he expected. It was the only time I had ever been sorry to have him say that because it cut our trip short by several days. And I was sure that, in view of the worsening conditions, I would never again get back to Peking.

Laden down with our purchases, neatly tied up in blue cotton bundles such as all the Chinese carried, we were driven out to the airport and left there. It was a lovely day and we stood out in the sun waiting for our plane. Suddenly down the road came a large company of soldiers on the double. Clutching each others hands, we retreated to the shelter of the plane, dead certain they must be the advance guard of the Communist forces. They were only Nationalist soldiers out for their early morning exercise! But it did make us recognize how deeply we had been affected by the tense atmosphere of Peking, and it helped reconcile us to the few extra days we had had to give up.

Roger got in that evening and the next day we flew up to Nanking to spend the night with the Ambassador. A lovely drive the following morning with chrysanthemums in full bloom everywhere and in the afternoon we went over to Ginling College to call on that darling little Dr. Wu whom I had met at the United Nations Conference. She was in the midst of a celebration of her 20th year as President of Ginling, but greeted Hester and me warmly and took time out to show us over the Recreation Building donated by my Alma Mater, Smith College.

Back to Shanghai the next day, to not too pleasant an atmosphere as the currency was deteriorating so rapidly it was necessary to call up the office each morning to find out what the rate of exchange was for that day. The official rate was 20-1, but 35-1 at the PX, and 40-1 on the black market, where we were not allowed to trade. So you never knew what you were paying for anything. You just made up your mind how much it was worth to you and then bought or not as the case might be.

In addition to this the Embassy had issued a warning "To all American Residents of Nanking and Environs: Military developments in North China have made it appear possible that hostilities may spread further south, with the result that normal transportation facilities may be disrupted; accordingly it is suggested that unless you have compelling reason to remain, you consider the desirability of evacuation while normal transportation is still available."

This was followed a few days later by an even stronger statement from John Cabot, our Consul-General in Shanghai which read: "All Americans in the Shanghai consular district who are not prepared to remain in areas where they now reside under possible hazardous conditions, should plan at once to move to places of safety. Facilities for movement are being arranged, and will be announced shortly."

Refugees were pouring into the city from the north by the thousands, rice was in short supply because the farmers refused to bring it in for sale with the uncertainty of the currency. There were a few minor riots around the shops which were suspected of hoarding. Mayor Wu appealed to Roger: could he have rice brought in from somewhere? Roger could, and did; by getting in touch with Sir Alexander Grantham who promised to divert some shiploads of rice en route from Burma and have it in Shanghai within a few days. It arrived and that particular situation was saved. But martial law and curfew were declared on the 11th just the same and anyone found on the streets between 11 P.M. and 5 A.M., would have to spend the rest of the night in the hoosegow unless they had a special pass, which we procured at once.

We felt that Washington had gotten the wind up too soon. All U.S. Government office equipment in Peking was ordered to be destroyed. All American Army dependents were ordered out of Peking and Tientsin on 12 hour notice. The result was that Admiral Badger had 13 pregnant women dumped on him in Tsingtao on only an hour's notice. He promptly put them aboard a hospital ship in the Harbor where they were to stay until he could get them started on their way home.

These proceedings were a little humiliating because the British had taken no steps at all. I was truly mortified when I was having my hair done by a Russian who said "Madame is going home very soon?" I said no, I was staying; to which she replied "Ah! then,—Madame is British,— I thought she was American" . . . and *this,*—from a Russian! Hester, Ed and I made up our minds to stay until we were actually ordered out; we would rather be on the spot and know what was going on, than be elsewhere and hear only alarming rumors.

While Carol was in England she had a "daily" who, when anything went the least bit wrong, always urged her to " 'ave a cuppa tea, dearie, it'll take yer mind off." As time went on, we, too, appreciated having our minds "taken off" even by a lizard. Or a choice booboo from one of the papers: "Captain Andre Gaston Houel, the French Military Attache, will be hot at a cocktail party on the 11th instant between 6 and 8 at the Peking Club." I cut it out and sent it to the *New Yorker* hoping they would publish it under the caption of "The Neatest Trick of the Week."

Another lovely distraction was the annual chrysanthemum show held in one of the parks. Hester and I went and there was such a mob trying to get in that I was pinned against the ticket booth and had to be extricated by an elderly Chinese who fortunately understood English. But once in, what a sight! Thousands of plants of every shape and color, many of them trained to form Chinese characters or grown through a wheel-like arrangement of bamboo with one huge blossom in each opening. Some of the plants must have been grown and trained for years; I saw one on which 160 blooms were growing from a single stem as thick as a small tree. Only the Chinese and the Japanese, I felt sure, would have the patience to work for and achieve such perfection.

Life from then on, I felt, could have been described in the words of the seasick traveler who when asked if he was enjoying his trip, replied "Well at least, something new is coming up every hour." The situation changed from day to day. Although Hester and I did not feel we were "living dangerously," we did take things seriously enough to have our trunks packed with all our purchases and the clothes we didn't need. We sent them off by ship along with the cabinets and table tops I had bought in Peking—it seemed foolish to take a chance on not being able to get them out later.

Quite a few people had left, mostly the elderly, the ill, or women with young children. Ed thought our only disagreeable experience might come from retreating Nationalist soldiers who were neither paid, housed nor fed. As they left, they might seize the opportunity to do a bit of looting. His instructions: "But if that should happen, Mrs. Lapham, and they did get by the guards at the gate, meet them with a beaming smile, give them cigarettes and beer, and if you *could* make a joke in Chinese, it would be most helpful—they have such a keen sense of humor!" I replied that under those circumstances, I doubted if I could even be funny in English and that my beaming smile would be only a frozen grimace.

However I wasn't going to worry about that, because I had had a brilliant thought; if a lot of the typists were sent home, I might be able to get a part time job. I said as much to John Sumner one night, and his reply was that from what he'd seen of me, he doubted if I could pass the FBI investigation! And this, his first facetious remark, surprised him so, he didn't speak again for ten minutes.

Roger, as usual, had been flying hither and yon—Peking, Tientsin, and stopping off at Tsingtao hoping to see Admiral Badger, but afraid he would not have the time, as the chartered plane he was in on that particular trip, had to make the landing in Shanghai before dark. However he was met by the Admiral's Aide, who brought him an invitation to lunch with the Admiral on board the "Princeton." The aide provided a helicopter to fly him over and land him on board. "A new experience" said my husband, "but a very interesting one."

Social life continued exactly the same as ever, except that all dinners broke up early on account of the curfew. You had not only to be indoors yourself, but allow your driver time to get off the streets as well.

One evening toward the end of the month, we dined with the Cabots. Jack was very tall and I thought a bit on the stiff side until I heard he was one of only four boys who had ever run away from Groton. His wife, Elizabeth, was charming and a most gracious hostess; but even she couldnt' have saved that dinner from being more or less of a debacle. In the first place I sat next to Jack and he asked at once when I was going home. I said I wasn't. I thought that his next remark was a hit below the belt: he asked if I realized that if I stayed and had to be gotten out, it would undoubtedly be at the expense of someone who was really needed. I countered by asking when his wife was going home. With a little hesitation he said not for the present. So I said I'd go when she did. Then he said "But, Mrs. Lapham, do you realize the risks you are running? You may not have heat, food, or even water—in which case your—er—sanitary facilities would be cut off." I said cheerfully that that didn't worry me a bit; we had lots of bushes in the garden and I was sure our "boys" could build a Chick Sale in no time flat. He never spoke to me again during dinner!

But I soon realized that he had to deal with a far more serious problem than my facetiousness—namely the guest of honor, a United States Senator, who was making a tour of the world in forty days, visiting eight countries and making an official report on their social, political, economic and financial condition.

The Senator's longest stay was to be four days in China. His first pronouncement was that we were allowing the British to "do us in the eye" here; his second, that the Dutch were appropriating all the Marshall Aid money to carry on the war in Indonesia, but he was going there, and he'd soon put a stop to that—all proclaimed at the top of his lungs. In addition, he had completely turned his back on the fine and prominent (but older) woman on his left, moved closer to the very young, very pretty wife of one of the ranking Chinese bankers on his right and put his arm across the back of her chair. Withdrawn as she tried to be, he devoted himself entirely to her. Mrs. Cabot collected the ladies as soon as it was humanly possible.

Then we had the Senator's wife airing her views at the top of her lungs. She wore an extremely low-cut, strapless evening dress, a style that hadn't reached Shanghai yet, but even if it had, none of us would have worn it. Chinese women dressed so modestly that we instinctively wore dresses which covered us a bit. She announced that all her clothes for the trip came from Hattie Carnegie, then she started her series of complaints: (1) the American authorities in Japan would not allow her to fly to China on a Military plane, but made her pay her own way on a commercial liner; (2) Ambassador Leighton Stuart had refused to let her send all the things she had bought back to the States by Diplomatic pouch (which happened to be against the law) so she would have to pay duty on them; and (3) the Ambassador had also refused to place his plane at her disposal to fly to Peking, and she "just couldn't go home and say she hadn't been there." (He really had a very good reason for his refusal—he didn't have a plane!)

Her next remark, to a room about equally divided between American and Chinese women, was that everyone knew the only reason we were giving aid to China was in our own so-called interest, and how did I feel about it? I turned myself loose and when I had finished, she said "Why, that's real inter-es-ting, Mrs. *Lapman,* and if your husband ever comes to Washington, I'm sure my husband could get him a few minutes with the President." Looking like the cat that had swallowed the canary, I said "How very kind of you! But it really won't be necessary, for Mr. *Lapham* is just back from Washington where he had an hour and a half with the President!" M-E-O-W? Oh! sure; but I had had all I could take and in fact quite a bit more. It was a little more than embarrassing to have Americans of that ilk in their ignorance tip the delicate balance of the *entente cordiale* which all the Agencies in China were trying so desperately to maintain.

Roger flew to Peking on December 5th and absolutely refused to take me with him. He thought it too risky, but I was ready to kill him in cold blood when he got back a few days later and said "Gee, Sport, you ought to have gone with me! All the dealers in the city swarmed around me urging me to buy any of their treasures for a song, just to get them out of the city and have them preserved in safe hands!" I knew I would never get another chance like that and I learned my lesson —never to take "no" for an answer.

The tenseness in the atmosphere increased. Although we did not have what the papers called "Shanghai jitters," we never knew where we stood from day to day. Both the Embassy and the Consulate had issued second warnings, not ordering, but urging all non-essential Americans to leave. Many did go although the evacuation ships were terribly overcrowded and there was no choice of a destination. Most of the women and children were sent to Santo Tomas in Manila.

Peking was completely cut off both by rail and by air a few days after Roger got out. Chinese by the thousands were swarming both into and out of Shanghai. We were told that the scenes at the railway station were appalling. Four people were crushed to death one day between those who were trying to get off the train and those who were trying to get on. The poor were going back to their native villages and the wealthy to Hong Kong.

We were given the location of our central meeting place in the face of a real crisis and told we would be allowed to carry 65 pounds of luggage including a pair of blankets and eating utensils. The rendezvous was fairly near 1803, but neither Ed nor I could have walked it so he had a ricksha on tap in case of emergency. Then we were told that in a few days all ECA personnel was to be moved into the Park Hotel where the Griffins and ourselves would each have a five room suite. Our servants would be permitted to take care of us.

The next gentle hint was that Mme. Sun-yat-sen was very inadequately housed and would be only too glad to move into 1803 if we had to leave. Of course, this was just a suggestion, no compulsion, but as the house belonged to the Bank of China, they could have forced the issue at any time they saw fit. I did hope she would like my very American style of furnishing if she did take over. We would naturally have had to walk out and leave everything "as was." All I could think of was how smart I had been not to buy solid silver!

Each letter I wrote home at this time was headed "1803 Avenue Joffre, probably for the last time." I really believed it, but after so many false alarms I made up my mind that *"Plus c'a change, plus c'est la meme chose."*

However, the idea of the Park Hotel was abandoned and the next spot chosen was the Broadway Mansions way downtown and across Suchow Creek. That plan lasted until it was discovered that five different sets of people shared in the occupation and operation of the Broadway Mansions: the American Army group, who had no idea of leaving, and we couldn't move in unless they got out; one of the banks owned the oil supply for the boilers, but the Navy owned the boilers and said they were planning to remove them; the Army ran the mess, but didn't feed civilians. So taking one thing with another, we were to be permitted to stay put until someone came up with another brilliant idea.

All my days were busy, getting ready for Christmas—mostly last minute shopping at the Bazaar for scrolls. I got three lovely ones—a landscape in soft greens and browns with a red bridge for an accent, and two of Su-bei-hung's "Eight Heavenly Horses" which were so gay you smiled involuntarily when you looked at them.

In the meantime Hester had been in the hospital for a minor operation and I had been out to see her every day. Once, however, I got there before she was ready to see me and had a rather grim experience. As I was waiting in the lobby an old girl came in and dissolved in tears. After a bit I went over to her, offered her smelling salts and aspirin, and asked if there was anything I could do. "Yes," said she promptly, "come up stairs with me, take a look at my husband and tell me if you think he is dying." I did my best to talk myself out of it, but no go; so up I went, and when I saw him, I thought he was dead then. She said Oh! no, he was breathing, but did I think he was going to die? Most fortunately for me, a friend of hers came along at that moment, so I was spared an answer. He did die the next day and on inquiry I learned that she was a well-known psychopath, if not a complete nut.

The day before Christmas I did what was probably one of the stupidest things ever in my somewhat chequered career. I started downtown to the ECA offices (which had moved from the center of town to the Glen Line Building on the Bund overlooking the River) to get some money for distribution to the servants. It was mid-afternoon. I should have been down and back in under an hour, but the further we drove, the worse the traffic. My driver tried street after street. But each one was a seething mass of cars, pedicabs, and pedestrians, who couldn't move backwards or forwards except by inches.

It took an hour and a quarter to reach the Bund and as we started to turn into it, there just wasn't any place to go in any direction. I didn't have my regular driver, who would never have allowed me to step foot out of the car, let alone suggesting it; but this one said "If Missy in a hurry, more better she get out and walk." Like an idiot I did. It was only eight blocks from the Avenue Edouard Sept to the office, so out I got.

I realized before I had walked a block that something out of the ordinary was going on. The crowds were something the like of which I had never seen; (100,000, the papers said the next day). There were two lines of them, one queued up in front of the banks trying to turn in their almost worthless paper money for gold bars; the second line sightseers or innocent pedestrians like myself. There was a row of armed police in between, doing a calm, firm job. It was certainly no place for me, but there was nothing to do but keep on going. Seeing a tall, serene Chinese woman just ahead of me who was making her way quite unhurriedly, I took hold of her skirt. She smiled pleasantly at me and nodded, so I trotted along behind her, while she said "Wah!" which apparently was "Open Sesame" and I finally reached my destination.

Roger greeted me cordially, and asked where I had been. I said, "Walking on the Bund—for eight blocks" and while he didn't say "all the fools aren't dead yet," he surely looked it. He then asked if I didn't know that seven people had been crushed to death there that morning. I did answer mildly that if I had known it, I wouldn't have come; but as long as I had come out of it safely, I couldn't help but be amused. I, who never walk a step that I can help, had picked that particular time to take my first exercise in Shanghai.

He sat me down firmly in a chair and said "You wait there." I did. When it was time to go home, the crowds were still so great that it took us an hour and a quarter to reach 1803. Incidentally, the Government suspended the sale of gold the next day until some safer plan could be devised. I was dying to buy one of the tiny gold bars myself and have it set in a ring, but Roger said no, because if anyone saw it I'd probably lose not only the gold bar, but also the finger!

Christmas came and went most successfully. We started the day cozily with breakfast in bed over a cheerful little open fire, then dressed, went down stairs, opened our presents, and had the household in to give them theirs. I had toys for Ea Te's four children including a veloci-pede which was too small for two of them and too large for the others, but was greeted with rapturous delight—as Ed pointed out, "You don't buy your children many toys on $25 a month." Roger gave them all money. Ea Te gave me Chinese dishes for "small chow." I also saw my cook for the first time! Quite a record after living in the house for three months!

All our gifts from home had arrived and we had many from Shang-hai friends—including a beautiful rosewood cabinet inlaid with carved ivory from Fu-Tso-Yi's right hand man and a jade figurine from Mayor Wu. Roger was quite upset because he couldn't return them without the donor's losing "face." He was told not to worry: he could give them something equally good at Chinese New Year the next month.

The rooms really looked lovely with the little fir tree Eleanor Deamer had sent me sparkling with electric lights. The tree surrounded with a dozen pots of scarlet poinsettias—at 25¢ a pot, if you please, and each with six blooms. There was a cut-out cardboard crèche on the mantlepiece and the rest of the living room was filled with plants and flowers. One plant was a dwarf cherry and another a dwarf plum. Both were covered with tiny white star-like blossoms. One flower arrangement was a combination of pussy-willows, poinsettias, chrysan-themums, and China lilies, all blooming out of season. Another one may seem very strange because it was composed of a pinky-purple cab-bage, chrysanthemums of the same shade, pussy-willows, and tiny tan-gerine oranges stuck on laurel branches. It was the most artistic ensem-ble I had ever seen!

We had a second tree in the hall, what species I never knew, but it looked like a "monkey-puzzler." Prickly as it was, Ed had covered it from top to bottom with gold and silver paper ornaments which Jane had sent me.

Our first guests were 20 Standard Oil boys who lived next door. They had heard there was a party and decided to come, though unin-vited, to wish us Merry Christmas. They left before our crowd began to arrive at 4:30, so they certainly didn't bother us: in fact for a while, it looked as if they might be the bright spot of the afternoon, because every ECA "Stateside" girl who came into the room, took one look at the little fir tree, went over and sniffed it and promptly burst into tears!

We had turkey sandwiches, "small chow" and drinks and gathered around the piano to sing Christmas carols. No one left much before nine. Roger made the hit of the day by distributing 38 neckties which he laid out on one of the beds and told each man as he came in to go up and choose one. As one of our San Francisco Columnists had written while Roger was Mayor, "his colorful ties looked like an explosion in a tomato-canning factory," or as one of our guests said "If we all wear our ties to the office tomorrow, we won't need any artificial light."

Twelve remained for dinner of roast pig and Cordon Rouge (from the Commissary at $3.30 a quart!) and everyone was off by 10:30—the curfew certainly shortened any evening entertainment.

The next day I went out to spend my Christmas checks from Mother Lapham and Roger. I took Hester with me to give her opinion of how I looked in a leopard skin coat. I was determined to buy one even though I had always said you had to be young, dark and beautiful to wear one. I went to the best store and tried one on. I saw Hester's mouth twitch before I saw myself in the glass; when I looked I knew why and burst into loud laughter. My original judgment had been correct: I had never seen anything more hideously unbecoming than that coat on me. That idea died a-borning.

Then Hester said she had to go to a jewelry shop to have her watch repaired. Snooping around while she was busy, I saw a jade ring that just rang a bell. It was jewel jade with tiny diamonds forming the Chinese symbol of longevity and set in heavy gold. I took it home on approval, wore it to a cocktail party that afternoon and asked a woman, who knew jade, what she thought of it. She said it was good, but not at the price asked and to go back and offer him half. I did the next day and without a word he took the ring and put it back in the case! I was crushed, but made up my mind to pursue it further later on.

Home in time to sit with Ed who had a short wave radio, and hear

Bing Crosby sing "White Christmas" from Los Angeles. And we both listened with tears running down our cheeks, not entirely due to the glass of Scotch in our hand.

There were lots of holiday doings, but the best invitation we received was for New Year's Eve. It read, "10:30 P.M.-5 A.M. Six double beds, and three singles available; make your own arrangements!" But we had a curfew pass, so didn't have to make ours.

New Year's Eve was a very gay affair held high in a penthouse overlooking the city. There was dancing including my husband's own individual brand and a Highland fling by the British Consul-General and the hostess.

One of the guests was a newly-appointed representative of the Bank of America, a Mr. Questa, who did nothing but lean against a door and look glum. I decided the poor soul was a lonely stranger, so went over and introduced myself. This was the conversation: Mr. Q: "Where do you come from?" Me: "San Francisco." Mr. Q: "Don't you wish you were back there now?" Me: "No, I'd much rather be right here." Mr. Q: "Liar!" Then he went back to leaning. A little later one of our charming ECA women, who had a lovely voice, was asked to sing. With a wink at me—she having tried her hand on Mr. Questa too— she sang Beethoven's *"In questa tomba obscura"* . . . he didn't get it, but I certainly did.

With our pass, we were able to leave about 3:30 A.M., so never did find out what "arrangements" were made about the double and single accommodations.

At a cocktail party at Hester's one day, I ran into the woman who had advised me about the jade ring. She asked if I had bought it and I said not yet, but I was still hoping. "You'll get it" said she, "just make some sort of an offer so the old boy can save face, and then you can buy the ring." She was a real character, and I never did find out if she was an American married to a Britisher, or had had first an American and then a British husband because she had both passports. After we finished talking about the ring, she said very abruptly "Mrs. Griffin tells me you want to play bridge; what kind of bridge do you play and what are your stakes?" I felt it was no time to be a shrinking violet and replied, "I play very good bridge and I guess I can play for any stakes you do." "Good," said she; "then I'll ask you for lunch and a game next Friday. But if you had said you played for a fortieth, I'd have known exactly the sort of a game you played and dropped the whole subject!" I went on Friday and found the ladies played for the same modest sum I did at home. I won $13 from the three of them and two more invitations—they could hardly wait to get back at me!

A few days later I returned to the jewelry store. On the way in, I noticed a wide bracelet, woven in two shades of gold, which I thought I could use nicely. So I asked to see it and, with a beaming smile, I said that naturally if I bought both the ring and the bracelet, he would give me a very good price. After a bit of bargaining, I got the two for only a few dollars more than the price of the ring alone; we both saved face. He was satisfied and I was tickled to death.

On the way home I saw a wonderful pair of red Russian leather high boots lined with white fur in a shop window. I went in, bought them and wore them home. Ea Te greeted me with a very expressive "Ai-yah!—Missy!" They were a real necessity. It had been cold lately and we still had no rugs in the house; all the windows were long French ones, and the floors were like ice. Roger thought they were really something and wanted me to order him a pair just like them. I did, only in black. He nearly wept when he saw them—he had expected them to be red. I told him the Chief of the Economic Cooperation Organization simply could not run around the streets of Shanghai in red boots.

As time went on, I felt a book could really be written about Ea Te. He was quite a character. It had been a great help to have Ed Bodman living with us to deal with Ea Te—particularly his accounts and his vocabulary. Ea Te's two favorite expressions were "More better" (no matter what I suggested Ea Te always had a "more better" idea) and

"Besso." It took Ed and me a long time to figure out the meaning of the latter. Finally we decided that it meant "formerly"; as "chicken 'besso' GY 20 a pound, now 80—more better we have something else."

When Roger planned to be out, Ed and I usually ordered "coolie chow" for dinner—a bowl of rice with small bowls of fish, meat, vegetables and soya sauce to choose from. It never failed that that would be the night that Roger would change his plans and come home, generally bringing several other men. It didn't make any difference to Ea Te—coolie chow stretches indefinitely. But Roger was not too fond of Chinese food and, as we had no deep freeze nor too many reserve stores, there was rarely enough in the house for more than one meal ahead.

Ea Te would never let me go anywhere outside of the compound on foot; "More better you take car, Missy; plenty soldier here now, plenty bad men; maybe grab your purse, maybe take you coat!" I think that the real problem was that the household would lose face if I walked. Roger seemed to agree with Ea Te. I always took a car even to go the two blocks to the English dairy where the only certified milk in Shanghai was sold at 40¢ a quart!

One long saga was about the "rec i-o" which was "plenty good Besso, but no work now. So he take to Rectician, who want GY 200, but no fix; so he no pay, then he find 'nother rectrician who fix good for GY 100, so I tell him he one smart boy and save me plenty money (50¢)."

I had two real visitations about this time, one from our Standard Oil boys who had a monkey they brought over for me to see. Unfortunately it got loose and led everyone a merry chase all over the house. Ea Te as usual directed the forces safely from the rear.

The second was a visit by a man I had met in Peking. He came to call, and stayed three hours and a half! He ended up by saying he had been trying to think who I reminded him of, and he had just gotten it: one of the most interesting women he had ever met. She was a Manchu princess and the mother of the Pearl Concubine, the favorite of the last Emperor and whom the Old Buddha shoved down a well because she had too much influence with him. I said coldly that I was glad he found me interesting, but both my daughters were married so I couldn't possibly be a concubine's mother. And I didn't expect either of them to be shoved down a well. He said, no, no!—that wasn't the point; it was the fact that I had so much vitality for a woman of my age! Whereupon I stood up, and being a gentleman he could do no less, held out my hand, said it was so nice of him to call on me. He got the idea and left, although I was sure he had had every idea of being asked to stay on for dinner.

The Griffins left early in January to go 'Stateside, Allen to report to Washington and Hester for a general medical check-up. She very kindly turned her car and driver over to me. The driver's name was Feng and he was known as "Homeside Feng" to distinguish him from another ECA driver who was "Officeside Feng." It didn't take me long to lose face with him; I stopped shopping at four o'clock, whereas "Missy G'liffin, she always shop 'til seven."

One dinner we went to rather amused me, because the host, a Socony-Vacuum man, was so deadly serious. He asked me to just go to any table and sit down and the men would join me. There were so few women in Shanghai those days he explained, they had to be rationed— six that night to twenty-four men. I said "Oh! how wonderful of you to give me a headline for my next story! I'm a newspaper correspondent, you know, and the caption for my article will be "Women Rationed In Shanghai!" He turned pale green, smiled feebly, and managed to stammer out that he hoped I wouldn't mention his name. I really intended to undeceive him, but he avoided me like the plague for the rest of the evening so I never had a chance to do it.

Although we had heard nothing more about moving out of 1803, the atmosphere continued to be tense and rumors were rife; the G'imo was going to resign; he was going to take a vacation; he was going to move the Government to Canton and so on. Nobody was going to do anything until after Chinese New Year which was due January 29

302

to last two weeks with every shop shut up as tight as a drum.

The American press must have been playing the situation up in a big way because I got a letter from a friend about then which read: "My dear, I worry about you a lot; are you really going to stay on? Could you get out if you had to? I suppose you are having the most extraordinary experience in the world, but do be discreet and don't wait to pull the whiskers of danger and death." Very kind of her, but the only whiskers I had ever tried to pull were my own.

As a matter of fact, while I wasn't afraid, things weren't too pleasant. The streets were crawling with soldiers who were neither fed, housed, nor paid, and had begun moving into unoccupied houses—and even occupied ones demanding food and lodging. So far they had left quietly when refused, but no one seemed to exercise any authority over them. And you couldn't help but wonder if you would be next on their list. There was also always the uncertainty that Roger would come home and say we were moving into Broadway Mansions the next morning at seven.

I had caught a terrible, bronchial cold after several days of pouring rain and was coughing my head off. A young Navy doctor assured me that I had a virus pneumonia and prescribed sulfa. I, in turn, assured him I had a bad go of bronchitis and sulfa didn't agree with me; a nice, old-fashioned mustard plaster would do the trick. If I had demanded a large shot of heroin, he couldn't have been more horrified. He insisted that I was to take sulfa every four hours day and night, but he did strap me up. The minute he was gone, I telephoned Elizabeth Cabot to ask her if she had any Colman's mustard. She did and sent it over with a stack of "whodunits." I made myself a nice, strong plaster, and in a matter of hours my cough had loosened and my disposition improved —fortunately, because Chinese New Year was only a few days off and I did want to enjoy it. "Enjoy" is a feeble word. I adored every minute of it.

First of all, Roger was able to repay his Christmas indebtedness with appropriate gifts: among them, a lovely silver cigarette case for

Mayor Wu inscribed in Chinese and English "From one Mayor to another with sympathy" and, for Fu-Tso-Yi's representative, a case of Scotch.

The house was filled with the traditional flowers—China lilies, Heavenly Bamboo, and a flowering shrub called Lu-mei, or the "12th Month Flower." The latter had pale yellow blossoms like a plum and a very delicate, elusive scent. You had to have the three in combination to have good luck for the coming year—the Year of the Ox, which everyone hoped would be happier than the departing Year of the Rat.

Firecrackers began going off early in the morning of the 29th, and never stopped day or night for three days. In the middle of that first afternoon, Ed came rushing in and said the Standard Oil boys next door were bombarding us, what should be do? "Bombard them back!", said I without a moment's hesitation. But we had no ammunition; so I gave #2 two dollars to buy some. He came back with such an armful of firecrackers as I had never seen. Each was 8 inches long, ½ an inch in diameter, and went off twice—first BOOM, and then BANG! No. 2 was the hero of the day because he held onto them for the BOOM and then tossed them over the wall of the compound for the BANG. All Ea Te's family and "f'lens" were on hand. One of the ECA men joined the fun, but held on to a firecracker too long. He blew his glasses off and said "My God! I've gone blind." We unearthed the glasses from the bushes with one lens cracked and he played bridge in them all evening. The cracked lens gave him a very odd, rather leering expression.

Roger was away, or perhaps he would have restrained Ed and me from what we did the next afternoon (unless he had thought of it himself). We drove out to Hung Jao to bombard Van Street and his housemates. We parked outside his compound and tossed firecrackers over the wall. We were a bit nervous because Van's Boxer tried to retrieve them before they had gone BANG. But it was nothing to the nervousness we engendered. Everyone was awakened from a siesta and thought the Communists were taking over. They rushed downstairs in every known state of deshabille. We really were apologetic. But they got over their shock and went up and dressed. Then they came down and served us liquid refreshment which we didn't feel we deserved, but partook of with enthusiasm just the same.

Minor excitement on the home front: our hen had begun to lay. Some time before, a hen and two roosters had flown into our compound, but the hen had never laid an egg. On the last day of the New Year, I missed one of the roosters and asked Ea Te, "What happened?" He replied, "Two-piece l'ooster, too much one-piece hen, Missy, so we kill, eat one-piece l'ooster, now one-piece hen lay egg." And by golly! It did! I had a fresh egg for breakfast every morning. The eggs did have a very strange colored yolk, probably due to the orange marmalade Roger had fed it every morning for breakfast.

3

DWINDLING SAND
IN THE GLASS

M Y next letter home, dated February 3, began: "The sands are running out of the glass fast now and the Shanghai interlude is nearly over. Roger came home last night and said we were to leave for the 'States on the 16th."

Paul Hoffman had been out earlier in the year and the report that he and Roger had turned in had been rejected. But even so, Roger was going to Washington to appear before the House Foreign Affairs Committee and the Senate Foreign Relations Committee. He got the names mixed up once, but was told they were easy to remember—the Senate was too old to have anything but relations. I was to be dropped off in San Francisco, and whether he, or I, or both or neither of us went back was an open question. So I shopped like mad, packed up everything I hadn't sent already, and sadly prepared to leave 1803, very much in doubt about ever seeing it again.

We had pictures taken of the house, inside and out, with Ed, us, and all the servants. A special one was made of amah with the light concentrated on her very pregnant-looking stomach. She resembled nothing so much as a nearly Italian Primitive of Jupiter visiting Danae in a shower of Gold.

I certainly wish I could have had my picture taken a day or two later when I had my hair done at Broadway Mansions. Something had gone wrong with the heating system and I was wrapped in my fur coat under the drier when a very large and pregnant cat jumped into my lap. My hands were on the table being manicured, my feet were under the table being pedicured, and I didn't know exactly what to do about the cat! At that moment the Russian woman, who was the head of the beauty shop, came over to offer me a cup of coffee. It was most acceptable, except that I had no place to put it. She asked if I objected to cats. I said no, I loved them, but not to the extent that I wanted them to have kittens in my lap. She reassured me that they were not due for another week. All I could hope was that the cat was equally sure of that fact. But what a composite picture it would have made! Me, the manicure girl, the little gold-toothed Chinese man at my feet, the drier, the cat and the coffee; my next year's Christmas card would have been a natural!

Ed was to stay on for a while at least, but the ECA staff was being reduced as rapidly as possible because the Mission was forbidden to operate in Communist-dominated territory, which was steadily increasing. My feeling was that the days of the Mission were numbered, and that if Roger did come back, it would only be to shut up shop. If he did, I intended to come with him. Otherwise I would have felt I had missed the last three installments of the best serial story I had ever read.

The last two weeks in Shanghai were busy ones, socially, physically, and mentally. Roger was hither and yon, Nanking, Tsingtao, and Taiwan (where he had his picture taken with two native Princesses and the native Chief. They appeared later in "Life" and, like Queen Victoria, I "was not amused" because he had taken off his necktie and tied it around his head to match the headbands the Princesses wore).

Roger got a laugh out of the G'imo the last time he was in Nanking. He had dinner with him and the Madame and recited the 28 provinces of China for him. My husband was never a linguist; his pronunciations must have been very strange indeed to have provoked even a smile from Chiang Kai-shek. The only word Roger was sure of was "Gambei!" (bottoms up when your host toasted you). Ed, who spoke good Mandarin, shuddered every time Roger said "Yang*tze*" instead of "YONgsa." Ed could do nothing about it because Roger insisted it had been "YANg*tze*" when he went to school and it was still good enough for him.

We left Shanghai quite literally in a blaze of glory—1803 popping with firecrackers and loads of people to see us off. Elizabeth Buell, Roger's secretary, was with us, and we three and two newspaper men were the only ones on the flight as far as Tokyo. Two and a half hours there and two and a half more in God-forsaken Wake. Then I discovered that my overnight bag with everything I needed in it, was missing and all I had were the clothes I stood in, my typewriter and a hatbox! So useful for a 48 hour flight!

I was so upset about it that Roger asked me with bated breath if I had all my jewerly in it, to which I was able to answer no, only the $165.00 worth of the "pearls" I wore in my mouth—(my spares). However, the bag turned up in Honolulu just as inexplicably as it had disappeared, and I was more than glad to see it. We went through customs in Honolulu and they opened everything, including my typewriter, to make sure that I had no plant concealed in its insides. With diplomatic passports, we paid no duty, even though I had declared both my jade ring and my bracelet.

We spent 12 hours in Honolulu and three more in Los Angeles because San Francisco was fog-bound. So we arrived seven hours late, weary, dirty, and not even sure what day it was after crossing the International Date Line.

It was good to be home again and to catch up with family and friends. But most of the latter couldn't have been less interested in where you had been, nor in the sort of a life you had been living. They thought I looked "remarkably well, considering what you must have been through" and then couldn't have been less sympathetic when I showed them the pictures of our house and our seven servants.

In Shanghai, I had asked one of the newspaper men what I should say that was really intelligent when people asked me about China. His reply was "China is a vast country with 450,000,000 inhabitants," and stopped there. I said "Well, go on," and he replied "That's all you will ever be permitted to say. After that they will begin telling you about the four days they spent in China in 1921, or wasn't it strange that Mary's seven month's baby weighed 9 pounds, or did people in China (if they could remember where you had been) play much Canasta?" How right he was!

One dear friend did ask me why ECA had been so successful in Europe and such a failure in China. I replied coldly that I did not consider it had been a failure in China, but if that was the general opinion, I might remind her that the annual appropriation for China amounted to one day's spending for Europe. True or false, I enjoyed making the statement because I knew she knew much less of the facts than I did.

Life from then on was such a series of "If's,"—*IF* Roger was held indefinitely in Washington, *IF* the situation in China deteriorated much farther, *IF* we went back, or *IF* we didn't. I apparently dwelt on the IF's to such a degree that someone told me the following "IFFY" story:

During the War, there had been a large American Air Force base very near an English Ducal castle. After entertaining the Commanding General one night, the Duchess had told him that she thought a great deal was being done both for the Brass and for the G.I.'s, but nothing for the Non-Coms; she would be glad to entertain his ranking Non-Com for the following weekend. So he picked his Top Sergeant and sent him over. Monday morning when the Sergeant got back, everyone gathered around and asked him what it was like. "Well, boys" said he, "it was one of those 'Iffy' times." "Come on, Sarg, come through." "Well, boys, I'll tell you; we et off'a gold plate sure enough, but *IF* the water had been as cold as the soup, and *IF* the soup had been as warm as the wine, and *IF* the wine had been as old as the chicken, and *IF* the chicken had been as young as the maid, and *IF* the maid had been as willing as the Duchess, why Hell, boys, I'd 'a been there yet."

After three weeks at home, Roger phoned and said I might as well come on to Washington. It looked as though the House and the Senate had both adopted as their slogan what everyone used to call the D. L. & W. Railroad—"Delay, Linger and Wait." He might be there indefinitely. So I went on for three very pleasant days in New York while

Roger went on to Boston for a Harvard Overseers meeting. Then he and I went back to the Carlton—not our old rooms on the second floor, but their twins on the third. All the old waiters and bellboys greeted us so cordially, it was like Old Home week.

There seemed to be two schools of thought about China. One was to give her an enormous amount of aid—$700,000,000 for Military aid, and $500,000,000 to buy silver for the Government (the suggestion of a Senator from Nevada!). That group insisted that the uprising in China was a purely agrarian movement and denied it was Communist aggression. The second group wished to write China off completely, allow what little money was left from the original grant to be spent and then let China go her own way.

Roger felt very keenly that aid should be continued as long as it was humanly possible; that good men who knew the Orient should be sent to China; and that the United States should not be the ones to draw a "Bamboo Curtain." I went to the House every time a hearing on China Aid was scheduled, but something else always took so long (the terrific black market deals in American automobile tires in Morocco, for instance), that the agenda never caught up with China.

We saw many old friends. The Vandenbergs, Louis Johnson and General Bedell Smith lunched with Roger one day, but I was cordially invited to leave, so didn't get in on that one. We had a pleasant dinner with Paul Hoffman, Charlie Stillman and John Sumner.

Another dinner party raised my blood pressure 100%: one with Mayor and Mrs. Robinson, Roger's successor as Mayor of San Francisco. I sat next to him and he started the conversation by asking me how much longer Roger was going to keep on wasting his time by "gadding around China, and butting his head into a stone wall?" Roger should come back to San Francisco where he belonged, and Mayor Robinson would give him a position "commensurate with his abilities." He would place him in charge of off-street parking!!!! He added it was too bad Roger had not run for a second term, for with the experience gained during his first term, he might have made a *real* contribution to the City!

I counted to ten, slowly, remembering what Jack Neylan had told me before I went on the witness stand, "You are a lady, Helen, and a lady never loses her temper in public." So instead of following my natural impulse and spitting at him, I said mildly that I felt Roger had made a fairly worthwhile contribution to San Francisco even in one term and was continuing to make one in China.

Roger was displaying the patience of Job at the continued postponement of the discussion of aid for China. He was finally rewarded by an appointment to appear before the Senate Committee. He came back pretty sunk. He felt that he had made a poor presentation and that the sentiment was definitely against any future aid. However, he did better before the House Committee the next day. He was aided by a eulogy from Helen Gahagan Douglas, of all people! He then felt that little if anything more could be accomplished and was anxious to have ten days in San Francisco before returning to China. So told me we would go home the following week.

My daily life at that time hinged on whether or not I was going to get back to China. Roger asked Elizabeth Buell in my presence one day if she was willing to take a chance on going back. She said she was and I piped up that I thought if she could go, I certainly could—and I was even willing to pay my own way! Roger laughed but didn't commit himself. Shortly afterwards he got a cable from Allen Griffin saying that, although Jack Cabot was very much against Hester's and my return, he saw no reason why we shouldn't. That tipped the scales. The very next day I heard Roger call his office and tell his secretary to get three airline tickets for Shanghai on the 20th. And right there I slipped a bit, for knowing my dear husband as well as I did, I should have said—doubtfully—"Well, I guess I can be ready by that time. Instead I said "Darling! how wonderful!" The answer: "Oh! well, yours can always be cancelled."

The ten days in San Francisco were busy ones, between dentist, oculist, booster shots, shopping for thin clothes, a permanent, and unpacking my trunks which had come from China. I wrapped up six boxes of gifts to send to various members of my family and distributed others by hand. Among the gifts was a set of cocktail napkins and "drippers" sent to a friend. She commented: "They're very pretty and will probably look better after they are washed!" I was a bit taken aback because they were the Chinese version of Venetian lace made of off-white linen thread and the color was their chief charm.

Roger was given a large dinner by his friends of the Pacific Union Club. When he hadn't gotten home at nine in the morning, I called Nancy to see if Roger Jr. knew what had become of his father. I said "Has Roger Jr. gone out yet?" "No!" said Nancy, "and what's more, he ain't even come in!" We finally located them both at the Club and were happily assured that they were on their last rubber of bridge! Roger Jr. told me later than Roger only went to sleep once, and then, with his eyes shut, pulled the only card out of his hand that could have set a doubled and redoubled contract. The two Lapham wives were slightly bitter, but less so than if their husbands had lost. Nancy, at least, had the satisfaction of being sure it was all her father-in-law's fault.

We left for China on the 20th, spending two nights in Honolulu en route. We were joined by Hester and Elizabeth Buell to continue on to Shanghai where we all arrived on a Thursday. We Laphams had only three suitcases and, of course, my beloved typewriter. Our packing had been done very carefully. I took only sheer necessities and nothing I cared much about. We knew we might have to be evacuated at a moment's notice with just what we could carry in by hand. I did take some odds and ends of jewelry to be made into clips by a marvellous Shanghai jeweler, but they could always go into my handbag at the last minute.

We had a completely uneventful flight and were met at the airport by various Chinese officials, photographers and ECA personnel. We were warmly welcomed by Allen, and very coldly greeted by Jack Cabot to whom I said, "Well, Jack, here's your bad penny." He rather grimly replied "Then make the most of your 48 hour stay, for it won't be much longer."

We were greeted with such a salvo of firecrackers at 1803, that I felt our lives were in far greater danger than they were in the flight across the Pacific. The servants were all beaming and the house filled with flowers. It was good to be home again.

The City seemed perfectly calm as we drove through it, but the news was not good. The GY, which had been 400-1 when we left, was now 700,000-1, or completely worthless, and nothing was accepted but American or Mexican silver dollars. Rice had reached an astronomical sum per picul. The worst news of all: two British gunboats, the "Amethyst" and the "Lion" had been shelled on the Yanktze below Nanking, obviously by the Communists.

The four of us were supposed to fly up to Nanking the next day to spend the night with Ambassador Leighton-Stuart, but word came that Hester and I were not to come and the men were not to spend the night. And how right the Ambassador was! All Nationalist officials, the police, and everyone connected with the Government pulled out of Nanking at midnight and the Commies walked in at eight the next morning! Phil Crowe, who had represented the ECA in Nanking had had a heart attack. He was flown out on a stretcher on the last plane just as the Commies took over the airport.

The papers announced flamboyantly that Shanghai would be defended to the "last drop of blood." To prove how seriously they meant this, a stockade of wooden pilings 8 or 10 feet high was being built around the city by day. But by night the Chinese cut down all of it they could reach for firewood! The "Old China Hands" said there was no use in getting the wind up; they had seen this kind of thing too many times. So they just shrugged their shoulders and said *Mei-fa-tso* —"it can't be helped."

That Saturday night we dined with Admiral Badger on board his flagship the "Eldorado" which was anchored in the Whangpu. He warned that we should be prepared to be evacuated by the following Wednesday or Thursday. He would place two Navy planes at the disposal of the ECA women and children, to be followed a day or two later by an LST for the luggage we couldn't carry.

Sunday morning we went to the Episcopal Cathedral for the Memorial Service for the British sailors killed on the "Lion" and the "Amethyst." It was the grimmest, but the most impressive service I had ever seen. The Cathedral was so crowded that the Honor Guard marching to the "Funeral March" from "Saul," could hardly get through the aisles. Most of the survivors and many of the wounded were present. Everyone sang "The Son of God goes forth to war" and "For all the saints." The service ended with "Last Post" on the bugle and "God Save the King" sung with the deepest feeling and the utmost solemnity.

Roger was in conference all that afternoon with Allen, Admiral Badger and others, but asked Ed and me to go down to the old Chinese City to buy him some scrolls. The city was perfectly calm and seemed normal in every way.

Roger had been in communication with Sir Alexander Grantham to ask if 95 refugees from Shanghai would be welcome in Hong Kong (answer guarded, but very unenthusiastic, as Hong Kong was already overcrowded) and Allen's remarks was "Well, I guess it was a Hell of a time to bring you girls out, but I'm still glad you're here in the middle of history—just as long as history doesn't catch up with you"—which reminded me of the comment of a California friend of mine who said, "My husband and I never go anywhere but Menlo, Montana and the hospital, but there's never a dull moment for the Laphams!"

Monday, April 25th, I went downtown early to have my hair done at Broadway Mansions. It was on the other side of Soochow Creek and the city was such a seething mass of humanity in a rather ugly mood I didn't dare risk being cut off from the one narrow bridge. So went directly to the office. Roger was more than glad to see me because word had just come that we were to be evacuated to Canton at seven the next morning. Could I be ready and, in quavering tones, how many trunks did I have? He was truly relieved when I said no trunks, just three suitcases apiece and my typewriter. Of course I could be ready.

I spent the afternoon packing one suitcase as intelligently as possible. There was the contingency that I might never see the other two again. Ea Te and Amah followed me around like a couple of lost souls, saying nothing but "Oh! Missy! Oh! Missy!" We planned to leave them plenty of rice and tinned stuff which they could always sell for more rice. But still I was heartbroken at walking out and leaving them and their four children—especially with the stigma of having worked for Americans.

Roger came home early to gather his belongings together, but the only bright spot in the day was an item in the "North China Daily News" which read: "Prince Aly Khan slightly injured one toe in an accident at Nice during the weekend. The injury will not delay arrangements for his marriage to film star Rita Hayworth, a member of the Prince's household is quoted as saying."

I sent it to Lewis with my own comment:

> *"Said Rita's Prince, laughing, 'Ho! Ho!;*
> *Ask Rita, she'll certainly know*
> *That I'm Prince Aly Khan,*
> *A most virile man,*
> *And for real fun, I don't use my toe.'"*

The next morning we got up at 5:30, had breakfast, and put the last things in the bags. Then we welcomed the ECA women and children who were to accompany us. Roger and Ed Bodman as interpreter would be in one plane with some of them, and Jimmy Grant in the other with the rest. Jimmy also spoke Chinese so that someone could talk in case of any untoward event.

There were eight cars in the convoy led by Marines in an armed jeep with the siren screaming all the way to Lungwha Airport. A Navy truck with all our luggage brought up the rear. We stood around for an hour or so while the luggage was sorted out and weighed up, and finally climbed aboard. We took off about 9 A.M. Roger, Hester, Elizabeth Buell, Ed, four women, four children, a police puppy and I were in the first plane; Jimmy Grant, nine women and three children including a three months old baby in the second. Allen stayed behind to bring all those who were left plus the office equipment and the rest of the luggage down on a destroyer a day or two later.

It had been a sad get-away from 1803 and the trip to Canton did nothing to raise our spirits. The plane was a bucket-seat job with three chairs in the aisle for the #1, #2, and #3 Missies. Fortunately, the chairs were firmly anchored because they had no seat belts. For four out of the five hour flight, it was the roughest one I had ever had. Hester and I sat clutching the arms of our chairs as we flew over, under, and mostly through, enormous cumulus clouds. We dropped, side-slipped, and bucked all over the place. Everyone except the five of us was sick— including the puppy. While I was not terribly frightened (I had called St. Christopher's attention to our predicament), neither was I as calm as Elizabeth. She put her head down and went to sleep, so she wouldn't know when we crashed!

At one point a piece of luggage broke loose and banged around the plane. When the whole atmosphere showed signs of becoming hysterical, I asked Roger if he didn't have a flask in his briefcase. He said he did but it was for emergencies! I said if this wasn't an emergency I didn't know one when I saw it. So he produced a pint of brandy which was passed around from mouth to mouth. It went around twice and all the women stopped being sick and the children stopped crying. Then the women sat up and powdered their noses, thus proving the truth of Ogden Nash's famous statement that "Candy is dandy, but liquor is quicker." The air flattened out shortly afterwards, due I am sure to my prayers of "smooth out the Heavens like a curtain." With everyone back to normal we were able to put up a good front when we landed in Canton.

Hester, Roger and I went directly to Mr. Samson's house. He was the local ECA director. So much had happened in the last week that it was almost impossible to believe that just a week before Roger and I were sitting in the Royal Hawaiian drinking iced pineapple juice and waiting for Hester and Elizabeth to arrive.

Allen arrived on Thursday and that night the four of us took the night boat "Fatshan" down to Hong Kong to meet the destroyer which was due the next day. We didn't get in until noon, but I still had plenty of time that afternoon for a sorely-needed visit to the beauty shop. With the damp heat on top of my new permanent, I looked more like a French poodle than Nancy and Roger's *Fouff*.

We had tea with T. V. Soong in his charming house on Repulse Bay. He was busily engaged in painting a watercolor of a very lop-sided house which he showed us. The subject house was really four-square, so his off-line picture may have represented inner confused thinking. We had dinner with Sammie at the Hong Kong afterwards; *piece de resistance* was a roast pheasant, carved, but completely reassembled with wings, head and tail feathers—a beautiful sight and tasting just as good as it looked.

While the men went off to meet all the office secreteriat on the destroyer the next morning, Hester and I went window shopping. We saw a very attractive looking woman coming toward us. "Wait a minute" said Hester, "I think I know her. . . . Aren't you Barbara Schurman?" "Yes," said she, "and you're Hester, wait a moment . . . Hyde!" They had been at boarding school together and had not met for 32 years! Barbara invited the four of us for dinner, gave us her address and then, just as we separated, each said simultaneously "What is your married name?" "Petrov" and "Griffin" were exchanged.

We had a most interesting dinner, although we had to leave at 10:30 to go aboard the "Fatshan" for the return trip to Canton. The ECA had chartered her to take care of the passengers from the destroyer. They thought it was a great lark, and sang and danced most of the night. But their tune changed in the morning because they were quartered at the Oikwan, Canton's 3 Star Hotel—third rate even by Shanghai standards. Four hours after they moved in, six of them turned up at Sammie's as a complaint committee. They were prepared for hardship, but not for squalor.

The committee demanded better accommodations. Roger said he would go over and investigate after lunch and asked me to go with him. Over we went to find conditions pretty much as they had described them. The rooms were small. There was no place to put anything you unpacked. The toilets did smell and the tubs were filled with dirty water. Also the elevator ran only to the 10th floor and many of them were on the 14th; every time there was a thunder storm, all the electricity went off and the elevator didn't run at all!

I inspected each room and listened to each complaint. One thing that I had learned as a Mayor's wife, was that if you listened quietly and sympathetically to people, they felt better even if you couldn't remedy conditions. So I just said I hoped we would be able to find them better accommodations later on and left. They all wanted to return to Shanghai, but I was able to tell them that the two hotels where they had been housed there, had just been taken over by Nationalist soldiers. That helped a bit.

I couldn't possibly blame them because my own impressions of Canton were not only confirmed but intensified. It was dirty and smelly, crowded with crippled or deformed beggars and dreadful looking children with running sores or flies clustered in their eyes. You used eyewash every time you got home, always wore gloves and washed them after each wearing; Canton was definitely my most unfavorite city in China.

We were invited to inspect a hospital one day. It was named Fong Ben, or Everybody Welcome, and had 800 beds, but no electric light nor running water! I didn't feel I could face it, but Hester did. She came home pale green from the sights she had seen—two mothers and two babies in one bed, for instance, and many on the very verge of death. But I did go with her one afternoon to work with the Mission Hospital ladies and we were handed canton flannel pajamas to baste together. As I can't see to thread a needle even with my glasses, I was more of a hindrance than a help; I kept one woman busy just keeping me needled and threaded. It was not too successful an afternoon; I did not fancy sewing on canton flannel with the temperature in the nineties and the humidity only a few degrees lower.

We did share one experience, however, which neither of us will ever forget. It was a visit to a child caring agency for war orphans run and financed entirely by the Chinese. The "Shelter" was the remains of a bombed out American Missionary compound. The first thing that met our eyes was a group of teenage boys hammering old tin cans flat to make plates or bend them into cups for the children's use. Next we came to some teenage girls ravelling out torn, discarded, moth-eaten sweaters to re-knit them into socks or sweaters for the smaller girls. Then we heard music and there in one of the more usable rooms was a group of younger boys playing on band instruments some kind soul had sent them from America. Clean and smiling, even though ragged and undoubtedly hungry (they got only two meals a day of rice and vegetables) they were playing the "Hymn of Joy" from Beethoven's Ninth. Could anything have been more touching? Our eyes filled, of course, but before the tears had time to fall they finished the theme; the little leader tapped with his drumstick, gave out a number, laughed at us out of the corner of his eye, and burst into "Yankee Doodle!" No matter how poor or miserable, I had yet to see a Chinese without a sense of humor; and right then and there I decided the Chinese would never become ideological Communists because I had yet to see a Communist who could laugh at himself.

Even though we felt at times as though we were living at the ends of the earth, we had quite a bit of social life: a dinner on board the "Wusueh," sister ship of the "Fatshan"; another given by Consul-General and Mrs. Ludden; and one by Lewis Clark, the Counsellor of the Embassy. And with the numerous letters I wrote, and the men drifting in and out of the house, and a bit of shopping, the days passed quickly too.

Hester was still in pursuit of the perfect pieces of gem jade on which she had set her heart and I was looking in a desultory sort of way for earrings to match my ring rather regretting the ones I had passed up in Shanghai as too expensive. Shopping, as I wrote when I was in Canton before, was not attractive. We always had to have an interpreter. We always gathered an enormously curious, garlic-smelling crowd of

Chinese and every shop, even the higher-class ones, always just plain stunk of urine. A fan and smelling salts helped a bit, but not enough to make it worthwhile to linger longer than was absolutely necessary.

Roger's request for an Army plane to be placed at the disposal of the ECA (made months before) had finally been answered. Roger, Allen and some of the others were to take the same trip to Northwest China that Hester and I had taken with Charley Stillman in October. So, even though we heard that Bangkok was even hotter than Canton (it was just before the monsoon), we decided that rather than sit and swelter in innocuous *desuetude* during the week that the men were away, we would fly down there.

We left Canton on the morning of May 12th. Although we had had our reservations for a week, we found only one seat for the two of us when we got on board the plane. The Chinese had gotten there first! The stewardess simply shrugged her shoulders and said *Maskee* ("it can't be helped"). A nice American newspaper man came to the rescue. He gave me his seat and stood up for the 45 minutes to Hong Kong; he said the ECA had always helped him and now it was his turn to help them. I went in to Hong Kong Airways to complain on my arrival, but the agent simply said I must be wrong; they never over-sold a plane unless there was an emergency so there must have been one that morning!

We spent the afternoon at the beauty shop, dined with the Petrovs and took off at 4:30 the next afternoon for a six hour flight to Bangkok. One of our fellow passengers would have made the gods weep. He was Mayor O'Dwyer's confidential Aide on a good-will tour of the world in 18 days. The tour was sponsored by 50 Trade Associations and he was supposed to represent Father Knickerbocker. He was dressed for the part just like the Quaker Oats man complete with wig, three-cornered hat, ruffled stock, knee-breeches and cane. As he only left the airport at three places and saw no one but photographers and re-porters, I could not see that he accomplished anything except to confirm the belief of all Asiatics that all Americans were crazy. He looked hot and dirty enough at the airport, but when he got on the plane and took off his hat, wig and stock and sat in a filthy undershirt, you were almost ashamed to be a fellow-American.

We landed safely in Bangkok and were met by one of the Secretaries from the Embassy who drove us the 18 miles to town on a beautiful night of full moon. The small hotel, where we stayed, was run by an ex-Navy man, who called it the "American Club" so he could pick and choose his guests. You could stay there only by introduction.

The rooms were small, but completely screened and immaculately clean. There was a single bath between each pair of rooms. My co-bath-mate was up and off early every morning, but Hester's was an Army Sergeant, who bathed and shaved for an hour each day, singing lustily the while. My "out" was a baby, who started yelling at 5:30 A.M. which didn't seem even to disturb his parents, but annoyed me considerably. However, the food was delicious and we revelled in fresh lichee nuts and mangoes. You can't have everything.

The first morning the Commercial Attache and his wife called on us. She took us to deliver our letters of introduction and to "sign the book" at the Embassy. We also left cards; although Ambassador and Mrs. Stanton were not at home, they got in touch with us shortly and invited us for dinner the following Sunday night. It was too hot to shop after lunch, so we came back and relaxed over a cooling lime squash.

That evening the Caltex representative came up and introduced himself and invited us to go with him early the next morning to see the Floating Market. We left at 6:30, took a launch for a couple of miles up the river and then wound our way up one of the innumerable small canals or "klongs" for an hour of sheer enchantment. It couldn't have been more fascinating—jammed and packed with little dugouts bringing their wares in from the country. The boats were filled with every imaginable kind of stuff: cotton sarongs, flowers, silver ware, tin ware, vegetables and fruit. The latter included durians which smell to High Heaven and are said to taste worse; but we were told the Siamese would sell anything they owned for them, because durians are supposed to be a most potent aphrodisiac.

The whole scene was colorful beyond words because the canals are highways and the natives lived in as much as on them. The little shacks and shops faced them; the women wash there. Men were even cleaning their teeth in them. I was sure that a "drop of that water on a dog's tongue would kill a white man." And the children! The little naked brown babies swam, dove, and tumbled around the water as if it was their natural element; I decided a couple of them I saw were so small they could hardly have been weaned.

Our Mr. Caltex was indefatigible. Late that afternoon, he took us to a Siamese style boxing matches—with no holds barred including kicking the opponent in the face if possible. The program was in English and the description of one fighter read as follows: "Forcible and ferocious fighter possessed style of either elbow strike or kick. Expert style advance rushly in attack and nearly in every round of fight. Always send opponent down by knock-out so hope he will create sensational seeingfor (sic) the fans."

We got back to the hotel just in time for dinner in a complete state of exhaustion, but not so Mr. Caltex, who promptly asked us to go and see some Siamese dancers that evening! We felt that he had already acted far above and beyond the call of duty, so we declined gracefully and fell into bed—rushly.

Between sightseeing, shopping and social activities, all our days in Bangkok were full to overflowing. Our sightseeing included the court-yards and public rooms of the Royal Palace, where we felt the shades of "Anna" and her King hovering over us. The little temple bells rang and the mammoth stone statues (brought down from China as ballast in old sailing-ship days) grimaced and leered at us. We saw the Emerald Buddha high in his golden shrine and like "mad dogs and Englishmen," we walked miles in the midday sun.

We saw the Golden Buddha and left some tikals to add another gold leaf to his enormous bulk. We lunched at the old Oriental Hotel on the river with the Dutch Consul-General and his wife, and at the only air-conditioned building in Bangkok, a restaurant called "Chez Eve." We dined at the Embassy with the Stantons, and were more than amused at the residence which was a curious mixture of Oriental spaciousness within, and General Grant architecture without—the whole building painted pistache green! There, we met several Siamese Princes, who seemed to be a dime a dozen, had a delicious dinner and thoroughly enjoyed our evening.

Our stay in Bangkok had the added attraction of being remarkably cheap; for the five days in the American Club, the bill, which included room, bath, meals, laundry and innumerable lime squashes was only $33.00 apiece!

We were called at 3:30 the morning of the 19th, drove out to the airport, and for the first time in history I saw Hester turned down! In spite of her lovely voice, which I had seen charm birds off of trees, and her charming manner, the Captain of the plane didn't seem to think he could detour 300 miles to fly over Angkor Wat, which she tried to persuade him to do. He said very mildly that he guessed he'd better keep to his schedule and that it was all over Communist dominated territory. In short, the answer was "no."

Our last week in Canton was a strenuous one. It included several farewell parties between trying to pack so intelligently that we would need to open only one suitcase until we got home. I was hot and tired and on the verge of being cross that last afternoon. Then Allen, who had left some papers pertaining to our visas, came and asked if I had "filled out my form yet"; I laughed and told him that the last time I had "filled out my form" was in 1918. Roger Junior had been born on the 11th of November and I hadn't filled it out since.

The day we left turned out to be one none of us would ever forget. We were scheduled to leave by the ECA plane at 9:30 A.M.. It was a horrid day of low clouds, wind and rain. I was a bit dubious about the flight because the Kaitak Airport is tricky at best and our rather cocky pilots had been in only once—and then under protest. Allen had insisted they go down the day before on a dry run.

There were loads of people to see us off, pressing farewell gifts into our hands—among them a beautifully carved ivory Chinese junk. We finally took off after shaking hands all around with everyone and flew to within ten minutes of Hong Kong. Then the weather shut down tight, our radio went off and we turned around and flew back to Canton! There was quite a wait at the airport to get a car and then to the Canton Club for lunch. It was the flattest anticlimax I had ever experienced and our friends were anything but glad to see us; "Why we thought you'd gone!" was the prevailing sentiment.

We took off again at 2:45 P.M. and got in . . . under a 200-foot ceiling in a veritable cloudburst. Even one of our cocky pilots got out, patted the ground, and said "Good Old Mother Earth! I sure am glad to feel you again."

Finally we got to the Gloucester Hotel. From then on it was a three-ring circus. Roger and Allen were in conference with Admiral Badger and others in one room. Hester had a tailor in another. I was buying watercolors from a woman in a third room. Everyone left at last and we bathed, changed, and got to an 8:15 dinner only half an hour late. Back to the hotel at 10:30 and into bed for a very restless night with mosquitoes rampant, no screens on the windows, no nets for the beds, and Roger and I ended up in the sitting room at four, smoking, drinking ice-water and scratching mosquito bites for the rest of the night.

Hester and Allen left in the ECA plane at 11 the next morning, bound for Taiwan, and Roger and I took off for Tokyo at noon. We arrived there at 11 P.M. and were met by two GHQ officers. They took us to the Imperial Hotel and put a car at our disposal during our stay. Tired as we were when we arrived, we felt as if we had died and gone to Heaven: an immaculately clean room, a bath with clear, boiling hot water and plenty of it, no mosquitoes, and weather cool enough to sleep under a blanket. Our enjoyment was so great we slept until 10 the next morning.

Later on, we went out in the promised car. I didn't like it at all because it had V.I.P. in enormous letters on the windshield. I wondered why people didn't spit at us as we drove around. But we escaped something at that: one of the Army Officers told us afterward, that if he had only realized that Roger ranked second to the Ambassador, he would have had the letters read "V.I.P.I."—"Very Important People Indeed!"

We lunched with Phil Le Fevre (Caltex, Shanghai) and several Army officers and I immediately asked where I could get culture pearls. I got the very discouraging reply that it was the last of the month, Miki-moto's new supply came in on the first of the next month and that by the 3rd, all the Army wives had cleaned him out! But then I heard that Mrs. Creighton, whom I had known in Shanghai, was in town and knew another place to buy pearls. So that afternoon Roger and I drove out to call on her and her husband. They were staying in a charming little Japanese Inn on the outskirts of town. She said she did indeed know a place to buy pearls, and would take me there the following morning. She did and I found what I wanted—a short string of large pearls for myself, a double string of smaller ones, and a very irregular (and inexpensive) string of baroques. Roger was a bit dubious about the legality of the whole deal, but I assured him it was not a black market operation. So the next afternoon after he had seen mine, he went out and bought some himself.

The last morning, I braved a department store by myself while Roger kept an appointment with General MacArthur. The monetary system was most confusing because the Army issued scrip for use at the hotel, but you had to have Japanese yen to shop anywhere else. Express checks were pounced on with such joy, but I was sure they were illegal and was very careful not to find out if they really were.

That evening, we dined with an Army officer and his wife. I took such a dislike to both of them that I could hardly sit through the evening. They were so scornful of the Japanese and so swollen with the pride of their own position. I felt if he were representative of the large part of our Army of Occupation, I was surprised that the Japanese didn't rise up and kill them all. It really left a very unpleasant impression in our minds.

We took off from Tokyo the evening of the 28th, arriving in San

Francisco on May 30th, 1949, after an easy flight. The trip was saddened by the news which we received just before we left: the Communists had entered Shanghai a month to the day from the time we had left. Home seemed very luxurious, but nevertheless I was conscious of a real pang at the thought that there was little if any possibility of my ever seeing China again. With the lowering of the Bamboo Curtain, I could see little but tragedy ahead for her. I felt that those who thought enthusiastically of the Communists as "Agrarian Reformers" had no conception at all of the ideological drive behind the occupation of more and more of the country and that many unforeseeable dark days lay ahead.

China is a large country and I should add that it is also a large subject both facts I knew from experience. There were so many things I had left unsaid in my journal-letters home: for instance, so little of the real accomplishments of the ECA and nothing of the Joint Rural Reconstruction Commission, which had had a splendid program, but not enough time to implement it. I have hardly touched on the amount of flying Roger and I did—110,000 miles for him, and 50,000 for me. Nor have I said nearly enough about the fine people we met, both Chinese and Americans, the Army, the Navy, the missionaries, the Consular Corps, and the American businessmen of Shanghai. Many were trying to promote good will for America under terribly difficult conditions. I feel very definitely that I have overplayed the lighter side of our Chinese sojourn.

China has a way of twining herself around your heartstrings, as those of us who have known her even in a small way can testify. There are many of us who have loved her from personal experience, and thousands of others who must hope as earnestly as we did to see her emerge from the dark cloud which overshadowed her then. I could not but feel that the thousands of students who had been trained in the Christian Colleges of China, would some day evolve a better form of Government than any she had had in the past, inspired perhaps by the motto Dr. Leighton - Stuart had chosen for Yenching University, "Freedom, through Truth, for Service."

4

NEW ASSIGNMENT:
GREECE

AFTER the stimulation, the excitement and the suspense of the year in China, the next year at home seemed to be so uneventful by comparison that one day just slid into another with only a few outstanding happenings.

Nancy and Roger's fourth child, Norma Preston Lapham, was born on June 27th. Roger made a speech before the Commonwealth Club advocating the recognition of Red China and saying that he thought we should keep men trained in Oriental affairs there as listening posts as long as it was possible. He was very careful to send a copy of the speech to the State Department; he did not wish to be accused at some future time of a leaning towards Communism.

Roger Junior ran for the Board of Supervisors, and was defeated, coming in sixth, as all five incumbents were reelected.

Everything else is a blank until the early summer of '50. Then we went East to our 45th reunions, mine at Smith and on to Roger's at Harvard. While we were still in New York, we received an invitation from the Shell Oil Company to go to England for a week to see our dear friend, Ruth Rieber, christen a new Shell tanker. Roger asked me if I wanted to go and I told him that was putting it mildly: a week in Europe for free with "Cap" and Ruth Rieber, what could be better! So he agreed, even though it meant that he would have to make a flying trip back to San Francisco first.

We took off early in July and were still over Long Island when the Captain announced that there was an oil leak. We would have to return to Idlewild after he had dumped several thousands gallons of gasoline in to the Sound. I was a bit fearful of it exploding and catching fire, but it apparently vaporized as it was ejected. We got safely back to the airport.

England was still so strictly rationed that "Cap" was taking over a dozen hams and a dozen sides of bacon as gifts for his many friends. We were each allotted three hams and three bacons. Customs looked at us a bit suspiciously, convinced that we were going to do some black marketing, but finally passed us through with no more than a warning. From there on we had the red carpet treatment.

We stayed at the Savoy and had a private train to take us to Liverpool for the launching. A reception and luncheon followed after Ruth had cracked a bottle on the tanker and sent the ship down the ways in style. It had all been so much fun that "Cap" said why not prolong the outing and spend a week in France? No good reason not to, so arrangements were made to fly to Paris a day or so later.

Meanwhile, on our last evening in England, Sir George and Lady Leigh-Jones gave a large reception and dinner (he was the President of Shell). "Cap's" ham was served. He sat next to some lady of title, who took one look at the ham and announced that she was going to make a pig of herself; she hadn't seen ham for four years and she was going to take two large slices now, and hope it would be passed again! At which point "Cap" asked if he might send her a ham. Tears came to her eyes, and she said "Do you really mean it? The King and Queen are dining with me tomorrow night. I haven't one thing in the house to feed them and they haven't seen ham in four years any more than I have." "Cap" added a side of bacon when he sent the ham around the next morning in admiration of the *Noblesse Oblige* spirit one saw in those find old English families.

We were off to Paris the next day for some hasty shopping, delectable meals, and a side trip on a chartered plane for a night in Biarritz where we had some good friends, the Bill Brewsters. Everything went swimmingly for Roger and me, but the Riebers had bedbugs in the plushiest of de luxe hotels and "Cap" was arrested as we drove into Spain the next day, for passing a car on a curve.

Back in Paris we stayed over a day to see the celebration of the Quatorze Juillet and have dinner with some friends in their penthouse on the Ile de la Cite. But beautiful as the illuminations were from there, with Notre Dame, the Arc de Triomphe and the Sacre Coeur all flood-lighted, there wasn't enough excitement for Roger. He insisted that we should all go to Montmartre and watch the people dancing and having fun there. So off we went, but every street was jammed and Roger finally jumped out of the car and announced he was going off on his own.

I am sure nothing more of note happened that summer until September when something I had hoped and prayed for occurred: a telephone call from Paul Hoffman asking Roger if he would take a two year assignment as Chief of the Economic Mission to Greece! Roger called me and asked how I felt about it. My answer: "When do we start?" He exploded: "Why, you haven't even thought about it! I think if it had been Timbuctoo, you'd have been just as anxious to go!"

We didn't actually leave San Francisco until the 8th of October, because there were many business and other details to be settled for such a long absence. Jack Peurifoy had just been appointed Ambassador to Greece and that was the determining factor in Roger's mind which made him accept his appointment. I was equally delighted, because, slightly as I knew her, I already loved Mrs. Peurifoy.

We went right to Washington where Roger was to be briefed, and where I found out I was to be too. I reported to the State Department to get my passport and be sworn to uphold the Constitution of the United States. Then followed an hour's briefing from a Miss Wilson, on loan from the State Department to the ECA. It was anything but a pleasant session. The thermometer was in the nineties and she treated me like a congenital moron.

Without asking me if I had ever lived abroad or even traveled, Miss Wilson started with a long spiel about how different living in a foreign country was from what I had been accustomed. She warned that I should be prepared with all possible household equipment including a record player and at least 50 classical records. Everyone in Athens was very musical, she advised, and at cocktail parties after just one drink all the guests sat down to listen to records. I interjected mildly that living in Athens must indeed be different: I had never seen anyone stop with one drink at a cocktail party and every one I knew preferred cocktail chatter to records; furthermore, I did not have a record player at home and I guessed I could get along without one in Athens. Was I taking a Frigidaire? No. All bedding, lamps, silver, and china? No. Did I have the right kind of clothes for my official position? Athens was much dressier than Paris and short dresses for dinner were not correct at all. I must take plenty of long ones and, of course, enough short ones for the aforesaid cocktail parties. Did I have a dressy cocktail hat? To which I said "Take a good look at my face; I'm not the fancy hat type." She almost burst out crying so I did promise to get a hat in Paris.

Then we went on to shoes and underwear. Was mine cotton? No; I had been married 43 years and hadn't worn cotton underwear since for all those years. But I had plenty of nylons, which had done me nicely in China and Greece couldn't be hotter than Shanghai had been. We touched briefly on Roger's clothes and then went to the all-important subject of calling cards; did I have any with me and what size were they? Also, were they engraved or printed? I said I had 200 engraved by the best stationer in San Francisco, but I had no idea of the size. Now I knew; the official card is 2 inches by $3\frac{1}{2}$, except for an Ambassador's which is $2\frac{1}{2}$ x $3\frac{3}{4}$. So I did sweetly agree to have new ones made for Roger with his official title, which were to read:

ROGER D. LAPHAM

Chief of Special Mission to Greece

Economic Cooperation Administration

Athens

with the type in three sizes, large, small and smaller.

She went back again and again to my clothes, until completely exasperated I said I had everything I owned and they would have to do. Finally, I said, "Miss Wilson, you have asked me if I have traveled or ever lived abroad; all of this information could have been given you on a slip of paper which it would have taken you five minutes to read. It would have told you what positions my husband had held and given a slight idea of what my social experience had been. You have asked me a great many questions and now I would like to ask you one: Have you ever traveled?" "Oh! yes," said she, "I spent a week at Haiti once, and I almost got to Paris last fall! And I wouldn't have time to read such a memorandum as you suggest, because I am briefing the women of 28 different countries."

She got in the last word. As I left she first said she did sincerely hope I wouldn't make too many *gaffes,* such as going down town in Athens in shorts or forgetting to seat the guest of honor at the host's right at dinner. Then she presented me with a book entitled "Formalities In the Foreign Service of the United States of America." I read part of it after I got home and got the first real laugh I had had all day. There were 20 pages of instructions marked RESTRICTED and contained such gems as: "HOW TO MAKE CALLS: Calling in the Foreign Service has the purpose of announcing an arrival and making the first move to create a new friendship. If the door should be opened by the lady of the house, drop the cards which you will have in your hand inconspicuously into the card tray which should be in evidence."

That afternoon we asked an Admiral and Mrs. Moore for cocktails. They were just back from Greece where he had been ranking Admiral. She was able to tell me all sorts of things she thought I should know—particularly about the two houses, one of which we were supposed to choose as our residence. We had heard by the grapevine that the State Department would very much like us to occupy the marble palace on which former Ambassador Grady had taken a five year lease, rather than the smaller, simpler house which had already housed two ECA Mission Chiefs. Mrs. Moore told me that the Grady house had any number of salons and rooms for formal entertainment, but only two bedrooms—one on the ground floor and one on the third floor—and was almost impossible to heat. The other house, while too small for large parties, had five bedrooms. It sounded far more my style. So I could hardly wait to see it.

We were off for Paris November 7th. It was a comfortable flight across although not much sleep. Roger was such an expansive sleeper on a plane that when his feet weren't in my lap, his head was on my shoulder with his loving arm cutting off my wind.

Elizabeth Buell and an ECA man met us and escorted us to the Hotel Continental where we had stayed 21 years before on our way home after the close of the Food Administration Program. I felt that absolutely no changes had been made in it since. Roger went to the ECA Headquarters in the old Hotel Talleyrand on the Rue Florentin right after lunch. I betook myself to my little milliner, Jane, to order Miss Wilson's "must" dressey cocktail hat. I was determined to find something which was a cross between her ideas and my face. I did; an always flattering black velvet with a sweeping Bird of Paradise at the side for which I had always yearned, but of course could not wear in America, so it was now or never.

Roger and I had a quiet dinner *a deux,* and to bed early, for we both needed sleep. We lunched the next day with Bill and Thelma Brewster and had dinner with "Ambassador" and Mrs. Katz. He was the head of the whole European ECA setup, had Ambassadorial rank and used it. I had just heard that Roger had it too, but couldn't imagine his using it. To both of us there is just one American Ambassador to each country and he is the one appointed and confirmed by Congress. I thought of the wonderful conundrum Lewis had told me before I left New York: "What is it that has two legs and sleeps with cats?" The answer: "Mrs. Katz and sometimes Mrs. Feigenbaum." I thought it was funny enough when I heard it, but not nearly as funny as after I had seen Ambassador Katz. He would have fainted with horror if such a thing had been suggested to him.

We flew from Paris in beautiful weather, but it was raining hard as we crossed the Alps at 21,000 feet altitude. I was glad it took only 40 minutes and not as long as it took Hannibal with his elephants. It was raining and blowing even harder in Rome and quite rough for half an hour. But then it cleared and the air flattened out. It was lovely and clear when we arrived at Athens at 2 A.M. to be met by Paul Jenkins, the #2 ECA man and several underlings who took charge of passports, baggage checks, etc.

Our first lunch was with the Peurifoys. Afterward, Betty Jane (Mrs. Peurifoy) took me to see the Grady residence we were supposed to take. The Peurifoys had been expected to use it as the Embassy residence, but had refused in favor of a smaller and much more charming house. When I saw it, I knew why. It wasn't my cup of tea either and I think I would have died of acute melancholia if I had had to live in it.

In the first place the house was in the heart of town with no grounds around it; secondly, it was too much like a very elegant mausoleum. The front was all white marble. The entrance hall was at least 60 x 40 feet paved in black and white marble squares and tastefully adorned with grim busts of Roman Emperors. The ceiling was 20 feet high and the furniture gigantic. On the right, there was a library, two reception rooms and a dining room with a table seating 30. On the left, another salon, then one bedroom, dressing room and bath; no other bedrooms except the two on what (because of the height of the ceiling) amounted to the third floor reached by a long narrow flight of winding stairs. The kitchen in the basement was the size of a skating rink. I was ready to say I'd take the other house sight unseen, rather than even consider living in this monstrosity. Fortunately, it appealed to Roger as little as it did to me.

The next day we went for cocktails at the other house, #9 Yasemion Street in Psychico, a suburb of Athens about 15 minutes from the heart of town. I fell in love with it at first sight for it was very reminiscent of 1803 Avenue Joffre, only more so. Five bedrooms instead of three, including a lovely guest suite. Although the dining room only held twelve at a pinch, there was a good sized living room, a large white marble terrace, a spacious library, and plenty of room for entertaining buffet style. The grounds were half a block wide and a whole block long, terraced down from one street to the one below.

I went out to see it in detail the following day and was rather appalled at what it lacked. Although there was plenty of furniture, there was no silver, no linen, 100 cocktail glasses and four old-fashioneds, almost no bedding, no pillows, and not a coat hanger, ash tray or vase in the entire house! Fortunately, our trunks would contain most of the deficiencies when they came, but in the meantime it was borrow from anyone who could lend us what we had to have before we could move in. Betty Jane said not to worry, everyone had done it in their turn, and it was expected. Our procurement officer promised to order silver, glass and china for us from Paris. So we begged, borrowed, and did everything but steal so successfully that we were able to move in a few days later.

The house was already staffed with a houseman who spoke Greek, English and French, (although he was born in Malta and was a British subject); a maid who spoke only Greek, and a so-called cook. As long as I had inherited them, I thought I might as well keep them on and wait until I saw how things worked out.

It obviously was going to be a very different life from the experience we had had in China. I could see it was going to take quite a bit of getting used to.

In the first place the office hours were so strange: 8 A.M.-2 P.M. and 3:30-6 P.M. on Mondays and Fridays; 8 A.M.-2 P.M. on Tuesdays, Wednesdays and Thursdays, and 8 A.M.-1 P.M. on Saturdays, which meant lunch never before 2:30, and generally nearer 3:00, after which everyone siesta-ed. Cocktail parties were from 7-9, and dinners, even at your own home, either at 9 or later. It meant quite a bit of adjustment.

The telephone service was very poor; it took ages to get Central and when you did, she either gave you the wrong number, or the right one was busy and you had to start all over again. Athens had been so swamped with the influx of refugees from the North during the Communist troubles that none of the public utilities had been able to keep up with the growth of the population.

We had both Commissary and PX privileges. The former was pretty good, except that everything in it was either frozen or powdered, but the PX wasn't nearly as good as the one in Shanghai. No Greek cook, I discovered, had any idea how to deal with frozen meat—at least not one of the four I had in the first three months. We got some pretty unsavory messes. Liquor came in tax-free, which was a boon, but there was only one place it could be bought and it was generally sold out by the fifth of every month.

Athens itself was an odd mixture of really lovely houses with slums next door. Even the American Embassy residence faced on a "Camp" where refugees from Turkey had been "Camping" since the early 'twenties! The general landscape and the trees were very reminiscent of Southern California: palms, pepper trees, oleanders, etc., even to the little flower stalls on the downtown street corners. Our house faced the very bare Mt. Hymettus, which we were variously told had been denuded of trees by (1) the Communists, (2) the Germans, (3) the Turks. Actually, it had been stripped of all trees in the 15th or 16th Century and aided, I was sure, by the peasants ever since. (Wood was scarce and worth its weight in gold, whereas marble was very inexpensive and used extensively even in the poorest houses and apartments.)

The first formal party given exclusively for us, was a reception given by the Peurifoys. We met many of the Diplomatic Circle there as well as many of the prominent Greeks. Mrs. Peurifoy was wonderful at their names: Mr. and Mrs. Costopoulos, Mr. and Mrs. Pezmazoglou, and all the rest rolled trippingly from her tongue. Many of them she had seen only once or twice before! I knew from the start it was beyond me—and it was.

There were two large dinners, one given by General Jenkins, the head of the American Military Mission, at which I sat between the Chinese Ambassador and the Spanish Minister. I talked China to one and practiced my Spanish on the other. The second was a dinner of 60 given by the Prime Minister, Sophocles Venizelos. I was between Averof, the Minister of Finance, who spoke perfect English, and Vice-President Papendreou who asked if I spoke French and said he preferred it. In my best French, I said I had heard he was the finest orator since Demosthenes; after a momentary pause, he said "Madame, you are right; I cannot deny it." After that the *entente* couldn't have been more *cordiale*.

The second weekend after we moved into our house, we flew down to Crete to take part in a ceremony celebrating the opening of 15 miles of new road connecting a remote part of the Island with the main road to the capital, Canea. We took off on a Saturday afternoon 24 strong— ECA men and one ECA wife, members of the Greek Government, two interpreters, young Venizelos (grandson of the "Grand Old Man" and the nephew of the Premier), and a Greek-American girl secretary who had been born in South Carolina!

We had a beautiful flight of an hour across the Aegean, and were met at the airport by a welcoming committee that included the Governor of the Island. We were given armfuls of flowers and started our drive to Canea, but stopping several times in small villages to receive more flowers, and to give the people a good look at the new Chief of Mission.

At Canea, we were lodged at the Venizelos summer residence. Roger and I each had an enormous bedroom with a bath between. The accommodations were very comfortably furnished—even a bedside lamp and sheets from B. Altman's with the pricemark still on them!

That night, we attended the Governor's dinner of 60 at eight o'clock. I sat between the Governor and a nice fat Greek General whose name was Napoleon Zervas. The Governor spoke no English and I couldn't understand Zervas. But I soon discovered they both spoke French; I called Napoleon *mon General* and all went swimmingly. Speeches topped off the evening with the Governor's first—translated—then Roger's. His, I thought, was a bit restrained. Later, he told me he had been instructed to save the fireworks for the next evening. At the conclusion of dinner, Roger and I were each given a present. His was a beautiful Greek knife in a sliver scabbard and mine, a tiny duplicate of it to wear as a lapel pin.

The experience of the next day was indescribably touching, one such as we had never had before and would never forget.

We left Caneá at nine with the Governor and Venizelos in our car and drove over about 30 miles of narrow, winding mountain road. We stopped at each little hamlet we came to — probably 15 in all. At each place the entire population was out to welcome us *"Kalos Orisate!"* Then they gave us flowers—roses, chrysanthemums, marigolds—and food—walnuts, almonds, honey, cheese—followed by tiny glasses of liquor called *raki*. We were warned to touch the *raki* to our lips only, because it was liquid dynamite.

At one of the places, there was a fine, tragic looking woman dressed entirely in black. She read a three page longhand document which Venizelos told us was a recital of what that town had suffered during the German occupation; a mile further on, we saw evidence of it . . . a white marble mausoleum containing the skulls of 170 men who had been taken out and machine-gunned in reprisal for the kidnapping and killing of a German General. The skulls were in a glass coffin in the center of the little building. All around the sides were the huge funeral wreaths of gold and silver leaves you see in every European cemetery. The woman was the widow of the *Nomark*, who had been killed; she was to wear black for the rest of her life. The mausoleum had been given by a Greek-American from New London, Connecticut, who had been born in the village. It was brought home to me that it is one thing to sit comfortably miles away and read of atrocities, but something else again to see visible evidence of them, or as one small boy said, "My papa's head in there!"

And so it went at village after village. "Village" is a misnomer; they weren't villages as we think of them, but just a cluster of a few houses spread along the highway with no shops, nothing except a small *taverna* with a trellis and a grapevine over the beaten earth court-yard. There the few poor old men, who were left, could gather for a cup of Turkish coffee or a glass of *retzina,* the native wine. Grinding poverty was all too evident, but how the faces of the men and women stood out! Strength, determination, and the will-to-endure and yet all of them overflowing with heartwarming enthusiasm at our coming.

We reached the terminus of the road where the ceremonies were to take place—Kampanou—at 12:30, and there was a crowd of at least 3,000 gathered for the celebration. The first part of it was the blessing of the new road. A table had been set up out-of-doors for an altar with candles, a cross, a glass of water, and a few little green sprigs of some plant. Two bearded priests put on their vestments, one crimson and one gold, and started to intone the service. All I could think was, did they have to have a beard to become a bishop, or did they make bishops of the ones who had the best beards?

The Bishop of Caneá was one of our party, and I was sure he told them to cut it short (the service, not the beard), because right in the middle, one priest nudged the other, who promptly skipped about five pages of the prayer book. Then they dipped the twigs in the water, sprinkled us, and gave us the silver cross to kiss. General Zervas rushed forward to cut the ribbon across the road which Roger was supposed to do, and we all progressed to the feast with five cameras going like mad.

People were everywhere; on the roofs, in the olive trees, on the hillside, and the confusion of seating the chosen few was terrific. I had Zervas on one side and the Bishop on the other. He spoke only Greek and German, so all we could do was smile and eat—to say nothing of drink. It was my first taste of *retzina,* and I thought that a mistake must have been made. It tasted like furniture polish! The real wines, however, both red and white were very good and so was *ouzo,* the aperitif, which tasted like licorice.

After the feast, which included barbecued lamb and suckling pig, the speeches began. Roger made a corker, saying it was their road; that they had all built it themselves—men, women and children—with no financial assistance from the ECA, just the loan of some equipment; that they were leaders in showing what could be done when everyone worked together. Then he emphasized that the road had to be cared for and kept in good condition just as their crops were. He ended by saying we had come 10,000 kilometers to see the opening of this road and that although we had arrived in Crete only the day before as strangers, today we had hundreds of friends—*"Zito Créta!"* ("Long live Crete!"). Then he hauled me to the mike and I said my two words of

338

Greek *"Efxaristo pole"* ("Thank you very much").

As it was then after 2 P.M., and we had left at 9 A.M., it was definitely time for me to find a "convenience." So I asked an English woman, the wife of the Greek construction Supervisor, where I could pay a visit. She said I would find it very primitive, but she would take me. She led me about 50 yards away to a hole in the ground behind an olive tree with a very transparent screen of rushes.

Some girls in native costumes did some dances for us before we left, and we got away by 3 P.M. There were also a couple of stops on the way back. At one of them, a man came up and told Roger he had lived in Los Angeles for 17 years! We got to the house by 7 P.M.—just in time to change for a dinner of 100 the Nomark was giving us. I had *"Mon General"* again and by this time we were pretty chummy. He said I must be a woman of great endurance; I think I would have preferred "of great charm," but perhaps his statement was more nearly correct.

The next morning we went up and laid some of our flowers on the "Grand Old" Venizelos' grave and then took off at 9 A.M. for Athens. As our bags went into the car, I discovered a large demijohn of wine and a live turkey being added. The wine was all right, but what was I supposed to do with a turkey on the hoof? Fortunately the hostess of the plane claimed it as we landed!

The next week was taken up with my presentation to the Queen and to the various Ambassadrice, under the auspices of Betty Jane, all of them set for 11 A.M.

The Queen received us at the summer residence of Tatoi, about 15 miles outside of Athens. She graciously met us at the door, so we didn't have to make the three regulation curtsies. The Queen was a petite woman of real beauty and great charm. It was difficult to believe that she was Kaiser Wilhelm's granddaughter. She kept us well beyond our allotted 20 minutes and, of course, we had to wait to be dismissed. So I decided to help out a bit, knowing how many others there were in the waiting-room. I said, "Before your Majesty dismisses us, I would like to tell you a little story I heard just before I came to Greece. A dear friend, who is a member of UNESCO, had just been to a meeting in Italy and was accosted by a Senator at a Washington cocktail party. "And what do you represent, Madame?" said he. "I represent UNESCO, Senator" she replied, whereupon, rolling his eyes towards Heaven, he said "Ah! Your brave little country. What a magnificent fight she put up, and how we all respect her." "Thank you, Mrs. Lapham" laughed the Queen, "I shall tell it to the King tonight and it will make him laugh, which he needs to do nowadays." Indeed he did! Because the Communists were still not entirely driven out of Northern Greece.

Of course, what Miss Wilson had neglected to tell me was that whenever you were near enough to shake hands with Royalty, you wore the left glove only, leaving the right hand bare to show you were carrying no concealed weapons.

All the other presentations followed a prescribed pattern: you arrived at 11 o'clock sharp; were given either sherry or some sticky, sweet drink; talked formalities for 20 minutes and left. However, the one with Lady Norton, the wife of the British Ambassador, differed slightly because she had forgotten we were coming. She had been gardening and came in very informally garbed. She immediately offered us tea, the usual British "elevenses" and then asked Betty Jane if she thought that having just had her face lifted was an improvement! "Clifford, my dear," she said "didn't even notice it. And I cawn't understand why. All the wrinkles around me mouth are now around me eyes."

We were due to go to Salonika by train the next weekend, but in the meantime a most marvellous invitation came—a reception given by the King and Queen for the Princess Elizabeth and Prince Philip. I was agog with excitement, especially as the Peurifoys had asked us to dinner first. But Roger was very luke-warm: he didn't have his tails with him (he did), his shirts didn't fit, his white tie was too short, etc., etc. I said I was going anyhow. Finally he agreed that if I could find him a shirt and tie that fitted him, he would go, too. I called up our procurement officer, who provided the necessary articles, and we went to something the like of which we would never see again.

The reception was held in the beautiful gold and white ballroom of the Palace. The Royal entourage entered at 11 P.M. to the fanfare of silver trumpets. At least 200 people were lined up along the walls of the room and the Queen and Princess Elizabeth made the circle, stopping to say a few words to many of the women as they rose from their curtsies. As I arose from my curtsy, the Queen said "I told your story of UNESCO several times with great success!" Imagine her remembering me and my story after seeing me once for only 20 minutes in a tailored suit!

She was perfectly radiant in a pale pink Dior dress that looked as if it had been sprinkled with star-dust. Her jewels were magnificent: an emerald and diamond necklace with emeralds much larger than pigeons eggs, emerald earrings and a diamond crown as well as various ribbons and decorations. The Princess Elizabeth was very slight, much prettier than her pictures, but lacked the warmth of the Queen. She wore a heavy white silk dress embroidered with golden wheat, a ruby and diamond necklace and a diamond crown, but a smaller one than the Queen's.

Then I had some terrible decisions to make: to which of the muchly bedecorated men, who followed should I curtsy? I had made up my mind to follow Betty Jane, but there was a problem. I found that trying to watch her with one eye, the men with the other and curtsy all at the same time, gave me a horribly cross-eyed expression. It was more difficult than rubbing your head with one hand and patting your stomach with the other.

After the Queen had made the circle, she paused opposite me in the center of the room, caught my eye, and indicated by the slightest inclination of her head that I was to present Roger, which I did. He had, of course, already been presented to the King. I asked him afterward if he had noticed her jewels. "No," said he, "I was looking at her eyes."

On December 1st, we left by train for Salonika at 7:15 A.M. in a pretty gloomy state of mind. We had just had a cable from Roger Jr. telling us that Mother Lapham had had a massive stroke and the outcome was doubtful. But the trip had been scheduled and we had to go. It was an inspection tour of the marvellous work of reconstruction that had been done on the railway, where the Germans had blown up all the tunnels and bridges as they retreated. We were a party of 25, ECA men and wives, Greek Minister of Transport, the General Director of the railway, etc. With our many stops to inspect the improvements, the trip took 12 hours. We arrived at Salonika just in time to get to the hotel and clean up and change for an 8:30 dinner given by the Minister of Transport. I sat beside him and found he spoke French, so it was an easy evening for me.

We were up and off early the next morning, again by train, to inspect some lignite mines, with a stop at a place called Berea. The name rang a bell in my mind and I realized that it was one of the cities St. Paul had visited. I saw so many of them from then on, I decided he had stayed more places in Greece than George Washington did in America. And never did I expect when I sang "There's a cry from Macedonia, 'Come and help us'" in the Bedford Presbyterian Sunday School, to actually be in Macedonia and see help given—in a more material way, I was sure, than the B. P. S. S. ever envisioned.

At the end of the railway line, a place called Amyndeon, we had a second cable from Roger Jr. It reported that Mother's condition had worsened. The 40-kilometer drive to the lignite mines over a very rough road was not a happy one.

We arrived back in Salonika in time to call on the Consul-General and the USIA representative. The latter turned out to be the nice young man Hester and I had met in Chungking, who had escorted us to the convenience and provided us with toilet paper! Roger and I had met him the night before, so I was all prepared with a small roll of toilet paper tied up in fancy wrapping. I presented it to him to the great surprise and slight dismay of his young bride, who thought it a very strange gift for her bridegroom. He appreciated both the gift and the joke.

Back in Athens, I had my second Greek lesson and I was finding the language very puzzling. It was by far the hardest I had ever tackled, especially as I did not even know the alphabet except the names of a few Greek fraternities—and Phi Kappa, naturally. Things were not what they seemed in Greek. Why "MPAP" should spell "Bar" was completely beyond me—even after it was explained that "MP" was "B" and "P" was "R."

That afternoon I was sitting in our little library when I saw a Greek Orthodox priest in the garden. Vincent, our houseman, came in to say he had asked permission to bless the house. Of course, I gave permission gladly. I went out and he made the sign of the cross on my forehead with the little green sprigs we saw used in Crete. I kissed his silver cross, gave him a small donation and he left. Later, I found out that it was Saint Barbara's Day and he was the priest of the little parish church dedicated to St. Barbara—one of my names. I felt sure I had received an extra blessing.

Ten of us took off by air the next morning for Alexandroupolis in Northern Thrace to inspect some of the ruined, but rehabilitated villages in that general area. We were met at the airport by Mr. Frisbie, the Field Service Director for that part of the country, and his charming wife.

The first village we visited consisted of 130 relocated families who had been forced to leave when it was completely destroyed by the Communist Guerrillas in 1947. ECA had provided some of the hard-to-get building materials and the Greek Government had given a modicum of financial help. Villagers had done the rebuilding themselves—the women participating just as fully as the men. There was no light, heat, water, or sanitation, but the villagers displayed their houses with great pride.

We visited two other villages that afternoon. They were nearer the border, so we were under the escort of an armed jeep. At each stop, the proceedings were much the same. A large crowd would greet us. At one village there was a sign reading "WELL COME" and a small boy read a short speech in English. Roger pushed me forward to say my few learned-by-heart words of reply in Greek. Then everyone pressed around to shake hands or even just touch him. With no thought of sacrilege, I understood for the first time how the hordes of people had felt about the Christ—that they could gain virtue if they so much as touched the hem of His garment. The villagers knew the benefits they had received from the Marshall Plan aid and Roger was the first Chief of Mission who had been able to visit any of the Field Service stations. To the people, Roger literally represented the unknown god.

After the singing and dancing with the children, we all progressed to the cobbled village square with its colorful blue and pink houses. From the balcony of the Town Hall, Roger made a speech saying how deeply he appreciated what Greece had suffered. He congratulated them for what they had accomplished with their own hands and always ended *"ZITO!"* and an approximation of the name of the town we were in. His Greek pronunciation was not the best; in fact, even "Psychicho" baffled him and usually came out either "Sickkico" or "Physico."

We left Alexandroupolis at 8:30 (the second day was more or less a repetition of the first), and reached Kavalla by 6:30 p.m. We stayed with the Frisbies, who had a bathroom with plenty of hot water!—and did we soak out stiffness, fatigue and dirt in it with joy and rapture.

We were up and refreshed after a wonderful eight hour sleep and off for a tour of the city. We visited the Chapel of St. Silas, the first place where St. Paul is supposed to have preached in Europe. From there we went to Philippi where we saw the prison from which St. Paul was delivered by an eathquake. I was certainly following in the footsteps of St. Paul, physically if not spiritually.

We took off at noon for our two hour flight back to Athens. It was mostly over the clouds, so we did not catch a glimpse of Mt. Athos, for which I was hoping because it is the only way I would ever see it. No females of any kind are permitted there except birds which they can't help. I was told that fifty years ago a cow wandered in and practically caused a major scandal.

New Year's Eve we spent at the McCauley's (ECA) and it was a gala evening of songs, supper and bridge. We got home at 4 a.m. We were both still asleep at 11 the next morning, when I woke up and suddenly realized that Roger was due at the Palace at noon to wish "Happy New Year" to the King and Queen in the full regalia of white tie and tails! I had ordered coffee which I handed him as I woke him and said "get up and climb into your glad rags, you've only got about half an hour to do it."

It was raining torrents and Roger hated full dress like poison under the best of circumstances, but to have to get into it on the morning after the night before . . . well, I thought I'd heard about everything, but I heard some good new words before I finished tying his white tie. It was really a pretty ridiculous business, standing in line for half an hour or so, just to shake hands and say *"Kala Chrystouneia"* and then spend another half hour waiting for a car.

One afternoon was most amusing. The Brewsters and Muriel King, ECA friends, called for us and took us out to the Kanakis Taverna, about 7 miles from Athens for lunch. They had been there many times before and were greeted rapturously by the family—Momma, Poppa, and so many grown children it was hard to count them. I asked Momma how many she had had and she said "Fourteen, fifteen, after twelve I lost count!"

The Taverna was a low, one-story, white-washed, rambling house built around a farmyard. Rooms had been added haphazardly as needed and all at crazy angles. You entered through the room where the huge casks of wine were stored. (They made their own wine and before we left we were asked to come out the next fall and help tread out the grapes.) Then you passed into the courtyard to a low, dark barn filled with pigs, lambs and chickens. It could easily have been a scene of the Nativity—even to the stalls for the beasts and the manger. Next to it was a shed with an oven where they baked the bread and beyond that the main house. There was also a garden filled at the time with daffodils and narcissus in full bloom.

By the time we had finished our tour of inspection it was raining, so we all crowded into the kitchen to eat in front of the open fire. There were five of us plus fat Momma, one son and at least three daughters. The kitchen was none too large, but so warm and cozy! Our first course was tiny fish—"just two hours out of the sea"—cooked over a fire made from the cuttings from the olive trees; the frying pan was poised on top of an iron tripod. We got them sizzling hot right out of the pan accompanied by plate after plate of French fries. Everything fairly melted in the mouth! Next came little lamb cutlets, three apiece, with more potatoes and all washed down with their own wine, which was a great improvement on *retzina*.

Then the singing started. Roger favored with "Oh! you *push* the damper in, and you *pull* the damper out, and the smoke goes up the chimney just the same." After the third rendition, everyone joined in and we all roared it out together. By this time, the rain had stopped and we adjourned to the countyard for dancing.

We left about 6 p.m., laden with flowers and eggs so warm I was sure they had gone out and squeezed a couple of hens to get them for us. It was a real experience, and I felt that the whole setting might have come right out of Homer.

January 12th, we started off with the Russell Drakes, a charming ECA couple, on a motor trip to Patras and Delphi via Corinth. Our first stop was for a look at the Corinth Canal. Nero conceived the idea in A.D. 67, but actual work on the canal did not start until 1881. It was opened in 1893. It is three miles long and 75 feet wide, with sheer rock walls 230 feet down from its bridges.

From there, we went on to old Corinth and ate a picnic lunch on the steps of the Temple of Apollo after we had been through the museum. It was lovely and warm sitting there in the sun and we thoroughly enjoyed it. We wandered around the ruins for quite a while after lunch, but I was quite willing to admit that I was either too deficient in imagination or education to appreciate them. When I was shown an unattached piece of marble and an amorphous lump of stone and told it was Hercules and the Nemean Lion, I just didn't get it. Roger didn't either, which made me feel a great deal better.

We reached Patras about 5 o'clock after a very pleasant 150-mile drive through a fertile country. The hotel was really luxurious. It had two rooms with baths, of which the Drakes had one and we the other.

The next morning, we were off to visit a very famous winery where they had casks of wine made for such notables as the Empress Elizabeth of Austria, Bismarck, and Queen Alexandra, locked away and never touched. The first thing we spotted was an award from San Francisco's Treasure Island Exposition. After we signed the book, we had a small glass of the *spécialité de la maison,* Movrodaphne. I don't like heavy sweet wine, especially at 10 a.m., but it was an 1884 vintage and I couldn't refuse to drink to the year of my birth!

We started for Delphi in a heavy rain without knowing the condition of the roads. Our caravan included two cars and a jeep. We were ferried across the narrowest part of the Gulf of Corinth—between two fine old Venetian forts guarding each side of the Strait—on a small LST. After landing we started on an 85 mile drive that was a honey of a mountain road most of the way—narrow, winding, mountain on one side and a sheer unguarded drop on the other. All of it was muddy and slippery with a good bit of it under water. We had an excellent driver, but even so I had callouses on both feet from putting on the brakes coming down the last 25 kilometers.

We reached Delphi in a very heavy rain. But at least we were on good, comparatively level paved road and as long as it didn't turn to snow we were all right; Delphi was 2500 feet up on the slopes of Mt. Parnassus. We had been told that the hotel was the best one in Greece outside of Athens, but that was a slight exaggeration. Our room contained two iron beds, one chair, one very small table, a washbasin and three hooks on the wall. There was no heat and the glacial chill was like nothing I had ever felt since Venice in March, 1931. We had a drink with our teeth chattering against the glass and then crawled into bed with all our clothes on—plus hot water bags and all the covers we could find including my fur coat! But even then it was too cold to rest, so we went downstairs for tea, another drink and dinner. Eventually the heat came up and we had a pleasant evening with an Englishman named John Hare, the Field Representative for that area.

Two interesting dinners followed shortly after the trip: one at the Chinese Ambassador's and the other at the Peurifoy's for the King and Queen. At the former we had all my favorite dishes—birds' nest soup, sharks' fins, sweet sour pork, and rice with all sorts of tidbits mixed through it, all of course eaten with chopsticks.

At the Peurifoy dinner, we were asked to be at the Embassy residence at 8:15 for an 8:30 dinner because everyone had to be assembled before the King and Queen arrived. There were 18 of us. During the 15 minute wait, most of the women were worrying about their curtsies. Then the Royal party arrived. It included the Queen's *Maitresse de Robes,* a charming older woman, and Colonel and Mrs. Levides. He was the *Grand Maréchal du Cour.*

I had discovered that it was a very wise idea to wear a full skirt if you had to curtsy; a few days earlier, meeting the King and Queen unexpectedly in a museum, I had made my curtsy in a tight suit skirt and split it right up to the knees! So now I had on a wide skirted, ruby and ivory striped satin dress and Betty Jane was in white chiffon with touches of jade green. The Queen looked more like someone out of a fairy tale than ever. She was in a *robe de style* of blue chiffon with an overdress of the same color—with raised velvet figures in warm brown which was perfect with her sapphire blue eyes and chestnut curly hair. Her jewels were four strings of pearls, a diamond pin, a couple of orders, and a huge emerald and diamond ring.

Betty Jane signaled me to come and talk to her and the Queen immediately asked me for another story. I told her the one about Molotov talking on the phone from Moscow to the French Foreign Minister in Paris with Stalin at his elbow. Molotov says "Nyet, nyet, nyet" shaking his head violently. Finally, he says "Da" and Stalin says "Vait a minute; vat for you say 'Da'?" To which Molotov replies "He asks me can I hear him."

It was not much of a story but it amused her and she said I must tell some of my stories to the King. I said I had already told her the only three respectable ones I knew and she laughingly replied, "You know some other kind? That is the kind the King likes best!" I could just see myself as the wife of the Chief of the Economic Mission stepping up to the King of Greece and saying, "Want to hear a good off-color story, Your Majesty?"

Roger went to Paris for a Mission Chiefs' meeting the next week, but I did not lack for entertainment. I was invited for dinner three out of the five nights he was gone. One was a most casual invitation from Mary Karolou, one of the Queen's Ladies-in-waiting: "If you're not doing anything Saturday night, we'd love to have you dine with us. The Peurifoys will bring you." I explained that Roger was away, but Mme. Karolou said she knew that and wanted me anyhow. When we got to the Karolou's I noticed that all the women but me had on a long left glove and I began to have a sneaking suspicion that Their Majesties were coming, too. So I said to Mary that I was sorry I had forgotten my gloves and she asked if I would be more comfortable if I had a pair. I got the picture and said "yes" and she procured them just as the King and Queen entered the room.

It was a small dinner of only 10, and couldn't have been more informal nor pleasanter. The conversation was fairly general, and I overheard Betty Jane telling the King that I was working hard at my Greek, so he asked how I was getting along. I said I was about to start a one-woman campaign for the elimination of the letter "H" (eta) from the Greek alphabet. It was written like an "n," pronounced as a long "e" and cropped up where you least expected it—for example at the end of my name which is "Elevh" in Greek. He laughed, so I warmed to my subject and went on to "s," remarking that it looked like a capital "E" at the beginning of a sentence, an "o" with a tail in the middle of a word and an English "s" with a tail in the opposite direction if it was the last letter of a word. And an "omega" looked like a "w" at the end of a word if was was a verb or an accusative plural, but not otherwise!

Of course, I had completely forgotten that one of the things I was briefed on in Washington was never to discuss modern Greek or politics at a social gathering, because: "The object of a reception or dinner is to promote good will, and one must not embarrass one's hostess by bringing up controversial topics of conversation." However, my hostess didn't seem to feel any embarrassment and the King immediately countered by mentioning some of the difficulties of the English language—words which were spelled the same, but pronounced differently, such as "bough," "cough," "though," "through," etc. I guess I didn't make too bad a *gaffe*.

In February Betty Jane and I had received an invitation from General Kells, the head of the port of Piraeus, to join the S.S. Independence when she put in to Athens on her maiden voyage and go with her to Cyprus, Haifa, Beirut and Alexandria. We had been toying with the idea of a trip to Egypt and we accepted with alacrity.

The first Port was Haifa where our Consul provided Betty Jane and me the use of his car for two hours of sightseeing. We had now lost St. Paul, but had picked up Elijah and Elisha. We were driven to Mt. Carmel where Elijah slew 400 prophets of Baal and threw them into the Brook Cherith; we picked scarlet poppies and pale pink cyclamen and saw the cave where Elijah was fed by the ravens. A very fine Carmelite Church was built over the cave which was under the altar, but accessible from the church.

Nazareth and the Sea of Galilee was next. It was a perfect day and the whole drive through Old Testament country was fascinating. The first part was through lush, fertile land of the Twelve Tribes of Israel. We passed the mountain from which Moses saw the Promised Land; Mt. Gilboa where Saul died, and other spots too numerous to mention.

Nazareth was an entirely Arab community that had been respected by both sides in the fighting as a Holy Place. Except for the little main street where you could picture Jesus as walking and finding it much as it was today, the other places left me somewhat cold. The cave of the Annunciation, the home of Mary and Joseph, and various other supposedly sacred spots, all had churches built over them and trashy souvenir shops at the entrances.

The Sea of Galilee was quite perfect and we ate our picnic lunch there in a truly divine spot high above the sparkling blue waters of the Lake. There was a little chapel in the foreground marking the place where Christ preached the Sermon on the Mount. It was called Mt. Beatitude; I found my knowledge of the Bible stood me in good stead when no one else could recite the Beatitudes except me. After lunch we drove down to where the Jordan flows out of the Sea. All of us dabbled our toes in it and picked up pebbles. Two of the women took bottles of water against future baptism. I didn't and was just as glad when the bottles exploded a day or two later.

The next morning we drove to Tel Aviv where we picked up Ambassador and Mrs. Davis and motored up to new Jerusalem. We lunched at the King David Hotel and then climbed up into the tower of the YMCA Building to look over at Old Jerusalem—which is in Jordan and can't be entered from Israel. That night we sailed for Cyprus, where we spent an uninteresting day and on to Beirut.

We were met by our Consul who offered us his car to go to Baalbek and Damascus where our Minister Cannon and his wife were expecting us for lunch. Baalbek was tremendously impressive; the ruins were on such an enormous scale and so different from the ones in Greece. We only had an hour or so there which wasn't nearly long enough, although at that I had done about all the walking of which I was capable. Then on to Damascus for a delicious lunch with the Cannons, and a bit of shopping and sightseeing chaperoned by an Arab from the Ministry.

A short plane ride took us to Jerusalem the next day. The sightseeing was intensely interesting although it involved a tremendous amount of walking. We saw the site of Solomon's Temple—now with a very beautiful Mosque on it—and the Mount of Olives. The Garden of Gethsemane, kept by the Franciscan Fathers, was a gem; filled with flowers and the most enormous olive trees I had ever seen. Then to the Stations of the Cross and the Holy Sepulchre and finally a well earned lunch. After lunch we drove over to Bethlehem. It was the most commercialized place of all with many beggars and swarms of men selling "holy relics." The Church of the Nativity was divided like Gaul into three parts—one for the Catholics, one for the Greek Orthodox, and one for the Armenians and each faith could hold services only in their own little corner. Tragic and ironical it seemed to have the birthplace of the Prince of Peace the scene of some of the fiercest discord ever known.

We were met at Alexandria as usual by our Consul and loaded into the train for the hot, dusty ride to Cairo. We had expected to stay at the Semiramis Hotel with the rest of the crowd, but were taken out to Mena House instead. It was an enormous pile on the edge of the desert with the Pyramids practically in its front yard. Our rooms were at the end of a tremendously long hall, very dimly lighted, the kind of diminishing perspective seen in a horror movie where some monster jumps out and throttles you at the end. The same awesome atmosphere prevailed in the dining room—a huge, darkish room in a strange combination of late Moorish and Mid-Victorian architecture. There were only two other people in it besides ourselves. Even a couple of pre-dinner drinks did little to lighten the prevailing gloom and we crept to bed hand in hand wishing we were any other place in the world.

Things took a turn for the better the next day, when some of our shipmates turned up for lunch. We all had drinks together on the porch overlooking the really lovely gardens, lunched together, and then made our way to the camels for a ride to the Pyramids and the Sphinx.

No sooner had we started than the boys began their constant song: "Give me American dollar Miss, to feed my family and bring you good luck." I finally gave mine one to shut him up, but no sooner had we started back than he began to whine for "little Gyptshan money to feed my camel." When I refused, he threatened to make the camel gallop. I said if he did I would report him to the American Express and we walked sedately in.

On our arrival at Luxor by train, the confusion at the hotel was indescribable. There were more people than had been expected, most of the rooms were not ready and everyone was complaining in no uncertain tones. We finally got organized, and started off on our trip across the Nile to the Valley of the Tombs of the Kings. It was about a six mile ride in cars, the latest of which was a Model-T Ford, and all of them held together with spit and string. They had to be cranked, none had brakes.

The country we passed through was the abomination of desolation—like Ezekiel's vision of the Valley of Dry Bones—just sand and rocky ridges with not so much as a blade of grass anywhere. We got to the Tombs in short order and got out into the blazing, glaring sunshine with a temperature of 107 or 108. There was a great deal of walking from tomb to tomb. The first one or two were very interesting, especially King Tut which was the smallest but in a wonderful state of preservation. But I soon began to feel that if you had seen one, you had seen them all. We had a box lunch at a terrible rest house swarming with flies, then on our way to some Queen's temple, we were beset with souvenir vendors who tried to sell me a bust of Queen Nefertiti. They asked $5.00 but came down to fifty cents. I should have bought it; on the bottom was neatly inscribed in English "Made 2000 B.C."

The next day made up for everything. It was twenty degrees cooler with a lovely fresh breeze from the river. We drove out to the Temples of Karnak in amusing little Victorias and there was plenty of shade to stand in while our guide lectured. The Temples—built in different periods—were in a wonderful state of preservation. They had been excavated only about 70 years.

I began to feel rotten the next afternoon—achey and alternating between shivering and dripping with perspiration. So I went to bed with aspirin, the last drink in the bottle of Scotch as a hot toddy, and with a bath towel draped around my back and shoulders through which Betty Jane ironed me with her electric iron. A twelve-hour sleep restored me.

We went to Ambassador and Mrs. Caffrey's for a dinner in honor of the King's sister, the Princess Faisiah. She was very late in arriving and we stood around for half an hour with no drinks served. In my weakened condition I had had it; so I said to the young Navy doctor, who was standing next to me, "I've had a sunstroke. Find me a place to sit down and get me a drink unless you want to see me drop at your feet." He tried to argue that if I had had a sunstroke I would be dead. I was in no mood for argument, and simply repeated that I had had a sunstroke and wanted a chair and a drink, both of which he found for me. So I relaxed in comfort until the Princess came in and it was time to make the circle. She was very lovely looking and wore an exquisite dress although the black velvet top and a white tulle skirt was slightly suggestive of a penguin.

On our return to Athens by plane, Roger met us and announced we were leaving for Rhodes the next day! I cannot say I screamed for joy. But I did think it wise to go if my husband wanted me to, or otherwise I might not be asked the next time.

And so to Rhodes. The object of the trip was to get the ECA to put up funds to make Rhodes the Paradise of the Aegean. It could well make that claim because it has just about everything to offer: a very even climate, fine scenery, wonderful old medieval buildings restored by the Italians who held the country from 1912 to 1945, fine roads built by them, good swimming, golf, tennis, and first class hotels.

The Governor and others met us, drove us around a bit and then delivered us to the Hotel des Roses where we had two hours of relaxation and a good dinner.

The next day, we did a tour of the city including the "Street of the Knights" and the famous "Castello." The latter was a huge fortress-castle surrounded by three moats and built by the Knights of St. John in the early 1300's. It had been restored and furnished by the Italians as a refuge for Mussolini, who was killed before he could occupy it. It even had tiled bathrooms with sunken tubs, bidets, heat and electric light; how they ever got plumbing and wiring through those three-foot thick walls was completely beyond my comprehension.

One event that we attended was a *Fete Champetre* with dancers in native costume. To everyone's great delight, Roger joined the dancers with his necktie around his head. The Governor said it was worth ten political speeches. As a matter of fact, he was made Honorary Mayor of the village of Ambona where the dancers came from; he was quite pleased until Asher predicted that within 24 hours he would be handed a statement of the village indebtedness, for which he would find he was responsible. I tried my few words of Greek on all the women, and found

that the phrase which made the biggest hit was *"exo thotheka engonia"*
—"I have 12 grandchildren."

On our return, Athens looked wonderful. Spring had come and the
flower stalls were filled with tulips, freesia and anemones. Even our own
garden was beginning to show color and the violets bordering all the
flower beds were in bud. #9 Yasemion never looked better and I had
a real feeling of homecoming. My table silver had arrived from Paris
and my new cook, even though no *cordon bleue,* was a great improvement, and she spoke French at least. I looked forward to our expected
visitors, Cap and Ruth Rieber, Jane Lapham, Kitty Murphy, and Jane
Swinerton, with the pleasant knowledge that they would be comfortable
and decently fed.

Our social life was a very active one. There were receptions or
cocktail parties almost every day and several dinners a week—sometimes
formal, but often just the Peurifoys and ourselves. The hours were
generally late and I wondered how Roger could keep up with it. He
was very busy with many conferences with the Government, the Ambassador, his staff and frequent trips to Paris for meetings of the Mission
Chiefs.

One thing Roger did manage to escape was the High Mass at the
Cathedral in celebration of Greek Independence Day. He would have
had to get into his tails at ten o'clock in the morning and stand up for
an hour during the service. It was March 25th, and happened to be both
Easter Sunday and Betty Jane's birthday. I went with the Peurifoys
and thoroughly enjoyed the most colorful sight. All the Royal family
were there, of course: "Tino" in his Boy Scout uniform, all the Diplomatic Corps in full regalia with decorations, and everyone else dressed
in their best. We had celebrated to the extent of hanging out Greek
and American flags.

In April, we had a marvelous day with the Dan Brewsters (a charming young couple; he was State Department on loan to ECA). We took
a 150-mile drive to Thermopylae and Lamia to celebrate the third Anni-

versary of Marshall Plan Aid and to see what it had accomplished in that part of the country. It was an interesting drive through Thebes, Livadia and many small villages where the whole population turned out to welcome the Ambassador and the Chief of Mission, who were in separate cars. It was very like the day in Crete, except that we were offered only flowers instead of food and drink (for which we couldn't have been more thankful). But the crowds were larger and most of the children in native costume. The enthusiasm was out of this world and, although I had had the same experience several times before, it still gave me the same thrill and the same choke in the throat. It was lovely and it was heart-warming and it was pathetic . . . for you knew the crowds had been standing lined up along the road for hours.

We stopped in one tiny settlement where there were probably not more than 30 people lined up. The two leading cars had passed right through, but Dania Brewster and I called a halt—from necessity—not knowing when another opportunity would present itself. In my best Greek I said *"Pou einai to meras?"* ("Where is the place?") That was the first sentence my teacher had taught me and she had assured me that it would get me the convenience I needed. It did. We were escorted to a nice hole in the ground thinly surrounded by a screen of reeds, and accompanied by several hens, two dogs and a pig.

We traveled up and over a 3,000-foot pass on a well graded, well-banked road—but with 30 or 40 hairpin turns—and down onto the Plain of Thermopylae. Thousands of years ago, the sea had come up to the foot of the pass; gradually the area had become a salt marsh. One of the big accomplishments of the ECA had been to drain and de-salt some 200,000 acres and plant it to rice, which had done so well that now, in the third year, there was enough of a crop for some to be available for export.

A large crowd was gathered on the Plain and a truly impressive ceremony took place: first, of course, the Archbishop with the usual chanting; then the American and Greek flags were raised; followed by speeches from a General, a Nomark, and Jack Peurifoy, who afterwards climbed a small hill and planted a commemorative tree. All this time a line of 300 soldiers formed a symbolic wall high on the surrounding hillsides as a token of Leonidas and his "Immortal Three Hundred," who sacrificed themselves to the invading Persians in 480 B.C. On the flat were 48 girls in costume to represent our 48 States, and one, who was a real beauty, as Greece. The troops marched past in review, and then we all got into our cars and drove a few miles to Antheile, where we were to have lunch and the Marshall Plan part of the day.

By that time it was half-past one and we were hungry. To our horror, we learned that speeches were to precede, rather than follow, lunch. That meant at least another hour—each speech, both Greek and American, had to be translated sentence by sentence. Two Greek Ministers spoke first, and then Roger.

Finally we had lunch—barbecued lamb with cold, congealed fat, cold boiled rice with a float of Greek olive oil (which always tasted rancid to me), green salad, which we had been warned not to touch, and the worst *retzina* I had ever encountered yet.

Also in April, Jane Lapham and her friend, Kitty Murphy, arrived from New York via Paris and Rome to visit us. We installed them in our really luxurious guest suite—bedroom, dressing room and bath—which had only one out; the water in the bathtub ran boiling hot and the cold water didn't run at all. When you wanted a bath, you had to fill the tub at least half an hour before you could even ease your body into it. Forewarned, they escaped being scalded.

The Russells, Jane, Kitty, Roger and I soon took off for Crete on what was supposed to be a totally unofficial visit. However, we were met by all the Brass as usual—the Governor, the Nomark and even part of the Army. We were allowed only a few minutes at the hotel; then taken on a tugboat ride around the harbor, followed by a walk around the city with a trip through the market. Back at the main square, Roger came out on the balcony of the City Hall and made a nice flag-waving speech which was well received by the large crowd which had appeared out of the blue.

The next morning, we drove out to see the Minoan ruins at Cnossus. The man in charge of the restoration, a fine Englishman named DeJong, took us through; so much work had been done on some of the buildings that you really had a picture of what they must have looked like in 3,000 B.C. Roger, always somewhat allergic to ruins, was in a good deal of pain from stomach trouble. So he retired to Mr. DeJong's house where he was petted and entertained by DeJong's attractive Scottish wife.

Roger fell into bed as soon as we got back to the hotel and I didn't wake him for the Governor's lunch. I knew it would not only be a strain, but would disagree with him violently. Kitty and Jane also tried to beg off. They said they couldn't face the food again, but Roger said they were part of the show, and the show must go on.

At the lunch, I sat on the Governor's right and, after consultation with the Governor, I was allowed to make Roger's speech for him. It was against tradition for a woman to make public addresses; so I said that perhaps a woman had to be married as long as I had, 43 years, to merit the right to speak in public. I presented Roger's regrets and said that we felt we had made many friends in Crete. I handed out a few other bouquets and sat down. It must have gone over all right, for the Archbishop said afterwards (through an interpreter) that he could see I was a good Christian woman. I didn't know exactly what his conclusions were based on, except for the fact that I had been married for 43 years. Perhaps he thought that ought to make a Christian out of anyone!

Dr. Gamalakis, a man of high reputation as a surgeon and a patriot —he had served with the Army in Northern Greece before the triumphant Germans swept in when he returned to Crete—came in to see Roger. His diagnosis: nervous indigestion and over-fatigue. But Roger could get up and come to dinner at the Doctor's house that night. The Doctor was probably the best known collector of Minoan antiquities in Greece. The first thing he had done on his return to Crete was to parcel treasures out to peasant friends to be buried for the duration; and just as well he did, for when the Germans came in they had photographs of all the important pieces, and demanded their immediate surrender. He told the invaders they had all been looted by the civilian population. They promptly threw him into jail and then went out to his country place and killed every living thing on it—even the dogs and cats, and wrung the necks of all the poultry without bothering to eat it. However, the Germans needed surgeons so badly that Dr. Gamalakis was released two days later on his promise that he would operate for the duration on anyone they sent to him.

After the war, his entire collection was dug up and returned to him bit by bit and we were privileged to see it that evening at his house. It included pottery, bronzes, over 3,000 seals of all sorts and descriptions, some very beautiful gold jewelry, and many other things too numerous even to remember. He gave us a short talk about his collection, presented Eleanor Russell, Jane and me each with 3rd century B.C. carved seal rings. Then he capped the climax by presenting me with a string of carved gold beads "as a token of love and gratitude to America." Roger thought them too valuable for me to accept. But the Doctor said nonsense; they were not very old, only from about 800 A.D. I took them with pleasure.

Home again in Athens, Kitty was leaving at one in the afternoon to join her husband in Paris. Beforehand, Betty Jane was to take her and Jane for an audience with the Queen at 11:30 a.m. I thought it would be at Tatoi, the summer residence where I had been presented and I didn't see how Kitty was going to make her plane.

However, the presentation, fortunately, was in the Palace in the city. Kitty had plenty of time to make her plane, and even to have a martini beforehand to give her Dutch courage. She had been so impressed with the Queen that she hardly needed it.

Dinner that night was at the Grande Bretagne with the Costopoulos. He headed the Bank of Greece and she was a most delightful woman. It turned out to be one of the best semi-official parties we had gone to. I had the Italian Ambassador, who was lots of fun, on one side. Mr. Tsaldaris, who was always in and out of the Government, on the other. The Greeks described his wife as "formidable." She had an enormous behind and, no matter what kind of costume she wore, there was always a huge bow across it.

The next week was Greek Holy Week which the Orthodox Greeks take very seriously: church twice a day, no meat or milk products sold in the stores, and from Friday morning until Saturday midnight, nothing to eat but olives and bread. For Good Friday evening, we had been invited to a room in the Grande Bretagne from which we could watch the parade which symbolized the burial of Christ. We had to walk the last few blocks as no cars were allowed through, the sidewalks were jammed and all the street lights muffled in black. Every window, every balcony and even the roofs were filled with absolutely silent people—all holding candles which they lighted as the procession appeared and all the lights in the buildings were turned off. To me the complete silence was more impressive than anything else. Greeks by nature are not given to silence.

Sharply at 9:30 we heard distant music. A few minutes later the solemn procession started to file by to the strains of Chopin's "Funeral March" which three following bands took up as the one ahead of it passed out of hearing. Every kind of an organization was represented, all marching in slow step in time to the music. Police headed the procession then: a detachment of Red Cross nurses; a Boy Scout troop in the form of a cross and each one carrying a flare; two ranks of priests carrying a coffin between them to symbolize the Christ being borne to His tomb; the Metropolitan, Archbishop and Bishops all arrayed in gorgeous scarlet and gold vestments just as they had come from celebrating a service in the Cathedral. Next were representatives of the Royal family, the Government, the Army and Navy. And finally, hundreds of people all carrying lights of some kind and all flanked by two rows of clergy dressed in red and white robes.

It was the most moving, impressive ceremony I had ever seen. It was heightened by the lack of any sound except the slow tramp of many, many feet. After it was over, our group broke up silently—no one had any inclination to stay and make polite conversation.

Saturday after the Mass from eleven until midnight, the Holy Week fast was over and the feasting began. From our verandah, we could see the little church of St. Barbara perhaps half a mile away, and at midnight all the bells rang; the people poured out of the church, each person again holding a lighted candle which had to be carried home without its going out to ensure good luck for the coming year. Bells rang all over the city, fireworks were shot off, and we stood and watched as groups of twenty or more left the church and went on their candlelit way, exchanging the greeting, *"Xristos aneste"* ("Christ is risen") and the answer, "He is risen indeed." John our driver told us that everyone went home to feast on roast lamb and wine, and danced and sang and celebrated all night.

5

PARIS IN SPRING AND
AMERICAN HOLIDAYS IN GREECE

IN May, we prepared for a trip to Paris. Betty Jane, who had never been there, was going with us. Lewis was to fly over, meet us there, and Jane would go home with him. We planned to stop off for a few days in Rome after five days in Paris.

We took off at 10 a.m. via TWA for a pleasant 3½ hour flight to Rome, half an hour there, and then flew completely blind over the Alps at 27,500 feet; it was the second time I had crossed them without seeing even the tip of an Alp. Jane did not care for it at all—particularly when smoke and a queer smell of burning rubber began to invade the cabin. She was especially annoyed because Betty Jane and I were asleep and didn't notice it. It was some slight thing wrong with the heating system and was soon remedied.

The airport at Geneva, our next stop, was a beautiful modern one with food, drinks and enticing shops featuring every possible kind of watches and clocks. We ran across some friends from San Francisco who were very sour because they had just been bumped off of our flight with no reason given. The reason, we felt, appeared almost immediately: Mrs. Roosevelt, her son Eliot, and his latest bride. The three Roosevelts got into our plane and Betty Jane commented: "If we crash now, we'll all make the headlines even if we don't get top billing."

The next morning, Betty Jane and I did a little light shopping and met Roger at the Ritz bar where we had lunch. Then went off *en masse* to meet Lewis. He was supposed to land from a Pan-Am flight at Orly, but when we got there we found the passengers had been transferred to a BEA plane landing at Le Bourget! So to Le Bourget we hastily betook ourselves, but no Lewis when the BEA plane got in. Roger suggested a liqueur while Jane went to check, and I duly watched the arrival of an Air France plane. I spotted Lewis and managed to reach him just as he was getting into a bus.

The next four days were busy ones with Roger spending a good deal of time at the ECA headquarters, but always meeting us for lunch at one of the marvellous restaurants. Betty Jane, Jane, Lewis and I did things like lunching at the Mere Catherine in Montmartre—and how delicious everything tasted after seven solid months of Greek food! We did all the little art shops from the *Place du Tetre* down, and they were just as fascinating as ever.

We lunched at the Crillon Bar on the last day. There were sad good-byes to Lewis and Jane, who were staying on a few days longer, and then we were off to Rome on a mid-afternoon flight.

A brief look at the shops the next morning, lunch with the Daytons —he, the Chief of the ECA Mission to Italy—and dinner by ourselves at the much touted Del Orso. We considered it a gyp joint with slow service, poor food, and what seemed to us very high prices—confirmed by the waiter when he brought Roger the bill with "Bad News" written on the back of it.

We had had a lovely vacation, but home looked awfully good, and we must have been missed; Vincent actually kissed my hand, the first sign of emotion I had ever seen him display, and I was very glad I had bought his wife a bottle of French perfume.

Socially busy weeks followed from then on including two cocktail parties: one to celebrate Norwegian independence and one to celebrate Yugo-Slav something. There was also a huge reception at the Peurifoys at which Betty Jane presented the women of AWOG (American Women's Organization of Greece) to the Queen.

At the Norwegian's Roger introduced me to General Frederick, the new head of the Military Mission. I talked to him for ten minutes and decided I could no longer monopolize the guest of honor. As I started to leave, he looked at me imploringly and said "Please don't go. I've met at least 300 people in the last two weeks, and you are the only woman in the room whose name I know." He went on to say that his predecessor, General Jenkins, had made so many engagements for him and he had been kept so late at cocktail parties that he hadn't sat down to dinner for three nights. So on the impulse, I invited him to come out and have a quiet family dinner with us. He accepted with alacrity and we had a very pleasant evening during which he told us some of his experiences, the most trying of which was spent at the Royal Palace. His invitation had read "Movies at ten, followed by supper." "And I," said he, "who never go to the movies under any circumstances, had to sit through 'Little Women' in Greek!"

At the Yugo-Slav affair, Alessandrini, the Italian Ambassador came up to me and shook hands saying "Madame, under ordinary circumstances I kiss the lady's hand—but tonight, in Communist surroundings —I do not think it fitting."

The reception for the Queen was a great success, even though it entailed two and a half hours of standing. The AWOG had all sorts of welfare projects beside assisting in the Queen's Fund for children and disabled veterans. Most of the AWOG had never seen the Queen before, let alone having had a chance to be presented to her. She came at 6:15 p.m. looking as charming as always in a crisp white pique dress with embroidered dots and scallops, a narrow gold belt, straw sandals strapped with gold, and a tiny hat mostly gold veiling.

On May 30th, we invited all the ECA personnel, their wives and their children (some 200, with about 30 children from 2-15 years old) for a big party at #9 Yasemion. We were blessed with weather and John had hired the iceman's donkey so the children could have rides. The cook commented: *"Il est comme le petit chat, Madame, pas jolie, mais un animal gentille et pas de tout sauvage."* Our grounds were admirably suited for donkey rides. There was a large stretch of level lawn with an ornamental pool in the center—just the right depth for wading—and a stone walk all around it.

John managed it beautifully, lifting the children on and off two or three at a time—"Once around for everyone." The ice-cream vanished faster than a rabbit-in-the-hat as the elders partook instead of sticking to the food and drinks provided for them. Apparently a good time was had by all as nothing like it had ever been done before.

Danny Peurifoy, aged five, kissed the donkey good-bye. Betty Jane said she DDT'ed him afterward When I went to pay the iceman, the donkey hire was $4.00 for four hours, so in a big-hearted way I tipped him 75¢ and then departed hastily; he was so pleased I thought he was going to kiss me. One child wrote me a darling note afterward which said "I had a good time at your party. I had five glasses of iced tea it was so good. I made many new friends and the donkey."

A high point was the arrival of the U.S. 6th Fleet—15,000 strong. Our canteen was staffed by all the American organizations in Athens— Army, Navy, ECA, Embassy, etc.—each of whom had a special day assisted by some of the British and a few fine Greek women. The ECA having the largest group, had the heaviest day—Sunday. We all did two 3-hour shifts, and from 2-5 p.m. at least 100 of the boys were in line constantly for hot dogs, hamburgers, coffee and doughnuts, postal cards and stamps.

The city government had allowed us the use of a fine playground, an ideal spot. It had a building equipped with a kitchen as well as a large open room with space enough for tables, chairs and dancing. The playground itself had a basket ball court, a ping-pong table, and even enough room for soft ball. The Navy supplied the food, coffee and a band, and the Greeks supplied enough carefully selected girls for the boys to dance with. We women sold cards and supplied advice and information. One boy sent seven cards all exactly alike, which read "This is a swell joint, having fun, wish you were here, Love and kisses" —six to girls and one to his mother!

I was on the 5-8 shift one Sunday when Betty Jane came in and said the Queen had just telephoned that she would like to visit the canteen unofficially. This raised the question of what the procedure should be to receive Royalty unofficially. We decided that just to have the Greek National Anthem played would be suitable. We asked the bandmaster if he knew it. "That and 47 more" said he and then had a roll played on the drums. In the ensuing silence, he announced, "Boys, the Queen is coming to visit us. We're going to play the National Anthem. And whether you know what it is or not, STAND UP!"

The Queen arrived accompanied by Mary Karolou and one of the Court Marshals. After the music was over and Betty Jane and I had made our curtsies, she indicated that she wished to make the tour alone. So she went around the room stopping at table after table to say a few words to the boys. We trailed along in the rear to pick up such comments as: "Gee, I always thought queens were old, but she sure is a looker" and "Gosh, I wish she'd stayed a little longer, I sure would have liked to ask that babe to dance."

Finally, one of the sailors plucked up enough courage to ask her to have a cup of coffee with him. She sat down at his table and another sailor immediately asked if he could take her picture. She said, of course, but not alone; she must have some of the boys with her. So four of them stood up with her, partly overcome with embarrassment and partly proud as Punch as about 20 cameras were leveled at her.

She inspected the kitchen arrangements, but when I asked her if she would like to try a hot dog, she said "Do I have to? I am just up from a three hour lunch."

She left in about half an hour, but shortly afterward the Court Marshal came back and said Her Majesty had changed her mind, and would like a hamburger. The girl behind the counter said "With or without?" The Marshal looked completely bewildered and said "With or without what?" "Onions and relish" said the girl, and he said he would go and ask. Returning a few minutes later, he said just one word: "With." So the Queen, Mary Karolou and he all departed proudly in the royal limousine, each munching on a paper-wrapped hamburger "with" while driving through the main streets of Athens.

By the end of this first week in June, it had warmed up in a big way. The bi-weekly trip to the commissary through the heat of town was something I really dreaded; the commissary had only a few slowly revolving ceiling fans and it was almost hotter inside than it was out of doors. Then, too, it meant coping with Vincent's shopping lists, which were sometimes difficult to decipher; "Mi-an-ese" I finally got after pronouncing it phonetically. But "Black Papper" eluded me, especially as it appeared on every list. I finally discovered it was Black Pepper; and began to wonder how on earth we could use so much, as well as two pounds of coffee each time, considering I was the only person in the house who drank coffee. I asked around a bit, in all innocence, and found out that while I could get pepper for 60¢ or 70¢ a tin, it retailed in the black market at about $3.00 a tin, and coffee at somewhere around $5.00 a pound. From then on there just never seemed to be any pepper or coffee in the commissary, no matter how often Vincent listed them.

June 15th was an unforgettable day. Ten of us left for Epidorous at 1:30 p.m. in Admiral Glass' launch, a 65 foot converted Navy boat. The 2½ hour trip down was pleasant, except that the engines were so noisy you could neither talk nor hear. We made an easy landing in a picturesque small harbor with a Byzantine church guarded by a single, tall sentinel-like cypress on a bluff jutting out into the sea. Many other small boats were there with friends from Athens aboard. All the natives were out to see the excitement. The little village of New Epidorous was charming with houses pink, tan or pale blue, each one with its own vine and fig tree. Bright pink oleanders grew everywhere in wild profusion.

It was a lovely drive winding up the narrow road to Old Epidorous which had been the center of the cult of Aesculapius in the 4th century B.C. The amphitheatre, seating 14,000, was still there in a remarkable state of preservation. There, we gathered to hear a concert by the Vienna Orchestra under the direction of Otto Klemperer. The amphitheatre had a rise of perhaps 100 feet and was said to have the most marvellous acoustics in the world.

It was a warm, beautiful night of full moon, and the program was a lovely one; two Mozarts, a symphony, and then Brahm's Variations on a Theme by Hayden. During the latter, Mr. Klemperer put on such a fit of temperament as I had never seen. First he waved one arm at a cellist, then both arms, stamped his foot, and finally turned his back on the orchestra and ceased to conduct for at least two minutes, during which time the orchestra, nothing daunted, kept right on playing!

Then came an intermission scheduled for 15 minutes, but which lasted for 35; we all thought they were hunting for ice to cool off Mr. Klemperer, but he finally returned to play the Beethoven 5th. All went well until the Scherzo, when a sudden cloud covered the moon and we had a cloudburst! Klemperer rose above it for a few minutes with every musician trying to shield his instrument with his coat and play at the same time. Klemperer gave up in disgust after five minutes of downpour and everyone raced for cover. Irena Yost had a steamer blanket which she shared with me. Arm in arm we ran, resembling the famous picture of Paul and Virginia fleeing from the volcano.

An event of the week was Lady Norton's "Gala"—a benefit ball given for some British charity at the Race Track Club House. Fortunately, it was a warm, moonlit night, for there must have been at least 1,000 people present. If they had all been forced indoors by a sudden shower such as we had at Epidorous, it would have been a complete fiasco instead of the brilliant success it was.

I had planned a dinner of eight beforehand, but collected an added starter in a most amusing way. Betty Jane had rung me up a few days previously to say Lady Norton had called her to ask if she could take Sir Clifford for dinner. The Peurifoys were coming to us, but Betty Jane assured Lady Norton that I could take her husband. Of course, I was delighted because Sir Clifford was most charming. So I rang the British Embassy at once only to be told that he thought he should stay at home in case his wife needed help with her party at the last minute. I saw him the next day, and he said "I say, is your invitation still open, for if it is I'd love to come. I told my wife I had refused, and she said 'Oh! my dear man, whatever for? I've been trying to park you out for dinner that night for a week!'" So he came along with the Peurifoys, Admiral and Mrs. Glass and the Costopoulos.

We got to the Club House a little after eleven, went up to the verandah on the second floor, found ourselves a table, and sat down and ordered drinks. Shortly after Ambassador Wen came up and said he couldn't find his table. I most cordially invited him to join us which he refused to do, and only found out at the end of the evening that we had his table. He knew, but was too polite to throw us out.

The King and Queen were there, and an hour or so later, the Queen danced by our table, fastened her eye on me, and said "Why isn't your husband dancing?" I was so staggered I simply said "Do you mean with you?" (not even "Your Majesty," or "Ma'am'). She smiled, said "Certainly," and danced away. I told Roger, who accused me of making it up. But I said no, it had been a Royal command! so he said "Boy, another bottle of champagne," took a drink to nerve himself, and then went over and asked her to dance. And after the first dignified round, did they dance! Everyone else got off the floor while Roger spun, twirled, and otherwise fancy-danced the Queen to the intense amusement of the crowd—including the King. Roger ended with a long glide and a low bow, and returned to our table amid loud applause. He was sweating freely. I asked him how he had dared to fancy-dance the Queen, but he said it was the last thought in his mind. After the first round she had said "And now do your stuff!" And what else could he do, even though he was frightened to death all the time that he would get tangled up in her skirt and trip them both.

A few days later, we had a reception for Secretary of Labor Maurice and Mrs. Tobin, plus all the Greek Labor boys. The cards read "From seven to nine" but the Greeks began arriving at 6:45 and consumed three cases of beer, a ham and a turkey besides innumerable sandwiches and "*dolmades*" before the guests of honor arrived at 8 p.m. I had over 1,000 sandwiches for 150 people, but even so Vincent came to tell me that the food was disappearing so fast there would be nothing left for the rest of the guests. So I told him to cut off the supplies to the Labor boys, they had had enough anyhow.

When the Tobins finally arrived, he was grabbed by a couple of reporters and interviewed for half an hour. Any thought of a receiving line went by the board. Jack Peurifoy finally rescued him, and although seething with rage, I apologized for the discourtesy of the reporters. Whereupon Tobin put an arm around my shoulders, and said "Dear Mrs. Lapham, you must remember that this is good publicity for your country—and mine."...Rats!

We were off by plane at 9:30 the next morning for Yannina for one of those "quiet, unofficial" weekends with Mike Adler, our Field Service man for that district in the far northwest of Greece.

We had a restful afternoon until six when we went for a drive around town visiting the ECA and the USIS headquarters. Then came a delightful hour and a half sitting under the trees at a taverna at the edge of the lake, watching a most beautiful sunset and drinking *ouzo* to prepare ourselves for the official banquet later on. It was quite a party—18 men, and me! I was sure that my presence was a mistake, but Mike said no, the dinner was in Roger's and *my* honor, and the only reason the men hadn't brought their wives was that it was cheaper to leave them home!

The next day was a long and hard one—12 hours to be exact. We motored north for 20 miles until we came to a plain marble column which had one word on it—*"OXI"* ("NO") which was the equivalent of the French, "They Shall Not Pass." It marked the farthest point of the Italian advance into Greece. Then we bumped and bounced over 20 miles of bad road, climbing 3,000 feet to a point very near the Albanian border. It overlooked a broad, fertile valley where an ECA irrigation project was under way. We retraced our route for several miles until we reached a garrison town and the monastery of Vellas where we were to eat lunch. Roger reviewed the troops and we both were decorated by the General with the badge of the regiment—a charging bull.

We lunched in the open under overhanging rocks and a huge fig tree. A mountain stream bursting out of the rocks made it not only beautiful, but cool. We started with *ouzo,* which we sorely needed by that time, and then I was led by the Bishop to inspect the barbecued lamb. Lamb by courtesy only! It was a tough old sheep and stone cold by the time I got it. As I couldn't even get a fork into it, I didn't risk my teeth, but made my lunch off of *"kokoretzi"* and ice cream. Mike had told me to lay off of the salad. The ice cream was made out of American powdered milk and ice cream mix with pistacho nuts and chopped-up cherries, and was really very edible. There were a couple of speeches after lunch, and then my dear husband suggested that I should thank the assembled company in Greek. Fortunately I was on to him by then, so had three or four little sentences of thanks I had learned in comprehensible, if not classic, Greek. They must have been understandable, for Mike waved away the interpreter he was in the process of summoning.

Back to the monastery for a siesta after lunch, and I would be willing to bet I was one of the very few women who ever slept in a monastery. And at that I didn't sleep, for the Bishop's room was pretty monastic and uncomfortable; the bed and pillows were hard as rocks, and the room itself slightly redolent of the waterless flush toilet close by.

If I had thought the morning was strenuous, it was fortunate I didn't know what the rest of the day was going to be like. We left the monastery at 4 p.m. and drove 40 miles to within three miles of the Albanian border southwest of where we had been earlier. En route we stopped at several small villages to be welcomed, decorated with flowers, and listen to long addresses while standing in the extremely hot sun. Finally we got to the military zone where Roger reviewed quite a large body of fine, tough-looking troops commanded by a young officer. His name should have been "Morning Hour" he had so much gold in his mouth.

Here, we picked up two armored cars as an escort. From then on with the jeep full of *gens d'armes,* we were quite an impressive convoy. Another 15 miles up, down and around, with me holding on with both hands so as not to be thrown off the seat. Finally, we reached the last village, Pogoniano, where the square was filled with people—and a four-page speech read by the Mayor and translated! Roger made a delightfully short reply.

At the square, there was a dance in our honor. It was performed by eight pretty girls in really beautiful native heirloom costumes. The headdresses were of some close-fitting white material looking like the Elizabeth Arden ads. The jackets were heavily embroidered in gold, and beneath them were wide Turkish belts with decorative silver knobs, and an apron-like skirt of white hand-woven wool. Dancing in a circle, they parted to let Roger and me in and round and round we went. All the music was sung, the ground was sloping as well as being stony and uneven, and it was no small job to keep the step and at the same time not turn your ankle on a stone. Roger and Mike were both tastefully arrayed in gaudy Honolulu-type shirts worn outside the trousers. The scene was most colorful! Roger ended the dance by doing a *pas seul* in the center of the ring.

After shaking hands with everyone in sight, we started for Yannina —stopping only three times to review troops and Boy Scouts and, finally, for a drink of Scotch from the flask Mike had thoughtfully brought along. We reached the hotel at 9:30 p.m., but the day wasn't over. A British Major joined us to play four-handed cribbage until quarter of one!

In going over my mail when I got home to #9 Yasemion, I found a charming note from one of the Greek Labor boys we had asked to the Tobin reception. It read: "Sir and Madam, I have the honor to thank you for your honorable request in your today reception and to ask you pardon because a sick keep me in bed and I am very sorry to not stay personally there." I only wished I could write as good Greek as he did English.

On the evening of July 3rd, Roger came home completely discouraged. Jack Peurifoy had just told him that as he, Jack, was to make the Fourth of July speech at the morning Open House at the American Embassy, it was up to Roger to make it in the evening after the picnic. Roger apparently hadn't an idea in his head, so he asked, "Why don't you write it for me, Sport?" I hadn't an idea at the moment either, but with my little typewriter under my fingers and a gin fizz at my side, I went to work. Here is how it came out:

"*One hundred and seventy-five years ago we Americans declared ourselves to be free and independent. We had passed through a long period of doubt, indecision and divided loyalty between our Mother Country, England, and our newfound conception of freedom—freedom from taxation without representation.*

"*Today we are anything but free from taxation, but at least we have a voice in voting those taxes. And we know that those taxes are to maintain that freedom for which we have fought in more than one war.*

"*The War between the States was fought to determine whether a nation can survive half-slave and half-free; the Spanish-American War to liberate a people suffering under the yoke of an oppressor.*

"*We fought the First World War to end all wars—to make the world safe for democracy—but it did not work out quite that way.*

"*During the Second World War, the Four Freedoms were widely proclaimed; Freedom from Want, Freedom from Fear, Freedom of Speech, and Freedom of Religion. All four of these we enjoy more abundantly in our United States than does any other people in the world today, and that is the very reason I feel most of us are here. Why have most of you left more comfortable homes or the life to which you and your families were accustomed? I feel there are two reasons for it, both of which give me the encouragement I need to continue my job: one is that no matter what endless discussions and dissensions go on at home, you still have faith in our essential Americanism. The second is that you have the spirit of the Old Crusaders, or translated into more modern terms, the feeling that you are carrying the basic ideals of American democracy into far countries.*

"*The old Crusaders fought for the physical possession of the Holy Sepulcher; but today we are not fighting for one inch of physical possession of any Nation's soil—but for the spiritual and inspirational possession of many Nations' future lives. We do it by material means, both military and economic, but we also do it as representatives of our way of life, as Ambassadors of good will.*

373

"I ask again 'Why are you all here?' And I think the answer, whether you know it consciously or not, is that—thank God, and I say it reverently—the old pioneering spirit of America is just as strong today as it was when the 'Mayflower' sailed from Plymouth for the New World; when Thomas Jefferson wrote the Declaration of Independence, and when our forefathers struck out from rocky New England for the rich fields of the Western Reserve over a hundred years ago to push even farther to the shores of the distant Pacific.

"We are just as convinced today of the truth that a nation cannot exist half-slave and half-free as we were when Lincoln voiced it. But today it has an even wider application; how can a world exist half-slave and half-free? I will not dwell on that part of the world that is not half, but wholly slave, so I will close by saying that I still have faith—faith in America and in our American way of life, faith that each and every one of you cherishes.

"God bless America!"

By the time I read it to Roger, between the sentiment and the gin, there wasn't a dry eye in the house. Roger said he wasn't sure he could get away with it. But he read it over the next morning, cut it a bit, and delivered it practically intact that evening, reading it very simply and quietly. It was well received and I was flattered that he had asked me to do it for him.

While we had been in Yannina, a delegation of club women from Texas had arrived in Athens to present a $500 scholarship at the University of Texas to the Government. Betty Jane said they were all the Helen Hokinson type, but presented the scholarship to Papendreou with great eclat, (though $500 would not even have gotten anyone from Athens to Texas); then the leader of the group said "Now Girls" and they all gathered around Papandreou and sang "The Eyes of Texas are upon You." Later that afternoon he resigned. Jack Peurifoy said he evidently couldn't stand the eyes of Texas, because no one knew of any political reason.

Life went on much as usual except that the temperature was steadily rising—95-97 on our sheltered marble porch, and 105-107 downtown, Outdoors on the verandah was bearable after six when the sea breeze came in, but the house had a flat topped roof, and upstairs was sweltering both day and night.

Ed Bodman turned up and we had a dinner of all the "Old China Hands" we could gather—11 in all. It was one of the best meals I had ever been able to offer my guests; the Swinertons, who were in Norway for the fishing, had sent us one of the delicious salmon they had caught. It had been smoked on the home grounds and was simply out of this world. I had the forethought to save out a good-sized piece for Roger and myself, which was just as well as by the time the dinner was over, all that remained of the salmon was the head, the tail and the backbone.

Roger and Jack Russell were due for a trip to Paris the following week, so Eleanor and I decided to visit Corfu. She had to take her two children with her—Julie, 10, and Jackie 4. After a pleasant two hour flight, we were met at the Corfu airport by the Nomark, Seriotis, and escorted to a brand new and immaculately clean hotel with comfortable beds, hot and cold running water in each room, and showers nearby.

Corfu and cats will always be synonymous in my mind. I had never seen so many cats! And this in spite of the fact that the Nomark told us the Italians had eaten them all during the occupation. But they must have left at least two and those two had not been idle.

At *ouzo* time, when we were having a drink on the sidewalk in front of the hotel, who should turn up but Mike Adler, newly arrived from Yannina. He took us to dinner at another out-of-door place, which compared to Athens was positively cold. When we returned to the hotel, I played three games of cribbage with him—winning one by 9 points and being skunked the other two. He refused to take the winnings he was entitled to, but did accept about 80¢ and left me with a bottle of Scotch to make up for it!

Mme. Thessyla, the Mayor's wife, took us to see the Achelleion, the palace built by Empress Elizabeth of Austria, and subsequently bought by the Kaiser who went there every spring. It was beautifully situated on a mountain top, dignified and impressive outside, but very baroque and German inside. There was very little of the original furniture left, except for a bicycle saddle seat on which the Kaiser had used to sit at his desk.

On the whole, I was a little disappointed in Corfu, about which I had heard too much as the "Island of Faery." There wasn't so much bomb damage but you could see what it must have been like in its heyday in the early 1900's. To me in 1951 it looked like a once beautiful woman who hadn't bothered to have her face lifted.

6

ATHENS: IN'S AND OUT'S

IT had now been nine months since we had reached Athens. It did not seem so long but individual days seemed long because of the intense heat and the dry wind full of invisible dust particles blowing straight from the Sahara. The sun blazed down and the sky was white without a cloud in it. You never went out of doors without some kind of head covering, and you put on dark glasses almost before you cleaned your teeth in the morning. One afternoon, it was 42 Centigrade on our porch, which multiplied by 9/5 with 32 added, came out at 107.3 Fahrenheit—and our porch was marble and the thermometer in the shade!

On one of my frequent days at the Peurifoy's swimming pool for a swim, I was surprised to see no one there. Jack told me that the Queen's lady-in-waiting had telephoned that the Queen and the two princesses would like to come at 5:30 for a swim, so everyone else had been shooed away. I offered to go too, but Jack said it wasn't necessary; Roger ranked next to him, so I stayed. When the Queen arrived I was in a quandary. Should I try to curtesy in a wet bathing suit and with bare feet? I decided against it, though I was sure Miss Wilson would have said it was a *gaffe*.

The Queen looked darling in a sky-blue bra and shorts, and swam as I did—breast stroke with her curly head well out of water. I had never seen two more natural nor obedient children than the two Princesses, aged 14 and 9. The Queen said "Out of the pool now, girls." She was answered by two "Oh! Mothers" to which she replied with one word "Out!" Out they came.

Afterwards we all sat around on the lawn drinking coca cola and eating commissary cookies from a pasteboard box. The conversation ranged from politics to obstetrics. At 8 o'clock I committed my second and worst *gaffe*. I arose and said "This is such an informal occasion, I hope your Majesty will excuse me," and left after asking Betty Jane if it was permissible. Roger and I had an 8:30 engagement, and the Queen showed no signs of going. John, our driver, was so horrified at my leaving before the Queen that I was really upset and hoped that I wouldn't be excommunicated.

The Queen and the two Royal children were there one afternoon when I was, and the pool was closed to all other guests. While we were sitting on the grass after our swim, shrieks began coming out of the Maternity Hospital that overlooked the pool. The Queen in horrified tones asked Betty Jane what was happening. "Oh! just a Greek woman having a baby," she replied, and the Queen said "Poor woman! she must be in agony." "Not at all," said Betty Jane, "the Greek women begin to yell the minute they get in sight of the hospital so they get plenty of anaesthesia, but the American women who go there don't make a sound, so they get none."

The Queen still seemed unconvinced until Betty Jane reminded her that she probably hadn't made a sound either when her three children were born. The Queen said she hadn't; which inspired me to tell her of my delivering my daughter's baby in my husband's car. This in turn inspired her to tell me of the miscarriage that her husband's sister had had in the airport at Rome. "Most embarrassing," said the Queen.

By the end of August, the heat had really gotten me down and I told Roger I would have to get out of it for a while. He allowed he was pretty fed up with it himself, so he cabled the Bill Brewsters, friends who had a villa in Geneva, to ask them to get us rooms at some hotel there. They cabled back at once inviting us to visit them even though they warned that it had been an unusually rainy summer in Geneva. Rain! The very thought of it was refreshing to the soul after the long days of cloudless, white-hot skies of Athens.

We took off one Wednesday afternoon and were met by the Brewsters with open arms. We were driven out to their charming villa on the south side of the Lake and it was so peaceful, so luxurious and so cool, it seemed too good to be true.

After our baths in great big tubs with plenty of crystal clear hot water, we went downstairs and had our drinks in front of an open fire. Thelma said "Now I will tell you our scheme of life; we don't appear before noon, we do not go in for any kind of social life, and we have made no plans for you whatsoever. The car is at your disposal and you may do as you please. We mostly just sit and enjoy the peace and quiet." Right up our alley after the somewhat hectic life we led in Athens! And from then on we enjoyed our long lazy mornings and the delicious meals prepared by the Brewster's French chef. We always did something for lunch and in the afternoons and generally played three rubbers of bridge in the evening, but we kept early hours and nothing could have been more to our liking.

I got home to sad news. Someone had hit our pet cat, Puss-puss, either with a stick or a stone and broken her leg at the shoulder. When she crawled into my lap on three legs and began to purr, I almost burst into tears. I took her to the doctor at the Naval Installation the next day, and he said there was nothing to do but put her out of her pain; however, there was a very good Greek vet and I could get his opinion if I wanted to. I did, of course, and he said he could cure her, but could not guarantee that she would not be permanently lame. He would keep her at his hospital for several days, and . . . 500,000 drachmas ($35.00). My driver John, who was interpreting, was perfectly horrified at the price and said I could have broken my leg much cheaper for I could have gone to the Navy Hospital for nothing. He must have spread the word of what I was paying for a cat as soon as he got to the house; the next day the entire household hit me for a raise.

After Puss-puss came home from the vet's, I spent most of the next ten days cat-sitting. She was swathed in bandages which had to be changed every day, and she objected violently with both teeth and claws. It took John, Vincent and me to do it. Frequently, it had to be done more than once, as she raced around on three legs just as spryly as she did on four, and would tear into the room with yards of bandage trailing behind her, and I had begun to feel like the woman who said she couldn't keep a canary; it was too great a responsibility.

One afternoon Roger came home waving a newspaper at me, and said "Look! Puss-puss has made the Publick Prints!" Sure enough, there she was right along with Premier Venizelos and Field Marshal Papagos, except they were on the first page and she was on the third. There was her picture with the vet, and a long article headed "Four-footed Aristocrat! Noted Athenian animal doctor sets leg of cat for Chief of Economic Mission!" Quite a promotion for our thrown-in-the-driveway alley kitten, but just possibly a bit of publicity for the vet. I got a copy of the picture from him which he inscribed as follows: *"A'la Clinique de Pettis Animaux à Athènes, la sympatique petite chatte de Madame Elene Lapham, se laisse soigner docilement par le sous-signé Docteur Vétérinaire Grecque, Pierre Kiappé."*

The doctor had done a good job, and Puss-Puss recovered without a trace of lameness, though after her long enforced stay in the house, she was more anxious to go night-roaming than ever!

Our next trip was to visit a very remote mountain village named Frangista which had been completely destroyed first by the Germans and then by the Guerrillas. It was a five hour drive from Athens via Lamiá to a spa called Ipati where we spent the first night in a very comfortable hotel. The next morning we were off by car with John Hare, the Field Service man for that vicinity, following us. After the first ten miles there wasn't a straight stretch of road of more than 30 yards; the road wound up and around the Pindar Mountains getting steadily worse with innumerable hairpin curves, lots of loose rock, and the roadbed itself indescribably bad.

We finally reached Frangista in time for lunch. Six hundred of the original seven hundred inhabitants had returned to rebuild it with material furnished by ECA, but a terrific amount remained to be done. It was by far the poorest village and the most miserably dressed people we had seen anywhere. A movie had been made of them and their work, and Roger was to present that with a plaque to commemorate it. The ECA was also installing a radio station and a generator plant.

We inspected the tiny new schoolhouse which was immaculately clean, but without heat, light or sanitary conveniences. We also saw the remains of the church—only a shell and belfry—but with the bell still functioning. It was rung for our arrival and departure. Then we had a remarkably good lunch of baby chickens. John Hare told me they probably wouldn't have any chickens or eggs the next winter, as they had killed all the chicks off for us. The village was snowed in each winter. John Hare was probably the only foreigner they saw from one year to another; it was easy to understand why they didn't miss a detail of our actions or our attire. How I wished I could speak enough Greek to be able to communicate with them!

After lunch the children sang and danced with Roger joining in. We listened to the first broadcast on the newly-installed radio, and then left for the 77 mile, four-hour drive back to Ipati. There we took a short rest and then to the Nomarks' dinner.

I had been carrying on an animated dinner conversation with the Nomark in French, when Roger broke in and asked me to tell him he had a present for him. Roger promptly removed his vivid red tie and gave it to the Nomark. I pointed out to him as he accepted it that he ran the risk of being taken for a "Red" when he appeared before his city council. The Mayor looked as though he were about to burst into tears, so Roger went back to the room and produced a tie that was just as green as the other one was red. Roger carefully pointed out that both ties came from " 'Ollywood." I never saw such beaming faces.

The day after we got home Roger brought Miss Wilson, the woman who had briefed me in Washington, out for lunch. He had warned her that I was highly critical of her briefing. So when she asked me what I had objected to in my talk with her, I said "Being treated like a congenital moron." To which she replied that she must not have been at her best that day. As a matter of fact, she had misled so many people that the Department had finally sent her abroad to see things as they really were. She couldn't have borne me any ill will, for she came to the cocktail party we gave for Mitchell, the Civil Service Commissioner the next day, and I was tactful enough not to ask her if she considered me properly dressed.

In late September, we flew up to Salonika to visit the Exposition which was being held there. We took John our driver with us as he said he had met people and seen them off at the airport hundreds of times, but had never flown himself. His first trip was highly successful, but he was a "little scary in the head, but all right in the stomacho." Furthermore, he would never forget it. His children and his grand-children would be told of his first trip by air given him by Mr. Lapham (he was still a bachelor), and thus "Mr. Lapham's name would never die."

We were met by Archie Johnson—the ECA Field Service man for that area—several Greek officials, and Stuart Campbell the Consul with whom we were to stay. The Consulate was delightful, a six-story build-ing on the waterfront, with three floors of offices, three of residence, and a beautiful view across the Bay to Mt. Olympus. The next morning, we went to the Exposition where we spent two hours and were trailed by a photographer who took Roger's picture in front of every possible exhibit.

We also drove out to the American Farm School to have lunch with the heads, a delightful Mr. and Mrs. House. It was founded in 1903 by Mr. House's father who had lived in that part of the country as a Missionary for 30 years. He decided there was a crying need for some sort of a foundation to train young Greek boys in agriculture and live-stock raising. He tried to get the approval of the Missionary Board, but they thought it too secular a prospect, so he resigned and started it himself on 17 acres and a shoestring. It had grown tremendously, and now graduated 60-80 boys a year, all of whom were pledged to go back and work in their own villages for three years. The Houses gave us a delicious lunch with fresh milk—the first I had had in Greece—home-made ice cream, and a big cocoanut cake with candles for Mrs. House's birthday.

I went on strike the next morning. Roger was going off to see some land reclaimed for growing rice. I had seen enough rice in China to last me nicely, and said I wanted to see something of Salonika. So Stuart Campbell took me on a sightseeing tour—Byzantine churches with good mosaics, Byzantine-Turkish-Venetian walls and ramparts, and a Roman arch built over the old road from Brindisi to Constantinople.

Late in the afternoon we went back to the Exposition where Roger was to make a speech in the ECA theatre—the real reason for the trip. It took up the problems of that whole northern region, particularly that of its being a one-crop country—tobacco—and the amount of good land devoted to the growing of a sub-standard crop. Cocktails with Archie Johnson and dinner with the Governor-General followed, and the next morning a visit to Anatolia College. We were shown around there by President and Mrs. Carl Compton. The buildings had been the head-quarters of the German Army during the occupation, and they had left them intact, though stripped of everything.

On our arrival home by plane that afternoon, everyone who had seen us off, met us. It was good of them, but really a great nuisance. It meant fifteen minutes of strained conversation and a great deal of hand-shaking and handkissing which I generally forgot and gave someone a good bump in the mouth with my fist. #9 looked very quiet and peaceful.

Our next excitement was Carol's visit. She came out on the "Constitution" with Betty Jane. They landed in Naples where Jack flew over in the U.S. Military plane to meet them. We met at the airport at 8:45 p.m. and it was certainly good to see Carol! We dined and talked late into the night.

I had a big buffet supper in Carol's honor and broke every rule in the State Department Social Guide book, which said never to entertain more than one Ambassador at a time. I had three—American, Italian and Chinese, as well as the Prime Minister and Mrs. Venizelos! It all worked out beautifully. Each Ambassador had a table of his own and seated according to protocol. No one was insulted and no one went home because he had been slighted. The only mistake I did make was the lack of a piano player. They all wanted to dance and all I had was a man who played the guitar and sang sad songs in Spanish.

The day after our party, Carol and I started for Delphi. It was a perfect day when we left, but about half way there it began to rain and poured so hard that I suggested giving it up and going home. Carol said no, so we kept on. Just before we reached Delphi the sun burst forth brilliantly, and the most beautiful rainbow we had ever seen arched across the valley. It was a complete double bow with the seven colors vividly clear and distinct and one end rested on the snow of Mt. Parnassus!

After a delightful tour of the ruins, we got back to Athens the next day in time for a late lunch and a good rest before going to a cocktail party at Ambassador Wen's. There we got stuck in the rattle-trap elevator along with Mrs. Venizelos, who raised the roof until someone came to our aid and got us going again.

There was a dinner at the Peurifoy's that evening for Gen. and Mrs. Omar Bradley, who had left Japan only a week ago, but looked as fresh and untired as daisies. It was a pleasant dinner of 24. But the men did not join the ladies until it was time to go home, so I have no impressions of the Bradleys except that he shook hands as if he meant it, and Mrs. Bradley was easy and charming.

During Carol's visit, we also went to Rhodes. Mr. Woods, the ECA man from Crete who was covering Rhodes while John Asher was on home leave met us. He drove us out to the Asher house, where we were to stay, and after lunch drove and walked us around some of the old cobbled streets while Roger took a siesta. At dinner in the Hotel des Roses that night, we seemed to accumulate most of the people in the dining room and had a lively evening—ping-pong and dancing that ended with a *"pas de deux"* by Roger and Carol to loud applause.

After a tour of the *"Castello"* the following day, we picked up Mr. Woods and started for Lindos, 55 kilometers away through lovely rolling country. Lindos literally burst into view with the force of an explosion.

There was a sudden turn in the road, and there it was—a mediaeval castle with crenellated walls high on top of a rocky hill and a little white village nestling at its foot. The Aegean, jade green and indigo blue, lay beyond as a backdrop.

Back at Rhodes, we attended a seated tea at the Governor-General's with a few local lights and all the "Brass" from two American destroyers that had come in that morning. We had a first and second sitting; the second consisting of the Governor-General, the Aide to the Spanish Ambassador to Turkey, who was there with his wife, and four Navy men who never spoke during the entire session. Dinner at the Hotel des Roses again, was followed by a fashion show, and a very exotic Cuban dancer, who disappointed everyone by not coming completely out of her dress which she always seemed on the verge of doing after just one more wiggle.

Helen Drake gave a delightful luncheon of ten for Carol at the Piraeus Yacht Club, which included some of the people we saw a good deal of, but whom Carol had not met before. That day, Roger came home very much exercised over an attitude of the Greek Government. I was sitting alone when he came in, and he paced up and down the little library relating the session he had just had with one of the Greek *Ministeres*. Roger was saying very emphatically, "I will not be double-crossed!" When Vincent came in with the cocktails, he saw Roger shaking his finger at me, and beat a hasty retreat! I called Vincent back and told him everything was all right, and then said to Roger it was one of the greatest compliments I had received in ages!

The last few days of Carol's visit passed quickly, what with various cocktail parties, a couple of visits to the Parthenon, several buffet suppers at different places, and some guests of our own. I was going back when Carol did as I had had an infection in my tear ducts and wanted to see my own oculist in San Francisco. Roger expected to go with us, too, but was held up at the last minute by a Chief's meeting in Paris on the 5th of November. He then planned to fly on to New York and Washington, and then West for three weeks in San Francisco.

I had five nice days in New York, then San Francisco for a busy month; getting the house runnning, twice-weekly trips to the oculist, shopping, fittings, Christmas present gathering, and, of course, entertained by all my friends. Roger was equally busy when he got there.

We returned to Athens in time for Christmas preparations. The day began with a late breakfast Christmas morning and opening our gifts in our sunny bedroom. At 2 o'clock, we dined with the Peurifoys, who had 14 of us including 6 young Navy officers from a destroyer which had just arrived in port. I had taken my book of Christmas carols with me, so after dinner we all gathered around the piano and sang. As the officers left one of them—a Texan—said "Thank you ma'am, for playing those songs. Ah sure felt Ah was right home again." I was glad I had thought of it.

A few days later, there was a phone call from the office to say a cable had just come in from the Griffins; they were arriving in Athens at 12:15 that day and it was then 11:30. They were a bit chagrined to land and find no one to meet them, but I got there shortly afterward, so all was well. It had taken the cable three days to get from Istanbul to Athens!

Saturday Hester, Betty Jane and I drove down to Piraeus to an exhibition given by local artists. We were told that we had been asked to "lend *éclat*" as the attendance had been very poor. We soon found out that "lend *éclat*" meant "buy a picture." Most of them were pretty impossible, but I finally found one I liked called "Admiring the Dowry." It was a typical Greek interior done in a primitive, Grandma Moses style. It was colorful and there was a cat curled up on the hearth that was the image of Puss-puss, so I bought it to have something to remember her by when we had to go home and leave her behind.

Sunday we did the Parthenon exhaustively with a guide in the morning and then came home to prepare for the Open House we were having for ECA that afternoon. Roger had decided to give a "Necktie Party," so had spread all his ties out on the floor a couple of nights before and selected 80 to give away. Kathleen Farrelly and I had folded and sealed them in envelopes and put them in a big basket with gay red ribbons on the handle. I had written a little jingle which Roger read after everyone was assembled:

> *"Step up my friends and take your pick;*
> *Some ties are thin and some are thick;*
> *Some ties are new and some are old,*
> *Some colors tame and others bold.*
> *There's one apiece—but Luck is blind—*
> *It's all pure chance, the one you'll find.*
> *But which of you won't take a chance*
> *Your manly beauty to enhance?*
> *So choose, my friends, the tie today*
> *That binds us close in ECA"*

The idea made a tremendous hit. I was quite pleased with the way it all went off, for the house was gay with crimson cyclamen plants, my little cardboard creche was on the mantlepiece, the lighted Christmas tree showed up well, and although there must have been 200 there at one time or another, they came and went at intervals and it was never too crowded.

On New Year's Day, Roger had to dress up in his white tie and tails and appear at the Palace to wish Their Majesties *"Kronia Pola."* We had early lunch as soon as he got home and changed, and then drove down to Sunion to see the Temple of Poseidon. We stopped at the Kanakis Taverna on the way back to distribute Christmas gifts—stockings, lipsticks and cigarettes to the numerous family, and a very special black and gold knitted stole for Momma (I told her it was the latest thing in New York, even though it had come from San Francisco).

We had been asked to a dancing party at the Levidis', and even though the invitations read "Black Tie," I was sure the King and Queen would be there. Sure enough they were. As I rose from my curtsy, the Queen asked me if I would be jealous if she danced with my husband.

387

I didn't want to insult her by saying "No," so I said I couldn't possibly be jealous of a privilege to which he had been looking forward. She wore a very bouffant gown of white satin embroidered in a vine-like pattern of pearl and crystal beads with little soft puffs of pink feathers for flowers. She lost a few of the feathers when she fancy-danced with Roger!

The Peurifoys, the Yosts and ourselves were the only Americans there—we hadn't felt that we knew the Levidis well enough to ask to have the Griffins invited—Betty Jane and I were the only two in the new short evening dresses which we had bought when we were home. Mine was black net with a spangled top. I had felt a bit naked in it before arriving, but not after I got there; one woman had nothing much above the waist except three fan-pleated ruffles.

Later in the evening the Queen asked me if I had gotten my dress in America and if I had a good modiste there. I told her I had gotten it ready-made which she found very surprising and asked if they ever fitted. I said they did, for they went by sizes and I was size 14. "Oh!" said she, "then they do not go by age? What size would I be?" I said "12," but Mary Karolou said firmly "14. You haven't seen her undressed."

January 27th was quite a day. We had been invited to the christening of Vincent's baby and a day or two beforehand he had asked me if my "little name" was "Elene"; I said it was, and he beamed broadly. It was to be the baby's second name—Nicolette Elene. I knew it raised the ante, but at that I was fortunate not to be asked to be godmother (as I was not a Catholic) for that is practically a life-long responsibility in Greece.

We got to the Cathedral about noon. In the ceremony, the godparents progressed by slow degrees from the center of the church to the font where so much water was poured over the baby's head they had to hold her upside down so as not to drown her. She gave one tiny squeak but that was all, which I thought truly remarkable. Roger and I each lighted candles, and then we were given a box of *dragées,* a holy medal and a macaroon, which we ate with gusto going home in the car.

I had worn my best clothes, my mink, and my cocktail hat with the Paradise, so as to make "face" for Vincent. He was beaming when he got home in the afternoon. I was sure I had done the right thing and was very proud of myself until he said that his friends were surprised that at our age we were so well preserved, and got around as well as we did ... *sic transit*.

One night there was a dance given by the Union of Greek Employees of the Mission and the Embassy at the Acropole Palace Hotel. Roger and I went taking Betty Jane with us as Jack was away. It proved to be quite a gay affair with plenty of liquid refreshment, and the account that Roger gave me the next day was so vivid that I shall quote it verbatim:

"After dancing with Betty Jane and several other Americans, I decided that in the interest of Greek-American friendship I should from then on dance only with Greek ladies. I found no difficulty picking partners. When you and the rest of our party left at 1:30 a.m., I was having too good a time to leave.

"Finally at 3:30 a.m., with three Greek men and three Greek ladies, we drove out to a taverna on the outskirts of the city where we found an orchestra playing their heads off to some 50-odd Greeks present. The only trouble was that the floor was concrete, and I found it rather tough on my feet after the hours of dancing at the Acropole.

"At the table next to us were two men and two girls, all of whom I took to be Greeks. But as I returned to my table after a particularly fancy dance, one of them said to me in perfect English, 'Better look out or they won't elect you Mayor of San Francisco again.' My answer, of course, was 'They won't have another chance.' I had to laugh at being identified in a place like that in my one night out on the town."

Finally at 6:00 a.m. they started home in the pouring rain, stopping on the way at a flower market to buy bouquets for the girls and a bunch of violets for me. He woke me up by dropping the cat on my stomach to present them. I muttered "Go to bed and take your cat with you."

One afternoon a man named Kavanagh came to ask Roger to be the official father of his bride-to-be, and give her away at a wedding the following Saturday night. He started the conversation by saying I didn't know him well enough to know how funny it was for him to be in the State Department. Then he said, "I know it was nervy of me to ask the Old Man to be Pappy to an unknown gal, but from what I'd seen of him I thought he was a good guy, so I took a chance." I agreed that it was funny for him to be in the State Department.

A few days before the wedding, the telephone rang, and a man's voice said "Hello, Helen, this is Cap." It was Cap Rieber. He and his daughter, Ruth, were in Athens—just back from Teheran via Istanbul, where he had been sent by the World Bank to interview Mossadegh on the oil situation. We picked them up at eight o'clock at the Grande Bretagne and brought them out to dinner and listened spellbound to Cap's description of his meeting with Mossadegh, and his visits to the oil fields.

Friday morning we took them on a tour of Piraeus, the Acropolis, etc., and though it was windy as always climbing up to the Parthenon, the wind was behind us and actually helped us up the steep ascent. Roger had to lunch with a couple of Government Ministers, so I brought the Riebers out to the house. I hope they enjoyed lunch more than I did; LOVE had entered Puss-puss'es life and we ate our meal to a chorus of cat-calls from her and her five gentlemen friends.

Later when the Brewsters came over for cocktails, Dania took one look at Puss-puss and said "Why didn't you tell me to bring Tommy over?" They had a beautiful half-Persian tom, and we had always talked of his being the father of "our" kittens. No sooner said than done. Dan went back to his house, and reappeared with Tommy in his arms. Dania and I, both dressed up to the nines, made quite a picture as each of us with a cat in arms escorted them to a trysting place in the laundry. Again the poor Riebers were in the middle of a cat-astrophy!

When we got home from dinner with the Riebers, we went down to the laundry room to see how the cats were getting along; as we opened the door Puss-puss shot out like a bat out of Hell with Tommy in hot pursuit. Apparently she would have none of him. The next morning when we went down to let them out, only Puss-puss appeared; Tommy was hiding in the rafters, so it seemed that Puss-puss was betraying her lowly origin in preferring alley cats to genuine blue-bloods. I sent Dania a pretty evening bag as a stud fee with the following jingle:

"OWED" TO THE BREWSTERS

"For 'Services Rendered'—(successful or not),
The Laps owe the Brewsters I'm sure quite a lot.
Picture Mr. D. B. carrying aforesaid Tom
Who would make of our Puss-puss a regular 'Mom,'
And Dania B. all dressed in her best
Conducting her cat to a fight or a 'fest,'
With Helen behind and clearing the decks
To sacrifice Puss on the altar of sex.

A feast or a famine? I wouldn't quite know;
And while I can't claim that your cat's somewhat slow,
MY cat's polyandrous—she left yours in haste
For four or five others more to her taste.

So are we related—a-kith or akin?
Only Puss-puss can say . . . and she's living in sin."

Saturday was a full day with a visit to the Commissary in the morning, picking up the Riebers and taking them to the airport for a one o'clock departure for Rome, a quiet afternoon, then calling for Betty Jane at 6:30 and going on to the wedding. The church was freezing cold, and again we waited half an hour. The groom was there, but the bride lost her way and arrived at 7:30, pale and trembling. Poor girl! I was sorry for her; it's bad enough to be married in a strange land you've never seen until 48 hours previously, to a bridegroom you hadn't seen for six months, and without another soul except him you had ever laid eyes on before, but to lose your way to the church in addition must have been the last straw.

Roger took her up the aisle in style. The only untoward feature was that all the ushers were in dinner clothes, and no one had told

Roger to wear them and he was in a dark blue suit. Too bad, as we were going on to dinner and he would only have had to change once instead of twice. The reception was small and pretty grim as no one knew anyone else. We didn't stay long but went home to change and then on to a lovely dinner given by the Costopoulos at the G. B.

It was a dinner of some 60, and I had two Ambassadors, the Spanish and the Austrian. The conversation was entirely in French, and while I could not understand the Spanish Ambassador's brand at all, I got on beautifully with the Austrian, talking mostly about Vienna and its charms. Someone said afterwards that they found him awfully *Ancien Regime*. Probably that was why I liked him.

The next day I wrote Mme. Costopoulo the following thank-you note:

> *"Bien chère Mme. Costopoulo:*
> *Votre diner hier soir—du plus beau!*
> *Si chic et si gai*
> *Notre seul grand regret*
> *Qu'il nous fallait partir si tot.*
> *Toutes les viandes étaient du mieux:*
> *Et les vins? Mon Dieu!—delicieux!*
> *D'en faire un part*
> *De tout cet éclat,*
> *Que mon mari et moi sont heureux.*
> *Amusant—mes Ambassadeurs;*
> *Ni de li'un ni de l'autre avais-je peur.*
> *D'etre enface de vous,*
> *Comme cela m'avait plut.*
> *Merci—du fond de mon coeur."*

Meanwhile there was a Greek holiday and Roger decided to take a long weekend for a tour of the Peleponnesus, which was the one part of Greece we hadn't seen. We were joined by the Aldefers of the MSA.

The first stop was Mycene about which no one knows too much. The ruins, dating from between 1400 and 1100 B.C. were only unearthed by Schliemann in 1876; he based their probable location from his studies of Homer. We had a picnic lunch there, sitting on ground which was carpeted with wild flowers; scarlet anemones, wild purple iris, and darling little blue grape-hyacinths that made me homesick for Atherton.

Dr. Aldefer, who had taught at Penn State, lectured interestingly on all the places we saw. But I thought he overdid it a bit when he insisted on pointing out orange and olive groves to me as though we didn't have them in California. At one point, he also called my attention to the ruins of a Frankish castle, telling me that the Franks had at one period invaded Greece. I said I did remember that as I had majored in history in college; his very bland reply was that that must have been so long ago, I had probably forgotten! I took a slight dislike to him from that moment.

Our next stop was Nauplion where we took a short motor launch ride to the island fortress of Bourtzi where we spent the night. It looked more like the setting for the first act of Hamlet than Elsinore did and when we saw our rooms, all I could think of were the lines from Hamlet—"The wind bites shrewdly, it is nipping cold." There was no heat except in the stone-floored square entry room where there was a black pot-bellied stove around which we all huddled.

The names of the places we drove through Sunday rang in my ears like bells; Argos: Jason, his Argonauts, and the "Argive Helen"; Sparta, Leonidas and his Immortal Three Hundred; and Mystra, a throwback to the Middle Ages, built about 1400 A.D. by the Byzantines at the height of their civilization. Modern Sparta is probably not more than 150 years old and the old city is gone altogether. But Mystra was something else again; although every house was a shell, the 14 churches were wonderfully preserved. I only saw two of them because they were strung out straight up hill for nearly a mile, and the walking was all over large and slippery cobble stones. Byzantine churches were Dr. Aldefer's passion, and he was bitterly disappointed that Roger and I faded as soon as we did. We took the car back to the main square, sat on the sidewalk outside of one of the tavernas in the sun, and drank *ouzo*.

At the taverna, we were joined by a fine-looking white-haired man who according to our driver came over to interpret. It was a carnival day, and he told us that the music we had been hearing came from the City Hall across the Square where the children were having a dance. Would we like to see it? We would. So he led us over and it really was a sight; some 175 children, ages 5 to 12, in fancy dress with all the proud mammas sitting around watching them doing the traditional Greek dances—and an occasional Samba! The Demark pulled Roger and me into the dance, but I cut out after a few rounds and left Roger with the children. And how they loved it, especially when he put on one of their hats and did a *pas seul*.

After half an hour the Nomark (Mayor) arrived and said that he would like to entertain us at an informal dance that evening. Sparta would lose face if the Chief of Mission was there and not offered a suitable welcome. We accepted with pleasure.

At 9:30 p.m., we were called for and formally conducted to the City Hall where a gay and amusing party had been gotten up for us on three hours notice. A short time after we arrived a charming group of young people blew in, all in carnival costume of some sort. They had been at a party of their own, but had been asked by the Mayor "to strengthen his party." They pulled us into the traditional dances, and Roger again was in his element doing his fanciest steps with gusto amid enthusiastic applause.

Roger had danced with every fat old girl in the room when at midnight the Mayor said he had an announcement to make. Would Mr. Lapham please step to the center of the room? Mr. Lapham did—and was made an Honorary Citizen of Sparta! It was seriously and impressively done, and was quite touching. Roger said afterward that an Honorary Citizen of Sparta was the last thing he ever expected to be, and he was sure it was conferred on him not in recognition of American aid but because he had danced with every woman in the room.

General and Mrs. Eisenhower arrived in Athens a day or so later. We were all excited because he had just made a clean sweep of the New Hampshire primaries. Betty Jane gave a luncheon of 14 for Mrs. Eisenhower, whom I found most charming and natural and with lots of "savvy," which is so important for anyone in her position. The other guests were the wives of the British, Canadian and Turkish Ambassadors, Mrs. (General) Hart, Mrs. (Admiral) Glass, and several Greek women whose husbands were members of the General Staff.

I sat next to Mrs. Unaydin, the Turkish Ambassadress, and we discussed Ann Bridge's latest book, "The Dark Moment." The heroine, Feride, was presumably based on Mrs. Unaydin, herself. She only shrugged and smiled when I asked her if this was so, but she did admit that Ann Bridge had stayed with her during the three months it took her to write the book.

That evening we went to a reception given for the Eisenhowers by the ranking Greek Brass at the Greek Officers' Club. As we approached the General in the receiving line, he caught Roger's eye, held up two fingers, and said "Two no trump without looking." The last time he had met Roger was at the Bohemian Grove; he had played bridge with him there and knew Roger's peculiar system of bidding. When we reached the General, he said the only thing he regretted was that his stay was so short he didn't have time for another game of bridge with Roger.

Our next visitors were Ray Lapham, Roger's Boston cousin, and his wife Madge. They had been on a cruise on the "Caronia" to South America and South Africa. Ray had a wild animal farm at Nashua, New Hampshire, and had been collecting animals for it everywhere en route. He had had an attendance of 500,000 the year before at 50¢ a head for adults and 25¢ for children. He also sold so-called *objets d'art*. When he got to Athens he was so taken with the plaster models of the Parthenon and busts of various gods and goddesses that he swapped two baboons and a snake for a crate of them.

It was time again for the Mass at the Cathedral in celebration of Greek Independence Day. It proved to be an even more brilliant spectacle than the year before. All the diplomats—except American, Canadian and Italian—were in full dress uniforms with decorations and resplendent with gold embroidery; Denmark in scarlet, France and Holland in blue, England and others in black, with the women beside them looking like modest little brown wrens. All the other men, except those in Army or Navy uniform, Government Ministers, Jack, etc. were in full evening dress.

We waited fifteen minutes, and then heard the cheering outside and the band playing the Greek National Anthem. The Royal Entourage entered to be met by a procession of the clergy in their gorgeous vestments. The King was in his Admiral's uniform, blazing with ribbons and diamond orders, carrying his Marshall's baton. The Queen wore a long brown dress with the blue ribbon of the Order of St. George, a single string of pearls, a diamond cross and a ruby pendant. Everyone stood during the whole ceremony and at the end the Metropolitan came forward to the Royal Family, held out a silver cross for them to kiss. They walked down the aisle to a spontaneous cheer of "Long live the King."

Easter Week proved to be Animal Week. Good Friday morning before I had had my coffee I heard Vincent's step approaching, then I heard "B-A-A-A" and thought he was being awfully playful. He came into the room carrying the homeliest lamb I had ever seen. It had a card tied around its neck saying, "Best wishes for a Happy Easter" from a Mr. Kananias who was the head of the Greek meat industry. A nicely dressed lamb all ready for roasting was one thing, but a live lamb on the hoof was something else again! I said, "Take it away!" and Vincent said, "What shall I do with it Madame?" I said I didn't know, but to take it away until I had had my breakfast and could think.

An hour later I heard a terrible rumpus from the kitchen and went down to find Vincent and Maria yelling at each other in Greek. I told them to keep quiet and tell me what it was all about; Maria wanted Vincent to kill the lamb on the premises, and he said he was engaged as a houseman and not as a slaughterer of animals. If she wanted the lamb slaughtered she could take it to the butchers herself. I agreed heartily with Vincent and told Maria to take the lamb to the butchers right away. I gave her 30,000 drachmas for the slaughtering, and she departed leading the lamb on a string, but muttering that we'd never get our own nice lamb back, but some old sheep the butcher would palm off on us.

When I went to the icebox that night, all that was left of our lamb were the legs and the chops. Vincent had taken the head, Maria the skin, and Puss-puss had feasted on all the left-over insides. Maria asked if we wanted it for dinner, but I told her I couldn't possibly eat an animal at night to which I had been introduced in the morning. We would save it for Easter Sunday when all the Greeks eat lamb after a black fast on bread and olives during Holy Week.

7

LAST DAYS IN GREECE

EARLY in May, Betty Jane and I slipped away together for two weeks in Italy. We were fortunate in two ways: the trip was a dark secret so that we didn't have all sorts of people wanting to go with us; and we were able to arrange a ride on a military plane to Florence. There we were met by Consul-General and Mrs. Reed who took us to our hotel, the Grand.

For the next week in Florence, we had a marvelous time sightseeing, taking in a symphony and an opera, visiting the Ufizzi Gallery and shopping. But the high point came with a lunch with ex-Queen Helen of Romania in her charming Villa Sparta half way up the hill towards Fiesole.

Betty Jane happened to mention to the King one night at dinner that we were going to Florence. He had promptly said, "Oh! then you must see my sister," and had sent her a cable. Queen Helen followed it up with a note on our arrival. She was very handsome, simple, charming—and frank. When I asked her when she bought the villa, she said "When Carol invited me to leave Romania and buy and settle in some other country, as we could no longer breathe the same air."

Queen Helen did much of her own gardening and concentrated on iris—a Florentine specialty. When she said she had a great deal of trouble with roses, I told her the story of the New England spinster who told her garden club she had quite a "prah-blem"; she loved roses, but had very little space, and did they think it would be all right if she put the Reverend Ulrich Bruner in the same bed with Dorothy Perkins? Queen Helen, unlike Queen Victoria, was amused.

Betty Jane and I had decided to go to Venice by bus in order to see the country, especially as it was described in the C.I.T. folders as a "delightful seven hour run, with an hour for lunch at Ravenna and an hour for sightseeing afterward."

We left the Grand Hotel at 8 a.m. and finally got under way after stopping at numerous hotels to pick up other passengers. Among them was a tall, blonde, youngish woman—probably Scandinavian. She raised a rumpus because she hadn't seen her luggage loaded. Reassured, she subsided into a nest of three coats—two cloth, one near-leopard and a fur stole.

We reached Ravenna at one and had a nice lunch chosen from a pricelessly translated menu which featured "Porc flancks with small pees" and "Cheese as you licke it to choice." Then the C.I.T. stewardess announced that the Po River was so high we might have to make a long detour to get across, and we would not reach Venice before 9 p.m. Would it be agreeable to everyone if we cut out the hour's sightseeing in Ravenna? Everyone agreed except the blonde Swede. She threw another tantrum. She had come to Ravenna to see the tomb of Galla Placidia, and she was going to see it, or tell everyone what kind of an outfit C.I.T. was. We were 29-1 ... but to the tomb we went after getting into the wrong church first. When we got to the right one, Betty Jane asked the sacristan right away where the tomb was, and he led us to it—a small mausoleum outside of the church. Meanwhile Blondie was searching the church in vain, and she never did see it which didn't hurt my feelings at at all.

The next day, we had a ride in a gondola, had our pictures taken with the pigeons and did a little mild shopping. We also listened to a concert in the Piazza San Marco but with difficulty. The competition between the bells on the Campanile and the two bronze figures on the clock tower was very keen. I felt that Browning's statement, "The air broke into a mist of bells" was the understatement of all time. The "mist," to my way of thinking, was a full gale.

We returned to Florence by train the next day. We had made return reservations at the Grand, but apparently now they had never heard of us. We were told that there wasn't a bed in the place. I pointed to the reservation I had made that they showed me, so they said, "Oh! you are Mrs. Lappami from Capri. You have a double without a bath." I said the name was misspelled, but it was my room just the same.

Betty Jane went up to sit in the room in case Mrs. Lappami appeared while I went out to check with the American Express on our reservations for Rome. I met with a slight disappointment. Because Betty Jane and I were the only reservations, they had cancelled the tour to Rome. We would have to leave by the regular bus—CIT—and spend the night in Perugia en route. We left at 7:30 the next morning with all our purchases crammed in our bags. The ride to Perugia took four hours and was pleasant, except for the fact that our good, but very fast driver burst into song out of a clear blue sky, driving with only one hand and holding a microphone (which he didn't need) in the other. We left Perugia after lunch the next day, and had a rather uninteresting five hour drive to Rome.

The next morning we walked miles in the Vatican, ending up with a long visit to the Sistine Chapel. Then we drove up the Palatine Hill to peek through the keyhole in the monastery gate which gives such a surprising view of St. Peter's. Betty Jane was slightly apprehensive when I coaxed her to put her eye to the keyhole. She was sure someone was going to squirt water through it, but gave a shriek of surprise and pleasure after she had summoned up her courage.

In late spring, we drove down to Piraeus and went aboard a Greek minesweeper for a three day cruise to the islands of Leros and Cos. Roger was to inspect two technical schools. The ship was a 1250 tonner, 220 feet long. Roger and I had the "deluxe quarters" in sick bay. It contained two iron bunks—one above the other—a wash stand, desk and a couple of chairs. We also had a supposedly private bath, but the door didn't lock. The toilet either flushed all the time or not at all, and, when the only toilet on the ship gave out, ours ceased to be private.

I took the upper bunk because I didn't think Roger would ever be able to make it. There was only a foot clearance between the sleeper and the welter of hot pipes above. The side of the upper bunk had to be hooked in place after you were in place. As Roger fixed it the first night, he laughed and said "You're not rocked, you're locked in the cradle of the deep, Sport."

On the island of Tinos that evening and we went ashore to see the famous ikon which was discovered 130 years ago through the dream vision of a nun. It was the center of a great festival every 15th of August. People came from all over Greece to see the ikon carried through the streets. We were led directly to the ikon. It was so completely covered with votive offerings of jewelry that you couldn't see it at all. One beautiful diamond pendant on a chain was draped across it. The ikon was also covered with earrings, pins, bracelets, and almost everything you could imagine—all under glass.

The entire church was filled with hanging lamps, each with a silver ship depending from it—as votive offerings. Most of the ships were very beautiful and I saw Roger's mouth watering; he had collected ship models for years, but had none like these.

We arrived on the island of Leros the next morning. We were greeted by the whole school drawn up in military formation and presented with flowers. Then we were taken to the main building for "limonada" and dreadfully sweet cakes. The tour of inspection followed. At 5:30 p.m., we were taken over to the parade ground to watch a soccer match and Roger kicked in the first ball, which he did successfully. After that the whole school marched and counter-marched across to where we were sitting. They gave Roger a metal paperweight they had made for him, raised the American flag, and then did more marching with each trade singing its own song. At the close of the ceremonies Roger shook hands with the 16 honor boys, and made a nice little speech about the impression the school had made on him. By that time it was 7 o'clock, and we went to our little launch with all the boys racing along as an escort. In fact, they showed strong signs of wanting to carry Roger on their shoulders, an honor he declined.

We crossed the Bay to the main harbor of the island and were met by the Mayor. We made a grand tour in the most delapidated cars I had ever seen and finally reached the capital, Parthene, about 8 p.m. What a sight it was! The little square was crammed with people who had probably been there for hours because of our late schedule. Roger made a very short speech from the flag-draped balcony of the Mayor's office. Everyone clapped and cheered, and then began to sing.

In the meantime, a Medieval castle high above the town on a hill was illuminated with oil flares in three tiers. On that clear night with a half-moon, it was truly a fairyland spectacle! Downstairs a group of high school girls danced for us, and as usual dragging one after another of our group into the dance. We had dinner at the men's club next door; with *ouzo* and hors d'oeuvre (good), followed by roast lamb and black walnut ice cream for dessert. I was sitting next to a French-educated Greek engineer who piled his ice cream on top of a raw cucumber! It was a 14-hour day before we were back aboard our boat anchored in the harbor.

On Cos the next morning, we visited a small school of only 110 boys. Then we were driven to the ruins of the great Medical School of Hippocrates dating from Roman times. It was on the side of a hill surrounded by tall cypress trees, and was really very impressive. Then we saw the sycamore tree under which Hippocrates lectured. It was in three pieces now, with the most enormous trunk I had ever seen outside of the redwoods, and still green and flourishing.

Dan Brewster had been ordered to Paris; Roger was going to Washington for consultation and then out to the Coast; we had had terribly hot weather, so I had decided to get away from it all and take a trip to where it would be cooler. I invited Dania Brewster to go with me. Our idea was to fly with Roger and Dan as far as Zurich, spend the night there, and then go on to Vienna the next day.

On the flight up, our pilot had a passion for sightseeing, so we circled the Acropolis, later on Vesuvius, then Rome and afterwards Pisa. Zurich was blistering hot. Our hotel was in the center of a circle of churches all of which had chimes and none of them synchronized. They played every quarter of an hour night and day with 15 minutes of solid noise at 6 a.m., and again at 8 a.m.

In Vienna we saw St. Stephen's and Schönbrun, and then we drove out through the "Wiener Wald"—the Vienna Woods of the waltzes—to Cobenzl, and lunched on the porch of the inn at Karlsberg. Our delightful guide was not the kind of person you could tip; when she asked if we minded if she took her dessert home to her daughter, we ordered the whole lunch for her to take home. She practically had tears in her eyes. She said she and her daughter had not tasted meat or sweets for over a year.

We went to the Hapsburg tombs—all 144 of them including Maria Theresa's and her husband's. It was a joint affair weighing two tons with four weeping figures seated at the corners, an angel blowing a trumpet high at the back, and Maria Theresa and Francis each sitting up on one elbow. The figures were looking at each other with expressions of "Fancy meeting you here!" Our guide explained that is was supposed to be the start of their resurrection as the "Last Trumpet is blown." When I looked at myself in the mirror after I had had my hair washed and set that afternoon, I was the living image of Maria Theresa with three tight rolls of curls on each side of my head. I decided I was not the rococo type, and combed them out the minute I got back to the hotel!

General Hays' Aide, Major Pinckney, met us in Saltzburg and took us to Berchtesgarten Hof for the night. The hotel was once a famous retreat of the Nazi higher-ups, and was now run by the American Army. We had two fine rooms with one of the most superb mountain views I had ever seen; across emerald green meadows to towering rock peaks with a little snow still left on the summits.

The next morning we drove to Obersalzburg where both Hitler and Goering had small summer places, and from where we could see the famous "Eagle's Nest" far, far above us. Both the houses had been demolished lest they become places of pilgrimage, but the remains of Goering's blue-tiled outdoor swimming pool were still visible. It was here that Dania and I were conscious for the first time of resentment against Americans. A group of German men and women were blocking our path and, far from moving aside to let us pass, they spread out forcing us into the ditch. They also muttered something in German with a sneering laugh. On the way back I said "Bitte" and walked right through them. I had had enough of their insolence.

The next morning, General Hays placed a car at our disposal to drive us to Munich. There we stayed at the Hotel Excelsior, an American Army hotel and a very definite come-down from the ones where we had been staying. The rooms with bath were $1.00 a day, payable in advance. They were faded, dingy and pretty grim; it had evidently been a second class commercial hotel before the war and was right across the street from the railway station. There were two signs on the wall of each room that read: "There are both male and female guests billeted on this floor. To avoid embarrassment it is requested that robes be worn (or appropriate uniform or civilian clothing) when going to and from the bathrooms and/or W.C." The other read:

ALL OCCUPANTS OF THIS ROOM ARE CHARGED WITH THE FOLLOWING: Towel, bath, 1; Towel, hand, 1; Sheets, 2; Blankets, 2; Case, pillow, 1; Pillow, 1; (and it was just as hard as the Greek pillows) Ashtrays, 1; Glasses, water, 1.
We hope you enjoy your stay in Munich.
Signed, Commanding General.

The next morning, we left for Geneva where I was to spend a week with the Bill Brewsters, and Dania one night before she returned to Athens to collect her children and her belongings en route to joining Dan in Paris.

Among the letters forwarded to me in Geneva was one postmarked Florence and signed "Helen." I thought "Who on earth can this be from? I don't know anyone in Florence named Helen." It turned out to be Queen Helen of Romania! When I wrote her my bread-and-butter letter to thank her for the luncheon, I had typed it and begun:

"Your Majesty:

"I have never written to a Queen before, so do not know if I am committing lèse majesté in typing this letter, but if you could see my handwriting you would be grateful, for I frequently cannot read it myself."

I went on to tell her how much I had enjoyed the egg dish she had given us, and had wondered what the ingredients were, and she had sent me the recipe with the following note enclosed:

"Dear Mrs. Lapham:

"Thank you so much for your delightful letter, it did make me laugh! I was so flattered by your compliments that I am enclosing the recipe for the eggs. As you see they are not at all complicated, there is no exotic base as you seemed to think unless my cook has not let me into the secret.

"It was so nice having you and Mrs. Peurifoy to lunch that day. If you ever happen to come here again, do let me know.

"With all kind thoughts,

Helen"

Back in Athens one Sunday Betty Jane and I went to the races. I had never been, and as we had invitations to sit in the Royal Box, we thought we ought to go. We got there late, but the first race I saw I placed a 20,000 drachmas bet. My horse, Number 11, came in and I won $2.45! On the big race, I got reckless and put 40,000 drachmas on Number 7. Number 11 came in again! I was furious that I had switched. Two days later I saw Admiral Glass, who had done my betting for me, and he said "Well you did all right Sunday; whatever made you think of that combination?" I said "Oh no, I shifted and bet on 7." "But my dear girl," he said, "they're the same stable, if either one wins, you collect. Have you still got the tickets?" Believe it or not, I found it still in the purse I had carried that day. He cashed them for me, and sent me 106,000 drachmas!

The weather continued hot and, in addition, water was rationed—coming on between 9 a.m. and 4 p.m. one day, and 6 p.m. until 3 a.m. the next. But finally the *mel-temmi*, the cool breeze began to blow. We went down to the Carlson's in Kavouri for a swim in the Aegean and a little bridge. It was deliciously cool—probably only 90 instead of 106—and I enjoyed it all thoroughly except Roger's insistence on playing goulashes. I loathe it because he said I always passed my cards wrong. As a matter of fact, I was sure I passed them more knowledgeably than he did.

On another Sunday, Senators Wayne Morse and Russell Long arrived. We had drinks on the porch with Jack and General Hart also there. At dinner, the conversation was mostly by Wayne. Poor Russell Long kept trying to get in a word or two about how he would have liked to vote for some bill, but couldn't because of his constituents.

Wayne was down on everything from the way Eisenhower's campaign was being run (which I think was sour grapes as he had expected to be nominated for the Vice-Presidency) to all foreign aid. I finally asked him if we Americans ever did anything smart. He replied, after a short pause: "Very rarely." That left me more depressed than ever. Just before I went to bed, I asked him if he couldn't say just one cheerful thing, and his answer was that as far as he had been able to ascertain, the MSA/G "wasn't too badly administered." I hoped he didn't change his mind after Roger briefed him on the situation in Greece the next morning.

About this time, we were asked out to the Kanakis taverna for lunch and then to tread out the grapes. En route, we passed donkey cart after donkey cart laden with grapes and now we knew their destination. Quite a crowd had already gathered, including Betty Jane, the Chinese Ambassador, Admiral and Mrs. Glass and many of the younger Embassy and MSA personnel. It was quite an experience!

We took off our shoes and stockings, stepped into a tub of warm water, and then into a small and very warm enclosure. It had a sloping floor for the juice to run out through an outlet at the lower end. The grapes were two or three feet thick on the floor and we danced on them to the music of an antique phonograph playing a traditional Greek dance. Everyone was holding hands, dancing round and round up hill and down on the slippery grapes, singing, trying to keep time to the music and to keep from falling down. It was quite a do!

There was a tub of water to wash our feet in as we got out, and then we all had our pictures taken holding one of the huge clusters of grapes. They were so enormous that they looked exactly like the pictures of the ones the spies brought home from Eschol in the "Story of the Bible" I used to pore over as a child.

All the way home the line kept going through my ear, "He is trampling out the vintage where the grapes of wrath are stored." But I will never believe that these grapes were the grapes of wrath. They were the ones that Timothy spoke of . . . "but use a little wine for thy stomach's sake and thine often infirmities."

The Phil Crowes invited me to go to Istanbul with them. It seemed my best chance, because Roger's resignation had been announced a few days before and we were to leave early in October. He was not going to have time to go to Istanbul and take me with him. We took off at 2:40 p.m. by BEA Viking for the three day trip. I had a nice whodunit all ready to read on the flight, but Irene Crowe produced John Dewey's "Introduction to Philosophy" and I didn't have the courage to bring it out of my bag.

On arrival, there was no one to meet us. Finally, a man from the consulate, who was there to meet someone else, took pity on us and drove us in from the airport. At the Consulate no cable had been received; they had never heard of us and we had no reservations. After a great deal of telephoning, they got us into a hotel called the Ipek Pala. It must have been third or fourth class even by Turkish standards. I had the only room with a bath, and the water ran both hot and cold. The floor was so dirty I wouldn't have put a bare foot anywhere near it—any more than I would have put on the clogs nor the bathrobe that were in the bathroom.

That night, we dined at a highly touted restaurant called Abdullah's. I had my promised caviar which was about a third the price it was in New York and about a third as good. I guess I like my caviar with trimmings, egg and onion and blinis and sour cream the way they give it to you at "21" and not just a little glass container of fresh caviar unaccompanied by so much as a lemon. Then I had a quail—at least, it said so on the menu. But I am pretty sure it was a sparrow.

Next morning we moved to the MSA guest house and had nice rooms overlooking the Bosphorus. An extremely helpful woman was the hostess; she not only planned our two days for us, but went almost everywhere with us. She was Turkish and also spoke many other languages. That morning, we did the Bazaar which was all covered and the largest one in the world. The saying is that if you go in on a Wednesday morning alone, you are lucky if you can find your way out by Thursday afternoon. At the end of two hours of walking, looking and shopping, we had bought exactly nothing!

Another swordfish lunch, and then what I really enjoyed more than anything else: a trip on one of the little river steamers up the Bosphorus as far as the Black Sea. Fortunately, we got to the wharf early and paid 10¢ extra for first class seats. We were jammed in like sardines for the first hour. We must have stopped at ten little landings and weaving back and forth from the European to the Asiatic side. We saw the Sultan's "new" palace—only 100 years old, but a great improvement over the old one. We also saw the old-time summer homes of the wealthy Turks and the Diplomatic corps—sadly shabby and in need of paint now, but they must have been something in their prime. There were many freighters anchored in the river and many little boats swishing back and forth. It was truly a fascinating experience!

We reached the entrance to the Black Sea in two hours, and what you saw there brought you up with a round turn: a swinging boom of bombs built from each side in such a way that a passage was left open for ships to go through in the daytime; the hinged section was closed at night. An LST was patroling one side and a gunboat the other. The Turks were not going to be caught napping if their traditional enemy tried to jump them some dark night.

The Crowes were delightful companions. Phil was widely traveled, very well-read, and as passionate an admirer of Kipling as I; we spent a great deal of time quoting his poems to each other. I, having learned the whole "Ballad of the Mary Gloucester," was like the brook and it was hard to stop me once I got started. I was sure Irene thought we were quite mad, but she was always charming and never seemed bored.

The next few weeks were busy ones. Our schedule was to leave on the 7th of October and return to San Francisco via the Far East. Some of our possessions were to go in trunks and boxes by ship; two suitcases were to be shipped ahead by air freight so we would have something to wear when we got home; and we planned to take only thin things with us and to travel as lightly as possible on our nearly three week trip.

The weather changed! And I was very glad the heat was over. Since Roger's resignation had been announced, we had been deluged with invitations and I had felt that if I had to work at breaking up the house all day and go out every night, I would be poured on the plane in a liquid condition.

Lee Barrows was to succeed Roger and his wife Irene came out one morning to go over the house, find out what went with it, and what I thought of my servants, whom she was planning to keep on. She thought that as a State Department house, everything in it went with it. I told her it did except for my personal possessions—my Chinese scrolls, my pictures, my vases and figurines, my nest of tables, etc.

She was quite miffed until I told her pillows, coat-hangers, ashtrays, vases, a breakfast set, and lots of books which we had read would be among the things I was leaving her.

Betty Jane and I had an appointment to say good-bye to the Queen at Tatoi, so I drove out with her at 5:30 p.m. If I hadn't lit another candle at Daphne the day before, I think we would both have been killed. She had an excellent driver and as we were going along a perfectly straight stretch of road, we saw a Greek Army truck coming towards us Hell-bent-for election. Panos drew as far off the road as he could and stopped, but it was impossible for us to turn out any further because of a ditch on the right and a culvert ahead. The truck careened and hit us—fortunately, only in the rear fender and neither of us were even thrown off the seat. In typical Greek fashion, the truck driver got out and said to Panos, "Why were you driving so recklessly?"

We had a delightful hour and a quarter with the Queen, who gave us tea. It was all very pleasant and informal.

Our last week in Athens was a busy one, what with getting everything that was to be sent ahead of us off, and either entertaining or being entertained. Tuesday the Barrows gave a big reception for us at the Grande Bretagne, which was lovely except for standing in the receiving line for two hours and shaking hands both coming and going.

Wednesday morning I finally nailed Roger to go through his clothes. By lunch every bed in the house was piled high and labelled "to send ahead," "to go by trunk," or "to give away." I couldn't have been more confused because the piles seemed so disproportionate that I was sure I had them mixed. Roger entertained his poker crowd that afternoon and they didn't leave until after seven. We were due at the Abbott's at eight and had to go to a cocktail party for Admiral and Mrs. Mc-Cormick in the meantime. I didn't see how we were going to make it and we didn't.

Thursday morning the whole MSA staff gathered in one of the big movie houses for an official good-bye to Roger and a welcome to Lee Barrows, just as they had two years ago to speed Paul Porter on his way and welcome Roger. He had warned me that this time he was going to call on me to speak to them in Greek, so I had prepared by three little sentences. My first was, "My husband is a bad man because he knows how little Greek I speak." Everyone laughed fortunately, because that gave me time to think of the other two.

We had the big official Government dinner that night—always a strain because I got Venizelos and he was hard to talk to; and Roger called on me to say "thanks" again in Greek. Venizelos made a most complimentary speech to which Roger responded easily and well, and then said his wife would finish for him in Greek. I rose to me feet and got on very well until the past part of the last sentence. So I turned to Venizelos and asked him what do I say now? He said, "Madame, I have no idea!" By that time I had remembered it, and was warmly received. All the Greek Ministers kissed my hand and congratulated me, so I guess I got at least an "E" for effort. We finally got home at midnight.

The next day, there was an informal lunch with the King. We got to Tatoi at one and were met by the King and Crown Prince Constantine. The King looked very stunning in his white Naval uniform, and apologized for the fact that it wasn't a real party; Her Majesty was in Germany, and though he had tried to get others, they all seemed to be out of town. A servant then came in with a tray on which there were two cocktails and two glasses of tomato juice which were passed to me first. I was in a quandary; which was I supposed to take? The King quickly came to my rescue and said, "Tino and I always take tomato juice," so I took my cocktail with pleasure.

Then the King reached around behind him and produced a box which he handed to Roger saying simply, "Here, I want you to have this to remind you of Greece, and in recognition of the fine work you have done here." It was the order of the Phoenix with a ribbon and a large star!

The four of us had a pleasant luncheon with much conversation between the King and Roger, and a desultory one between Tino and me. I asked him if the *"bombe"* on the menu was a dangerous one, but he said "Oh! no Madame, it is a *spécialité de la maison,* and quite, quite safe; but you must take some of the center, for it is chocolate and very delicious."

That night we had a buffet supper for forty Division Chiefs, their wives and secretaries. I decided at the last moment to seat the tables which was quite a job because we had six extra women. We were still at it when our first guests arrived so we promptly roped them in to help. So many of the different groups had wanted to entertain us that there just weren't enough nights to go around, so we had asked for the privilege of entertaining them ourselves instead. The universal comment was, "Oh, I'm so glad you haven't torn the house to pieces yet. We were afraid it would be completely stripped." It would be by the next day, and by that night I hoped everything would be completely packed— and perhaps a bit of room for some of the things I might have overlooked.

The hints of our Greek servants during that last week left a slightly unpleasant impression. We were going to leave them many clothes, and a good bonus, but not the 170 gold pounds Vincent would have liked to buy a small piece of ground, nor whatever Maria needed to build a small house, nor Koula's dowry, nor put up for John's buying himself out of 18 months' Army service, etc. Maria even went so far as to gather all the kitchen utensils together and said, "Madame, as you are leaving, I shall take all these with me, yes?" I told her they were Government property, and she could take nothing—not even an old unusable coffee pot.

We went out to the Kanakis Taverna to say good-bye and then returned for a simple, early supper. The next day we refused all invitations, and had a quiet evening. The McCauleys had a small dinner for us Tuesday night before we left for the airport, just the Drakes and the Carlsons, and we were due to take off at midnight. The last few weeks had been so hectic that I felt we would both heave a sigh of relief as the plane left the ground.

I had one keen disappointment. The wine from the grapes that I had trodden out was not aged sufficiently for me to be able to take it home. So after all, I can't offer, "Try some of this wine. I made it with my own feet."

We got to the airport a little after eleven, and people began pouring in until there must have been between forty and fifty. It was heartwarming to have that many friends who would turn up to see you off at midnight. Several of them brought champagne, but Adrienne Long—one of the secretaries—capped the climax; she brought her kitten, "Marybelle," whom I had given her, to say good-bye. It was the hit of the evening. Admiral Lappas brought a huge sheath of roses from Venizelos, so that when I got on the plane, I felt as though I should be stretched out somewhere with it and "Rest in Peace" on my bosom.

Well . . . the Song of Greece was ended, but the Melody will continue to linger on for the rest of our lives. True, I never felt the same love for Greece that I did for China, but I wouldn't give up our two years there for anything!

Η ΕΛΛΑΣ ΕΡΓΑΖΕΤΑΙ ΜΕ ΤΗΝ ΒΟΗΘΕΙΑ ΤΟΥ ΣΧΕΔΙΟΥ ΜΑΡΣΑΛΛ

Κρητικοί καί Κρητικοπούλες μέ ἐθνικά κοστούμια ὑποδέχονται μέ τοπικούς χορούς τόν Ἀρχηγό τῆς Ἀποστολῆς τοῦ Σχεδίου Μάρσαλλ στήν Ἑλλάδα καί τήν Κα Λάπαμ (στό ἀπάνω μέρος τῆς εἰκόνας) πού παρευρέθηκαν στά ἐγκαίνια τοῦ νέου δρόμου ἀπό τό χωριό Πρασσές στό Κάμπανο. Τό ἔργο αὐτό ἔγινε μέ βάση τό πρόγραμμα Πρόνοια — Ἐργασία καί μέ τήν ἐθελοντική ἐργασία τῶν κατοίκων τῆς κοιλάδος τοῦ Σελίνου. Ὁ κ. Λάπαμ ἐχαρακτήρισε τό ἔργο σάν ἕνα λαμπρό παράδειγμα τοῦ προγράμματος αὐτοβοηθείας πού τόση σημασία ἔχει γιά τήν ἀνόρθωσι τῆς Ἑλλάδος.

52/1-12-50

ΔΗΜΟΣΙΕΥΕΤΑΙ ΜΕ ΤΗΝ ΣΥΝΕΡΓΑΣΙΑΝ ΤΗΣ ΕΛΛΗΝΙΚΗΣ ΚΥΒΕΡΝΗΣΕΩΣ ΚΑΙ ΤΟΥ ΓΡΑΦΕΙΟΥ ΠΛΗΡΟΦΟΡΙΩΝ ΤΗΣ ΑΜΕΡΙΚΑΝΙΚΗΣ ΑΠΟΣΤΟΛΗΣ ΤΗΣ Δ.Ο.Σ.

The Laphams were treated enthusiastically by the press of Greece during their residency and travels there as evidenced by this feature coverage in a major publication.

413

ABOVE — Forgotten words of a banquet speech in faltering Greek are deftly turned to delight the audience. Mrs. Lapham simply turns to Greek Premier Venizelos and asks what to say next.

RIGHT — A page from one of many voluminous Lapham family scrapbooks records Roger Lapham's arrival in China as Chief of Mission for the ECA recovery program there.

American Aid Chief Arrives

SINWEN TIENTI No. 42

地天聞新

天地有另中聞新新 聞新是皆問地天

中華民國卅七年六月十六日出版 ·第四十二期·

·美國經濟合作總局司長樸漢普抵滬下機前與歡迎者揮手·

415

*Roger Lapham poses in 1948 with the house staff of
their official residence at 1803 Avenue Joffre in
Shanghai. The staff of seven — plus fluctuating numbers of staff relatives — cost US$116 per month. The
staff was headed by the Lapham's beloved #1 Boy, Ea
Te, shown standing to the right of his wife.*

IV

RETIREMENT ROVINGS

(1953 — 1966)

1

THE LONG WAY HOME

O UR air route returning home to San Francisco was via Karachi, Beirut, Calcutta, Bangkok, Hong Kong, Manila and Honolulu with a few stays at various way points.

Our four days in Hong Kong were out of this world. We stayed at the Repulse Bay Hotel and immediately contacted the Gilpatrics. He had been Deputy Chief of the ECA Mission when Roger arrived in June, 1948. Then we got in touch with H. J. Shen, whom we had known so well in Shanghai, and from then on we didn't have a dull moment.

Another thing I had done when we got in Sunday was to ask at the desk to have a good tailor make three shirts for Roger out of the beautiful Greek hand-woven silk Bodasaki had given him for Christmas. The tailor arrived about ten and said "can do" to the shirts—and also to a sharkskin dinner jacket and thin black trousers that Roger needed. But he insisted on one fitting. Could we come to his shop at five? We could and, getting into the spirit of the thing, Roger promptly ordered two English woolen suits made for Stateside wear—all to be done in two days and for a total sum of under $200!

I met Mrs. Gilpatric the next morning to change all the foreign money Roger and I had left over; lira, French and Swiss francs, a few pounds sterling, and seven Turkish pounds. One whole street is money changers and you shop around to see who will give you the best rate in H.K. dollars which then were 6.20 to the U.S. dollar. The first man wouldn't take my Turkish pounds, but the second said they had a Greek who did the exchange on all the Middle East/currency so I should talk to him. I did in my best Greek. On the strength of it he gave me $1.65 for my $2.50 and invited me to have coffee with him.

419

We had lunch with the Gilpatrics at the Parisian Grill on the strength of the counterpart funds I had collected. I ate at least a dozen delicious Sydney oysters, which are the best in the world—a little smaller than bluepoints but much sweeter and saltier. Then Roger and I went to call on Keswick, the former head of Jardine-Mathieson. It was one of the leading firms in the Far East and had been ousted from Shanghai where we had known him. We had heard he had written a book entitled "What I Know About China." Roger asked him to let him see it. He smiled and gave him a beautifully bound book . . . all the pages were blank!

We also had dinner with the Hank Liebermans. He was the New York Times correspondent for the Far East and the kind who went all over gathering the news himself and drawing his own conclusions rather than depending on cafe gossip. He had a charming young wife who had studied Chinese painting and did some really lovely things. I wanted to buy one but Hank laughingly said he was still well able to support his family and she would give me one with pleasure. He would not allow her to sell it and possibly become independent of him. She gave me a charming picture of Hong Kong Harbor in the rain which had everything in it I wanted to remind me of Hong Kong.

The other quests were Jenkins, the Reuter's man, and the U.P. man and his wife. The conversation was well worth listening to and we got a lot of information on what was going on in Red China.

Wednesday we lunched with the Whiting Willauers. He was General Chennault's right hand man. That afternoon the Gilpatrics gave us a delightful cocktail party of about 20 at the American Club and I think everyone there was an "Old China Hand": Bob Drummond from Peking, Nixon from Canton, H. J. Shen from Shanghai, Keswick and the Willauers. It was such a pleasure to see them all again that I would have liked to sit down and talk to each one indefinitely.

The last day we had lunch with Jerry O'Donnell, who had a charming home out beyond Repulse Bay. From there we went to the Peninsula Hotel in Kowloon where we had asked Ea Te, our beloved #1 boy in Shanghai to meet us. He was so glad to see us it was pathetic and all he could say was "Oh! Master—Oh! Missy!" He looked older and sadder, and no wonder. His wife and five children were still in Shanghai and he could neither get them out, nor was he making enough money to support them even if he could get them to Hong Kong. Roger slipped him a parting present, but he still looked pretty sad when we left.

We took off from the Kai Tak airport at 4:00 P.M. in a DC-4 and landed at Manila at 8:30 in a pouring rain, to be met by the Russells. Up we went to the Manila Hotel and then out to the Russells for late dinner. Eleanor had always referred to their place as "our Tree House," so I had always pictured them climbing into a tree by a rope ladder *á la* Swiss Family Robinson. It wasn't quite like that, but you did go up a flight of steps to enter the first floor. The whole set-up was most delightful: an open verandah living room, dining room screened with sliding blinds of wood and Philippine shell, two nice bedrooms, and everything just as airy as it had to be in this climate.

Jack had told us that we and they were to spend the weekend at Baguio as guests of Ambassador and Mrs. Spruance. I was delighted. I had heard of Baguio ever since I could remember and was most eager to see it. It is about 160 miles from Manila, but 5,000 feet up and has such a different climate you feel you are in another world. The drive up was extremely interesting—through small villages and finally a climb for the last 25 miles up and up through a gorge that could be in Colorado or the Sierras, to pines and cool weather. The view was superb with velvety mountains on all sides and the residence surrounded with all kinds of flowers—orchids, poinsettas, begonias and azaleas, all blooming at once.

The residence was Virginia Colonial style, both spacious and gracious. The Spruances couldn't have been more hospitable. She was a lovely looking woman with snow white hair, my generation but considerably younger. He gave the impression of quiet strength, which I guessed came more from being a four star Admiral, than eight months as Ambassador. It was in this house that the Japan's surrender of the Philippines was signed. We had the room that Yamashita occupied.

421

He was later hanged and, as Roger was very restless during the first part of the night, I thought it might be Yamashita doing a bit of haunting.

Typhoon warning #3 was up when we drove back to Manila and no one knew just where "Trix" was headed for. Probably it is because of this impossibility of predicting what typhoons are going to do that they are all named alphabetically for women. It rained and blew hard during the night, but not enough to be alarming. By noon the next day it had veered to the south so we were able to go to a Harvard Club lunch. Roger spoke informally and well, mostly about his experience as an Overseer, Conant's program, and other matters relating to Harvard.

Thursday morning we heard that our Pan-Am plane, which had been held in Guam waiting to see which way "Trix" was going to jump, had just arrived and would take off at nine that evening as scheduled. So I got most of my packing done before Eleanor called for me to do some last minute shopping.

We took off right on time after a final farewell to the Russells and the Sycips. I took a sleeping pill and slept the sleep of the just—we had berths—waking up only for a brief look at Guam, and then getting in another lovely couple of hours of sleep before landing briefly at Wake Island.

Arriving in San Francisco after a stop at Honolulu, we found Roger and Nancy, Miss Wild and Mr. Davidson (Roger's secretaries) waiting to greet us and mighty good they looked! A warm welcome was waiting at the house from Christena, and I had never seen anything as lovely as 3680 looked when we walked in; the rooms were filled with flowers from one and another, everything was spic and span, and on the practical side, Lew Ming, who had been with Mrs. Sutro who lived next door, had provided us with another excellent cook.

2

VISITS WITH THE PEURIFOYS AND
ROGER IN MAYO CLINIC

WE were back home at 3680 just in time for our 45th Wedding Anniversary, October 30th. I collected a few friends to come and drink our health—about twenty guests. A few couples stayed on to eat cold turkey with us, a folksy sort of thing.

During the first few weeks back at 3680, I was still in the process of orienting myself: never quite sure when I first woke up each morning whether I was in Athens, Hong Kong, Manila or San Francisco. But I quickly got "back into the swim" with plans for Christmas and the New Year of 1953.

The four Lewis Laphams came out for Christmas, and I was very careful to have again everything just as they remembered it—the big green tree with all sorts of colored balls and lights on it in the living room, and the little white one with nothing but silver balls with the creche under it in the hall.

The next event was Ruby Carlson's wedding to George Knoll. He had been courting her more or less since we had met him in Guaymas, and he had finally told her the time had come when she had to "fish or cut bait." She wisely chose the former. It was a pouring rainy day and we got to the church in Burlingame early. Roger started up the aisle to be a guest at someone's 4 o'clock wedding in the church unaware that Ruby's was to be at 4:30 in the chapel. I took off after him, and finally caught him as he neared the front pew. There was a reception at Mother Lapham's house and then we took off for Monterey through one of the worst downpours I had ever seen. We ended up at the Hotel Munras for a very late dinner and afterward I found myself seated on the piano á la Helen Morgan singing at the top of the voice of which I had none.

We were off to Sea Island early in January for a meeting of the Business Advisory Council at Sea Island. We had a really delightful time. Mrs. Alfred Jones, whose husband owned the hotel, invited us all out to her ranch for an outdoor dinner with the main feature roasted oysters—served with cotton thick gloves to hold them and a good strong pick to get them out of the shell. I made my meal off of them, to Mrs. Jones' delight. (She told me that the week before she had entertained some convention there, had ordered eight dozen oysters, and not one had been eaten!)

At our outdoor dinner, Mrs. Snyder, whose husband was a Cabinet officer, was in fits because he had not appeared. He finally did and this is what had delayed him: the swimming pool was flush with the lawn and he stepped in it in the dark! He had had to borrow dry clothes from the host.

One of the big moments of my life came on March 25th. We were asked to the celebration of Greek Independence Day at the Civic Auditorium. Before we left Greece Roger had asked me if I had any unfulfilled desires, and I had said that I had two: one was to revisit Peking; the other was to sing the Greek National Anthem on the stage of the Civil Auditorium with George Christopher. Roger said there was nothing he could do about the first, but he thought the second might be managed. It was. Of course we sang only the first of the 28 verses. I stood up and fairly bellowed in George's ear—to make sure that *he* knew that *I* knew the words. Then after Roger had spoken I said a few well chosen words in Greek—courtesy of the Berlitz School, which must have been all right, because the Orthodox Bishop came up and kissed me and I got a good hand from the audience.

During the summer of 1953, Lewis was made Executive Vice President of the Grace Line. After that there wasn't much excitement until December, when Roger became 70. He planned to give himself a big party at the Pacific Union Club. But Nancy put her foot down, and said that if he did, she would come despite no women being allowed inside the Sacred Precincts. He would have the embarrassment of seeing her thrown out. So he agreed to a party at home, but no women over forty-five were to be invited. Furthermore, they must all be dancers. Never did I learn what "Girls" meant in so short a time. One favorite plaint was, "But I've only been 46 for two weeks!" Roger Jr.'s invitation was a gem: it pictured a speedometer with the needle on 70, and one line underneath it read, "I'm hitting seventy." The party was a huge success until at 2:30 A.M. Garrett McEnerny arose, all six-feet-six of him, and announced it was time for everyone to go home. No one dared refuse!

After a winter of life which had been—to quote my sister's colored cook—"too daily," Roger and I made a six week's trip which included two weeks with the Peurifoys in Guatemala, then Mexico City, San Antonio, New York, and Washington.

We left San Francisco February 12th (1954) and spent two days in Pasadena during which time Roger went to Santa Anita on a pouring rainy afternoon and won almost enough money on a "mudder" to make up his losses on the other races. Then we flew via Pan-Am on an eight hour non-stop flight to Guatemala City, and with a strong tail-wind got in twenty minutes early for the first time in the history of those flights.

It was heart-warming to see the Peurifoys again after our year and a half separation, and we found them their old friendly, delightful selves. Everyone we met said how truly fortunate Guatemala was to have two people of their caliber and to see the Embassy buzzing after several years of a teetotaler, non-entertaining bachelor Ambassador.

We were delightfully entertained and met some most attractive people. But the two outstanding features of the trip were visits to Tiquisate, and the following weekend to Chichicastenago. That ride down to Tiquisate on the single-unit Diesel car was really something— a drop of 5,000 feet in not much over 100 miles. It took five hours because there seemed to be only one kilometer of straight track in the whole distance.

Roger and I took a car on our trek to Chichicastenago, an Indian village about 140 miles away in the mountains. The first 70 kilometers were paved road, and the rest hard surface. But it was also very hard driving because of the hairpin curves and steep grades—up to 8,500 feet in one place, down to a river, and so on for the whole distance. Added to this the Indians on their way to market were strung out all along— and across—the road. They were carrying enormous loads and driving pigs, chickens, donkeys or children.

At one point our driver drew off the road beside a very sheer drop and said "And now I tell you a most u-nique and inter-es-ting thing. Right here President Arevuela and two Russian ballerinas went over the side—Jesus Christ—and he only President for one year—poor man." (I heard afterward that it wasn't the right spot, that the car had caught on a tree, everyone was hauled up and Arevuela continued to be President for another six years.) Our driver's next remark was, "And now Lady, we are coming to a very bad road—what you call cord-u-roy. It is bad in this car, but in a jeep—Jesus Christ—you better have your own teeth."

Back in San Francisco, I was sure Roger had a stomach ulcer, and he went on to the Mayo Clinic. He found he did have one, so he came back for me and to attend to some business, and then we both headed back to Rochester.

Carol flew out to be with me for the operation and was I glad to have her there! The doctor's prognosis had been anything but encouraging; he said that there was every indication that the ulcer was malignant, and that I must not be too optimistic. He gave Roger only about a 50-50 chance of survival. I told the doctor that he didn't know the Dearborn constitution, but I did, and that I was sure Roger would come out all right.

Roger was operated on the second morning. Carol and I waited two hours before we were summoned to the floor where the operation had taken place, and we had had no word of any kind in the meantime. After we had sat outside a laboratory for about twenty minutes, a man came out carrying a pieplate covered with a napkin which he whisked aside and showed me what I thought was a slice of raw meat.

"That," he said triumphantly, "is your husband's ulcer." I thought I was going to faint, but Carol had smelling salts handy, so all I did was burst into tears and ask in a feeble voice if it was malignant.

"Oh! no," said he. "Didn't anyone tell you? You should have known that long ago." He said that Roger probably would not be conscious for at least two hours. So we left, had a drink, which we both badly needed—lunch, and then went back to the hospital.

Roger was in his room, but still unconscious, so we just sat there waiting. St. Mary's was a Catholic hospital and there were crucifixes over each bed plus a Murillo of the infant St. John and a lamb on the wall at the foot of his bed. All of a sudden Roger awoke, and pulled himself up a bit from the pillow. He took a look at the picture, said "B-A-A" in a loud voice, and then lapsed back into slumber. (The next day Roger still somewhat groggy said, "Sport, yesterday St. John was feeding the lamb.")

When Roger was moved to the hotel, a dismal place, he still had to go to the clinic every day, get a number, and wait sometimes an hour or more before it was called. He couldn't keep anything on his stomach, even the milk he was supposed to have every two hours. In addition, I couldn't get milk at the hotel between 10 A.M. and lunch time, and 2 P.M. and 6 P.M. I was worried sick, but could get little comfort from his doctor who said nausea was quite common after an operation of this kind.

Finally, I got so worried when it came near to the time that the doctor said Roger could go home, I sent for Lewis; not that there was anything he could do, but I needed someone to talk to and possibly take a little of the strain off of me. Lewis stayed two or three days, and then we took off for home. It was a miserable trip with a long wait in Chicago, and Roger actively sick again there.

Roger got worse instead of better after we got home. His local doctor sent him right to the hospital in an ambulance, had a consultation, and looked pretty grim about the whole situation. Now the doctor feared a blockage of some sort, so my poor dear had to go through X-rays again. He was on intravenous feeding and only semi-conscious most of the time. After two days, the doctor—who was a gloomy Gus if ever there was one—said cautiously that things looked a little better, and from then on Roger picked up rapidly.

When he came home from the hospital I brought a nurse with me, and said she was to stay as long as *I* wanted her. She was a cute little English trick who had wonderful control over him. She saw that he had the proper nourishment every two hours, and not the whisky and soda he kept demanding. I kept her for three weeks until he was really himself again—except that he weighed 152 instead of 180. (Naturally, he had to have all his clothes refitted.)

In spite of all he had been through—and it had been touch and go at the Franklin Hospital for a couple of days—he regained his health rapidly enough to go to his camp at the Bohemian Club Grove in July —drinking nothing but milk, of course.

In September, I went back East for the wedding of my nephew, Eliot Loomis, to a charming girl, Susan Leonard, who lived in the country quite near Providence. Dorothy and Dana were there, of course. It was a sweet, simple outdoor ceremony, a nice small reception after-wards, and then Dorothy, Dana and I drove in to a hotel in Providence. The next day we drove around the countryside, ending up at a fine seafood restaurant where we ate steamed clams and broiled live lobster to our heart's content.

Later, we drove down to New Haven, where I was getting off to spend a few days with Carol. She had rented mother's house for the summer. Ernie was to meet me at New Haven to drive the 40 miles or so to Washington (Conn.). By the time we got there, it was blowing great guns, and leaves and branches of trees were falling in all directions. We learned from the radio that it was a hurricane that was sweeping all of New England. Washington just got the tail end of the storm. But that was bad enough and caused a great deal of damage, including Ernie skidding his car into a huge fallen branch of a tree and ruining the car.

It seemed beyond coincidence that the two devastating New England hurricanes were named after my two daughters, Carol and Edna, and that years later when we were in Japan, a threatening typhoon was named Nancy. I was surprised that our family could stir up so much trouble.

On my return from the East, Roger was invited to be one of the Civilian guests on the carrier "Essex" on a trip to Honolulu. Meanwhile, the Peurifoys had been ordered to Thailand against Jack's will. He said things were just beginning to calm down in Guatemala after the revolution, people had gotten used to him, and he thought there was still a great deal of work for him to do there. However, he was summoned to Washington where President Eisenhower put it on a personal basis—only Jack could do the work that had to be done in Thailand. Jack's comment was that if that were the case, "God help the State Department."

The Peurifoys were to sail on the President Cleveland a few days after Roger left, and it occurred to me to join them and meet Roger in Honolulu. I made my reservation for a single room with bath, but when I got on board, I found that I had been assigned a deluxe suite opposite the Peurifoys—all very pleasant, as I was paying minimum rates for maximum accommodations. We had a good four and a half day trip, found some bridge players, and enjoyed all the amusements provided for us.

Roger met us on arrival, draped us with leis, and then I was driven out to the Surfrider to deposit my things. Later we went with the Peurifoys to Pearl Harbor for a cruise of the Harbor before lunch with Admiral and Mrs. Stump, he being the Commander in Chief of the Pacific (CINCPAC). After lunch we took the Peurifoys sightseeing and back to the ship for a 6 o'clock sailing. We had a wee doch and doris in the Peurifoy's suite with the Anschuetz joining us. They, too, were on their way to Thailand as career Diplomats. After they sailed, Roger took me back to Pearl Harbor to a rather raucus dinner at the Officers' Club.

Roger had all sorts of briefing on Naval activities including a tour of the Island to see all the installations, a dive in a submarine, etc. And he was always through in time to take me out for dinner somewhere. I really felt it was like a second courtship!

3

AROUND THE WORLD
(1955)

FOR some time Roger, the Swinertons and we had been discussing the idea of taking a long trip together. We finally decided on a trip around the world to last about three months. Roger and I both had our 50th reunions coming up in June, and of course we wanted to be home by then.

Honolulu was our first stop. We took a small plane over to the Island of Maui, where Paul Fagan met us and drove us to his charming house at Hana, where we spent the next three delightful days. On the fourth day, Paul chartered a plane to fly us back to Honolulu, where I put in one of the busiest days I had ever had: repacking, luncheon and cocktails on the other side of the Island, dinner in Honolulu, and finally bed.

The following morning we flew to Guam where Alfred's firm was doing some construction work, and he wanted to see how it was going. The project manager and his wife met us and conducted us to the guest hut, which—after the luxury at the Fagans—was an awful come down. There were two beds, two chairs and a table in each room, and the noise from the construction starting at 6 a.m. made sleep impossible. One of the two nights we spent there, we had dinner with Admiral and Mrs. Murphy, who were delightful. My dinner partner was a young geophysicist, and I thought of course he had something to do with geography. But no. He was investigating snails on Guam. His real field was anthropoid apes. So I said I was hoping to see lots of loose monkeys on this trip, and he said, "Weren't all monkeys loose?" That didn't seem to be getting us anywhere, so I turned and talked to the man on my other side.

431

The next stop was Manila. We were met by the Russells, and driven up to the hotel for breakfast where we found Jack Peurifoy and Charles Yost in the dining room on their way to Baguio for a Seato Conference. We had lunch with the Brenns—he the Chief of the FOA Mission. It was a dull affair until going down the stairs on the way home, Alfred slipped on the third step. He shot down the rest of the way on his back, and neatly knocked my feet out from under me and I sat down hard on the tiled floor. Roger and Jane, who were ahead of us, thought it was the funniest thing they had even seen, but we were really sore for the next couple of days.

That evening Admiral Goodwin sent his launch for us, and we had a lovely 25-minute moonlit trip across the Bay to Sangley Point. Mrs. Goodwin must have been a woman of "infinite-resources-and-sagacity"; she didn't know for certain that the four of us were coming until noon, and fifteen minutes before dinner four British diplomats literally dropped in. They had been flying from Singapore to Hong Kong, but couldn't land there, so had to make Manila instead.

The next day Jack Russell took the men to call on President Magsay-say, and Eleanor R. took Jane and me to lunch at a very attractive hotel overlooking a large lake in the crater of an extinct volcano. The follow-ing day we went to a lunch given by the Sycips at the Bankers' Club. The Mayor of Manila, Lacson, was there. Jane Swinerton set next to him and he told her a story in Spanish at which she laughed so hard, he asked her if he should repeat it in English. This was the story:

"Ladies and Gentlemen: you have all heard of Evita Peron. Well, she was in Europe and was received by the Pope—why, I would not know. Then she went to Madrid where a parade was scheduled in her honor. But instead of cheering, the crowds cried *'Puta, puta,'* ('whore'). She was highly insulted, and asked the General with whom she was riding to do something about it. 'Do not worry, Senora,' said he, 'I *too* have been retired for ten years, but they still call me General!' "

At Hong Kong, we stayed in the Repulse Bay Hotel, where we had our old, lovely room. There was one drawback: a water shortage and

432

the water was on only between 5 and 8 p.m. No matter where you were or what you were doing, you had to stop and return to the hotel in time to have a bath.

Shopping, the men did themselves proud on shirts and suits. Roger ordered a purple silk one which he said he had always wanted to do, and which was almost bright enough to satisfy him, and not too noisy to horrify me.

Cocktails at the Maurice Rices (State Department, Greece), on the lawn overlooking Deepwater Bay was another event. The Rices' little dachshund came up and poked his nose against my ankle, and if I had known that a cobra had been killed on that lawn only a day or two before, I would probably have had the screaming heebie-jeebies.

We dined with H. J. Shen, and though I had asked him to make the Chinese dinner a short one, I counted at least 15 courses. We all had our pictures taken after the dinner. The photos came out pretty well, except that Jane felt that she was the living image of Eleanor Roosevelt.

More lunches, cocktail parties, and dinners by friends occupied the next two days, and then we were ready for our visit to the Peurifoys in Bangkok, where Jack was Ambassador. Jack's smiling face greeted us as we landed and he got us through Customs in no time. He drove us to the Embassy Residence, about 18 miles from the airport. It was set in spacious grounds, and less than a five minute walk to the Guest House where we were staying.

There was a luncheon at the Peurifoys the next day, and then an outdoor reception for U Nu (the Burmese Prime Minister) at the Burmese Embassy. I never saw more beautifully decorated grounds, with fairy lights strung in patterns all over. We had dinner at the Meaders (State Department), afterward, with cocktails on the lawn. They handed you a cocktail for one hand and then, either Skeetaline or a pillow case to save your feet and legs from mosquitos.

The next morning we made a trip to Angkor Wat—Jane Swin, Betty Jane, Mary Louise Lowrey, Roger and myself. Betty Jane was taking Alfred's place, for he said he had seen Angkor twenty years before, and he didn't believe it had changed much. We were called at 5 a.m. to go to the airport. There our passports were taken up, and we filled out various papers in more detail. Finally our passports were handed back in a most casual fashion. I got one containing the picture of a young Siamese girl which I refused to accept, so the clerk gave me the choice of the rest. I did find mine, but Betty Jane's never showed up until Roger went and picked it up off an odd table.

Breakfast shortly after take-off consisted of coffee, an orange, a banana, a piece of cold chicken, a meat pie, a piece of pound cake and a Hershey bar, but no knife, fork, spoon, nor napkin. The flight was a short flight and followed by another long wait at the airport for passport examination. Finally we loaded into a black Maria type of bus, which promptly broke down. Eventually we arrived at the Grand Hotel. It was grand in name and price only, and offered such confusion around the desk as:

"Monsieur and Madame Lapham did not want a room with a so large double bed? *Mon Dieu, que faire, que faire.*"

"Mme. Peurifoy wanted a room to herself? *Mon Dieu!* We have one single lady, five single gentlemen, and only three double rooms. *Que faire?*"

Mme. Peurifoy did not care at all who occupied two of the rooms, but insisted on having one to herself. It was finally settled by Jane Swin and Mary Louise sharing a room. The rooms when reached were definitely on the primitive side—especially the bathrooms, with plumbing but no water.

We finally drove off to the temples, where we discovered there was a great deal of walking to do in the heat of the midday sun. We said "I pass," found a small booth and sat there drinking warm beer with small pieces of (probably contaminated) ice in it.

Roger went to bed right after lunch. Fortunately, our afternoon was more to my liking. We took busses to the various temples, walked through them for a quarter of a mile or so, and then were met by the car on the other side. We got back in the late afternoon, tired, hot and dirty, but still no water. Every American was gathered around the hotel desk complaining and all the concierge could say was *"Le courant électric ne foncionne pas, but ayez patience*—in another leetle fifteen minutes, all will be well."

Of course it wasn't, so at five I put my finger on the bell and kept it there until a large can of hot water was deposited at the door. Then I found out there were no stoppers in either the basin or bathtub. However, I managed to clean up—avoiding the black beetles in the can. When I saw Roger cleaning his teeth with that water, I shrieked with horror, and promptly substituted Evian.

We had a final tour the next morning, and this time Roger did go to see more temples of a different era. But he did not get out at all our stops. I came back to the bus at one point, to find Roger sitting in the rear seat with an ever-growing crowd of children and adults gazing at him. He was laughing like a banshee. I watched for a few minutes, and found he was slipping his lower denture out for them, and they were simply fascinated. The rest of the crowd came back, and as a parting gesture, he slipped out his uppers. It brought down the house.

The next ten days in Bangkok were taken up with social events, shopping, and sightseeing. We went to Jim Thompson's fascinating silk shop, where Roger went crazy buying ties, cummerbunds, silk yardage to take home to the girls, and suiting for himself of bright golden bronze. We were also taken to Jewel street, but all the stones, though very cheap, were so flawed that no one who knew anything about gems would think of buying one. I did get a pretty "Princess ring" for Edna, with the nine precious stones in it (very small ones), and a good topaz for Carol at another place.

Danny had a party for his 9th birthday one night, and the picture, "Annie Get Your Gun," was shown afterward. It did make us feel old; Roger and I were the only two in the room who had actually seen Buffalo Bill in his wonderful Wild West Shows.

We were off again on March 21st, after a lovely, lovely twelve days. No couple could possibly make their guests feel more at home, make plans they thought you would enjoy, or leave you free to go about your own business as the Peurifoys did. The four of us were eternally grateful to them.

The flight to Colombo on KLM was the drinking-est I have ever had. Breakfast was coffee, hot chocolate, and beer. We played bridge for a very short time, and it was time for the pre-luncheon drinks—anything you asked for, then burgundy and champagne served with the lunch and liqueurs afterward. We got into Colombo right after lunch, to be met by Ambassador Phil Crowe (China), and driven to the best hotel, the Galle Face. It was right on the Indian Ocean, and just as English as possible—even to the horrid glazed toilet paper, called by all the inhabitants the Gall Stones, for reasons which became rapidly obvious.

On Saturday the 26th we left in one of the Embassy cars for a four-day tour of the Island. Each little village seemed to go in for one product only: rice paddies cultivated by boys and water buffalos, miles of coconut trees, rubber trees, manioc, bananas, papaya, and cashew nuts, and climbing pepper plants (a great surprise to me, as I had no idea that pepper grew on vines). We had a fine picnic lunch by the roadside, and then we saw our first elephant! He was standing in a stream on three legs, having his off hind foot washed by his mahout. And right after that we began to catch up with monkeys. They had black faces and very long tails, which curled like a hind-side-before question mark when they sat down. They were very loose indeed.

At Polo-na-ru-wa there were some "famous" ruins, but after Angkot they didn't even rate. We drove around a bit, until a sudden shower drove us into a very nice rest house. There we sat on the porch, had a beer, and watched dozens of monkeys swinging from tree to tree, and scampering across the roof of our porch to find shelter. I found them much more interesting than the remains of dead kings' palaces.

Retracing our steps for 45 miles, we came to Sigiriya which was noted for a sheer rock rising 800 feet up from the plain. My dear husband got away from me before I woke up the next morning, and climbed it on an empty stomach and in blazing heat. He was lame for days afterward and could not get out of the tub without assistance.

Kandy was the next stop. After settling into our rooms at the Queen's

Hotel and luncheon, Jane and I went sightseeing. We ended up at the Temple of the Tooth, where Buddha's tooth is displayed once a year for three days. The tooth, about an inch and a half long with a light brown patine, was displayed hanging from a gold upright in a crystal dome on an altar heaped high with flowers. Two gorgeously attired priests in attendance did nothing except rush everyone through as fast as possible and kick the offerings of flowers under the altar. The crowd was very *émotioné,* some of them almost in a trance. No one seemed to resent the presence of us unbelievers.

From Colombo, we went to Bombay for two days and left the third morning for New Delhi and the Imperial Hotel. We were met at the airport by the Grants (China) and driven to their house where we were joined by a General and Mrs. Chaudhuri. They were a delightful couple whom the Swins knew. He was a fine looking man, and she one of the loveliest creatures I had ever seen; small, dainty, and beautifully dressed in saris. They had spent a part of their honeymoon with the Swinertons in Woodside 17 years before, and now was their first big chance to repay that hospitality, which they certainly did for all four of us.

The Grants, the Chaudhuris and Caltex planned a trip to Kashmir for us which was most helpful. The Chaudhuris recommended us to several army friends who lived in Srinigar and engaged a house boat for us. Meanwhile, the Swins and I left for Agra the next afternoon. Roger stayed saying he had gone to Angkor with us, and it was Alfred's turn to go to Agra. It was a four-hour, hot, dusty drive and not particularly interesting except for the people and the animals.

We didn't arrive in time to see the Taj by sunset, but did see it after dinner by full moonlight. It was an indescribable experience; the Taj looked like a huge iridescent bubble floating in space. When we explored it the next morning, it looked unpleasantly like all the replicas of it you have seen since you were a child. On closer inspection, however, the lacy marble work was exquisite and the building, itself, far more interesting than it looked at first blush.

After a number of other side trips, we finally arrived in Kashmir. We were met by Ismail, the owner of the "Jacquiline," and driven directly to the boat. It was moored to the Bund on the Jhelum River—very much more satisfactory for my early-rising husband than being in a boat on Dal Lake, where you had to take a water taxi every time you went ashore. For the rental of the boat with five servants and all meals, we paid $3.00 a day apiece. Of course we paid extra for our drinks, taxis, and firewood. And we needed plenty of the latter as it turned very cold the last few days of our stay. The "Jacquiline" had a living room, three bedrooms, and three bathrooms with "Cold and Hot Running waters" and "Sanitary fittings," which consisted of two old fashioned commodes. The cook-boat was moored astern and all food brought in was on the run along a catwalk on the outside of the boat.

The first afternoon, Roger and I took a walk along the Bund and it was really an incredible sight: huge chenar trees lining the water front, and behind them all sorts of spring flowers including iris, forsythia and Persian lilac, and across the river, the snow-covered Himalayas came down to the water's edge. On our return to the boat, we were besieged by vendors selling everything from "postcards" to terrible furs. They came by water in little boats with lovely names—"Gin Bitter," "Lovely Happy," "Trifalgar," etc. Window shopping the next morning, we were particularly taken by two shops named "Suffering Moses" and "Sabana the Worst."

During our stay, we took a trip to Gulmarg. It was about 25 miles away, and had been the favorite hill resort of the British, and later the Americans on leave. But now it was all but deserted. The first part of the trip was by car, and the last three miles straight up 2,000 feet on little hill ponies with Roger, Jane, and Ismail aboard. The rest of us were carried in "dandies" by porters. Other porters carried the lunch and, of course, the rug and pillows we never went out without. For their day's work, the porters got the equivalent of 30 cents apiece! We each tipped them a rupee (20 cents) and would have gladly given them more except that Ismail said that it would upset their whole scale of living.

Gulmarg was really a beautiful spot in a saucer-shaped depression in the mountains. It consisted of small cottages and a hotel with "Highly Competitive Rates." We picnicked sitting on a tee of the snow-covered golf course. The men threw bread to the multitudinous crows despite the wives' disapprovals—justified when a hawk swooped down between Jane and Roger and snatched a piece of meat off one of their plates.

On another day, we engaged two decrepit held-together-by-baling-wire taxis for a 55 mile trip to the Bringhi River. There the Swins had rented a fishing spot on a racing, tumbling stream, clear as crystal, and cold as the mountains from which it came. They also rented rods and tackle and went to work. The only trouble was that Jane lost two sections of her rod four times. When I tried it, I had two strikes but landed neither fish; the top fell off the rod both times. Fortunately, Ismail and his crew produced enough trout for the four of us. It had been just caught and bought, I suspect, from the guard at the entrance of our portion of the river. The trout was served sizzling hot from the frying pan, and I never tasted anything better.

The next day we went shopping, and got an education in the Kashmir materials. The finest is woven from goose down and is very expensive—$250 for a blanket, "so fine it will go through a ring." (I declined saying that I didn't spend my time pulling blankets through rings.) The next grade is Pashmina from the softest ibex wool; the third grade is the familiar cashmere and the last grade, the very coarse—but warm —material that the men wear as shawls.

Following the Kashmir sojourn, we returned to New Delhi, for hectic repacking and sorting out what was to be sent home by steamer, by air, and what was to be kept with us. Alfred also battled with the Albertson Agency representative over the bill he presented. It simply said, "For services rendered, $128.00" with no itemized list of any kind. Alfred made the man sit down and go over the amounts item by item. The bill ended up at exactly $19.00! The man shrieked, "I will report you to the Albertson Agency," whereupon Alfred said "Then you'd better be quick about it, before I report that their agent in Delhi is a crook."

In Karachi we were met by Mr. Butts, the Caltex man, who took us to the "best" hotel, the Metropole. He called for us in time for a drive around town and to the very British Club for drinks; then to his house for a nice home dinner, and finally to the airport to go to Baghdad by Air France. We got to Baghdad safely at 6:00 A.M. and the next morning Jane, Roger and I, went out to see the famous Golden Mosque. We also went for tea at the Embassy, and met an attractive couple named Goodhue from Boston with whom we dined later accompanied by the Counselor to the Embassy, and had a very amusing evening. Early the next morning we made the four-hour flight to Teheran.

We were met by a delegation of ex-ECA Greeks, and Neville Huffman, a Standard of Cal man, who devoted himself to us during our stay. After lunch a Mr. As'as from Point 4 took us around sightseeing. We went to the old Gulistan Palace to see the Peacock Throne that had been captured or stolen from Delhi centuries ago. It still had the original jewels—emeralds the size of pigeons' eggs, rubies, pearls, gold, etc. The huge reception room it was in had cabinets all around the walls with *objets d'art,* ranging from the truly beautiful to the incredibly terrible, such as a bronze statue of a lady with a clock in her stomach presented by Queen Victoria.

After much sightseeing, entertainment and a trip to Shiraz and Isfahan, we headed for Istanbul. We arrived at midnight in thin silk suits. It was colder than Greenland and for the first time, there was no one to meet us. All of us but Roger had been to Istanbul before, so we did very little sightseeing—just a couple of mosques and tea at Roberts College. Our trip through the East was over, and fascinating as it was, I think we were all ready to see something green and clean in Europe.

We left for Athens in the morning and immediately went out to #9 Yasmeion where Russell Drake, who was now Chief of Mission lived. There, I learned the meaning of the term "A full house." Roger and I had our old room; the Swins the one next to us; Paul Porter, down from

Paris had the single guest room; a Swedish couple, whom Russ had cordially invited to visit him any time, had picked that particular weekend to arrive and had the guest suite; and Russ had a small room, which had been the scene of the accouchement of our Puss-pusses' kittens.

The house had been considerably refurbished since we were there. Vincent was no longer there, but Koula was and Roger swept her into his arms and gave her a resounding kiss to the accompaniment of a storm of her giggles.

On May Day, we went out to the Kanakis Taverna. It was old home week with kisses for every Kanakis in sight regardless of age or sex. That night there was a cocktail-buffet party that Russ gave. Everyone who was left in Greece whom we had ever known was there, and we met quite a few newcomers as well.

We left for Geneva the next morning. We stayed at a hotel but had most of our meals with the Bill Brewsters, did a little shopping, and had three good days there. Then on we flew to Paris, arriving in time to open our CARE Package from Cabot Brown. It contained a bottle of Scotch and one of Bourbon, and a carton of cigarettes apiece. We dashed around to the Ritz to lunch with the Camerons, ending with *Fraise de bois,* and *creme d'Issigny.* What a treat!

Copenhagen was the last stop before heading home. We did a little sightseeing and shopping and had lunch at a most attractive restaurant called the "Seven Little Houses"—it might have been just that, because one small room led to another. It was so cold and windy that there was little temptation to go out, until Mr. Wiggins (Caltex) called for us to take us to lunch. Later, we joined Mrs. Wiggins and her two young children and we all went to the circus. Roger was not too enthusiastic, but I had been before, and knew how good it was: wide, roomy chairs, you can smoke, there is only one ring to watch, and every act is the best of its kind. In one act, there was a juggler standing on a ladder who kicked six cups and saucers onto his head. Roger sat so far forward on his chair, that I was afraid he would slip off. He enjoyed it a great deal more than even the two children did!

441

Our trip around the World ended with the long polar flight from Copenhagen to Los Angeles on S.A.S. We had traveled about 33,000 miles on fourteen airlines making forty landings and takeoffs.

Our trip had been made easy for us by so many different people: Point Four men, Caltex, the airlines, the friends we knew, the friends of friends we met, and above all, Mr. Huffman of Standard of Cal. It was a wonderful, wonderful trip with our pathway smoothed for us all the way around the world and it gave us the happiest memories for the years ahead.

4

OUR GOLDEN WEDDING ANNIVERSARY
AND ROYAL VISITORS

WE arrived home from our trip around the world to receive sad news. After 23 years of marriage, Ernst wanted to divorce Carol so that he could marry the Swinerton's daughter. It was a terrible blow to us, and almost as much a one to the Swinertons. Carol said she had fought it for three years, but there was nothing left to fight for. She was going out to Glenbrook, Nevada, and would get her divorce after her six weeks stay there.

I went up to be with her for a weekend, and Maria, who had spent most of her summer with her cousins, the Deamers, went up later on to be with her mother for the last two weeks. Maria was very peeved that her mother would not let her play the slot machines; the last night, Maria had a dollar in ten cent pieces and put them in herself, but let Carol pull the handle. Unfortunately, according to Carol's point of view, they hit the jackpot with the last dime and collected about $14.

We went East in the spring, and got word the day after we arrived back home that Mother Lapham had died. It was a blessing in a way, for she had been paralyzed and speechless for six years. I had loved her dearly and had always been very close to her.

Ruby (Carlson) Knoll and I had the job of breaking up the house. We wrote all the children and grandchildren to send in a list of what they wanted. We tried to be as fair in the distribution as possible, but we had several conflicts of interest to solve. Roger flew right back to New York for the funeral services in New Canaan where she was buried in the Lapham plot.

Less than three months later, Jack Lapham, his granddaughter,

443

Joyce, her fiance, and an old college friend of Jack's were all killed in
a plane accident. They were coming in for a landing at a flying field
on his ranch at Bandera, about 50 miles from San Antonio. Roger and
I were down at the Cypress Point Club giving a big dinner there that
night when Mark Thomas telephoned Roger what had happened. With
infinite courage, he sat through the dinner and the evening which
followed without telling anyone.

Then in August came more tragic news: Jack Peurifoy and Danny
had both been killed in an automobile accident south of Bangkok.
Betty Jane was left alone except for 14-year-old Clint, who was a cerebral
palsy case. He had also been in the car and had been badly hurt. Clint
probably escaped because of his disability he did not stiffen up auto-
matically as the others probably did during the accident.

Roger cabled at once that either he or I, or both of us would fly out
if Betty Jane wanted us. She cabled back not to come, because she was
leaving in a few days on a plane assigned to her by the Navy and would
lay over for eight or ten hours in San Francisco. She would be very
glad to have us meet her at Moffett Field, the Navy airbase, and spend
that time with her. Jane Swinerton in the meantime, had telephoned
to ask if we wouldn't all come to stay at her home in Woodside.

When Betty Jane arrived, she said she would like to go to the Swinertons. Arrangements were made for the care of Clint and his dog,
and we drove on over to the Swin's. When Jane asked Betty Jane,
"which would you rather have first, a bath or a drink?" She instantly
replied, "A drink first, then a bath, and then perhaps another drink
after that. Would that be all right?"

Betty Jane talked about Jack quite naturally. The question of sabotage had been gone into thoroughly as it was a Thai condemned truck
that had no brakes which had run into him. But after careful investigation it had been decided that it was really an accident. It had happened
near a small bridge where neither car could turn off as the road was
high-crowned with rice paddies on either side. We saw her off at midnight, and thought again what a perfectly wonderful person she was
to be so calm and controlled after the terrible loss she had suffered.

The next excitement was the Republican Convention of 1956 with all the meetings held at the Cow Palace. And did the eastern newspapers have the time of their lives over the name! One of them referred to it as the *"Palais de Vaches,"* and another said that as the Sheraton chain had just taken over the Palace Hotel here, it should be called the "Sheraton-Cow Palace."

December brought the news that Jannie van Oosten had been secretly married to a girl named Marion Elman the preceding March! His family had not wanted him to marry until he was out of the Navy and had completed his last year at college. At any rate, she was a dear girl—very quiet and not at all self-assertive. She had a wonderful influence on Jannie—not by saying much, but just looking at him and saying "Oh! Jannie" whenever he became too flamboyant.

One day I was home and we had a slight earthquake around 8 A.M., a stronger one about 10 A.M., and a corker at 11:45. I rushed to stand in the nearest doorway, so that if the ceiling fell I would be protected. I threw my arms around Nonie, who had joined me from another room, and literally shook with fright.

I had called some kind of a meeting for 3 P.M., and just after everyone was seated, we had another good hard shake. Three of the women started for the front door. There were slight tremors around five, another at eight, and another really hard one at midnight. I was so frightened I crawled into bed with Roger. But as I usually slept under two very thin blankets and he slept under three heavy ones, I was in a dripping perspiration in five minutes. So I returned to my own bed, feeling I would rather be fatally shaken than boiled to death.

A few months later, I got a notice to serve on the jury for the first time in my life. When I took the little card down to City Hall, I was excused for being over 65. Roger was so incensed at my being let off, that he threatened to go down to the Board, and tell them that no matter what my age, I was a great deal more fit to serve than most of the people they had on their juries. I wouldn't have minded serving, if it hadn't meant reporting every morning at 10 A.M. only to be excused because Roger had been President of the A-H, and Mayor of San Francisco.

The months rolled on, with Roger's going up to the Bohemian Grove for the Jinks the last two weeks in July as usual. In the meantime we were both working hard on the invitation list for the big party we planned to have in October to celebrate our Golden Wedding Anniversary. Roger went through the lists of members of the P.U. Club, the Bohemian Club, and the Cypress Point Club, and early in October we sent out invitations far and wide. I think that everyone accepted unless they were bedridden.

We had taken two large rooms at the St. Francis Hotel, as well as the dining room, because we planned to have all the family and all the out-of-town guests for dinner first. I cautioned Roger to be careful about everything—his driving, how he got into and out of the tub, etc. And then six days before the party I stood up to go into dinner without realizing that my left foot had gone to sleep and turned my ankle badly! The doctor bandaged up my ankle, and said I was to have X-rays the next day; if they showed a break, he would put me into a walking cast. I told him he didn't have a prayer; that I had paid $32.50 for a new pair of slippers dyed to match my dress, and I was going to wear them —come hell or high water. Fortunately, nothing was broken—just torn ligaments. But I must admit it was pretty painful standing to receive our guests for nearly two hours.

Podesta and Baldocci, whose reputation was nationwide, did the flowers and they outdid themselves. They had green trees in the rooms with golden balls and stars hung in them, and huge standard vases of chrysanthemums in all shades of gold in all three rooms.

The real date of our Anniversary was the 30th, but we actually had our party on the 26th because it was a Saturday night. People accepted from all over the country and beyond—New York, Washington, Baltimore, Houston, Hawaii, and Spokane. The little dinner we had planned turned out to be 80 or more. Roger Jr. seated the tables for me, and did a wonderful job. I had a son on each side of me, and Roger, a daughter.

Mr. and Mrs. Roger D. Lapham on their Golden Wedding Anniversary, October 30, 1957.

ABOVE — The entire Lapham family including children, their spouses and grandchildren photographed in the living room of 3680 Jackson Street, San Francisco, on the Golden Wedding Anniversary.

BELOW — Unexpected congratulations which included flowers and this card came from President Dwight D. Eisenhower on the Lapham's 50th Anniversary.

Please accept my sincere congratulations on your 50th wedding anniversary with best wishes for many more years of happy companionship.

Dwight D Eisenhower

The rest of the family were scattered around, each with a table of their own.

The Editor of the Call-Bulletin got out an entire edition just for our guests. It was headed "LAPHAMS WED FIFTY YEARS" and entitled the Special Golden Extra. It contained pictures of Roger and myself from our honeymoon right through his entire career, as well as pictures of our whole family—some taken with us and some of each family separately.

In spite of the fact that we had said "No gifts please" on our gold-printed invitation, we were overwhelmed with flowers, a beautiful silver-gilt covered cup from our friends in town, an old loving-cup from friends in Pebble Beach, a wonderful illuminated scroll from our old Greek hands, and above all things!—an invitation to our wedding that somebody had saved for fifty years.

One of the papers asked Roger to what he attributed the success of married life for fifty years, and Roger's reply was, "To my wife's tolerance." Was he right! I had systematically spoiled him from the day we were married.

I had wanted to send the Eisenhowers an invitation, but Roger said it was foolish. It would be just another thing to throw in the White House waste basket, so I didn't do it. Were we embarrassed on the evening before the party when we got a special delivery letter from them congratulating us on our anniversary. I answered it in a little jingle which read as follows:

> *My dear Mr. President: as you're not a resident*
> *Of our beautiful town on the Bay—*
> *I really don't see—it completely beats me*
> *How you knew of our Great Golden Day.*
> *With no invitation to our celebration,*
> *(And the life that you lead must be hard),*
> *How could you take time to make all our bells chime*
> *By sending that wonderful card?*
> *It's our proudest possession, and t'will be an obsession*
> *To show to our friends far and near,*

So from Helen and Roger, that Artful Card-dodger,
Our thanks Mr. President dear.

I got a very nice acknowledgment of it from the White House, signed "Frederick Fox, Special Assistant" which said "Your letter dated November 9 in response to the President's greetings on your fiftieth wedding anniversary was gratefully received. Most correspondence coming to the President is in demanding prose, so your delightfully metered thank-you was pleasing not only to him, but to everyone here."

Needless to say, I did no dancing at my own party, but everyone came to my table to talk to me and Roger danced enough for the two of us. Our youngest guest was Nora Lapham, aged 8, and our oldest, Fred McNear, aged 80. There was every graduation of age in between. I stopped the music at 2:30, much to Roger's disgust, for he said it was a good party and why stop it? But we had served a buffet supper and I figured that everyone of our more than 400 guests had had plenty to drink. We eventually got home around 3 A.M.

There were so many thank-you letters to write that Roger suggested that I write jingles which he would have printed for each group, but could be sent individually. So I did, and here is the one I liked best:

Dear Friends of former days in Greece,
Like Abou Ben Adhem—"May your tribe increase."
To all you friends we love and know,
Our thanks (we hope) are properly expressed below.

The Greeks around their temple plinths
Planted sweet-scented hyacinths
To give to cold immortal stone
A warmer beauty than its own.
The temples stand—the flowers are gone,
But still their fragrance lingers on
And penetrates our life today
With perfume of some bygone May.

All friendships have this rare perfume
Which heightens joy and lightens gloom;
And you, our dears, perhaps don't know
How much you mean to us; and so
I'll say that when we started to unroll
That bright, illumined scroll,
Our hearts, our eyes were filled with tears,
Caused by your love for us, my dears.

A Golden Wedding comes but once in any life,
And if you've passed through love and joy
    and strain, and stress and strife,
Through fair and foul, or rough and sunny weather,
But still as one—grow ever close together,
And friends from far away or those from nearer here
Unite to show they love and hold you near—
All we can say is "Thanks; we know you wish us well,
Dear love, dear friends—from H. and R. D. L."

David Lapham wrote us a wonderful poem about various famous people in history, and each of the four verses ended up with the line, "She never stood a Lapham fifty years," the fifth verse ended with "Accept this medal from your humble peers. By God YOU stood a Lapham fifty years." The poem was accompanied by a gold clip set with tiny rubies from Edna Lapham and all her family. It was probably the most expensive present I had ever received, because I had to buy a gold circlet for my neck to hang it on, and earrings and a ring to match. Our children together gave us a lovely old French clock—with new works—and a gold bracelet with a small gold ball which opened up to reveal a tiny picture of the four children inside. Dorothy wrote us a song. Dana made us two watercolors illustrating our past lives and the newspapers played it up in a big way. The Board of Supervisors even passed a resolution in our honor. All togther, it was a real occasion!

We left right after Christmas for New York, to be on hand for Pat and Nora Macfarlane's wedding on Long Island. It was a sweet simple little service in a smallish, white, 18th century church. Pat's best man was his brother, Ernie, and Nora's attendant was her sister Susan.

The reception afterwards was different and very interesting. Nora's grandfather was a Norwegian, so the wedding cake in many, many layers, was decorated in Norwegian style. Nora made a lovely bride, and Pat a handsome bridegroom. They went to Nassau on their honeymoon, and on their return went to Miami where Pat had been assigned for his last year with the Coast Guard.

Carol rang up one day to say that she was not going to Europe with Pui Folger as she had planned, but was going to be married instead! It was not to be to the man who had been attentive to her all winter (and with whom I did not think she would be happy), but to Ed Valentine, whom she had known for years! He liven in San Marino and was a childless widower. Nothing, absolutely nothing could have made me happier.

Ed was very anxious to be married in church. Carol, who had been baptized an Episcopalian while we lived in Atherton, was interviewed by a group of churchmen including the Bishop. They finally gave her permission to be married in Church, because she was the innocent party in her divorce and was an Episcopalian.

Carol and Ed were married August 8th in the Chapel of Grace Cathedral. Pat gave her away, and Maria was her only attendant. Bill Valentine was his brother's Best Man, and said he was sure it was a very rare thing to be the Best Man at two weddings of the same girl— for he had been Ophie's Best Man when Carol married in '32. Carol wore a silk print dress and a tiny hat to match, and looked lovely— indeed she and Ed made a stunning couple. After the wedding there was a small reception at our house with quite a few friends and relatives present. The whole wedding and reception were happy occasions, for both families were pleased with the choice of Ed for Carol, and Carol for Ed.

Norma Bartlett died early in September. She had not been well nor going anywhere for some time, but said there were two things she was determined to do—one was to see the film "American in Paris" for which her son had done the sets, and the other was to go to Carol's wedding. She didn't actually get to the wedding, but was at the house when we all came back from the church. Those were the last two times she was out.

For the rest of the summer, it was nothing but the "Right to Work" —Proposition 18 on the ballot. The high point of the campaign was Roger's hour-long debate on TV with Harry Bridges 22 years after their memorable one during the waterfront strike. This time no one asked me if Roger was wearing a bullet-proof vest! The Proposition was snowed under at the polls—as it was in the five other states on which it was on the ballot.

During the last of November, the Queen of Greece and her elder daughter, Sophia, arrived on an unofficial visit. I had known about the visit in time to ask Betty Jane up after having received assurance from Mayor Christopher that he would make sure that the Queen had time for a date with Betty Jane. So on the 24th of November, Roger, Betty Jane and I gathered in the Mayor's office, and we all went down to the Rotunda of the City Hall to hear her speak. She did beautifully.

After the ceremonies, Mary Karolou said that the Queen would like to see Betty Jane and me in her apartment at the Mark Hopkins. When we entered her suite, she asked "But where is Mr. Lapham?" I said he didn't know that he was invited, and she said "Of course, but can you find him?"

I knew he was at the P.U. Club with young Lewis Henry. So I phoned him, and told him to bring Lewis along, and I would explain to Her Majesty. Sophia was about Lewis' age and I thought it would be very nice for both him and Sophia. They came over, we all had a glass of sherry, and then Her Majesty asked, "Where should we have lunch?" I was really stumped until she added that she loved Chinese food. I decided to take her to Johnny Kan's.

We were in a party of nine including the Queen, the Princess, a man from the Greek Embassy in Washington, an expert on nuclear physics —whom the Queen had really come out to see—Mary Karolou, Lewis Henry, Roger, Betty Jane and myself; two Secret Service men ate at another table. When the Queen asked what to order for lunch, the little Chinese waiter behind me muttered to take the regular lunch. So I told Her Majesty that I thought the regular lunch would be satisfactory.

It was not an entirely relaxed lunch. When the Queen found out that Lewis Henry was a reporter, she was horrified. The Queen pointed out that this must be a completely off the record party. Roger assured her that Lewis would respect her wishes. Then Sophia never said a word and L. H., whom I had never seen gravelled for lack of matter, had a bit of hard sledding with her.

After lunch, the exodus began. The Queen arose and started for the exit, Mary K. and the Princess followed her, the Greek from Washington almost knocked them down in his anxiety to get to the door, the nuclear scientist followed—and who was left to pay the bill? . . . my dear husband! And when the waiter asked if that hadn't been the Queen, that meant an even larger tip than Roger had planned on giving. And poor Lewis Henry with a clean newspaper scoop in his hands and bound not to use it!

The Queen then wished to walk through Chinatown, so I took her past the best shopping district. The only purchase any of them made was an explosive cigar that Sophia bought for her father! The Queen did stop in at one jewelry and objets d'art store where she took a fancy to a rose quartz incense burner. She told me to ask the price, and the proprietor said in very bored tones "$1,500." He showed no interest in our party whatsover. As we all trailed out, I couldn't resist saying to him "If you had taken a little more interest in us, you might have made a good sale. That was the Queen of Greece who wanted to know the price of the rose quartz burner." He practically wilted.

454

5

NEPAL, SOUTH AFRICA, SOUTH
SEAS AND SOUTH AMERICA

ROGER JR. was sworn in as President of the San Francisco Planning Commission on the 3rd of January, and shortly after that, Roger developed a thirst for travel. All we had to do was to settle on a place. While we mulled it over a letter came from Helen Drake in Nepal, where Russ was stationed, asking us to come out and visit them! I wrote and accepted with alacrity warning that if we came it would have to be for two weeks. Helen wrote back that she expected us to stay a month.

We started off for Nepal via Honolulu, Hong Kong and Calcutta, the only place one could obtain a visa for Nepal. The flight from Calcutta to Kathmandu was pleasant enough except for the last 20 minutes. We went through a very narrow, jagged pass to finally land on a very short runway. I didn't like it!

The Drakes met us and gave us a wonderful two weeks exploring by automobile the only two good roads that led out of Kathmandu. One of the roads was so dusty that Helen Drake had to vacuum clean us before she would let us back into their apartment in the "palace" they occupied.

Our visit ended in a burst of glory. Dag Hammerskjold was in town on a two-day visit. When he left in the King's plane for New Delhi, he took us along as hitchhikers. As a result, we had the greatest thrill of our lives: Hammerskjold was a sightseer and for more than an hour we flew through the Himalayas, even circling Annapurna! It was a breathtaking sight—one very few people had made and perhaps ever would.

A terribly nice thing happened about three months after we got home. I had taken two rolls of pictures on our wonderful flight through the Himalayas, but only two or three of them turned out well—most of them were largely wing with a quarter of an inch of mountain in the background. So I had written Dag Hammerskjoeld and asked if I might borrow a couple of his negatives, as he had been taking pictures in the cockpit with a telescopic lens. I got no answer, until one day a large package arrived from Washington. Opening it I found four wonderful 8 x 10 pictures of the mountains we had passed on our flight!

Shortly after our return, Lewis resigned from the presidency of Grace Lines, to go with the Bankers Trust as Chairman of the Executive Committee. Roger went around saying he didn't raise his boy to be a banker, but in the same breath said he was sure there was not a banker in New York who had had so much experience in so many different lines as Lewis had.

In August, Roger flew off with a golfing group, who called themselves "Antefogasta," to play at Jasper Park, B.C. All went well except: they could not land at the Park because of bad weather and had to motor in the last 50 miles; and Roland Tognazzini, returning to his room to get his luggage, found a large black bear finishing up the fruit and sugar on his table. Tog said he didn't know which was the more frightened, he or the bear.

Roger got back from the B.C. trip at midnight and took off at 8 A.M. the next morning via Pan-Am on a courtesy one-day flight to Honolulu for lunch and back. It was the maiden flight of one of the first jet planes, and about 85 men were invited. My Dearie was powerful tired when he got home!

That fall (1960), Roger began to have an itchy foot again. We decided to take Betty Jane with us; she had just lost her 18-year-old son, who had had cerebral palsy. So she went with us to South Africa, where we visited Phil Crowe, who was then Ambassador there.

The whole trip was a great success, except that Roger was coughing his head off most of the time, and we had an awful stay at that horrible Semiramis Hotel in Cairo, a city I at once added to the list of others that I did not care to ever see again—Canton, Calcutta, Baghdad and Karachi.

On our return home, Roger continued to cough badly. He had also gotten very thin, and I was really worried about him. He was finally persuaded to see a doctor. In the meantime, Nancy and I had made plans for a three week trip to Portugal and Spain. We were to leave in late September. But Roger came home with the news that his doctor had said he had TB in both lungs; but his next remark was "But you must go to Spain just the same." What a position to be placed in!

His doctor said he did not need to go to a sanatorium, or even have a nurse, because our house was built so that he could have a suite— bedroom, bath and sitting-room with an open fire—at his sole disposal. But there would be no one with authority over what he should or shouldn't do if I went abroad. In my despair, I telephoned Betty Jane Peurifoy, and she said she would gladly come up and take charge while I was gone. I said "Oh! Betty Jane, I think it is asking too much of you" but she said "To leave Tulsa in September? Don't be silly." So she came the day before I was due to leave. Her doctor said that as long as she had been with Roger during the most contagious stage of the TB and had not caught it, she was immune. So Nancy and I started off, planning to spend one night in New York, and then take off for Lisbon.

We arrived at the Ritz in Lisbon and had two of the most palatial suites I have ever seen; each had a huge bedroom, a small sitting room, an enormous closet, a large bathroom, and a dressing room—and all for $22 a day for the two of us!

We went right to bed as soon as our bags arrived, and did not wake up until it was time for tea. Then we went down to the Hotel Aviz where all the passengers from the first commercial flight of the Pan-Am line had visited; Roger had been one of them, courtesy of Cap Rieber, and had told me that all of them had signed an illumined scroll, which was hanging in the bar. We finally located the scroll and the bartender claimed he remembered my husband perfectly. "Very white hair, very red face," he said. I guess he really did remember him!

The next morning, was asked for a car with an English speaking driver, and got a very good one—except that he was so anxious that we overlooked nothing and that he talked every minute. He took us on several all-day tours and found good restaurants for us. One of them was right on the beach beyond Estoril. It not only had delicious fish, but also a dog with two noses—and I took a couple of snapshots to prove it! We also visited the museum where the Royal carriages were kept —one of them with a nice seat which lifted and had a silver *pot de chambre* underneath, and another which had been made in Danbury, Connecticut, in the 18th century.

We had found Lisbon so charming, the shopping so good and so reasonable, that we were really sorry we could be there only four days. We bought linens, rugs, and old blue-and-white tiles to be set in iron for small tables. The food was good everywhere we went—the fish, the langouste and the langoustine particularly delicious.

Then we flew from Lisbon to Madrid. Getting through Customs was difficult. The first thing the man opened was Nancy's duffle bag, in which she had heavy clothes, ski boots, etc. for Tonia, who was at school in Strasburg. On the very top was one of those head models with her wig carefully fitted to it. The man was completely baffled, took it out and asked, *"Que es esta?"* Nancy replied *"Por mi cabeza."* He searched a little further, came across some very personal items, and told us to close everything up.

Going into the Ritz was like Old Home Week, for we saw the Witters and a Dr. and Mrs. Bruck, all from San Francisco, almost as soon as we got there. The men were partridge shooting, and we certainly were charmed by their prowess. They not only gave us a partridge dinner at Horcher's—one of the best restaurants—but also left us eight when they departed.

Nancy also had a letter to a Srta. Muneca Topete, who was one of a family of eight and in her thirties. She wanted to get away from home, and do some things on her own. She didn't advertise as a guide, but was passed on by word-of-mouth from one client to another. She took us to all sorts of little out-of-the-way restaurants as soon as she discovered we preferred them to the posh ones. She also took us to the Flea Market one Sunday, and put us on to dressmakers and other things we would never have been able to find on our own.

The chief reason we had wanted to come to Spain was to get evening dresses for Tonia's coming out in December. I found a beauty: aqua blue, the bodice embroidered all over in turquoise and pearl beads. We did go in for practical clothes, too, and were very satisfied with our purchases.

We got a good car and driver, and took two all-day excursions into the country. One of them was to the Escorial where we had a good lunch at the Hotel Felipe II, and followed by a visit to the Valley of the Fallen *(Valle de los Caidos),* where the most beautiful cathedral had been hollowed out of solid rock and topped by a 400-foot high cross.

With the Prado just across the street from the hotel, we went there several times, and I even found a picture of Murillo's St. John as a child with the lamb. I sent it to Roger to remind him of his "B-A-A" at the hospital in Rochester. We also went to a bullfight and Ernest Hemingway sat very near us. We guided our actions by his: when he said, *"Olé!,"* we said, *"Olé!,"* and when he was silent, so were we.

I heard daily from Betty Jane, and she reported that Roger was making a quicker recovery than we had expected. He was gaining weight. Because he had never taken any anti-biotics, everything that they gave him worked and at one time he was taking 28 pills a day!

After our return home, Roger was confined to the second floor for several more months and then allowed downstairs once a day.

Roger made his own "debut" at Tonia's coming-out party at the St. Francis. The Mark Thomas' daughter, Julie, came out at the same time, and it was a good party in spite of the fact that Tonia had her leg in a cast because she had broken it skiing.

Roger Jr. had rented a golf cart for her so she was mobile. Her cast was decorated with a large blue and green tulle bow in the same material as the decorations. Roger rode around the ballroom in the golf cart with Tonia and got her back safely, which was really quite a surprise to me. My husband was not a good driver in any kind of vehicle. But he mostly sat at a table and received so much attention that he was quite miffed when I insisted on taking him home at half-past twelve. When we got to the house, he told the cabbie "Let Mrs. Lapham out, and take me back to the St. Francis!" Fortunately the taximan was on my side and refused to do it.

By January, he was allowed downtown to his office each morning, and by April he was permitted to play nine holes of golf. He also could give up a few of the 28 pills he had been taking daily.

Toward the end of summer after the Grove (Roger went, but stuck nobly to milk, which he called his "white champagne") he began to get restless for travel again, and started plans for a trip to Asia. There was to be a meeting of the various Asia Foundation men who worked in the various countries of Asia. That gave him a peg to hang his hat on. Dr Brown said he could go, but not for more than five or six weeks. He really wasn't fit to travel around at that time, because almost everything we did tired him terribly.

We invited Betty Jane to go with us and she accepted. We took off early in October for Tokyo, Hong Kong, Singapore, Australia and the Fiji Islands, where we took a five day cruise on what was erroneously described as a "Luxury Yacht" in the brochures.

The stay in Hong Kong was not too successful either. The social entertainment almost exhausted him and there was the endlessly long walk to our horrid bed-sitting room at the Repulse Bay Hotel. Our travel agent had engaged a suite for us at the Gloucester Hotel in town, but Roger would have none of it, because he wanted to stay at Repulse Bay for old times sake. He asked the Foundation to make reservations for us there. Someone did but never looked at the rooms. The long walk was the last straw to long, and, for Roger, tiring days. One night, he was so all in, that he practically cried as he undressed. I was more than glad when we were able to move on to the greater comforts of Singapore.

Late in January 1962, we went down to Pebble Beach for the Crosby "Clambake." The weather was bad as usual, but this year it outdid itself. There was the worst snow storm within the memory of the oldest inhabitant! With three inches of snow on the greens, the finals had to be postponed until the next day. We drove back to the city that Sunday afternoon, and it snowed lightly all the way. It was cold enough for the snow to stay on the ground. In San Francisco, it was the heaviest snow in 30 years.

Finding out early in February that Betty Jane Peurifoy could go with us, we made reservations for a trip to South America. We flew down the east coast, across the Andes and up the west coast terminating at Miami.

On our way down, we joined the Swinertons and their friends, the Bill Millers, whom we had met in Africa. We met some other friends in Buenos Aires and then continued by air over the Andes. After visits to Santiago and Lima, we went on to Quito to see our beloved grandson, Ernst Ophuls, who was really the excuse for the whole trip.

Ernie met us at the airport and we were lucky enough to have a full four-day visit with him. He was waiting there for an important part of his airplane to be shipped from the United States. We met all the people with whom he worked—the two priests he stayed with in Quito and the heads of Caritas, the Catholic order of foreign aid. Seeing Ernie was all we wanted because the 8,500 feet of altitude there was not too good for Roger and me.

We saw very little of Quito, but did have our pictures taken at the monument marking the equator. Roger posed in one hemisphere and I was in the other.

Seeing Ernie in South America was a tremendous thrill. I feel that I cannot say enough about him, his spiritual devotion and his love for his airplane. To quote from a letter received once from him: "I am doing what I want to do. I am luckier than most; not all have the abilities that fit this work, nor the circumstances of life, nor the graces to do it."

He became a Catholic during his two years at Gonzaga University. When he first began his work as a lay brother, he expected to be appointed to Africa, so began the study of Swahili. He amused us greatly by appearing at the house one night, and saying to me with a broad grin, "I'll bet you don't know how to ask to go to the bathroom in Swahili!" I replied no, but that I could do it in Greek (*Pou einai to meras?*); Swahili was definitely not on my language list with the exception of two words, *"Simba"* (lion) and *"Bwana."*

His assignment was changed to South America, so he spent two years studying Spanish, and every possible kind of airplane work—including taking a plane to pieces and putting it together again. He finally got off in November, 1961, with all sorts of airplane licenses, allowing him to do night flights, carry passengers, etc. His job was flying supplies to Mission outposts in other parts of the country across the Andes.

Then tragedy struck in June of 1962. Beloved Ernie died of an atypical polio in Quito. He had had hepatitis but had recovered when he came down with polio. He was completely paralyzed and died 48 hours later. Carol had been in touch with Quito. Ed had ordered an iron lung flown down from Panama, but it hadn't even been sent before Ernie died. Carol left before it was realized how critically ill he was, and he died before she got there. The funeral Mass was the day she arrived. He was allowed to be buried in the vault with the Brothers in spite of the fact that he was only a layman.

Carol stayed there several days, meeting all those whom he had worked with, and being flown over to Tena by his partner. Ernie must have made a tremendous impression in the seven months he was there for they named the little hospital they were building in Tena after him —"Hospitale Ernesto Ophuls." How thankful Roger and I were that we had had that wonderful visit with him in March. I think that if he had lived, he would eventually have become a priest.

Ernst Ophuls, a grandson, photographed shortly before his tragic death of polio in Ecuador in 1962. The Senior Laphams had visited him there three months earlier on their South America trip.

1971 — Helen Abbot Lapham

464

6

"THE SHACK" AT PEBBLE BEACH

W E now had a real interest to take us down to Pebble Beach often. Nearly a year earlier, Roger had bought a beautiful piece of property there on Roger Jr.'s advice. After much family consultation and a little urging from Junior, Senior finally said he would build on it. He claimed I had said that we had owned three houses, but had never built one and I would like to build. I am certain I never said it. The last thought in my mind was to try to keep house in two places.

Roger agreed to pay for the building on the condition that Roger, Jr. attended to everything—architect, plans, construction, furnishing, etc. Roger refused to take any other responsibility. Roger Jr., Nancy, George Rockrise, the architect, and I fussed over plans for six months. The only change I would have made when the house was ready was to have had two servants rooms instead of one.

Our property ran down to the first fairway of the Cypress Point Golf Club, so we had a beautiful view of greenery as well as a full sight of the Bay beyond. The house took a whole year to build mainly because of a contractors' strike right at the beginning and the work stopped for three months.

That September, Pat and Nora Ophuls, who were then in Abidjan on the Ivory Coast, had a baby girl—Julie. She must have been a darling from her pictures; but alas! she lived only three months, and died from some dreadful pneunococcus bugs.

In October, Nancy and I flew away on another of our three-week trips to Portugal and Spain. We had our same driver in Lisbon, stayed at the Ritz again and found the shopping just as good. Tonia came on from her school in Strasburg to be with us for a few days, and we did some of the things we had done before: Toledo, Valley of the Fallen, etc., and Tonia was duly impressed.

On our Christmas cards that year, we used a picture of Roger and me sitting on the steps to the monument over the Equator—he in the Northern and I in the Southern Hemisphere. The day after Christmas, we went south to Maria's debut at the Valley Hunt Club. Maria looked very stunning in a lovely white and silver brocade dress. In the meantime, the Jan-Roger van Oostens had had a baby boy, which elated them because their other child was a little girl, Gay.

I named the Pebble Beach house "Lapland"—but Roger always called it "The Shack." When it was finished, we had two housewarmings; the first for the caddies and their wives, and all the employees of the Cypress Point Club. There was hardly any furniture in the house, but more than plenty of food and drink. By the time Roger and I left at 8 P.M., I don't think that anyone missed the lack of chairs—nor us. Nancy and Roger Jr. continued to host the party, and we heard the next day that it had not broken up until 1 A.M.

Two weeks later, we had our second housewarming with about 80 invited, most of whom came. Betty Jane came on from Tulsa. Before the party, we had the house blessed by the Episcopal Minister from Monterey. The Orthodox priest had blessed our house in Greece when we moved in, and I thought it such a lovely idea, that I decided to do it again in Monterey.

As time went on, and all the furniture and other things that we had ordered arrived, the house looked better and better. Everyone who saw it was most enthusiastic. Our prize possession was a pair of old San Francisco traffic lights. Nancy saw them advertised and bought them for Roger to be placed in our parking area. They did not change from red to green, which was probably just as well.

Two sadnesses occurred shortly after the housewarming. Our dear friend, Alfred Swinerton, died rather unexpectedly of emphysema. A month later Dorothy's husband, Dana Loomis, also died. She came out to see me in July, and probably the change of scene did her good—although quite naturally, she tired easily and her nerves were worn pretty thin.

While she was with us, Pat and Nora Ophuls stopped off to see us with their Abyssinian cat, Haji. They were en route to Japan, for a two-year assignment to the language school there. It was what he had put down as first choice when his term was up in Abidjan, but he hadn't really expected to get it. They were more than pleased.

In November of 1963, President Kennedy was assassinated in Dallas and the whole country was shocked beyond words. I heard the news in the beauty shop of the Mark Hopkins, where one of the customers had a transistor radio, which we all gathered around. Then a man's voice said, "Ladies and gentlemen, the President is dead." It just didn't seem possible!

We sat glued to the TV for the next three days admiring tremendously the dignity and courage with which Jackie Kennedy faced her loss. As time went on, we all thought more and more of the dignity with which the Kennedy's filled their role, and admired them more and more in retrospect—even if we hadn't voted for JFK in the first place.

All sorts of things happened from then on. Pat and Nora had a son a little prematurely. He was very thin and weighed only a little over four pounds. We all put in some anxious moments as the baby, Nicholas, went down below four pounds. He was kept in the hospital until he was over five pounds, and from then on he flourished.

In June, Roger, Betty Jane, Nonie and I flew to Hana Maui, and had ten good days there. Nonie was in Seventh Heaven, because the church was only a very short distance away; she could go every morning and still have a swim before breakfast.

The week before we left home, I had turned my ankle and fallen in the middle of Sacramento Street, and broken the fifth metatarsal bone.

It was not in a cast, but I had to walk with a cane—with difficulty. We had a lovely cottage near the main building (and the bar) with two large bedrooms, two baths, and two lanais. Nonie was in a cottage not too far away.

All went well except that Roger slept practically all the time, rousing only for drinks and meals. However, one day he did charter a small plane, and we all flew over to Hawaii. We lunched at the Volcano House, drove around the volcano crater, and then back to Hilo for the return flight to Maui. One other afternoon we took a long drive to the Seven Pools. Those two trips were really the greater part of our activity, except for cocktails with Helene Fagan at her lovely home above the Inn.

We got back home for Julie Thomas' wedding at the little Episcopal church in Monterey. The reception was held at the Thomas home in Carmel Valley. It was in the garden and Jean had planted everything months before, so it was a blaze of glory.

The next excitement was Tony Lapham's engagement to Burks Bingham of New York and Southampton in July, 1964. They were married in September that same year—and what a do that was! Roger, Nonie and I flew on for it, and everything was made as easy as possible. Our room reservations had been made by the Eastern contingent, and Cap. Rieber put a plane at the disposal of the guests to fly down to Southampton in 25 minutes, instead of taking three hours by train.

The bride was a lovely girl, and it was a wedding deluxe in every way; I never saw such presents, nor such wonderful treatment of guests. A huge marquee had been built on the lawn back of the house, with heaters, plenty of tables, and chairs, two bars, and two orchestras. Roger in his well-known badge—a red sweater around his neck—danced with the bride and they were warmly applauded.

In October 1964, we went down to Pebble Beach to celebrate our 57th wedding anniversary. We received a most wonderful gift from the Heinz Company, where Lewis was on the Board. It was a huge box with a sample of many of their 57 products along with a luncheon set, playing cards, and other things too numerous to mention.

Sometime later on, we went to a San Francisco restaurant, the Alouette, for dinner and asked the headwaiter for one of the tables against the wall where there would be less noise. But he said all the tables were reserved. We had gone very early, so Roger said mildly that he thought we would be through and out before most of the other people arrived. The waiter repeated that all tables were reserved; Roger became angry and rose saying, "Then we will eat somewhere else." The waiter replied, "That's all right with me—on your way!"

It was a rather unpleasant little scene, but nothing like what Herb Caen the columnist made out of it. He wrote that Roger had socked the waiter, and that the waiter had said "Well Mr. Lapham may be a rich man, but he is no gentleman." Needless to say we never went there again.

Later on in the spring, we went up to Portland to Judy Chace's (Roger's great niece) wedding and then on to Seattle to see the Van Oostens and our great-grandchildren. They were as cute as could be, but Roger, the little boy, was almost as wild as his father before him. We took one day off, and flew over to Victoria, lunching at the good old Empress, and then taking a long drive afterwards.

Then Dorothy and her daughter, Esther Harris, came out, and we all went down to Pebble Beach while Roger was at the Grove. Roger had Lewis Henry as his guest, and Roger Jr. took Tony. So the whole tribe came out—Jane, Melissa Bingham and Burks—and the men all came down from the Grove to be with us during the week.

Lewis and Jane gave a large dinner at the Club, and as Dorothy and Esther had not come prepared for that sort of a festivity, they had to borrow evening dresses; Dorothy, one of mine, and Esther, one of Jane's. Jane, the darling, said it seemed so much better suited to Esther than it did to her, that she gave it to her. As a matter of fact, I gave mine to Dorothy, too, but mine was a good old stand-by and Jane's was brand new.

Lewis H. had planned to stay on at the Club and do some serious writing. But the day after we had all left, he complained to Nancy, who had also stayed on, that he didn't feel very well and his face was sore. The next day, he was worse. She took a good look at him and said, "Mumps." She took him back to San Francisco where he had a really bad case, and was laid up for a full two weeks.

About this time there was a puff for Roger Jr. in the Examiner entitled "Roger Lapham Jr.—one of the few social figures who takes an active interest in political affairs." He had been the head of the Planning Commission for three years. One of the old-timers, whom Roger had appointed to the Board, Julia Porter, told me he was the best presiding president they had ever had.

Roger went to the Grove as usual and after his return, we went down to Santa Barbara where the Van Oosten family gathered. The main purpose of the trip was so that we could have four generation pictures taken. I had pictures from the time Roger was a baby until he was a great grandfather, and could have had them in my own family too, as my grandfather was alive when Lewis was born, but it never occurred to me.

That fall, Jerd, who was going to City College and was on the football team, asked me to come to just one game and see him play. The seats had no backs, it was a steep walk down to them, and it always turned cold in the late afternoon, so I was armed with a cushion to sit on, a heavy coat, and Daniel's arm to help me down the steps. I really enjoyed the game—especially when City College team won 34-0!

Another happy thing happened that fall. Betty Jane won a door prize of a round trip to San Francisco at some bazaar. She used it to come visit us. And how fortunate it was that she came!

We all went down to Pebble Beach for the weekend and while there had dinner with a widower friend of ours, Arthur Stewart. His party was at the Cypress Point Club and after dinner he asked if he might take her over and show her his house.

That was just the beginning. In January we were told that they were to be married early in April! Betty Jane commented that Roger and I had done a great deal for her but she never expected us to provide her with a husband!

EPILOGUE

In the middle of April 1966, the Van Oostens—Jan, Edna and Elinor —came up to stay with us for a few days. On Saturday the 16th, Roger left the dinner table early. He started upstairs, and a minute or two afterward we heard a terrible crash; we all rushed out to find Roger on the floor among the potted plants at the foot of the staircase.

Nonie telephoned Dr. Brown, who arrived in a few minutes, and found that Roger had a fractured skull and a broken leg. He called an ambulance, took Roger to the hospital, and came back three hours later to say that he was dead. Roger had probably suffered either a stroke or a heart attack on the way upstairs, and fallen over the banisters from the landing half-way up, and landed on his head. The rest of the evening is a complete blank to me, except that I know Nancy came back with Dr. Brown when he came to break the news to me.

Roger Jr. had flown to New York that morning, but took the first plane back Sunday morning. Carol also arrived Sunday and the funeral was planned for Wednesday morning—a private ceremony, by invitation only, at the lovely little Kit Stewart Chapel of the Calvary Presbyterian Church. Roger Jr. made all the necessary arrangements, Carol and Edna telephoned all the invitees. Nancy arranged for the flowers— of which, thank goodness, there were not too many, as we had said in the funeral notice, "Contributions to the Children's Hospital of San Francisco preferred" (eventually they amounted to over $6,000).

It was a glorious spring day for the funeral. The little chapel was full and Dr. Howie came back from Washington to preside. The only part in the arrangements I had was to insure Dr. Howie's being there, and saying that I wanted the pall to be maidenhair fern with a cross of red roses on it.

After the services, I invited most of the people to the house for a drink and sandwiches, as Roger had always insisted I should do. Practically everyone there said it was the most uplifting and inspiring funeral service they had ever attended.

I was completely dry-eyed through all those days mostly because Roger had had his wish—dying quickly and not having a stroke to linger for years as his mother had, paralyzed, speechless, and helpless.

The telegrams and letters poured in. I had over six hundred, and both Lewis and Roger Jr. had about two hundred apiece. Roger's secretary Kirsten Troeger, and his former secretary, Mr. Davidson, both helped me; I wrote some myself, dictated some, and had Kirsten reply to most of the telegrams with a little formula I had thought out myself. They were all answered within six weeks.

Then I had to make over my life, and get used to living alone. The hardest hours were from five to seven each evening when I no longer had Roger's homecoming to look forward to, and our sharing drinks together. Getting used to that was one of the hardest things I had to do.

Dr. Brown had told me early in 1965 that he doubted if Roger would live to see his eightieth birthday. But he had seen that one, and three more besides. I was in a measure prepared, as he had arteriosclerosis, and the last months had just been a question of when.

We had shared many happy experiences, and made many fine trips together, but now . . . my "Roving with Roger" was ended.

৩৯

"So he passed over, and all the trumpets
sounded for him on the other side."

—John Bunyan in *Pilgrim's Progress*, 1678